Śrī Brahma-saṁhitā

FIFTH CHAPTER

OTHER TITLES BY ŚRĪLA NĀRĀYAṆA MAHĀRĀJA:

The Nectar of Govinda-līlā
Going Beyond Vaikuṇṭha
Bhakti-rasāyana
Śrī Śikṣāṣṭaka
Veṇu-gīta
Śrī Prabandhāvalī
Śrī Bhakti-rasāmṛta-sindhu-bindu
Śrī Manaḥ-śikṣā
Bhakti-tattva-viveka
Pinnacle of Devotion
Śrī Upadeśāmṛta
Arcana-dīpikā
The Essence of All Advice
Śrī Gauḍīya Gīti-guccha
Shower of Love
Dāmodara-līlā-mādhurī
Śrīmad Bhagavad-gītā
Śrīmad Bhakti Prajñāna Keśava Gosvāmī – His Life and Teachings
Five Essential Essays
Śrī Harināma Mahā-mantra
Secret Truths of the Bhāgavata
My Śikṣā-guru and Priya-bandhu
Jaiva-dharma
Śrī Vraja-maṇḍala Parikramā
The Origin of Ratha-yātrā
Śrī Bhajana-rahasya
Rays of the Harmonist (periodical)

For further information, please visit www.igvp.com or www.gaudiya.net

ISBN 81-86737-10-3
First printing – 5000 copies, May 2003

śrī śrī guru-gaurāṅgau jayataḥ

Śrī Brahma-saṁhitā

FIFTH CHAPTER

With the full commentary (*ṭīkā*) of **Śrīla Jīva Gosvāmī**,
the most expert disciple of Śrī Rūpa and Sanātana,
president of the Viśva Vaiṣṇava Rāja Sabhā,
and protector of the Śrī Brahma-Mādhva-Gauḍīya *sampradāya*,
in the third disciplic generation from *kali-yuga-pāvana*
Śrī Kṛṣṇa Caitanya, who descended to perform His own *bhajana*
and distribute to others the ultimate goal of devotion to Śrī Kṛṣṇa

With foreword, explanations of Śrīla Jīva Gosvāmī's
commentary, and purports (*tātparya*) by the eminent personality
Śrīla Bhaktivinoda Ṭhākura,
in the eighth disciplic generation from Śrī Kṛṣṇa Caitanya

With a foreword by the effulgent *ācārya*
and founder of Śrī Caitanya Maṭh and Śrī Gauḍīya Maṭh,
Prabhupāda Śrīla Bhaktisiddhānta Sarasvatī Gosvāmī Ṭhākura,
in the ninth disciplic generation from Śrī Kṛṣṇa Caitanya

Compiled and with expanded commentary by
Śrī Śrīmad Bhaktivedānta Nārāyaṇa Mahārāja,
under the shelter and guidance of *ācārya-kesarī*
Śrī Śrīmad Bhakti Prajñāna Keśava Gosvāmī,
founder of Śrī Gauḍīya Vedānta Samiti
and in the tenth disciplic generation from Śrī Kṛṣṇa Caitanya

Vṛndāvana, Uttar Pradesh, India

Table of Contents

Śrī Śrīmad
Saccidānanda Bhaktivinoda Ṭhākura

śrī śrī māyāpuracandro jayati

For the reader's interest

It is stated in *Śrī Caitanya-caritāmṛta* (*Madhya-līlā* 9.234, 237–41):

sei dina cali' āilā payasvinī-tīre
snāna kari' gelā ādi-keśava-mandire

mahā-bhakta-gaṇa-saha tāhāṅ goṣṭhī kaila
'brahma-saṁhitādhyāya'-puṅthi tāhāṅ pāila

puṅthi pāñā prabhura haila ānanda apāra
kampāśru-sveda-stambha-pulaka vikāra

siddhānta-śāstra nāhi 'brahma-saṁhitā'ra sama
govinda-mahimā jñānera parama kāraṇa

alpākṣare kahe siddhānta apāra
sakala-vaiṣṇava-śāstra-madhye ati sāra

bahu yatne sei puṅthi nila lekhāiyā
'ananta padmanābha' āilā haraṣita hañā

After accepting the renounced order, Śrī Śacīnandana Gaurahari resided briefly in Śrī Purī-dhāma, and then began His tour of South India on the pretext of visiting the holy places of pilgrimage. After visiting Kanyākumārī, He arrived in the holy place called Vetapānī, located in Mallāra Deśa, where He had *darśana* of Śrī Raghunātha and then took rest for the night. A band of gypsies from the nomadic Bhaṭṭathāri community, who had made their camp there, captured Kālā-kṛṣṇadāsa, Śrīman Mahāprabhu's servant and associate, by alluring him with women. However, Mahāprabhu rescued him by the power of His divine opulence, and then immediately proceeded to the sacred banks of the Payasvinī River.

After taking evening bath in the river, Śrīman Mahāprabhu went for *darśana* of Śrī Ādi-Keśava. While beholding the deity, He became absorbed in ecstatic love and began to dance, sing and recite prayers and verses. When the scholarly devotees and thousands of pilgrims there saw Him, they were all struck with wonder. After taking *darśana* of the deity, Śrīman Mahāprabhu noticed that some devotees, who were immensely learned and realized in philosophical principles, were lecturing on this book, the Fifth Chapter of *Śrī Brahma-saṁhitā*. He was overjoyed to hear this devotional treatise, and after reading only a few verses Himself, He was unable to maintain His composure. The eight symptoms of transcendental ecstasy, such as tears, horripilation and trembling, became manifest.

Indeed, *Brahma-saṁhitā* is unprecedented and unique among the literature of the *bhakti* tradition. It is filled with descriptions of the paramount glories of Svayam Bhagavān Śrī Govindadeva, and with knowledge of the essential reality of the Supreme Personality and the essential reality of *bhakti*. It is as if a vast ocean has been bottled in one succinct treatise. Here one will find the collected essence of all Vaiṣṇava scripture, including the Vedas, the Purāṇas, *Bhagavad-gītā* and *Śrīmad-Bhāgavatam*. Śrīman Mahāprabhu had this great literature copied very carefully, and then He brought it back with Him to Śrīdhāma Jagannātha Purī.

I have no right to say anything more about this text. Nevertheless, I simply wish to suggest that if this literature is accepted in the category of extremely ancient scriptures, it is exceptional evidence to support the doctrine of *kṛṣṇa-bhakti*. Alternatively, one may argue that Śrī Caitanya Mahāprabhu must have written it Himself, since no mention of this scripture can be found anywhere in this region of Northern India. If such an opinion were to be established conclusively, what could possibly be a greater source of joy? The reason is that, in the Vaiṣṇava world, every last doubt about philosophical conclusions would at once be dispelled upon the discovery of a thesis of established philosophical truths written personally by Śrīman Mahāprabhu. Whatever one's opinion may be, this *Brahma-saṁhitā* is worshipable for Vaiṣṇavas, and is also worthy of their thorough study.

Śrī Bhaktivinoda Ṭhākura

Śrī Śrīmad
Bhaktisiddhānta Sarasvatī Ṭhākura Prabhupāda

śrī śrī guru-gaurāṅgau jayataḥ

Feelings of appreciation

It is common knowledge that *Śrī Brahma-saṁhitā* was not propagated in India prior to its being collected by Śrī Gaurasundara. Rather, the literary composition that had been widely popularized throughout the nation was *Śrīmad-Bhāgavatam*, the *sātvata-saṁhitā* (compilation for those in pure goodness) that was previously spoken in Naimiṣāraṇya. The word *brahma* means both "Veda" and also "the factual substance or reality established by the Vedas," which is none other than the Supreme Personality and Enjoyer, Śrī Kṛṣṇa, or Śrī Govinda. The understanding of the word *apauruṣeya* ("not of human origin," or "divine") is considered marginal if the word is used to confound the mundane conception by eliminating the irrelevant ("*neti neti*"), but does not refer to the Supreme Personality and Enjoyer, Śrī Kṛṣṇa.

Śrī Caturmukha Brahmā discarded mundane considerations from within the Vedas, which are called *apauruṣeya* (of divine origin), and then described in a *saṁhitā* (compilation) of one hundred chapters whatever essence of pure *bhakti* he had been holding in his heart in connection with the Supreme Enjoyer. Among those chapters, this Fifth Chapter is most worshipable for Gauḍīya Vaiṣṇavas because it is extremely practical and advantageous for the living entity. Especially from the point of view of the Śrī Brahma *sampradāya*, the factual substance of reality has been revealed in the four original verses of *Śrīmad-Bhāgavatam* by the mercy of Bhagavān.

The Supreme Personality can never be included in the category of insignificant worldly material enjoyers. The distinction between the two is that the Supreme Personality Śrī Kṛṣṇa is the absolute controller of all predominated potencies, whereas the individual living entity is completely bound by the Lord's potencies. Thus, the word *apauruṣeya* (not of mundane origin), is applied to Śrī Kṛṣṇa from the perspective of the conditioned living entity (*puruṣa*) who tries to conceive of Him who is beyond material existence. It is stated in the first verse of the *Śrīmad-Bhāgavatam*:

janmādyasya yato 'nvayād itarataś cārtheṣv abhijñaḥ svarāṭ
tene brahma hṛdā ya ādi-kavaye muhyanti yat sūrayaḥ
tejo-vāri-mṛdāṁ yathā vinimayo yatra tri-sargo 'mṛṣā
dhāmnā svena sadā nirasta-kuhakaṁ satyaṁ paraṁ dhīmahi

Śrīmad-Bhāgavatam (1.1.1)

I meditate upon Śrī Kṛṣṇa, who is the Absolute Truth and the original cause of the creation, maintenance and annihilation of the mundane universes. He is directly and indirectly conscious of all manifestations, and He is independent, because there is no other cause beyond Him. It is He who first imparted the Vedic knowledge unto the heart of Brahmājī, the original living being. By Him even great sages and demigods are placed into illusion, as one is bewildered by the illusory representations of water seen in fire, or land seen on water. Only because of Him do the material universes, temporarily manifested by the reactions of the three modes of nature, appear factual, although they are unreal. I therefore meditate upon Him, Śrī Kṛṣṇa, who is eternally existent in the transcendental abode, which is forever free from the illusory representations of the material world. I meditate upon Him, for He is the Absolute Truth.

The transcendental abode (*dhāma*) referred to here is categorically distinct from any material location. The word *dhāma* means "shelter" and also "light." One cannot see without light, and this verse confirms that the basis of illumination is a Person who is the object of worship, and is seen by the very same light. The foundation of illumination, the Supreme Transcendental Enjoyer Śrī Kṛṣṇa, exists splendidly and eternally along with His paraphernalia in the supramundane *dhāma* that lies beyond all comprehension of the conditioned souls who are entangled in transitory relationships within the material nature.

In the impersonal conception, the seer and the seen are ultimately considered to be one. This conception has arisen on the basis of the experience of limitation and incompleteness in the mundane realm, but this experience is irrelevant. The deluding material potency cannot disable her own controller, Viṣṇu, who is the Supreme Lord of Vaikuṇṭha and equipped with immeasurable power. The impersonal conception, which is thoroughly mundane, has been ousted entirely by the considerations described in the Fifth Chapter of this treatise.

The trend of thought presented in *Brahma-saṁhitā* is worthy of our profound investigation. We should therefore distance ourselves from the mundane point of view, in which scriptural descriptions of instrumental and ingredient causes may be considered to be indecent. This scripture was not contrived for the sake of delighting the minds of crude persons through vulgar devices. Rather, it has manifested for the purpose of infusing spiritual strength into the hearts of those who are debilitated by the onslaught of their own perverse inclinations.

The doctrine of the worship of five deities[1] was created as a result of a distorted vision of the substance of Godhead. This incorrect vision arose from the predominant pursuit of four conceptions, namely ordinary religiosity, economic development, sense gratification and liberation. The five concluding verses of *Brahma-saṁhitā* convey this point clearly and meticulously, and also elucidate the genuine philosophy concerning the substance of Godhead. By the grace of Sudarśana (the original auspicious vision of Bhagavān), one may acquire eternal wisdom through

[1] Sūrya, Gaṇeśa, Śiva, Durgā and Viṣṇu are worshiped together in the system known as *pañcopāsanā*.

careful study of these verses. The attainment of such wisdom renders one entirely devoid of antagonism towards the conception of Śrī Dhāma (the spiritual abode, full of all transcendental opulence). This antagonism is manifest as the tendency to propagate the defective philosophy that the Absolute Truth is formless and impersonal.

By good fortune one may be acquainted with the unique qualities of the self-effulgent transcendental abode that lies beyond Devī-dhāma and Maheśa-dhāma. That abode is *nirasta-kuhaka*, devoid of the darkness of nescience. The affairs of transcendence lie beyond material nature, and there is no room for the relative deception of the mundane world in that realm of eternal joy. It is for this reason that the treatise describing this transcendental phenomenon is called *Apauruṣeya-saṁhitā*.

Human beings whose hearts are polluted can be delivered from the tendency to enjoy inert matter by the power of the process of devotional service in practice (*sādhana-bhakti*). It is impossible for those who are ensnared in mundane sense enjoyment to take shelter of pure devotion. Such persons are only fit to undergo distress while being confined to the field of fruitive activities in the material world. The living entity's lusty desires for material enjoyment can only be dispelled by singing the glories of Kāmadeva, the transcendental Cupid. However, if one equates this excellent Kāmadeva with the inferior mundane lust, one will suffer an adverse effect instead of deriving benefit.

Our recitation of *Brahma-saṁhitā* will be considered successful when we become the followers of Caturmukha Brahmā and attain the mercy of Bhagavān, and when we can become the receptacles of love of God through singing these divine hymns in praise of Śrī Kṛṣṇa. At that time we will be able to understand that Śrī Rādhā-Govinda, the embodiments of sweet human-like pastimes, exist in the form of Śrī Gaurasundara. Śrī Gaurasundara resides in the most elevated realm of service to the genuine supreme predominating enjoyer, who possesses all opulence.

In the lower half of Goloka, two-and-a-half *rasas* (devotional mellows) are present in relation to Śrī Nārāyaṇa. Maheśa-dhāma lies below this, and below that again lies Devī-dhāma, the mundane realm that consists of fourteen planetary systems. The residents of Devī-dhāma, who are wandering throughout the universe, attain withdrawal of their material desires in Maheśa-dhāma. The conception of desirelessness that can be attained in Maheśa-dhāma eternally shines forth through the myriad variety of services available in the transcendental abode. That resplendent myriad of services is embodied in this *Brahma-saṁhitā* which describes the fifth and ultimate goal of human existence, namely the ultimate limit of the nectar of love for Śrī Śrī Rādhā-Govinda. Śrī Gaurasundara exhibited the extent of His magnanimity in His pastime of bestowing *śrī kṛṣṇa-prema*, by collecting that nectar and personally distributing it to the souls of this world.

Śrī Siddhānta Sarasvatī

Śrī Śrīmad
Bhakti Prajñāna Keśava Gosvāmī

Nitya-līlā-praviṣṭa oṁ viṣṇupāda *Śrī Śrīmad Bhakti Prajñāna Keśava Gosvāmī Mahārāja, the lion-like founder of Śrī Gauḍīya Vedānta Samiti, initiating spiritual master of Śrī Śrīmad Bhaktivedānta Nārāyaṇa Mahārāja, and* sannyāsa-guru *of Śrīla A.C. Bhaktivedānta Swami Prabhupāda.*

nama oṁ viṣṇu-pādāya
gaura-preṣṭhāya bhū-tale
śrī śrīmad bhakti-prajñāna-
keśava-gosvāmi-nāmine

govindam, ādi-puruṣaṁ, tam ahaṁ bhajāmi
govindam, ādi-puruṣaṁ, tam ahaṁ bhajāmi
govindam, ādi-puruṣaṁ, tam ahaṁ bhajāmi

veṇuṁ kvanantam aravinda-dalāyatākṣaṁ
barhāvataṁsam asitāmbuda-
sundarāṅgam
kandarpa-koṭi-kamanīya-
viśeṣa-śobham
govindam, ādi-
puruṣaṁ, tam
ahaṁ bhajāmi
govindam,
ādi-puruṣaṁ,
tam ahaṁ
bhajāmi
govindam
ādi-puruṣaṁ
tam ahaṁ bhajāmi
aṅgāni yasya
sakalendriya-vṛtti-
manti,
paśyanti pānti
kalayanti ciraṁ
jaganti.
ānanda-cinmaya-sad-ujjvala-vigrahasya,
govindam, ādi-puruṣaṁ, tam ahaṁ bhajāmi
govindam, ādi-puruṣaṁ, tam ahaṁ bhajāmi
govindam, ādi-puruṣaṁ, tam ahaṁ bhajāmi
govindam, ādi-puruṣaṁ, tam ahaṁ bhajāmi
govindam, ādi-puruṣaṁ, tam ahaṁ bhajāmi.

Śrīla A.C. Bhaktivedānta Swami Prabhupāda was the first to make Śrī Brahma-saṁhitā well-known all over the world. By his inspiration the Radha-Krishna Temple Album made the prayers of Brahma-saṁhitā heard in millions of homes outside India. He gave many lectures elaborately explaining various verses of Śrī Brahma-saṁhitā, and republished the first English edition of his gurudeva, *Śrīla Bhaktisiddhānta Sarasvatī Prabhupāda. All who read this English edition and benefit from the deep illuminations of Śrīla Bhaktivinoda Ṭhākura and Śrīla Jīva Gosvāmī are forever indebted to this great personality who brought the flood of Śrī Caitanya Mahāprabhu's* prema-saṅkīrtana *movement to the western world, and in eleven short years made "Hare Krishna" a household word.*

Śrī Śrīmad
Bhaktivedānta Nārāyaṇa Mahārāja

śrī śrī guru-gaurāṅgau jayataḥ

Introduction

[*translated from the Hindi edition*]

Śrī Brahma-saṁhitā was revealed by Śrī Brahmā, the original *guru* of the Brahma *sampradāya*, and the great-grandfather of the universe. It was collected and propagated by Śrī Caitanya Mahāprabhu, who is adorned with the sentiment and complexion of Śrī Rādhā. This scripture, which is full of brilliantly effulgent transcendental jewels in the form of many philosophical conclusions of *bhakti*, is an incomparable devotional scripture. Not only does it stand out among Śrī Gauḍīya Vaiṣṇava literature, but also within the entire body of sacred Indian texts received through oral tradition, such as the Vedas, the Purāṇas, the *Vedānta-sūtra*, *Bhagavad-gītā* and *Śrīmad-Bhāgavatam*. It is a matter of unlimited jubilation that today we are presenting the aforementioned *Brahma-saṁhitā* before our readers in Hindi, the national language of India, by the causeless mercy and inspiration of our *paramārādhya guru-pāda-padma, oṁ viṣṇupāda aṣṭottara-śata* Śrī Śrīmad Bhakti Prajñāna Keśava Gosvāmī Mahārāja.

It was my most worshipable Śrī Gurudeva's heartfelt desire that the Vedic devotional scriptures, especially the exceptionally beneficial Gauḍīya Vaiṣṇava devotional literatures, should be published profusely in Hindi and in all the other prominent languages of the world, and that they should simultaneously be distributed widely. By his mercy and inspiration, more than forty *bhakti* literatures have already been published in just a few short years. These include *Bhagavad-gītā* with Śrīla Viśvanātha Cakravartī Ṭhākura's commentary; Śrīla Bhaktivinoda Ṭhākura's *Jaiva-dharma*, *Śrī Caitanya-śikṣāmṛta*, *Bhajana-rahasya* and

Śrī Sanmodana-bhāṣya commentary on Śrīman Mahāprabhu's *Śikṣāṣṭaka*; Śrīla Rūpa Gosvāmī's *Upadeśāmṛta*; Śrīla Raghunātha dāsa Gosvāmī's *Śrī Manaḥ-śikṣā*; and several texts by Śrīla Viśvanātha Cakravartī Ṭhākura, such as *Bhakti-rasāmṛta-sindhu-bindu*, *Ujjvala-nīlamaṇi-kiraṇa* and *Bhāgavatāmṛta-kaṇā*. Most of these editions have also been translated into Hindi and other prominent languages of the world. Continuing in the same line, the publication of this Hindi edition of *Brahma-saṁhitā* today is a source of immense joy.

Brahmājī is the great-grandfather of the world, the original poet, and the presiding deity of the creation. When he appeared from Garbhodakaśāyī Viṣṇu's lotus navel, he saw nothing but darkness in all directions, and he became confused about his duty. By the mercy of Bhagavān, he heard the sound "*tapa*," and began to perform severe austerities.[2] When Brahmā's austerity was mature, Bhagavān's intrinsic nature of eternity, knowledge and bliss manifested in his heart by the mercy of the Supreme Lord. This has also been mentioned in the auspicious invocation or opening verse of the *sātvata-saṁhitā Śrīmad-Bhāgavatam*: "*tene brahma hṛdā ya ādi-kavaye* – by the mercy of Bhagavān, transcendental knowledge of the Supreme Lord, who is the proprietor of unlimited potencies and the embodiment of eternal cognizance and bliss, was manifested in Śrī Brahmā's heart." Consequently, his prayers in glorification of Svayam Bhagavān Śrī Kṛṣṇa, which he composed after he had personally realized

[2] According to *Brahma-saṁhitā*, by the mercy of Śrī Kṛṣṇa, Brahmājī received the eighteen-syllable *mantra* (the Gopāla *mantra*) through the medium of the transcendental Sarasvatī, and he began to perform *tapasya* in the form of *mantra-japa*. As a result of his dedication to the *mantra*, he later received *kāma-gāyatrī* through the medium of Śrī Kṛṣṇa's flute-song. By the influence of that *kāma-gāyatrī*, Brahmājī attained the status of being twice-born, and he began to glorify Śrī Kṛṣṇa with prayers that fully embodied the essential conclusions of the Vedas.

the Absolute Truth and which contain perfectly conclusive statements revealing the essence of all the Vedas, are called *Brahma-saṁhitā*.

There are one hundred chapters in this epic scripture. The essence of the entire text has been kept in this, the Fifth Chapter, just as if the ocean had been stored in a jar. The totality of established truths contained in all the Vedas, Purāṇas and Saṁhitās, and in the *Mahābhārata*, *Śrīmad-Bhāgavatam* and other authentic Vaiṣṇava literature, is included within this great monarch of scriptures. When the most munificent Śrī Śacīnandana Gaurahari was traveling in South India for the benefit of the world, He arrived in Trivendram, the capital of Kerala Pradesh, intending to take *darśana* of Śrī Ananta Padmanābha. On the way, He came across the temple of Ādi-Keśavajī on the banks of the sacred Payasvinī River. There He became overjoyed to hear the highly qualified devotees of that place reciting the Fifth Chapter of *Brahma-saṁhitā* and, after having a copy made, He took it with Him. That Fifth Chapter is now celebrated by the name *Brahma-saṁhitā*.

One should understand that there is no necessity of writing anything new about this regal scripture. Śrī Jīva Gosvāmī, who is the Gauḍīya *sampradāya-ācārya* on philosophical conclusions of the Absolute Truth, has analyzed the subject matter of *Brahma-saṁhitā* in his *Digdarśanī* commentary, and has revealed its immaculate glories to the fullest extent. Also in regard to this great, sacred Vaiṣṇava text, Śrīla Kṛṣṇadāsa Kavirāja, the author of *Śrī Caitanya-caritāmṛta*, has written:

siddhānta-śāstra nāhi 'brahma-saṁhitā'ra sama
govinda-mahimā jñānera parama kāraṇa

alpākṣare kahe siddhānta apāra
sakala-vaiṣṇava-śāstra-madhye ati sāra

Śrī Caitanya-caritāmṛta (*Madhya-līlā* 9.239–40)

As far as the final spiritual conclusion is concerned, there is no scripture equal to *Brahma-saṁhitā*. Indeed, that scripture is the supreme revelation of the glories of Śrī Govinda, for it reveals the topmost knowledge about Him. Since all conclusions are briefly presented in *Brahma-saṁhitā*, it is essential among all Vaiṣṇava literatures.

In addition to this book of philosophical conclusions, Śrī Caitanya Mahāprabhu also brought with Him from South India a book describing Kṛṣṇa's pastimes, namely *Śrī Kṛṣṇa-karṇāmṛta*. At the time of Śrī Ratha-yātrā, the devotees who were not His pastime associates (*līlā-parikaras*), and who had come from various Northern Indian provinces such as Śrīdhāma Vṛndāvana, enthusiastically copied these two texts and took the copies with them when they returned. In this way, both books were propagated throughout India. In this regard, it is stated in *Śrī Caitanya-caritāmṛta*:

pratyeka vaiṣṇava sabe likhiyā laila
krame krame dūī pustaka jagat vyāpila

Śrī Caitanya-caritāmṛta (*Madhya-līlā* 11.143)

Indeed, each and every Vaiṣṇava copied the two books. By and by, the two books were broadcast all over India.

As mentioned before, Śrīla Jīva Gosvāmī, the *ācārya* of Gauḍīya philosophical conclusions, has written a commentary on this superlative text. That commentary is entitled *Digdarśanī*, and it is pregnant with highly confidential devotional conclusions. The commentator appeared in the village of Rāmakeli in the Māladaha district of Bengal in approximately A.D. 1507 as the son of Śrī Anupama (Śrī Vallabha Mallika), who was the younger brother of the renowned Śrī Sanātana Gosvāmī and Śrī Rūpa Gosvāmī. When Śrī Caitanya Mahāprabhu came to Rāmakeli to give His *darśana* to Śrī Rūpa and Sanātana, Śrī Jīva, who was at that time just a babe in arms, had the good fortune to have the Lord's *darśana* and touch His lotus feet.

From early childhood Śrī Jīva was grave in character and wealthy in intelligence. While he was still a boy, after completing his study of grammar and other subjects, he completely renounced his home life to go to the divine lotus feet of Śrī Nityānanda Prabhu in Śrī Māyāpura Yogapīṭha, the holy appearance place of Śrī Caitanya Mahāprabhu. Śrī Nityānanda Prabhu bestowed His causeless mercy upon Śrī Jīva by taking him for *darśana* of the sixteen *krośas* (32 square miles) of Śrī Navadvīpa-maṇḍala. Śrīla Bhaktivinoda Ṭhākura has given an interesting account of this occurrence in his book *Śrī Navadvīpa-dhāma-māhātmya.*

Śrī Nityānanda Prabhu gave Śrī Jīva the order to go and stay in Śrīdhāma Vṛndāvana with Śrī Rūpa and Sanātana. On the way to Vṛndāvana, Śrī Jīva spent some time in Vārāṇasī studying texts on logic and Vedānta under the guidance of Śrī Madhusūdana Vidyāvācaspati. After that, when he arrived in Śrīdhāma Vṛndāvana, he became the fully surrendered disciple of Śrī Rūpa Gosvāmī, assisting him in various ways in the momentous work of writing authentic scriptures.

When Śrīla Rūpa and Sanātana Gosvāmīs disappeared, Śrī Jīva Gosvāmī became the undisputed emperor of all the Vaiṣṇava *ācāryas* in Vraja-maṇḍala, Gauḍa-maṇḍala and Kṣetra-maṇḍala. It was only after receiving instructions from him that Śrī Narottama Ṭhākura, Śrīnivāsa Ācārya and Śrī Śyāmānanda Prabhu became immensely influential in propagating *harināma-saṅkīrtana* and the literatures of the Gosvāmīs throughout Bengal, Assam, Manipura and Orissa. Śrīla Jīva Gosvāmī wrote twenty-five invaluable texts, including *Śrī Harināmāmṛta-vyākaraṇa*, *Ṣaṭ-sandarbha*, *Krama-sandarbha* (a commentary on *Śrīmad-Bhāgavatam*), *Gopāla-campū*, *Mādhava-mahotsava*,

Laghu-vaiṣṇava-toṣaṇī (a commentary on the Tenth Canto of *Śrīmad-Bhāgavatam*) and *Śrī Brahma-saṁhitā Digdarśanī-ṭīkā*.

The profound and confidential philosophical conclusions of *Brahma-saṁhitā* are practically incomprehensible without the help of the *Digdarśanī-ṭīkā* of Śrīla Jīva Gosvāmī, whose esoteric and penetrating insights are, however, also extremely difficult to understand. Śrīla Saccidānanda Bhaktivinoda Ṭhākura, the eternal associate of Śrī Caitanya Mahāprabhu, is the Bhagīratha who caused the Gaṅgā of *bhakti* (*bhakti-bhāgīrathī*)[3] to flow once again, inundating the entire world with *prema* in this modern age. He has conferred great welfare upon the Vaiṣṇava world by translating the *Digdarśanī-ṭīkā* into Bengali, and writing a commentary of his own entitled *Prakāśinī*. With the help of his purports, one can easily have access to the hidden moods of the original text, and to Śrī Jīva Gosvāmī's deep considerations.

Śrīla Bhaktivinoda Ṭhākura appeared near Śrīdhāma Navadvīpa, in the village of Ulā, in a highly educated and religious family, and was manifest in this world from 1838 to 1914. He was educated in Mahānagarī, Calcutta and was fluent in several languages, including Sanskrit, Bengali, Hindi, Oriya and English. This great personality rediscovered Śrīdhāma Māyāpura, the site of Śrī Gaurasundara's appearance place, which had been lost in recent times. He is also the worshipable father and *śikṣa-guru* of *jagad-guru* Śrī Bhaktisiddhānta Sarasvatī Prabhupāda, the world-famous preacher of *harināma-saṅkīrtana* and the instructions of Mahāprabhu. He has written about one hundred books, including *Śrī Caitanya-śikṣāmṛta*, *The Teachings of Śrīman Mahāprabhu*, *Jaiva-dharma*, *Śrī Kṛṣṇa-saṁhitā*,

[3] Mahārāja Bhagīratha's austerities to bring the holy river Gaṅgā to this Earth planet are described in *Śrīmad-Bhāgavatam*, Ninth Canto, Chapter Nine. Because she came to this Earth in response to Mahārāja Bhagīratha's austerities, Gaṅgā-devī is also known as Bhāgīrathī.

Bhāgavatārka-marīci-mālā, Śrī Harināma-cintāmaṇi, Śrī Bhajana-rahasya and *Datta-kaustubha*. Although his language is simple and natural, his mood is profound and mature. His purports to *Śrī Brahma-saṁhitā* are extremely deep and full of ecstatic transcendental emotions. Especially in his elaborate explanation of the word *nija-rūpatayā* in the thirty-seventh verse, he has performed the astonishing and formidable feat of perfectly reconciling Śrīla Rūpa Gosvāmipāda's philosophy of transcendental paramourship (*parakīya-siddhānta*) and Śrī Jīva Gosvāmī's philosophy of transcendental wedlock (*svakīya-siddhānta*), through a meticulous and subtle analysis of both.

My dear Śrīmad Bhaktivedānta Tīrtha Mahārāja has made a highly laudable effort to assist me in translating the original Hindi edition from Bengali. Actually, it is only due to his enthusiastic insistence that I gave priority to the publication of this devotional text over the publication of all others. Also worthy of praise are the valiant efforts of Śrīmad Bhaktivedānta Mādhava Mahārāja, Śrīmān Puṇḍarīka Brahmacārī, Śrīmān Purandara Brahmacārī and Śrī Omprakāśa Vrajavāsī (M.A., L.L.B.) in rendering various services such as presenting the manuscript, word-processing, proof-reading and so on. Śrī Bhūdhara dāsa has rendered service to Śrī Śacīnandana Gaurahari by his generous financial support. Our request at the lotus feet of Śrī Śrī Guru-Gaurāṅga and Śrī Śrī Gāndharvikā-Giridhārī is that they bestow their profuse blessings upon all of these devotees.

I have confidence that this text will be revered among the faithful *sādhakas* who are thirsting for devotion, and also among the intelligentsia. It is my heartfelt aspiration that they may enter into the immaculate *prema-dharma*. My most worshipable *śrī guru-pāda-padma* feels pain upon seeing the distress of others, and he is the embodiment of the Supreme Lord's mercy. May he and Śacīnandana Śrī Gaurahari be pleased with us and bestow upon us the qualification to render the services that fulfill their innermost heart's desire. This is our only grief-stricken prayer at their divine lotus feet. What need is there to say more?

Begging for a slight trace of the mercy
of *śrī guru* and Vaiṣṇavas,

Śrī Bhaktivedānta Nārāyaṇa

śrī śrī guru-gaurāṅgau jayataḥ

Preface

This first English edition brings to light many deep insights into the scriptural conclusions of our Gauḍīya Vaiṣṇava *ācāryas*. In particular, this is the first time that a full expanded translation of Śrīla Jīva Gosvāmī's erudite Sanskrit commentary (*ṭīkā*) has been presented in English alongside the purports of Śrīla Bhaktivinoda Ṭhākura, titled "Tātparya." Śrī Śrīmad Bhaktivedānta Nārāyaṇa Mahārāja's presentation of Śrīla Jīva Gosvāmī's commentary (titled "Ṭīkā translation") is based on Śrīla Bhaktivinoda Ṭhākura's original Bengali translation of Jīva Gosvāmī's commentary. Śrīla Nārāyaṇa Mahārāja has also given his explanations in the subsections titled "Vivṛti" and "Bhāvārtha," as well as in the Bhāvānuvādas, which delve deeply into the inner meanings of Śrīla Jīva Gosvāmī's commentary for certain select verses. The entire *ṭīkā* of Śrīla Jīva Gosvāmī has been presented in transliterated form in a special appendix.

Śrī Brahma-saṁhitā is by nature a deeply technical scripture which discusses a broad array of topics, some of which may at times appear highly esoteric. We have tried to remain true to the original Sanskrit, Bengali and Hindi sources without unnecessarily burdening the reader with Sanskrit terminology. Those who are interested in the precise Sanskrit terms used for English phrases may refer to the English Glossary, which lists English phrases alongside their Sanskrit equivalents.

In many places terms such as Goloka, Gokula and Śvetadvīpa are used in a way that may at first seem confusing to the reader. These should be understood according to their context. These transcendental place-names all have specific meanings, but they are also used to refer to Śrī Kṛṣṇa's divine abode. When the eternally manifest abode in the spiritual world is mentioned, it is usually called Goloka, and when it is manifest within this material world, it is called Gokula. But Gokula also refers to that place within Goloka in the spiritual world which is predominated by sweetness and there is an absence of any moods of opulence or reverence – in that Gokula even servitude is not without intimacy and familiarity. Similarly, Śvetadvīpa generally refers to the section of Goloka in the spiritual world where the eternal pastimes of Śrī Śacīnandana Gaurahari are taking place. That Śvetadvīpa is manifest within this world as Navadvīpa. Śvetadvīpa also refers to the outer part of Goloka in the spiritual world which is predominated by a mood of opulence, and where Rādhā and the other *gopīs* have a *svakīya* (married) relationship with Kṛṣṇa. Just as all names may be taken to refer ultimately to Śrī Kṛṣṇa, so all the various names such as Goloka, Gokula, Brahma-dhāma, Mahā-Vaikuṇṭha-dhāma and Svarga may all be taken to refer to Goloka Vṛndāvana.

One example of the same name having different meanings according to context has been given by our *gurudeva*. If we say, "Rāma was going with Sītā," it is apparent from the context that we are referring to Bhagavān Śrī Rāmacandra and His consort Sītā-devī. On the other hand, if we say, "Rāma is a bad boy," it is also apparent that we are talking about a human boy named Rāma. It is not necessary to say, "Rāma, who is God Himself, was going with Sītā," as this is obvious from the context.

This English edition has been translated from the Hindi edition of our *gurudeva, rūpānuga-varya* Śrī Śrīmad Bhaktivedānta Nārāyaṇa Mahārāja. First and foremost we are indebted to Śrīla Gurudeva, by whose grace our darkened eyes may receive the divine vision of the all-effulgent eternal abode described herein, and the ever-youthful Divine Couple Śrī Śrī Rādhā-Kṛṣṇa who preside there. Most of the translation was done by Śrīpāda

Bhaktivedānta Āraṇya Mahārāja. Śrīpāda Bhaktivedānta Mādhava Mahāraja answered numerous questions which arose in translation and final editing. Credit also goes to Śrīpāda Bhaktivedānta Bhāgavata Mahārāja, Śrīpāda Jñāna dāsa Vanacārī, Pūjanīyā Śyāmarāṇī dāsī, Śrīmān Kṛṣṇa-kāruṇya Brahmacārī, Śrīmān Kṛṣṇa-prema dāsa, Śrīmān Prema-vilāsa dāsa, Śrīmān Jaya Gopāla dāsa, Śrīmān Ananta-Kṛṣṇa dāsa, Lavaṅga-latā dāsī, Mañjulālī dāsī and Vicitri dāsī for their efforts in translating, editing, typesetting, proofreading, entering corrections, graphic design and layout. Special thanks go to Śrīmān Gopīnātha dāsa for his generous support in providing facilities at Gopinath Bhavan, Vṛndāvana, and for providing computer equipment needed to complete this and other books. Finally, the printing of this long-awaited first edition has been made possible largely through the generous contributions of Govinda dāsī.

ATULA-KṚṢṆA DĀSA

Verse 1

ईश्वरः परमः कृष्णः सच्चिदानन्दविग्रहः ।
अनादिरादिर्गोविन्दः सर्वकारणकारणम् ॥१॥

īśvaraḥ paramaḥ kṛṣṇaḥ
sac-cid-ānanda-vigrahaḥ
anādir ādir govindaḥ
sarva-kāraṇa-kāraṇam

Anvaya

kṛṣṇaḥ – Vrajendra-nandana Kṛṣṇa (is); *paramaḥ īśvaraḥ* – the Supreme Controller, that is to say the controller of all other controllers, and the original source of all incarnations; *sac-cid-ānanda vigrahaḥ* – His body is endowed with the three potencies of existence, knowledge and bliss (*sandhinī, saṁvit* and *hlādinī*); *govindaḥ* – (He is) known as Govinda, meaning He to whom service should be rendered through the senses, and He is the presiding deity of the practical process of devotional service (*abhidheya-tattva*); *anādiḥ* – without a beginning; *ādiḥ* – the original form of all else; *sarva-kāraṇa-kāraṇam* – the cause of all causes, or the original form.

Translation

Śrī Kṛṣṇa, Govinda, is the embodiment of eternity, knowledge and bliss. He is the Supreme Personality of Godhead, the controller of all lesser controllers, and the source of all incarnations. He has no beginning or origin, though He is the source of everything and the cause of all causes.

Translation and explanation of Śrīla Jīva Gosvāmī's ṭīkā (bhāvānuvāda)

I offer my obeisances to Śrī Śrī Rādhā-Govinda, by whose grace I have been inspired with the desire to comment upon *Śrī Brahma-saṁhitā*. May the glory of the beautiful form of Śrī Kṛṣṇa arise most excellently within my heart.

It is impossible for me to illuminate the thoroughly consistent, genuine purports and pleasing considerations within the heart of the greatest of sages, Śrī Brahmā, but he is nonetheless my only refuge.

Although this *Brahma-saṁhitā* is complete with one hundred chapters, still this Fifth Chapter, being the condensed essence of the entire book, brings the subject matter within our grasp.

The deep philosophical considerations in *Śrīmad-Bhāgavatam* and other *śāstras* that are seen by persons endowed with immaculate intelligence are all found collected together here. This brings extreme jubilation to my heart.

In order to deliberate further on what I described elaborately in *Śrī Kṛṣṇa-sandarbha*, I am touching upon the content of this scripture with full, thoughtful deliberation.

The following verse of *Śrīmad-Bhāgavatam* has been ascertained to be the defining statement (*paribhāṣā*): "*ete cāṁśa-kalāḥ puṁsaḥ, kṛṣṇas tu bhagavān svayam* – all the incarnations of Godhead are either plenary expansions or expansions of the expansions of the Supreme Person, but Śrī Kṛṣṇa is Himself the original Personality of Godhead."

Similarly, in the verse at hand, Kṛṣṇa has also been called the supreme controller, or the controller of all other controllers (*īśvaraḥ-paramaḥ*). Other incarnations of Kṛṣṇa are also called controllers (*īśvara*); therefore, only the origin of all incarnations, Śrī Kṛṣṇa, has been called the supreme controller (*parameśvara*).

It is stated in *śāstra*, "Let me try to understand Śrī Kṛṣṇa, who is the supreme controller of all controllers, the supreme worshipable deity among all worshipable deities, the supreme progenitor of all progenitors, and the master of the entire creation."

In this first verse, the word *kṛṣṇa* is the subject, and all the other words take the role of adjectives. All the famous perfect authorities, including Śrī Śukadeva Gosvāmī, have established Śrī Kṛṣṇa as the source of all incarnations by phrases such as "*kṛṣṇāvatāra-mahotsava* – the great festival of Śrī Kṛṣṇa's descent." The invocation of *Sāmopaniṣad* also supports this through the *kīrtana* of Kṛṣṇa's names in verses such as *kṛṣṇāya vāsudevāya devakī-nandanāya.*

At the time of Kṛṣṇa's appearance, when Gargācārya came to Nanda-Gokula and performed Śrī Kṛṣṇa's name-giving ceremony, Garga Ṛṣi said, "O Nanda, your son has appeared in previous ages as well. He came in a white form in Satya-yuga, a red form in Tretā-yuga, a yellow form in Kali-yuga, and now in Dvāpara-yuga He has appeared with a blackish complexion. Therefore this boy's name is Kṛṣṇa." In that statement of Gargācārya, the phrase *kṛṣṇatāṁ gataḥ* means *kṛṣṇa-svarūpatāṁ gataḥ*, entered into Kṛṣṇa's original form. It is evident from this statement that all the incarnations attain identity with Kṛṣṇa by entering into Kṛṣṇa's original form.[1] This conclusion is supported by the logic of filling a pot with milk. Just as a pot is full of milk, so the *śāstra* is filled with the names of Śrī Kṛṣṇa. The all-in-all, the Supreme Truth, the supreme non-dual reality has been called Śrī Kṛṣṇa.

In the *Prabhāsa-khaṇḍa* of the *Padma Purāṇa*, there is a discussion between Śrī Nārada and Kuśadhvaja, in which the following verse has been cited: "*nāmnāṁ mukhyatamaṁ nāma kṛṣṇākhyaṁ me parantapa* – O subduer of enemies, the name

[1] In *Śrīmad-Bhāgavatam* it is described that Śrī Kṛṣṇa descended along with all of His expansions and incarnations. When He performed certain pastimes such as slaying demons, these were carried out by the Viṣṇu forms within Him.

Kṛṣṇa is foremost amongst all My names." Therefore it is said in *Śrī Kṛṣṇa-aṣṭottara-śata-nāma-stotra* in the *Brahmāṇḍa Purāṇa* (2.3.36.19):

sahasra-nāmnāṁ puṇyānām
trir āvṛttyā tu yat phalam
ekāvṛttyā tu kṛṣṇasya
nāmaikaṁ tat prayacchati

The result that comes from reciting the entire *Viṣṇu-sahasra-nāma* (Thousand Names of Viṣṇu) thrice is attained by reciting the name Kṛṣṇa only once.

In this way the specific glories of the name of Kṛṣṇa have been highlighted. In the present verse also, Brahmājī has offered prayers to Śrī Kṛṣṇa by the name Govinda. Govinda is Śrī Kṛṣṇa Himself – the protector of cows, *gopīs*, cowherd boys and all the residents of Vraja. To illuminate this special quality of His, He has been called Gavendra, Lord of the cows. Kṛṣṇa's supremacy is proven by the logic of giving free rein (*mukta-pragraha-vṛtti*)[2] and solid evidence from scriptures. Adjectives such as *īśvara* in the first verse also specifically confirm this point.

Śrī Kṛṣṇa's supremacy is also pointed out through His endless qualities. For example, Śrī Gargācārya has said:

āsan varṇās trayo hy asya
gṛhṇato 'nuyugaṁ tanūḥ
śuklo raktas tathā pīta
idānīṁ kṛṣṇatāṁ gataḥ

[2] *Mukta-pragraha-vṛtti*, or the logic of giving free rein, is the process of deriving all possible meanings of a word or, in other words, taking the derived meanings of a word to their utmost limit. Applying this process to names of Śrī Kṛṣṇa establishes His supremacy.

bahūni santi nāmāni
rūpāṇi ca sutasya te
guṇa-karmānurūpāṇi
tāny ahaṁ veda no janāḥ

Śrīmad-Bhāgavatam (10.8.13, 15)

O Nanda Mahārāja, your son has many qualities and activities, in accordance with which He has many names at different times. This is known only to me and to no one else. In every *yuga* He appears in different incarnations, and now He has appeared as Kṛṣṇa.

All the incarnations who have appeared since the beginning of the creation, such as Śukla, have come within Kṛṣṇa (*idānīṁ kṛṣṇatāṁ gataḥ*); that is, all incarnations have combined together in Kṛṣṇa. Therefore Kṛṣṇa's superiority is revealed by His status as the actual agent. All the *avatāras* are only forms of Kṛṣṇa. From the verse beginning *bahūni santi nāmāni rūpāṇi*, it is understood that all names and forms are names and forms of Kṛṣṇa. Thus, His distinguishing uniqueness is also proven by His qualities.

Furthermore, the following verse exclusively describes Śrī Kṛṣṇa, and cannot be applicable to anyone else:

kṛṣir bhū-vācakaḥ śabdo
ṇaś ca nirvṛtti-vācakaḥ
tayor aikyaṁ paraṁ brahma
kṛṣṇa ity abhidhīyate

Mahābhārata (*Udyoga-parva* 71.4)

The word *kṛṣ* is the attractive feature of the Lord's existence, and *ṇa* means spiritual pleasure. When the verb *kṛṣ* is added to *ṇa*, it becomes Kṛṣṇa, which indicates the Absolute Truth.

The verbal root *kṛṣ* indicates all that exists (*bhū-vācaka*), and *ṇa* indicates attraction that negates everything else (*nirvṛtti-*

vācaka). The combined form of these two is Śrī Kṛṣṇa. In the *Gautamīya-tantra* – one of the Sātvata-tantras, which are all primarily concerned with the worship of Śrī Kṛṣṇa – there is a similar verse in the description of the eighteen-syllable *mantra* (2.60):

kṛṣi-śabdasya sattārtho
ṇaś cānanda-svarūpakaḥ
sukha-rūpo bhaved ātmā
bhāvānandamayas tataḥ

> The word *kṛṣi* indicates "existence or truth," and *ṇa* refers to the embodiment of natural bliss. The combined meaning is "one whose existence is characterized by bliss" or "one who attracts all and bestows bliss upon them."

Such is the constitutional nature of Śrī Kṛṣṇa; He is the embodiment of happiness and His very nature is the topmost transcendental bliss. Many meanings can be derived from this name. The verbal root *bhū*, found in the verse at the bottom of the previous page, refers to existence. The meaning can also be taken in this context as "attraction." In the *Gautamīya-tantra*, the word *bhū* has been accepted as a statement of existence. For example, both syllables of the Sanskrit word *ghaṭa*, which refers to a narrow-mouthed waterpot, are required to distinguish it as the word that refers to "waterpot." Thus, when we say *ghaṭa*, it is understood that we are referring to a waterpot. Although the word *paṭa* (cloth) differs from *ghaṭa* by only one syllable, it is completely distinct from the word *ghaṭa* and the object referred to by *ghaṭa*. Similarly, in the present context, *bhū* and *sattā* can only proclaim the all-attractiveness of Śrī Kṛṣṇa. Furthermore, *nirvṛtti* can only be taken to mean "bliss" (*ānanda*). The two words together (*tayor aikyam*) give a distinct meaning, according to the grammatical rule of giving preference to the composite meaning when two words refer to the same subject. This is the etymology of the word *kṛṣṇa*.

Tayor aikyaṁ paraṁ brahma: When combined, the words for undivided existence (*sattā*) and unbroken bliss (*ānanda*) indicate that Parabrahma, who is supreme in every possible way and who is the greatest of the great, is called Kṛṣṇa. But here, taking the verbal root *kṛṣ* as meaning "attractive," and taking *ṇa* as *ānanda*, one should understand that the description of their inseparable nature has been given in the mood of relation between cause and effect, and not by the grammatical rule of taking them as referring to the same subject.

The logic of "ghee is life" (*āyur ghṛtam*)[3] is used to show that in the form of Śrī Kṛṣṇa, existence has an abundant measure of attraction. It is stated in the *Viṣṇu Purāṇa* (1.12.55):

bṛhatvād bṛhaṇatvāc ca yad brahmaṁ paraṁ viduḥ

One who is great and makes others great is Parabrahma.

It is also stated in the *śruti*:

atha kasmād ucyate brahma bṛṁhati bṛṁhayati ca

What is Brahman? Brahman is one who is great and who makes others great.

The impersonalists accept that the words *sattā* (existence) and *ānanda* (bliss) mean the same, but such logic is inconsistent. The literal meaning of the word *sattā* (existence), being a statement of the existence of the Supreme Being, indicates that all sages and saints are attracted to Śrī Kṛṣṇa. In the *śruti* it is said: "*sa deva saumya idam agram āsīt* – O Saumya, before the creation, only the eternal form (*sat-svarūpa*) of Bhagavān existed." Bhagavān, whose intrinsic form and nature are eternal, has both complete bliss and complete attraction. Thus, it is certain that the word *kṛṣṇaḥ* in this first verse of *Brahma-saṁhitā* is a noun and

[3] According to this logic, since ghee is a life-giving substance, it may be said that ghee is life (*āyur ghṛtam*). But the statement "ghee is life" is not literally true.

the other words are adjectives. The impersonalists use the analogy of the tree, but in the phrase *vṛkṣa-taruḥ*, there is no relationship of noun and adjective since both words refer equally to "tree." Therefore, the impersonalists' statement that *sattā* and *ānanda* have the same meaning is completely irrational. The verse from the *Gautamīya-tantra* is explained thus.

In the first half of this verse beginning *īśvaraḥ paramaḥ kṛṣṇaḥ*, the most attractive personification of bliss, who is distinguished by His inconceivable energies, is called Śrī Kṛṣṇa. The all-attractiveness of Kṛṣṇa's form and His quality of being the original form of all pleasure are mentioned in the second half of the verse. Here the word *sarva* refers to the living entities, because Śrī Kṛṣṇa attracts them and makes them blissful. The cause of this is love (*bhāva*). Thus, Śrī Kṛṣṇa is He who is always immersed in the joy of love (*premānanda*) and who immerses others in it as well. Therefore, the word *kṛṣṇa* can only refer to the embodiment of bliss, who is supremely attractive due to His form and qualities. The word *kṛṣṇa* finds its limit in Devakī-nandana (Kṛṣṇa, the son of Devakī). The all-attractiveness of Śrī Kṛṣṇa is mentioned in the *Vāsudeva Upaniṣad*: "*devakī-nandano nikhilam ānandayet* – Devakī-nandana Kṛṣṇa gives bliss to all moving and non-moving living entities." In this first *śloka* of *Brahma-saṁhitā*, the word *ānanda* (bliss) is not declinable according to the rules of Sanskrit grammar and is therefore independently meaningful. Thus this word *ānanda* should not be taken out of context. It has been used to indicate Śrī Kṛṣṇa. As Bhaṭṭajī has said:[4]

labdhvātmikā satī rūḍhir
bhaved yogāpahāriṇī
kalpanīyā tu labhate
nātmānaṁ yoga-vādhataḥ

Śrī Kṛṣṇa is clearly specified as Parabrahma in *Śrīmad-Bhāgavatam*: "*gūḍhaṁ paraṁ brahma manuṣya-liṅgam* – Śrī Kṛṣṇa is Parabrahma hiding in human form." "*Yan mitraṁ paramānandaṁ pūrṇa-brahma sanātanam* – Śrī Kṛṣṇa is the friend of the cowherd folk headed by Nanda Mahārāja. That very Śrī Kṛṣṇa is Parabrahma, the supremely blissful, ultimate and eternal Absolute Truth." In the *Viṣṇu Purāṇa* it is stated: "*yatrā-vatīrṇaṁ kṛṣṇākhyaṁ param brahma narākṛtiḥ* – Parabrahma, who is known as Kṛṣṇa, descended and exhibited His human-like pastimes." In *Bhagavad-gītā* it is said: "*brahmaṇo hi pratiṣṭhāham* – I am the basis of the formless and imperishable Brahman." And in *Gopāla-tāpanī Upaniṣad* it is said: "*yo 'sau paraṁ brahma gopālaḥ* – He who is Parabrahma, the Supreme Spirit, is Gopāla (Kṛṣṇa)." These scriptural statements clearly establish the supremacy of Śrī Kṛṣṇa as Parabrahma.

The description here is in accordance with the first verse of *Brahma-saṁhitā*. Śrī Kṛṣṇa is that *īśvara* who is replete with names, forms and qualities. *Īśvara* means one who keeps everything under His control and who is able to accomplish anything. This is also inferred in the *Gautamīya-tantra*, where another meaning of the word *kṛṣṇa* is found:

athavā karṣayet sarvaṁ
jagat sthāvara-jaṅgamam
kāla-rūpena bhagavāṁs
tenāyaṁ kṛṣṇa ucyate

[4] "The etymology of a word may be stolen away by its conventional meaning, but how can a word destroy its own derivation? It may still be understood according to its derivation." This statement by Kumārila Bhaṭṭa asserts that words may always be analyzed according to the components from which they are derived. Sanskrit words are derived from verbal roots, and the etymology or derivation of words is an important part of Sanskrit grammar. Words still take on a conventional meaning based on usage, but this does not preclude breaking words down into their original components.

That Bhagavān who in the form of all-devouring time draws along all moving and non-moving living entities is called Śrī Kṛṣṇa.

"*Kalayati niyamayati sarvam iti hi kāla-śabdārthaḥ* – one who regulates everything in the form of time is called *kāla*." In *Śrīmad-Bhāgavatam*, the great devotee Śrī Uddhava has expressed his opinion thus:

svayaṁ tv asāmyātiśayas tryadhīśaḥ
svārājya-lakṣmyāpta-samasta-kāmaḥ
baliṁ haradbhiś cira-loka-pālaiḥ
kirīta-koṭīḍita-pāda-pīṭhaḥ

Śrīmad-Bhāgavatam (3.2.29)

Bhagavān Śrī Kṛṣṇa is that personality who is complete and indivisible, who has no equal or superior, who is the master of all three planetary systems, whose desires are completely satisfied by His supreme Lakṣmī, and to whose lotus feet all the universal authorities, such as the millions of Brahmās, bow down their millions of heads in order to attain the fulfillment of their desires.

This is also supported by *Bhagavad-gītā*: "*viṣṭabhyāham idaṁ kṛtsnam ekāṁśena sthito jagat* – through only one of My expansions, I pervade and support this entire universe."

It is also stated in the *Gopāla-tāpanī Upaniṣad* (21): "*eko vaśī sarvagaḥ kṛṣṇa īḍyaḥ* – Śrī Kṛṣṇa is one. He controls everyone, knows everything and is worshipable by all." Such an *īśvara* can be referred to as *parama*. *Para* means "the most excellent" and *mā* means "Lakṣmī, the sum total of all potencies." Therefore, one who is eternally accompanied by the most excellent Lakṣmī, namely Śrī Rādhā, is called *parameśvara* Śrī Kṛṣṇa. For example, it is stated in *Śrīmad-Bhāgavatam*: "*reme ramābhir nija-kāma-samplutaḥ* – Bhagavān Śrī Kṛṣṇa enjoyed His pastimes with Śrīmatī Rādhikā and the other *gopīs*." Also: "*nāyaṁ śriyo 'nga u nitānta-rateḥ prasādaḥ* – the great fortune attained by the *gopīs* in the pastime of the *rāsa* dance with Śrī Kṛṣṇa was not available for the queens of Dvārakā headed by Rukmiṇī and Satyabhāmā, nor for the Lakṣmīs of Vaikuṇṭha or Devaloka, not to mention the demigoddesses of heaven."

Furthermore, in *Śrīmad-Bhāgavatam* it is stated: "*tatrātiśuśubhe tābhir bhagavān devakī-sutaḥ* – Devakī-nandana Śrī Kṛṣṇa began to look even more beautiful amidst all those *gopīs*." In the latter part of this *Brahma-saṁhitā* (56), we will find: "*śriyaḥ kāntāḥ kāntaḥ parama-puruṣaḥ* – in Goloka Vṛndāvana there is only one hero, namely *parama-puruṣa* Śrī Kṛṣṇa. Lakṣmīs, in the form of *gopīs*, are His beloveds." The *Gopāla-tāpanī Upaniṣad* confirms this: "*kṛṣṇo vai paramaṁ daivatam* – Śrī Kṛṣṇa is the only supreme worshipable deity."

In the same way that Śrī Kṛṣṇa is the Supreme Person (*parama-puruṣa*), He is also the original person (*ādi-puruṣa*).

śrutvā 'jitaṁ jarāsandhaṁ
nṛpater dhyāyato hariḥ
āhopāyaṁ tam evādya
uddhavo yam uvāca ha

Śrīmad-Bhāgavatam (10.72.15)

After conquering all directions, Mahārāja Yudhiṣṭhira was contemplating how to defeat Jarāsandha, who appeared to be invincible. At that moment Bhagavān Śrī Kṛṣṇa, the original personality (*ādi-puruṣa*), suggested a method that He had heard from Uddhava.

Commentators on this verse have confirmed: "*ādyo hariḥ śrī-kṛṣṇaḥ* – the original Hari is Śrī Kṛṣṇa."

In *Śrīmad-Bhāgavatam* (11.29.49), the supremacy of Śrī Kṛṣṇa and His status as the origin of everything are both mentioned: "*puruṣam ṛṣabham ādyaṁ kṛṣṇa-saṁjñaṁ nato 'smi* – I offer my obeisances to Śrī Kṛṣṇa, who is the origin of all, the eternal and supreme personality (*puruṣa*). He is the origin (*ādi*) because He is the source of all incarnations, though He is beginningless."

In the *Gopāla-tāpanī Upaniṣad* (21) it is said: "*eko vaśī sarva-gaḥ kṛṣṇa īḍyaḥ* – Svayam Bhagavān Śrī Kṛṣṇa is He who is one without a second, who controls everyone, who can go anywhere, who is omnipotent, who knows everything and who is worshipable by all." In the Upaniṣads it is stated: "*nityo nityānām* – there is one Supreme Eternal amongst all eternals, one Supreme Consciousness among all conscious beings. Although He is one, He fulfills the desires of all."

According to the statements of *śruti*, He is the origin of everything and the cause of all causes. He is also the cause of Kāraṇodakaśāyī Mahā-Viṣṇu, who is the creator of the material world. For example, in *Śrīmad-Bhāgavatam* (10.85.31) Mother Devakī says to Śrī Kṛṣṇa:

yasyāṁśāṁśāṁśa-bhāgena
viśvotpatti-layodayā
bhavanti kila viśvātmaṁs
taṁ tv ādyāhaṁ gatiṁ gatā

I take shelter of Govinda, who is the indwelling supersoul of the entire universe. O original Puruṣa, Your plenary portion is the great Lord of Vaikuṇṭha, Nārāyaṇa, whose further partial expansion is Kāraṇodakaśāyī Viṣṇu. Material nature is a partial manifestation of His potency. The creation, destruction and maintenance of this world are accomplished through the modes of ignorance, passion and so on, which are only constituent portions of this material nature.

It is also stated in Brahmā's prayers (*Śrīmad-Bhāgavatam* 10.14.14): "*nārāyaṇo 'ṅga nārāyaṇa-bhū-jalāyanāt* – O Kṛṣṇa, You are the origin of Nārāyaṇa. *Nāra* means 'the collective group of living entities,' and *ayaṇa* means 'You are the shelter.' *Bhū* means 'the shelter of all the worlds' and *sākṣī* means 'one who knows past, present and future.' Nārāyaṇa is Your part and parcel; He is one of Your pastime expansions (*vilāsa-mūrti*). This is Your constitutional nature, which is indivisible. If Your nature is indivisible, how can You take shelter of water that is divisible? To answer this doubt, it is said that Your divisibility is not factual, but it seems to be so because of *māyā*. Although You are indivisible, You seem to be situated in divisibility by the influence of Your inconceivable potency. Even though this is true, Your form as Nārāyaṇa is not a false imaginary form like Your universal form. Therefore, Nārāyaṇa is Your limb, and You are His fundamental origin."

In *Bhagavad-gītā* (10.42) it is also stated: "*viṣṭabhyāham idaṁ kṛtsnam ekāṁśena sthito jagat* – this entire world exists on the basis of one of My expansions." The etymological meaning of the word *kṛṣṇa* has also been proven here. As described previously, His all-attractiveness and His supremely blissful nature have been indicated by the combination of both *kṛṣ* and *ṇa*. He is one without a second; there is no other entity or truth besides Him, nor can anyone be compared to Him. That is why He is the non-dual Supreme Truth, who is one without a second and the cause of all causes. There is no separate substance or energy that can be imposed on Him, because nothing else has any existence separate from Him or independent of Him.

It is also said in the *śruti*, "*ānandaḥ brahmeti* – Brahman is the original form of bliss." "*Ko hy evānyāt kaḥ prāṇyād ya ākāśa ānando na syāt* – if He were not the original form of bliss, how could anyone else maintain their life?" "*Ānandād dhīmāni bhūtāni jāyante* – all living beings have been produced from this blissfulness."

na tasya kāryaṁ karaṇaṁ ca vidyate
na tat samaś cābhyadhikaś ca dṛśyate
parāsya śaktir vividhaiva śrūyate
svābhāvikī jñāna-bala-kriyā ca

Śvetāśvatara Upaniṣad (6.8)

He does not have any mundane work to perform, nor does He possess material senses. There is no one like Him, and certainly no one is greater than Him. He has an eternal and natural superior energy which is manifested in various ways and which is the source of knowledge, strength and activity.

Someone may say, "According to etymology, 'Śrī Kṛṣṇa' certainly refers to the all-attractive supreme *ānanda*, but this analysis does not establish that He has a personal form, because bliss has no form; it is unembodied." This is partly true, but Bhagavān Śrī Kṛṣṇa is the supremely original perfect form of *ānanda*. That is why He has been called *sac-cid-ānanda-vigraha* in this first verse of *Brahma-saṁhitā*. Śrī Kṛṣṇa is the embodiment of concentrated existence, knowledge and bliss.

In Brahmā's prayers in the Tenth Canto of *Śrīmad-Bhāgavatam* (10.14.22) it is stated: "*tvayy eva nitya-sukha-bodha-tanau* – the entire world is temporary. That is why it is dreamlike, ephemeral, insentient, dull and distressful. On the other hand, You are the embodiment of eternity, knowledge and bliss, infinite and unlimited. The creation and destruction of this world takes place only by the influence of Your inconceivable illusory energy, but even so, the world appears to be reality."

The *Gopāla-tāpanī Upaniṣad* (1.1) and the *Hayaśīrṣa-pañcarātra* also give evidence for Śrī Kṛṣṇa's *sac-cid-ānanda* form:

sac-cid-ānanda-rūpāya
kṛṣṇāyākliṣṭa-kāriṇe
namo vedānta-vedyāya
gurave buddhi-sākṣiṇe

I offer my obeisances to Śrī Kṛṣṇa, who is the concentrated form of eternity, knowledge and bliss; who is the subject matter defined by Vedānta; who effortlessly creates, maintains and destroys the entire world; who frees His devotees from the five types of suffering beginning with ignorance; and who is our *guru*. As *guru* He inspires the intelligence of all, and He is the witness of our activities. Unto that Śrī Kṛṣṇa I offer my obeisances again and again.

In the *Śatanāma-stotra* section of the *Brahmānda Purāṇa*, it is also said: "*nava-vraja-janānandī sac-cid-ānanda-vigrahaḥ* – Śrī Kṛṣṇa, who is the concentrated form of eternity, knowledge and bliss, increases the *ānanda* of Śrī Nanda-Vraja, and all the residents of Vraja." Later, it will be stated: "*sattvaṁ khalv avyabhicāritvam ucyate* – Śrī Kṛṣṇa is pure transcendental existence. His existence can never be inhibited."

In *Śrīmad-Bhāgavatam* (10.2.26) the same conclusion has been established by the statements of the demigods, headed by Brahmā: "*satya-vrataṁ satya-paraṁ tri-satyam* – O Bhagavān, whatever You desire becomes reality (*satya-saṅkalpa*). You are true to Your vow (*satya-vrata*) because You are responsible for manifesting Your own desires (*saṅkalpa*). Truthfulness is the means to attain You, and therefore You are the Supreme Truth (*satya-para*). You are unchanged during creation, maintenance and destruction. You are truth itself. You are the root cause of the five major ingredients of creation: earth, water, fire, air and space. After these elements are again manifested during creation, You are present within them as the indwelling Supersoul, and after the devastation only You remain. You are the origin of both truthful speech and equal vision. Therefore, we are taking shelter of You, who are the original form of the Absolute Truth."

This conclusion is also supported by the statements of Mother Devakī:

naṣṭe loke dviparārdhāvasāne
mahābhūteṣv ādibhūtaṁ gateṣu
vyakte 'vyaktaṁ kāla-vegena yāte
bhavān ekaḥ śiṣyate śeṣa-saṁjñaḥ

Śrīmad-Bhāgavatam (10.3.25)

At the time of devastation at the end of Brahmā's life, the eternal time factor destroys all moving and non-moving objects in the world. The five gross elements beginning with earth revert to their subtle state, and all manifested objects disappear into their unmanifested form. Only You remain.

Furthermore, *Śrīmad-Bhāgavatam* (10.3.27) states: "*martyo mṛtyu-vyāla-bhītaḥ palāyan sarvāl lokān nirbhayaṁ nādhyagacchat* – the entities of this mortal world are terrified of the great snake of death. Although they flee throughout all the planets headed by Brahmaloka just to find shelter, they cannot become fearless anywhere. However, if such a fearful living entity associates with a liberated soul, then by the influence of devotion to You he attains the shelter of Your lotus feet and becomes liberated from the fear of the material world forever. Even death abandons him and flees far away."

Śrīmad-Bhāgavatam (10.14.18) states: "*eko 'si prathamam* – before the creation, only I existed." Brahmājī has also said: "*tad idam brahmādvayaṁ śiṣyate* – in the end, only the indivisible Supreme Spirit remains." In *Bhagavad-gītā* it is said: "*brahmaṇo hi pratiṣṭhāham* – I am also the basis of that Brahman."

yasmāt kṣaram atīto 'ham
akṣarād api cottamaḥ
ato 'smi loke vede ca
prathitaḥ puruṣottamaḥ

Bhagavad-gītā (15.18)

I am beyond the manifest nature, and I am also superior to the unmanifest. That is why I am celebrated throughout the world and in the Vedas as Puruṣottama.

Bhagavān is eternally masculine (*puruṣa-tattva*); He is not feminine or impotent. When the conception of masculinity (*puruṣa-tattva*) is understood, the mistaken conception of His being feminine or neuter cannot remain. Amongst all the *viṣṇu-tattva* expansions, Puruṣottama Śrī Kṛṣṇa is the most excellent.

In the *Gopāla-tāpanī Upaniṣad* (23) it has been said:

janma-jarābhyāṁ bhinnaḥ sthāṇur ayam
acchedyo 'yaṁ yo 'sau saurye tiṣṭhati
yo 'sau goṣu tiṣṭhati
yo 'sau gāḥ pālayati yo 'sau gopeṣu tiṣṭhati

Bhagavān is without desire. He is not affected by the six transformations, namely birth, death, hunger, thirst, old age and sorrow. He is Parabrahman and always exists in a form that never deteriorates. He is the central feature of the solar system (*sūrya-maṇḍala*, or Sauri). He protects and nourishes the wish-fulfilling cows, surrounded by His cowherd boy companions. He also performs His pastimes in the cottages and groves on the banks of the Yamunā, who is the daughter of the sun-god Sūrya. Even death personified is afraid of Him. That Supreme Personality is Śrī Govinda.

Here one should understand the word *saurye* to mean the Saurī, or Yamunā River, and also Śrī Vṛndāvana, which is situated on its bank.

Having discussed the eternal form (*sat-svarūpa*) of Śrī Kṛṣṇa, we will now establish the cognizant nature (*cit-svarūpa*) of that form. Śrī Kṛṣṇa's original form is self-manifested, so He can also manifest others.

In *Śrīmad-Bhāgavatam* (10.14.23), Śrī Brahmā says: "*ekas tvam ātmā puruṣaḥ purāṇaḥ, satyaḥ svayaṁ jyotir ananta ādyaḥ* – O Bhagavān, You are the only truth because You are the *ātmā* of all *ātmās*; that is, You are situated as *paramātmā* in everyone's heart. You are different from the perceptible world around us. You are the root cause of the creation, maintenance and destruction of this world; You are the primeval personality and the eternal supreme reality; You are completely immersed in eternal bliss; You are the embodiment of nectar, beyond all material designations; You are supremely pure, or in other words free from the modes of material nature; and You are self-illuminating, endless and indivisible. You are the supreme non-dual Absolute Truth (*advaya-jñāna-para-tattva*)."

In the *Gopāla-tāpanī Upaniṣad* (1.24), it is stated:

yo brahmāṇaṁ vidadhāti pūrvaṁ yo
brahma-vidyāṁ tasmai gā pālayati sma kṛṣṇaḥ
tāṁ hi devam ātma-vṛtti-prakāśaṁ
mumukṣur vai śaraṇam amuṁ vrajet

In the beginning of creation Parameśvara first manifested Brahmā, and then, in the forms of Matsya, Hayagrīva and other incarnations, He delivered the Vedas from sinking into the ocean of devastation. He gave instructions to Brahmā on spiritual science. He is the supreme worshipable deity, and He is self-manifest in His eternal form as Śrī Kṛṣṇa. All devotees take shelter of Him.

In the *śruti* it is stated: "*na cakṣuṣā paśyati rūpam asya* – it is not possible to see Him with these material eyes." *Katha Upaniṣad* (1.2.23) states: "*yam evaiṣa vṛṇute tena labhyas tasyaiṣa ātmā vivṛṇute tanuṁ svām* – He manifests Himself in the hearts of those who are surrendered to Him." The self-manifested original form of the Supreme Personality is Svayam Bhagavān Śrī Kṛṣṇa. He is therefore called the form of knowledge, which means that He is self-manifest.

Śrī Kṛṣṇa is also the original form of bliss (*ānanda-svarūpa*). The purport of *ānanda-svarūpa* is "*sarvatobhāvena nirupādhika-*

parama-premāspada – He is in every respect the supreme abode of *prema*, without any material designations."

It is stated in *Śrīmad-Bhāgavatam* (10.14.49) that after Mahārāja Parīkṣit heard Brahmājī's prayers, he inquired from Śrī Śukadeva Gosvāmī: "*brahman parodbhave kṛṣṇe* – O *brāhmaṇa*, how is it that the residents of Vraja had such *prema* for Śrī Kṛṣṇa, which they did not possess even for their own sons?"

Śrī Śukadeva Gosvāmī replied, "O King, every living entity only holds his own self (*ātmā*) dear. Besides one's self, all other objects of affection such as sons and wealth are dear in a secondary way, not directly, and only because of fondness for the *ātmā*. Living entities who have accepted a material body have more attachment for their own selves than for their sons, wealth, house and other paraphernalia. Therefore, all living beings are most attached to their own selves. In this world of moving and non-moving entities, any sense of happiness is due to the *ātmā*. The conclusion is that one should understand Śrī Kṛṣṇa to be the original Self (*ātma-svarūpa*) of all living entities. He mercifully appears in this world for the benefit of all. The entire universe is the external form of Śrī Kṛṣṇa; in other words Śrī Kṛṣṇa is the root cause of everything. Thus there is nothing that is not related to Him."

Śrī Vasudeva has described his own realization of this:

vidito 'si bhavān sākṣād
īśvaraḥ prakṛteḥ paraḥ
kevalānubhavānanda-
svarūpaḥ sarva-buddhi-dṛk

Śrīmad-Bhāgavatam (10.3.13)

O Prabhu, You are the Supreme Controller beyond the material nature, and You are that Supreme Personality who enters within everything. You are the original form of pure knowledge, and You are directly the Supreme Godhead, Bhagavān.

It is also said in the *śruti*: "*ānandaṁ brahmaṇo rūpam* – *ānanda* is the form of Brahman." Therefore, on the basis of all the evidence compiled from *śruti*, it is established that Śrī Kṛṣṇa is the form of eternity, knowledge and bliss (*sac-cid-ānanda-vigraha*). One should understand that Śrī Kṛṣṇa's form is His very self, and Śrī Kṛṣṇa's self is His form; *vigraha* is *ātmā* and *ātmā* is *vigraha*. This is the conclusion of all scripture. Bhagavān Śrī Kṛṣṇa is His eternal, original form, so the idea that He is materially embodied like the conditioned souls, or that He has accepted a material form from the illusory energy (*māyā*), is totally erroneous.

Śrī Śukadeva Gosvāmī has remarked:

kṛṣṇam enam avehi tvam
ātmānam akhilātmanām
jagad-dhitāya so 'py atra
dehī vābhāti māyayā

Śrīmad-Bhāgavatam (10.14.55)

O King, you should understand that Śrī Kṛṣṇa is Parabrahma and Paramātmā, the soul of all living entities. He has mercifully descended for the benefit of the whole world in such a way that He appears to be an ordinary person with a physical human body that can be perceived by the senses of the living entities. Although His pastimes resemble those of a common person, He is not an ordinary human being.

The human-like activities performed by Bhagavān during His manifest pastimes in this world are called *mādhuryamayī-līlā*, meaning that these pastimes are full of sweetness. His pastimes are manifested in this world only out of compassion for the living entities. In this *Śrīmad-Bhāgavatam* verse, the word *māyā* means "mercy." In the *Viśva-prakāśa* dictionary, the word *māyā* has been defined as either "deceit" or "mercy."

Now that the supremacy of Śrī Kṛṣṇa has been firmly

established on the basis of *śāstra* and logic, His absorption in His pastimes will be discussed. His pastimes are of two types: *aiśvaryamayī pura-līlā* (pastimes related to transcendental opulence) and *mādhuryamayī vraja-līlā* (the sweet pastimes of Vraja). He performs His *aiśvaryamayī-līlā* while residing sometimes in Mathurā-purī and sometimes in Dvārakā. At that time He is called Yādavendra or Vṛṣṇīndra. When the pastimes of His infancy, childhood and adolescence take place in Vraja, He is called Vrajendra-nandana or Govinda.

In *Śrīmad-Bhāgavatam* Śrī Sūta Gosvāmī has said:

śrī kṛṣṇa kṛṣṇa-sakha vṛṣṇy-ṛṣabhāvani-dhrug
rājanya-vaṁśa-dahanānapavarga-vīrya
govinda gopa-vanitā-vraja-bhṛtya-gīta-
tīrtha-śravaḥ śravaṇa-maṅgala pāhi bhṛtyān

Śrīmad-Bhāgavatam (12.11.25)

O Kṛṣṇa, O friend of Arjuna, O chief among the descendants of Vṛṣṇi, You are the destroyer of those political parties who are disturbing elements on this Earth. Your prowess never deteriorates. You are the proprietor of the transcendental abode, and Your most sacred glories, which are sung by Vṛndāvana's cowherd men and women and their servants, bestow all auspiciousness just by being heard. O Lord, please protect Your devotees.

In this *śloka*, Śrī Sūta Gosvāmī has introduced his worshipable deity Śrī Kṛṣṇa as the friend of Arjuna. This indicates Śrī Kṛṣṇa's intense affection for the Pāṇḍavas, which renders Him subordinate to them. It is also clear from the sequence of address in this verse that He has even more affection for the Yādavas (Vṛṣṇis). Śrī Kṛṣṇa not only destroyed the kings who were oppressing the Earth, He also protected the Pāṇḍavas and the Yādavas and maintained them in every respect. Śrī Sūta Gosvāmī is also saying, "You have still more affection for the Vrajavāsīs than for the Yādavas, and amongst the residents of Vraja, You have shown the most affection of all for the Vraja damsels. When Your dear devotee Uddhava came to Vraja, he repeatedly offered prayers to the dust of the lotus feet of the *gopīs*."

Śrī Brahmā considers that the form of Bhagavān that is most desirable for him is his own worshipable deity, Śrī Govinda. Later in this *saṁhitā*, Śrī Brahmā offers prayers beginning with the verse *cintāmaṇi-prakara-sadmasu kalpa-vṛkṣa-lakṣāvṛteṣu*, wherein he glorifies his worshipable Lord, Śrī Govinda, who is always endowed with His transcendental names, form, qualities and pastimes.

In *Śrīmad-Bhāgavatam* (10.27.20), the cow Surabhī performs *abhiṣeka* (ceremonial bathing) of Śrī Kṛṣṇa, giving Him the name Śrī Govinda: "*tvaṁ na indro jagatpate* – O You who possess inconceivable and unlimited energies, O indwelling soul of the universe, O creator of the universe, O infallible Acyuta, O Śrī Kṛṣṇa, O master of the universe, You are our only worshipable deity. You are the real Indra (monarch) because you are the maintainer of cows, *brāhmaṇas*, saintly persons and demigods. O Soul of the universe, You have descended to the surface of the Earth planet to remove her burden. The father of the worlds, Brahmājī, has engaged us in performing the *abhiṣeka* of You, who are worshipable for all." After saying this, Surabhī, along with Indra and the great sages, performed the *abhiṣeka* of Kṛṣṇa. Surabhī bathed Śrī Kṛṣṇa with her own milk, and Indra and the sages offered the pure waters of Mandākinī (the celestial Gaṅgā), which had been brought there in the trunk of Indra's elephant Airāvata. In this ceremony they gave Śrī Kṛṣṇa the name Śrī Govinda (*Śrīmad-Bhāgavatam* 10.27.19–23). After describing this *abhiṣeka*, Śrī Śukadeva Gosvāmī has also prayed: "*priyān na indro gavām* – O Indra (master) of the cows, Govinda, be pleased with us." Calling Him master of the cows does not minimize Him or decrease His position. On the contrary, it establishes His unrivaled monarchy, because it is stated in the *Go-sūkta*:

gobhyo yajñāḥ pravartante
gobhyo devāḥ samutthitāḥ
gobhir devāḥ samudgīrṇāḥ
sa-ṣaḍ-aṅga-pada-kramāḥ

All the different types of sacrifice have come from the cows of Goloka Vṛndāvana; the demigods have come from those cows; and the Vedas with their six limbs have also appeared from those cows.

Since Śrī Kṛṣṇa has descended from Goloka-dhāma, the planet of cows, He is the master of the cows. In the *Gopāla-tāpanī Upaniṣad* (35), Śrī Brahmā relates to the sages headed by Sanaka how he has prayed to his worshipable deity:

govindaṁ sac-cid-ānanda-vigrahaṁ
sūrabhū-ruha-talāsīnaṁ satataṁ sa-marud-gaṇo 'haṁ toṣayāmi

Along with the demigods headed by Indra, I offer praise to Vāsudeva, who is eternally ornamented with pure transcendental qualities and pastimes. Although He is the Supreme Truth, one without a second, He is also the embodiment of eternity, knowledge and bliss, resplendently situated beneath a desire-fulfilling tree in Śrī Vṛndāvana-dhāma.

Brahmājī has also prayed in the Tenth Canto of *Śrīmad-Bhāgavatam* (10.14.34): "*tad bhūri-bhāgyam iha janma kim apy aṭavyāṁ yad gokule* – the Vedas are still searching, even today, for the dust of the lotus feet of Bhagavān Mukunda, who is the very life and soul of the residents of Vraja. My life will be successful only if I can take birth in any species whatsoever in this earthly forest of Vraja, or in a border region of Gokula, so that I may be completely bathed in the foot-dust of the residents of Gokula."

Here the words *bhagavān mukundaḥ* directly refer to Vrajarāja-nandana, Kṛṣṇa, the son of Nanda Mahārāja. This form is found only in Vraja.

Brahmājī has also prayed:

naumīḍya te 'bhra-vapuṣe taḍid-ambarāya
guñjāvataṁsa-paripiccha-lasan-mukhāya
vanya-sraje kavala-vetra-viṣāṇa-veṇu-
lakṣma-śriye mṛdu-pade paśupāṅgajāya

Śrīmad-Bhāgavatam (10.14.1)

O Prince of Vraja, You are worshipable for the whole world. O Nava-Ghanaśyāma, Your yellow upper garment beautifies Your dark, fresh raincloud-colored limbs like a steady streak of lightning. Your ears are decorated with ornaments made of *guñjā* berries, and Your head with a crown of peacock feathers. A garland of forest flowers and leaves adorns Your neck, a morsel of rice mixed with yogurt is in Your hand, Your eyes are shaped like lotus petals, and Your appearance with Your flute and buffalo horn is exquisitely beautiful. Your lotus feet, which are the shelter of Lakṣmī-devī, are very soft and full of affection for Your devotees. You are always moving here and there in Vṛndāvana forest with Your soft lotus feet to enjoy Your pleasure pastimes. All glories unto You, son of Nanda Mahārāja, who tend the cows. Please accept my obeisances.

Thus Śrī Kṛṣṇa's supreme opulence is expressed by names such as Govinda. This is the significance of the name Govinda in this first verse of *Brahma-saṁhitā*.

After Śrī Kṛṣṇa's status as controller (*īśvara*) and Supreme Controller (*parameśvara*) has been established, in conclusion, His unique qualities are being described. In an explanation of the ten-syllable *mantra*,[5] the *Gautamīya-tantra* (2.18–19, 22–23) reveals the following:

[5] This is identical to the eighteen-syllable *gopāla-mantra*, except that it does not contain the words *kṛṣṇāya* and *govindāya*.

gopīti prakṛtiṁ vidyāj
janas tattva-samūhakaḥ
anayor āśrayo vyāptyā
kāraṇatvena ceśvaraḥ

sāndrānandaṁ paraṁ jyotir
vallabhena ca kathyate
athavā gopī prakṛtir
janas tad-aṁśa-maṇḍalam

anayor vallabhaḥ proktaḥ
svāmī kṛṣṇākhya īśvaraḥ
kārya-kāraṇayor īśaḥ
śrutibhis tena gīyate

aneka-janma-siddhānāṁ
gopīnāṁ patir eva vā
nanda-nandana ity uktas
trailokyānanda-vardhanaḥ

Śrī Govindadeva is famous throughout the Vedas, upon planet Earth and among the cows. He nourishes them and is always with them. Although complete with incomparable opulence and sweetness, He is absorbed in enjoying His independent pastimes while surrounded by herds of cows. He is celebrated in all worlds and throughout the Vedas, which means that He steals the hearts of the residents of Vraja in Śrī Nanda-Gokula. His complexion is like a fresh monsoon raincloud, and He expands His endearing pastimes, the sweetness of which is continuously sung in a loud voice by all the Vedas and throughout the worlds. Only that Śrī Kṛṣṇa, the moon of Gokula, the cowherd boy who carries a flute, is worthy of the name Govinda.

On examining the mood that Brahmā expresses in this verse, it seems that he surrendered himself fully unto the lotus feet of Śrī Kṛṣṇa from the very beginning. However, as the ecstatic mellows of *prema-rasa* increased in his heart, his greed to realize the sweetness of Śrī Kṛṣṇa also increased. Therefore he began to offer himself to Kṛṣṇa's form of Govinda, meaning Vrajarāja-nandana, the son of the King of Vraja, and Gopāla, who is the treasure of the life of Mother Yaśodā. Moreover, when Brahmājī's mood increased and matured completely, with his heart immersed in and relishing *prema-rasa*, he became desperate to attain the supremely beautiful fresh youth, Śyāmasundara – the expert dancer who, being surrounded by the lotus-eyed damsels of Vraja, bewilders the mind of Cupid. At that time, intoxicated by the incomparable nectar of *gopī-prema*, Brahmājī offered his life to Śrī Kṛṣṇa's form as Gopījana-vallabha. His heart was so thirsty for *gopī-prema* that he could not be satisfied by uttering only *kṛṣṇāya svāhā*, or even *kṛṣṇāya govindāya svāhā*. Helplessly overwhelmed with *prema*, he began to utter *kṛṣṇāya govindāya gopījana-vallabhāya svāhā*. When Brahmājī spoke thus, his intense yearning was fulfilled.[6]

In the aforementioned verses from the *Gautamīya-tantra* that explain the ten-syllable *mantra*, the word *gopī* has been derived from the verbal root *gup*, meaning "to protect and maintain." Therefore the special energy that bestows *prema* and maintains the devotees is called *gopī*, or *hlādinī-śakti*. Śrī Rādhā is that *hlādinī-śakti*, so one should understand that the word *gopī* refers to Śrī Rādhā. Also, in the statement *gopī tu prakṛtī rādhā janas tad-aṁśa-maṇḍalaḥ*, the word *jana* refers to those *gopīs* who are

[6] Here Śrīla Jīva Gosvāmī describes Brahmā yearning for that *gopī-prema* which has been described as unattainable even for Brahmā and Śaṅkara. To reconcile this with other statements of Jīva Gosvāmī and of *Śrīmad-Bhāgavatam* that Brahmājī practiced the eighteen-syllable *mantra* to get power for creation, we can understand that later Brahmājī may have been in the association of high-class Vaiṣṇavas like Nārada and others, and then he was regularly and repeatedly chanting these names. Then, he may have achieved *prema* as described here. It may be that the Brahmā described here is a special Brahmā who is now liberated, but other Brahmās have not received *gopī-prema*.

direct expansions of Śrīmatī Rādhikā's divine form. So *gopījana* refers to Śrīmatī Rādhikā and Her own direct expansions such as Lalitā and Viśākhā. Thus the word *vallabha* (beloved) can only refer to their most dearly beloved sweetheart, *prāṇa-priyatama* Śrī Kṛṣṇa.

The word *vallabha* means "one who gives inspiration," "the instigator," or "the lover (*ramaṇa*)." That hero who enjoys supremely sweet pastimes with the *gopīs* is Śrī Gopījana-vallabha. Gopījana-vallabha also means the *pati* or sole refuge of the *gopīs*, and specifically *prāṇapati*, the only shelter of the life's breath of Śrī Rādhikā, who is always surrounded by Her *sakhīs* headed by Śrī Lalitā and Viśākhā. Nanda-nandana Śrī Kṛṣṇa is the crown-jewel among connoisseurs of ecstatic transcendental mellows (*rasika-śekhara*). As Madana-mohana, the enchanter of the god of amorous love, He is elegantly present in Śrī Vṛndāvana with Śrīmatī Rādhikā, who stands in the midst of Her supremely beautiful, ever-fresh, lotus-eyed friends. Therefore only this budding youth, the Madana-mohana form of Śrī Kṛṣṇa – also called Govinda or Gopāla – is actually Śrī Gopījana-vallabha. Gopījana-vallabha is the eternal form of Śrī Kṛṣṇa who is always held in Śrī Rādhikā's loving embrace. Therefore it is automatically understood that *gopījana-vallabha* refers to the Divine Couple, Rādhā-Kṛṣṇa Yugala.

aneka-janma-siddhānāṁ
gopīnāṁ patir eva vā
nanda-nandana-ity uktas
trailokyānanda-vardhanaḥ

Gautamīya-tantra (2.23)

The purport of this verse is that those *gopīs* who had been performing *sādhana* for many lifetimes attained Nanda-nandana Śrī Kṛṣṇa as their husband or beloved paramour, who is dearer than life itself. He increases the bliss of all the three planetary systems, and He is the ever-fresh Kāmadeva, who awakens transcendental desire in the heart of every living entity in the universe, and then fulfills it. He increases the spontaneous, transcendental dedication in the hearts of the devotees, and He increases the *prema* of His dearmost associates. That original form of Bhagavān Śrī Kṛṣṇa is the ever-new deity of amorous love in Vṛndāvana.

This same Śrī Kṛṣṇa is thus the worshipable deity of the first *guru* of our *sampradāya*, Śrī Brahmā, who is seated upon a lotus flower.

The word *prakṛti* in the previously quoted verses from the *Gautamīya-tantra* indicates the illusory energy called *māyā*, which is the shelter of all the principal ingredients, beginning with the aggregate of primal matter (*mahat-tattva*) from which all the universes are manifested. Śrī Kṛṣṇa is the highly concentrated form of condensed bliss, and He is supremely effulgent like a blue sapphire. *Īśvara* means *vallabha*, beloved. Another sense of the word *īśvara* is "one who is everywhere" or "one who pervades the *vraja-gopīs'* hearts, minds, intelligence and so on." The fundamental meaning of *prakṛti* (dominated energy) is Śrī Kṛṣṇa's intrinsic personal potency, which is radiantly present as the *gopīs* of Vraja, and famous by the name of Mahā-Lakṣmī in realms such as Vaikuṇṭha, which are situated far beyond this material world.

The word *aṁśa-maṇḍala* (circle of expansions) is generally interpreted as a reference to the *catur-vyūha*: Vāsudeva, Saṅkarṣaṇa, Pradyumna and Aniruddha. However, in this context, one should understand *aṁśa-maṇḍala* to mean the expansions of Śrī Rādhā (*kāya-vyūha-rūpā*).

In *aneka-janma-siddhānām, aneka* means "many;" for many lifetimes the *gopīs* have been perfect in their *prema*. This proves that both the *gopīs* and Śrī Kṛṣṇa have taken birth many times before.

It is stated in *Bhagavad-gītā* (4.5): "*bahūni me vyatītāni janmāni tava cārjuna* – O Arjuna, both you and I have already taken birth many times." Similarly, the *gopīs* and Nanda-nandana Śrī Kṛṣṇa have also taken birth many times.

Gargācārya has also said (*Śrīmad-Bhāgavatam* 10.8.14): "*prāg ayaṁ vasudevasya kvacij jātas tavātmajaḥ* – O Nanda Mahārāja, at some time in the past, this son of yours appeared as the son of Vasudeva." This is also logical. Although Śrī Kṛṣṇa is the son of Nanda Mahārāja, He had appeared previously in the mind of Vasudeva Mahārāja (*Śrīmad-Bhāgavatam* 10.2.16): "*āviveśāṁśa-bhāgena mana ānaka-dundubheḥ* – the expansion of Kṛṣṇa appeared in the mind of Ānaka-dundubhi, Vasudeva Mahārāja." In the same way, Śrī Kṛṣṇa also appeared in the heart of Vrajeśvara Nanda Mahārāja, but there is a specific distinction between the two appearances. The partial manifestation of Śrī Kṛṣṇa who appeared in Vasudeva's heart is called the full manifestation (*pūrṇa-prakāśa*), whereas the form who appeared in Vrajeśvara Nanda Mahārāja's heart is called the most complete form of Śrī Kṛṣṇa (*pūrṇatama-prakāśa*). Just before the appearance of Bhagavān Śrī Kṛṣṇa, Nanda Mahārāja began to have His *darśana* in his heart and everywhere else.

The appearance of Śrī Kṛṣṇa in the heart is not sufficient to attain Him as one's son, however. Intense parental *prema* is also absolutely necessary. Such pure fatherly love is only found in Vrajarāja Śrī Nanda Mahārāja. Bhagavān may appear as one's son, but unless pure parental love is present, this does not constitute a relationship in which one genuinely feels, "Kṛṣṇa is my son." Although Varāhadeva appeared from the nostril of Brahmā, He is not considered the son of Brahmā, because Brahmājī had no parental love for Him.

Knowledge of Kṛṣṇa's opulence is an obstacle for the spontaneous love based on a relationship resembling intimate relationships with dear ones in this world. Vasudeva has knowledge of Kṛṣṇa's opulence, and Vrajarāja Nanda has pure parental love. Śrī Kṛṣṇa is present according to the degree of one's *prema*. Since the highest pinnacle of *prema* is found in the *gopīs*, Śrī Kṛṣṇa is manifest to the superlative degree among them. Thus the purport of the ten-syllable *mantra* also ultimately refers to Nanda-nandana Śrī Kṛṣṇa.

Śrīla Bhaktivinoda Ṭhākura's commentary: Śrī Brahma-saṁhitā-prakāśinī-vṛtti

pracura-siddhānta-ratna, saṅgrahe viśeṣa yatna
kori' brahmā śrī-kṛṣṇe stavila
ei granthe sei stava, mānavera suvaibhava
pañcama adhyāye niveśila

śrī gaurāṅga kṛpā-sindhu, kali-jīvera eka bandhu
dakṣiṇātya bhramite bhramite
e 'brahma-saṁhitā'-dhana, korilena uddharaṇa
gauḍa-jīve uddhāra korite

nānā-śāstra vicāriyā, tāra ṭīkā viraciyā
śrī jīva gosvāmī mahodaya
śrī gauḍīya-bhakta-gaṇe, mahā-kṛpā-pūrṇa mane
e grantha arpilā sadāśaya

sei vyākhyā anusāre, āra kichu balivāre
prabhu mora vipina-bihārī
ājñā dilā akiñcane, e dāsa harṣita mane
baliyāche kathā dui cāri

prākṛtāprākṛta bhedi,[7] *śuddha-bhakti-saha yadi*
bhakta-gaṇa korena vicāra
kṛtārtha hoibe dāsa, puribe manera āśa
śuddha-bhakti hoibe pracāra

bhakta-jana-prāṇa-dhana, rūpa, jīva, sanātana
tava kṛpā samudra-samāna
ṭīkāra āśaya gūḍha, jāte bujhi āmi mūḍha
sei śakti karaha vidhāna

śrī jīva vacana-caya, puṣpakali śobhāmaya
prasphuṭita koriyā jatane
guru kṛṣṇe praṇamiyā, śuddha-bhakta-kore diyā
dhanya hoi – ei icchā mane

It was by Śrī Kṛṣṇa's mercy that the four-headed Śrī Brahmā received the eighteen-syllable *mantra* through the medium of divine Sarasvatī (*daiva-vāṇī*). Then he performed worship by means of *mantra-japa* for a prolonged period of time. As a result of this worship, he received the *kāma-gāyatrī-mantra* through the sound of Kṛṣṇa's flute and attained twice-born status. Then he offered prayers to Śrī Kṛṣṇa with invaluable jewel-like statements that embodied the essential conclusions of the Vedas. For the benefit of all living entities, these precious jewels have been collected together in the jewelry box of this scripture, *Śrī Brahma-saṁhitā*, whose Fifth Chapter is especially full of the most valuable jewels. Śrī Śacīnandana Gaurahari, who is the ocean of compassion and the only friend of the living entities suffering in Kali-yuga, found this book while traveling in the holy places of Southern India, and carefully kept it with Him. Then, after having many copies made, He gave it to His associates. Later, Śrī Jīva Gosvāmī wrote a beautiful, comprehensive commentary on this book, full of examples and conclusions from various scriptures, and mercifully gave it to the devoted followers of Śrī Caitanya Mahāprabhu.

[7] An ability to differentiate between the mundane and the transcendental arises by the influence of *bhakti*. Only one endowed with such powers of discrimination is qualified to read and explain these commentaries in the line of Śrī Caitanya Mahāprabhu.

Considering *Śrī Brahma-saṁhitā* with Śrī Jīva Gosvāmipāda's commentary to be extremely beneficial for the devotees, my Gurudeva, Śrī Vipina-bihārī Gosvāmī, ordered me to write a further explanation of the aforementioned commentary in readily accessible language. Taking his order on my head, I have included several additional points of consideration in my *Tātparya* (purports). If the faithful devotees study this book with pure and simple hearts, keeping in mind the difference between the mundane (*prākṛta*) and the transcendental (*aprākṛta*), then this servant will consider his life successful and *śuddha-bhakti* will be propagated everywhere.

O Rūpa Gosvāmī, you are the life and soul of the devotees! O Sanātana Gosvāmī! O Jīva Gosvāmī! Your mercy is like an unlimited and fathomless ocean. The significance of your commentary on this *Brahma-saṁhitā* is also extremely profound. Therefore, have mercy on this foolish person. Kindly invest me with the power to comprehend this commentary and express its hidden meanings. The statements of Śrī Jīva Gosvāmipāda are elegant like a row of tender flowerbuds. It is my internal desire to make those fragrant flowerbuds blossom so that, after offering *praṇāma* to *śrī guru* and Kṛṣṇa, I may offer them into the lotus hands of the *śuddha-bhaktas*.

Purport by Śrīla Bhaktivinoda Ṭhākura (Tātparya)

Only Śrī Kṛṣṇa, who is endowed with His own eternal names, form, qualities and pastimes, is the topmost transcendent reality. His eternal name, Kṛṣṇa, indicates the supreme existence, characterized by the attractive power of love. Śrī Kṛṣṇa's own eternal form is the embodiment of concentrated eternal existence, cognizance and bliss. His dark complexion is enchanting and He holds a flute in His two hands. Although He is the Supreme Master, by the influence of His inconceivable potency He appears in His original form in medium-sized or human-like proportions as a fresh youth, the best of dancers, in the simple dress of a cowherd boy, playing upon a flute. Therefore His eternal form is full of astonishing transcendental qualities that have the power to attract everything. He is naturally the supreme predominating male enjoyer with His own transcendental senses. All contradictory qualities, including features which could not ordinarily coexist, are simultaneously fully present and coexisting harmoniously within Him. Concentrated existence (*sat*), cognizance (*cit*) and bliss (*ānanda*) are exhibited most elegantly in Him.

His expansions, known as Īśvara, Paramātmā or Viṣṇu, who manifest the material universes, are merely partial expansions of Śrī Kṛṣṇa's original form. Therefore only Śrī Kṛṣṇa can be called the Supreme Controller, Parameśvara. Although His transcendental senses and qualities are distinct from each other by the influence of His own inconceivable energy, they are combined together in their appropriate places to make the most beautiful, unprecedented spiritual form.

Śrī Kṛṣṇa's form is His self, and His self is His form; there is no difference between Śrī Kṛṣṇa's self and His form. The *śrī vigraha* of Śrī Kṛṣṇa is the very form of the condensed principle of eternality, cognizance and bliss (*sac-cid-ānanda*). Therefore the impersonal Brahman, which is the formless, diluted *sac-cid-ānanda-tattva*, is merely the bodily effulgence of the aforementioned condensed *sac-cid-ānanda-tattva* Śrī Kṛṣṇa, while the thumb-sized form of Paramātmā situated in the hearts of all living beings, who is the universal witness and regulator, is a partial expansion of that Supreme Absolute Truth Śrī Kṛṣṇa. Thus, the concentrated *sac-cid-ānanda* form of Śrī Kṛṣṇa is beginningless and without origin. He is the origin of Brahman and Paramātmā.

Śrī Kṛṣṇa's beauty shines splendidly through His pastimes as

Go-pati (owner of the cows), Gopa-pati (the chief of the cowherds), Gopī-pati (the beloved of the *gopīs*), Gokula-pati (the protector of Gokula) and Goloka-pati (the Lord of Goloka). That very Śrī Kṛṣṇa, who is also served by numerous Lakṣmīs or goddesses of fortune, is called Govinda.

Śrī Kṛṣṇa is the cause of all causes in the form of the dominant principle (*puruṣa*) and the predominated principle (*prakṛti*). The glance of His expansion, namely the *puruṣa-avatāra* Kāraṇodakaśāyī Mahā-Viṣṇu, inspires the inferior material nature to give birth to the mundane universes. Through the marginal energy of Kṣīrodakaśāyī Viṣṇu or Paramātmā, innumerable living entities are manifest, just as unlimited particles are manifest in the rays of the sun. This *Brahma-saṁhitā* establishes the ontology of Śrī Kṛṣṇa, and therefore the utterance of His names in this first verse constitutes the auspicious invocation of this book.

Verse 2

सहस्रपत्र–कमलं गोकुलाख्यं महत्पदम् ।
तत् कर्णिकारं तद्धाम तदनन्तांश–सम्भवम् ॥२॥

sahasra-patra-kamalaṁ
gokulākhyaṁ mahat-padam
tat-karṇikāraṁ tad-dhāma
tad-anantāṁśa-sambhavam

Anvaya

mahat-padam – the best of Śrī Kṛṣṇa's abodes, the residence of *go-gopa-gopī* (the cows, cowherds and *gopīs*); *gokula-ākhyam* – called Gokula; *sahasra-patra-kamalam* – has the form of a thousand-petaled lotus; *tat-karṇikāram* – the pericarp, or central seed-vessel of that lotus; *tad-dhāma* – is Śrī Kṛṣṇa's internal abode, where Śrī Nanda-Yaśodā and the other *gopas* and *gopīs* reside; *tat* – this Gokula; *sambhavam* – is manifest; *ananta-aṁśa* – by a special manifesting power of Ananta, who is the plenary portion of Baladeva. (In other words the pericarp of the thousand-petaled lotus, which is the abode of Śrī Kṛṣṇa, is manifest from Baladeva, who is called Ananta in His plenary expansion.)

Translation

Śrī Gokula-dhāma is the superlative realm of Śrī Kṛṣṇa. It is eternally manifested by Śrī Baladeva, of whom Śrī Anantadeva is but a partial expansion. This eternal, transcendental abode of Gokula exists in the form of a divine lotus flower with thousands of petals. Śrī Kṛṣṇa's own residence is the pericarp,[8] situated in the center of the whorl of that lotus.

[8] The Sanskrit word *karṇikāram* means the pericarp of a lotus flower. This is the central seed-vessel, which roughly resembles an inverted cone.

Ṭīkā translation

Śrī Kṛṣṇa's qualifications as the supreme controller, the embodiment of bliss, and the cause of all causes have been described in the previous verse. Now in this verse, His own eternal residence is being described. This abode of Śrī Kṛṣṇa, Gokula-dhāma, is exquisitely manifest in the form of a lotus flower with thousands of petals. The speciality of this place, which fulfills all desires like a wish-fulfilling gem, is that just as Śrī Kṛṣṇa is *sac-cid-ānanda*, this abode is also *sac-cid-ānanda*. Just as Śrī Kṛṣṇa is all-pervading, vast and all-illuminating, so this abode has similar qualities. This realm is called the supermost world of all, and it is also sometimes referred to as Mahā-Vaikuṇṭha.

In order that no one will harbor any doubts in this regard, it is said that the name of this abode is Gokula, or "the place that is inhabited by *gopas* and *gopīs*." In this context, it is stated in *Śrīmad-Bhāgavatam* (10.10.39): "*bhagavān gokuleśvaraḥ* – Bhagavān Śrī Kṛṣṇa is Gokula-pati, the Lord of Gokula." The same type of description has been made in this second verse of *Brahma-saṁhitā*, and we will proceed to elaborate upon it from this point on. The expansive, internal realm where Bhagavān Śrī Kṛṣṇa eternally resides with His associates, such as His father Nanda Mahārāja and His mother Yaśodā, has been called Gokula-dhāma.

Thus, the abode where Śrī Kṛṣṇa resides along with all the inhabitants of Vraja is also described here. Then, to acquaint us with the constitutional nature of that abode, it is said to be manifested by Śrī Anantadeva, a partial expansion of Śrī Balarāma. Here in this verse, the word *sambhava* may be taken to indicate *āvirbhāva-viśeṣa* (the special appearance of the divine abode), in the sense that it is eternally manifested by a personal expansion of Śrī Baladeva. Following this understanding, *anantāṁśa* then refers to Ananta, the partial expansion of Baladeva.

Alternatively, one may interpret this expression to mean "whose partial expansion is Ananta," namely Śrī Baladeva. Thus the sense becomes, "That abode is the residence of Śrī Baladeva, who lives there along with Śrī Kṛṣṇa."

Tātparya

Goloka-dhāma or Gokula is not any kind of created material place. Rather, it is eternally manifest. This divine abode has been called *anantāṁśa-sambhavam* to indicate that it is manifest from the *śaiṣī-śakti* (Bhagavān Śeṣa's potency) of Śrī Kṛṣṇa, who is unlimited in nature. The purport is that this abode is manifested by Baladeva Prabhu, whose partial expansion is Anantadeva or Śeṣa Bhagavān. Śrī Kṛṣṇa's pastime expansion, Śrī Baladeva, is the reservoir or shelter of this *śaiṣī-śakti*, and all spiritual and material universes have manifested from Him.

Śrī Baladeva's unlimited nature is exhibited in two ways: first, spiritual infinity manifest as unlimited transcendental abodes; and secondly, mundane infinity manifest as unlimited, inert material worlds. An analysis of the material worlds, which comprise one-fourth of Bhagavān's opulence, will be presented later, in the appropriate place. The infinite spiritual manifestation with its unlimited transcendental worlds comprises three-fourths of Bhagavān's opulence, and is untouched by lamentation, mortality and fear. It is fully illuminated, being entirely composed of completely pure, conscious existence. This manifestation of transcendental magnificence is called the immensely opulent spiritual realm, Mahā-Vaikuṇṭha or Paravyoma-dhāma. This Mahā-Vaikuṇṭha-dhāma is completely beyond the purview of the inert material nature, and exists splendidly and forever in the midst of the transcendental effulgence (*brahmajyoti*) on the other side of the Virajā.

This transcendental abode also has two features, namely the upper and lower manifestations. The higher feature is the realm of human-like sweetness (*mādhurya*), and the lower is the realm of extraordinary opulence (*mahā-aiśvarya*). The manifestation that is characterized by sweetness is known as Goloka-dhāma or Gokula-dhāma. This divine abode, which is divided into various subsections according to specific devotional mellows, is exceedingly elegant and charming. It is also sometimes called Mahā-Nārāyaṇa-dhāma or Mūla-Nārāyaṇa-dhāma. Therefore, the Gokula aspect of Goloka[9] is the most excellent abode of all. This one abode is resplendently situated in the spiritual realm in the form of Goloka, and in the material world in the form of Gokula. In his *Bṛhad-bhāgavatāmṛta*, Śrīla Sanātana Gosvāmipāda has written a *śloka* which reconciles the entire body of scripture:

yathā krīḍati tad-bhūmau
goloke 'pi tathaiva saḥ
adha urddhatayā bhedo
'nayoḥ kalpate kevalam

Just as Kṛṣṇa performs His playful pastimes in Gokula in the material universe, similarly He also performs the same pastimes in the Goloka of the upper region. Therefore, there is no difference between Goloka and Gokula.

One should simply understand that whatever is situated in Goloka-dhāma in the spiritual realm is also splendidly present in Gokula, Śrī Kṛṣṇa's place of pastimes within the material universe.

Śrīla Jīva Gosvāmī has written in the glossary of *Ṣaṭ-sandarbha*: "*goloka-nirūpaṇaṁ; vṛndāvanādīnāṁ nitya-kṛṣṇa-*

9 There are different *prakoṣṭhas* (chambers) within Goloka, wherein different types of relationships between Śrī Kṛṣṇa and His devotees predominate. Goloka in the spiritual realm is full of opulence, but within Goloka there is also an inner section called Gokula, which is predominated by sweetness. This is described in detail later in this book.

dhāmatvaṁ; goloka-vṛndāvanayor ekatvaṁ ca – Goloka and Gokula are non-different, but by the influence of Śrī Kṛṣṇa's inconceivable potency, Goloka is situated in the highest territory of the spiritual universe, and the Gokula that is located in Mathurā-maṇḍala is situated in the mundane universe of the one-fourth manifestation that has arisen from the material energy." If the transcendental abode is of the three-fourths manifestation, how can it be situated in the inferior material world of the one-fourth manifestation? This cannot be understood by the meager intelligence of a conditioned soul; one can only become acquainted with this truth by the influence of Śrī Kṛṣṇa's inconceivable potency. Gokula is a transcendental abode, so although it is manifested in this universe of five material elements, it is not confined by any kind of limitation that might be imposed by mundane time and space. Its unlimited, radiant existence is the supreme principle of Vaikuṇṭha, but the material senses and intelligence of the conditioned soul perceive the transcendental Gokula in a mundane way, because the conditioned soul is always absorbed in the inert material nature.

A cloud may cover the eyes of an observer, but it cannot cover the sun. Still, a person in the shade of that cloud sees, by ordinary vision, that the sun is covered by a cloud. Similarly, the conditioned soul, whose senses and intelligence are covered by material defects, inevitably superimposes the qualities of the material nature upon the transcendental abode of Gokula. Only one whose relationship with material nature has already been completely severed as a result of extremely good fortune can have a vision of Goloka in Gokula, and of Gokula in Goloka. The impersonal knowledge that is derived from the philosophical process of the gradual elimination of the material (*neti neti*) gives rise to satisfaction in the self, but such enlightenment can never afford one a vision of the transcendental realm that is situated above the non-differentiated Brahman. The impersonal Brahman is only a limited feature of the knowledge (*cit*) aspect of *sac-cid-ānanda*.

Thus, it is impossible to see Goloka or Gokula through the endeavor for impersonal knowledge because, in their search for the Absolute Truth, the adherents of such dry knowledge rely on their own subtle power of vision, rather than depending on the mercy of Kṛṣṇa, which is imbued with inconceivable potency. The endeavors for knowledge of the nature of the self are also useless in the matter of attaining Goloka Vṛndāvana. Similarly, endeavors in the *yoga* system, which comprise a limb of *karma*, also do not deserve Kṛṣṇa's mercy. Thus, these two types of endeavor cannot give rise to realization of the transcendental pastimes, which are situated above the oneness of impersonal liberation, and are separate from it. Only those who take exclusive shelter of the process of pure, unalloyed devotional service (*śuddha-bhakti*) are competent to receive Śrī Kṛṣṇa's mercy, which is endowed with inconceivable potency. One's relationship with material nature is dispelled only by Śrī Kṛṣṇa's mercy. Then the good fortune to have a vision of Gokula will arise.

The perfection of *bhakti* is also of two types: *svarūpa-siddhi* and *vastu-siddhi*. In the stage of *svarūpa-siddhi*, Goloka is seen in Gokula; and in the stage of *vastu-siddhi*, Gokula is seen in Goloka. This is an extremely confidential mystery. The attainment of the first rays of the sun of *prema* is called *svarūpa-siddhi*. After *svarūpa-siddhi*, both the gross and subtle material coverings of the *sādhaka-jīva* are removed by the mercy of Kṛṣṇa, and he then takes birth as an associate of Śrī Kṛṣṇa in the place of His pastimes. This is called *vastu-siddhi*. Whatever one's level of realization may be, as long as one has not attained perfection, Gokula will be seen as different from Goloka. Śrī Gokula, the unique seat of transcendental pastimes, is Śrī Kṛṣṇa's eternal abode, which is replete with endless varieties of enthralling features and fashioned in the shape of a lotus with thousands of petals.

Bhāvārtha

Brahmājī has defined the intrinsic form and nature of the transcendentally sportive Śrī Kṛṣṇa, and now he is describing Gokula, the supramundane seat of Kṛṣṇa's pastimes. Śrī Gokula-maṇḍala, whose *svarūpa* (intrinsic form) resembles a thousand-petaled lotus flower, is the eternal adode of Bhagavān Śrī Kṛṣṇa, the son of Nanda Mahārāja. The soil there is made of desire-fulfilling gems (*cintāmaṇi*), so Gokula has the form of a lotus made of *cintāmaṇi*. It is called *mahat-padam*, which means "the greatest or most excellent place of all." Alternatively, the word *mahat* (great) can indicate that Śrī Kṛṣṇa is Mahā-Bhagavān, the ultimate feature of God. His *pada* (abode) is the topmost portion of Mahā-Vaikuṇṭha. This is the sense of the word *mahat*.

One may object, "But the word *pada* can be interpreted in so many ways." In order to dispel this doubt, it has been stated definitively by the use of the adjective *mahat* that this *pada* (abode) is called Gokula. Here, in the conventional sense the word *gokula* means the abode of the *gopas*, or cowherd community. According to the logic of *rūḍhir yogam apaharati*, wherein the conventional meaning steals usage from the other legitimate interpretations, the word *gokula* is understood to mean the abode of *go* and *gopa* (the cows and cowherd community); however, other interpretations are not invalid. With this intention, it has been stated in *Śrīmad-Bhāgavatam* (10.10.34): "*bhagavān gokuleśvaraḥ* – Bhagavān Śrī Kṛṣṇa is the Lord of Gokula." Thus, it is appropriate that such an explanation has also been made in *Śrīmad-Bhāgavatam*, a favorable scripture that was manifest later. Gokula-dhāma is a worthy residence for Śrī

Kṛṣṇa and the Vrajavāsīs such as Nanda and Yaśodā, and that is why the word *mahat* has been used.

Now the meaning of *mahat-pada* is being explained in terms of its *svarūpa* (intrinsic form and nature). Gokula can be called the *mahat-pada* because it is manifested from Ananta, an expansion of Śrī Baladeva, or because it has arisen from an intensified portion of spiritual effulgence. Alternatively, Gokula-dhāma may be called *mahat-pada* because it is the residence of Śrī Balarāma, of whom Ananta is a mere part. Gokula has also been called *mahad-dhāma* because of Śrī Kṛṣṇa's appearance in the pericarp of that thousand-petaled lotus.

Verses 3–4

कर्णिकारं महद्यन्त्रं षट्कोणं वज्रकीलकम् ।
षडङ्ग षट्पदी–स्थानं प्रकृत्या पुरुषेण च ॥
प्रेमानन्द – महानन्द – रसेनावस्थितं हि यत् ।
ज्योतीरूपेण मनुना कामबीजेन सङ्गतम् ॥३॥

तत् किञ्जल्कं तदंशानां तत् पत्राणि श्रियामपि ॥४॥

karṇikāraṁ mahad-yantraṁ
ṣaṭ-koṇaṁ vajra-kīlakam
ṣaḍ-aṅga-ṣaṭ-padī-sthānaṁ
prakṛtyā puruṣeṇa ca
premānanda-mahānanda-
rasenāvasthitaṁ hi yat
jyotī-rūpeṇa manunā
kāma-bījena saṅgatam

tat-kiñjalkaṁ tad-aṁśānāṁ
tat-patrāṇi śriyām api

Anvaya

karṇikāram – the center of that thousand-petaled lotus which is the central part of Vraja; *mahad-yantram* – is a great and unique mystic device; *ṣaṭ-koṇam* – with six corners; *vajra-kīlakam* – of which Śrī Kṛṣṇa, who is completely transcendental and who is the possessor of all potencies, is the pivot in the form of a thunderbolt, which is as brilliant as a diamond; *ṣaḍ-aṅga-ṣaṭ-padī-sthānam* – in that place is manifest the king of *mantras*, composed of eighteen syllables with six limbs in six divisions; *prakṛtyā puruṣeṇa ca* – and therein are situated the original potency and the original enjoyer; *yat hi premānanda-mahānanda-rasena avasthitam* – that Gokula, whose nature is the bliss of pure, spiritual love, is the abode of supremely blissful transcendental mellows; *saṅgatam* – it is endowed; *kāma-bījena* – with *kāma-bīja*; *jyotī-rūpeṇa* – and the effulgent; *manunā* – *kāma-gāyatrī-mantra*; *tat-kīñjalkam* – the saffron filaments of the lotus; *tad-aṁśānām* – are the supremely loving devotees, who are personal expansions of Śrī Kṛṣṇa's *svarūpa*, and who are none other than Kṛṣṇa's intimate (*sva-jātīya*) *gopas*; *tat-patrāṇi* – all the leaves of the lotus; *śriyām api* – are the groves of Śrī Kṛṣṇa's beloveds headed by Śrī Rādhā.

TRANSLATION

The pericarp, or central part of that transcendental lotus, is Śrī Kṛṣṇa's abode. It is characterized by a six-pointed device (*yantra*), presided over by the predominated and predominating principles (*prakṛti* and *puruṣa*). Like a diamond, the omnipotent, radiant, transcendental *kṛṣṇa-tattva* is present as the central pivot. The eighteen-syllable king of *mantras*, which has six integral parts in six sections, is manifest in the form of a hexagonal place with six divisions.

This pericarp of the eternal abode called Gokula is the six-pointed realm of Śrī Kṛṣṇa's residence. The filaments are the residences of Śrī Kṛṣṇa's supremely loving parts and parcels, the intimate *gopa* friends who consider Him their very own. They beautify all four directions, forming an enclosure. The expanded petals of this lotus are the special sub-forests of the divine abode that belong to Śrī Kṛṣṇa's beloved Śrī Rādhā and the other *gopīs*.

ṬĪKĀ TRANSLATION

In these two verses, starting from *karṇikāram*, there is a description of the chief seat among the many seats of the divine eighteen-syllable king of great *mantras*, which is attended by all other *mantras*. The setting of this seat is characterized by a vast device, whose facsimile is drawn everywhere in the form of a symbolic diagram (*yantra*) for the sake of formal worship. Now the *svarūpa* of that device is being described.

This *yantra* has six corners, which are made by the overlapping of two mutually reversed triangles, and the middle is decorated by the pivot in the form of a brilliant thunderbolt. The purport is that the central portion of the thousand-petaled lotus is embellished by a diamond stud in the form of the *bīja-mantra* (*klīṁ*). In this *mantra* (verse 3), the syllable *ca* indicates the four-letter *kāma-bīja*, which is situated as the central pivot of the pericarp. What is the necessity of the six points? In response to this question, it is said that these six limbs constitute the locations of the sixfold integral parts of the divine eighteen-syllable invocation. Therefore the *yantra* is exhibited with six corners, and is presided over by the predominated and predominating principles (*prakṛti* and *puruṣa*). *Prakṛti* is present as the abode of the *mantra*. That *prakṛti* is also Śrī Kṛṣṇa in person. He has been called *prakṛti* in this context because He is the cause of *prakṛti*.

In remembering the presiding deity of this *mantra*, it is stated thus: *kṛṣṇaḥ prakṛtiḥ*. The significance is that Kṛṣṇa is *prakṛti*. *Puruṣa* also refers to the personality who is present in the form of the presiding deity of the *mantra*. Therefore, in this *mantra*, Śrī Kṛṣṇa presides as *prakṛti* and *puruṣa*. He is experienced in four ways: as the cause of the *mantra*, as the syllables of the *mantra*, as the presiding deity of the *mantra*, and as the personality who is to be worshiped by the *mantra*. Among these four conceptions, Śrī Kṛṣṇa is presented here as the cause of the *mantra* and the presiding deity of the *mantra*, and He has been described previously as the worshipable deity (*ārādhya-devatā*) in the verse *īśvaraḥ paramaḥ kṛṣṇaḥ sac-cid-ānanda vigrahaḥ*.

How He is experienced in the form of syllables will be mentioned later in the verse *kāmaḥ kṛṣṇāya* (verse 24).

In the *Hayaśīrṣa-pañcarātra*, it is stated, "O *brāhmaṇa*, enlightened visionaries of the truth say that the words of a *mantra* and one who is indicated by those words – that is, the *mantra* itself and its deity – are one, or non-different."

In the *Gopāla-tāpanī Upaniṣad*, it is also stated, "Just as the air within the body is one, and yet is known by various names and forms – such as *prāṇa*, *apāna*, *udāna*, *vyāna* and *samāna* – similarly Bhagavān Śrī Kṛṣṇa, the benefactor of the universe, is also present in five integral parts in the form of *mantra*."

There are some rare references mentioning that the presiding deity of this *mantra* is Durgā-devī. This is because potency and the possessor of potency are non-different. For example, in the *Gautamīya-tantra*, it has been stated:

yaḥ kṛṣṇaḥ saiva durgā syād
yā durgā kṛṣṇa eva saḥ
anayor antarādarśī
saṁsārān no vimucyate

Kṛṣṇa is Durgā and Durgā is Kṛṣṇa. Those who see any difference between these two are never liberated from the endless chain of birth and death.

Therefore, in this quotation, Śrī Kṛṣṇa's own internal potency has been referred to by the name of Durgā. This Durgā is not the Durgā who is a partial manifestation of *māyā*. In the *Nirukti* dictionary it is mentioned: "*kṛcchreṇa durārādhanādi-bahu-prayāsena gamyate jñāyate* – that personality who is known with great endeavor by the performance of extremely severe *sādhana* is called Durgā."

It is also stated in the *Nārada-pañcarātra*:

jānāty ekā parā kāntā
saiva durgā tadātmikā
yā parā paramā śaktir
mahā-viṣṇu-svarūpiṇī

yasyā vijñāna-mātreṇa
parāṇāṁ paramātmanaḥ
muhūrtād eva devasya
prāptir bhavati nānyathā

ekeyaṁ prema-sarvasva-
bhāvā śrī-gokuleśvarī
yathā mugdhaṁ jagat sarvaṁ
sarva-dehābhimāninaḥ

She who is the highest, most excellent potency, or Mahā-Viṣṇu-svarūpiṇī, whose very self is Kṛṣṇa (*kṛṣṇātmikā*), and who is the best of all His beloveds, is called Durgā. One who realizes Her surely attains the supreme Paramātmā, Bhagavān Śrī Kṛṣṇa, in less than a moment; there is not even the slightest doubt in this regard. She is Gokuleśvarī Śrī Rādhā, the full embodiment of spontaneous love and the personification of *mahābhāva*. Bhagavān Śrī Kṛṣṇa, who is the supreme *īśvara* of all existence and the God among gods, is attained by Her mercy. Śrī Rādhā is Kṛṣṇa's internal potency, and She performs worship of Her most beloved Śrī Kṛṣṇa with the entire wealth of Her devotion and service. [Alternatively, Her most beloved Śrī Kṛṣṇa always engages in Her worship with the entire wealth of His devotion and service.] That very Śrī Rādhā, the dearmost internal potency of Bhagavān, is known only to those who perform extraordinarily difficult worship. Therefore, saintly persons refer to Śrī Kṛṣṇa's beloved mistress of undivided *rasa* by the name of Durgā.[10] His covering potency, Mahāmāyā, is the controller of all the mundane worlds, and it covers and

[10] The name Durgā is derived from *duḥ*, meaning difficult, and *gā*, meaning to go.

bewilders the entire population of living beings who identify with their material bodies.

The following statement by Śrī Durgā can be found in the *Sammohana-tantra*:

yan nāmnā nāmni durgāhaṁ
guṇair guṇavatī hy aham
yad vaibhavān mahā-lakṣmī
rādhā nityā parādvayā

The name Durgā, by which I am known, is Her name. The qualities for which I am famous are Her qualities. The majesty with which I am resplendent is Her majesty. That Mahā-Lakṣmī, Śrī Rādhā, is non-different from Śrī Kṛṣṇa. She is His dearmost sweetheart and the crest-jewel of His beloveds.

Thus, the *svarūpa* that is the embodiment of transcendental love, bliss and supremely ecstatic transcendental mellows, who is the pinnacle of *mahābhāva* and who is the self-illuminating effulgence in the form of *mantra*, is called Śrī Rādhā. The expression *kāma-bījena saṅgatam* means that *kāma-bīja* is included in that *mantra* which is the origin of all others, *kāma-gāyatrī*. However, in some places it is stated that *kāma-bīja* is completely independent of the *gāyatrī-mantra*.

In this way, after describing Śrī Kṛṣṇa's divine abode, Śrī Brahmā describes the covering of that abode in the half *śloka* beginning with the words *tat kiñjalkam* (verse 4). If the *dhāma* is in the form of the pericarp of a lotus, then the filaments of that lotus form the lines of its enclosure. The word *kiñjalka* (filaments) has been used to indicate that there is a row of peaks, or that the lines of the enclosure are endowed with peaks, which surround the *dhāma* in all four directions. One should also understand the expression *tat-tad-aṁśānām* to indicate the Supreme Personality Śrī Kṛṣṇa's expansions such as His *gopa* and *gopī* associates.

Gokula is that abode in which Śrī Kṛṣṇa resides with His intimate associates who have a similar mood and are the vessels of the highest love. In describing Gokula, the abode of such associates, Śrīmat Kṛṣṇa-dvaipāyana Vedavyāsa said:

evaṁ kukudminaṁ hatvā
stūyamānaḥ sajātibhiḥ
viveśa goṣṭhaṁ sabalo
gopīnāṁ nayanotsavaḥ

Śrīmad-Bhāgavatam (10.36.15)

After the killing of Vṛṣabhāsura, Śrī Kṛṣṇa, who is a festival for the eyes of the *gopīs*, entered the cowherd village along with Baladeva. At that time the cowherd folk began to praise Him with poetry of their own composition.

The petals of this lotus are the abodes of His most beloved sweethearts, the *gopīs* headed by Śrī Rādhā, and are in the form of sub-forests. That Śrī Kṛṣṇa's beloveds are called *gopīs* has been clearly stated by the use of the word *gopī* in His *mantra*, and among all the *gopīs*, Śrī Rādhā is the most excellent. Just as Śrī Kṛṣṇa is the origin of everything, while being personally without beginning, similarly Śrī Rādhā, being non-different from Śrī Kṛṣṇa, is also the origin of everything, while being without origin Herself.

It is therefore stated in the *Gautamīya-tantra*:

devī kṛṣṇamayī proktā
rādhikā para-devatā
sarva-lakṣmīmayī sarva-
kāntiḥ sammohinī parā

Śrī Rādhikā is the Supreme Goddess (*para-devatā*), the exclusive abode of Kṛṣṇa's loving pastimes (Devī), and the shelter of all goddesses of fortune (Mahā-Lakṣmī). She is the most beautiful. Her inside and outside are nothing but Kṛṣṇa, and She is incessantly absorbed in Kṛṣṇa. She is the embodiment of all splendor, and is the enchantress of Śrī Kṛṣṇa's heart.

Furthermore, Śrī Rādhikā is the supreme ruler of Vṛndāvana, as stated in the *Matsya Purāṇa*:

vārāṇasyāṁ viśālākṣī
vimalā puruṣottame
rukmiṇī tu dvārāvatyāṁ
rādhā vṛndāvane vane

Viśālākṣī reigns in Vārāṇasī, Vimalā-devī in Puruṣottama-dhāma, Rukmiṇī in Dvārakā and Śrī Rādhā in Vṛndāvana.

Similarly, it is also stated in the *Ṛk-pariśiṣṭa*: "*rādhayā mādhavo devo mādhavenaiva rādhikā vibhrājante janeṣvā* – the handsomeness of Mādhava is enhanced by Rādhā, and the exquisite loveliness of Rādhā is heightened by Mādhava."

Tatra patrāṇām: One should understand that in the central section where the lotus petals of that Gokula-dhāma join together, there is a multitude of paths as well as the residences and pastures of the cows. Gokula is one undivided lotus flower in which everything is incorporated. Thus, dairy farming is also splendidly present there. Gokula-dhāma is described as a thousand-petaled lotus in other places in *śāstra* as well. For example:

sahasrāraṁ padmaṁ dala-tatiṣu devībhir abhitaḥ parītaṁ go-saṅghair api nikhila-kiñjalka-militaiḥ. kavāṭe yasyāsti svayam akhila-śakti-prakaṭita-prabhāvaḥ sadyaḥ śrī-parama-puruṣas taṁ kila bhaje.

Gokula-dhāma is a thousand-petaled lotus, on whose petals are situated the residences of the *gopīs*. There are dwellings for innumerable cows in all four directions. I render service to the Supreme Personality, Śrī Kṛṣṇa, the son of the Chief of Vraja, who is radiantly present along with all His beloved *gopīs* on the pericarp of the transcendental lotus.

Here it is correct to read the expression *go-saṅghaiḥ* as *go-saṅkhyaiḥ*. Thus it is understood to indicate the community of *gopas*, because the *Amara-koṣa* dictionary has described many meanings of the word *go*, such as *gopī* (cowherd damsel), *gopāla* (cowherd), *go-saṅkhya* (community of cowherds), *godhu* (one who milks cows), *gābhīra* (calf) and *ballava* (cowherd boy-friend). The central part of the pericarp, situated in the middle of the lotus, is indicated by the word *kavāṭa*. The fundamental purport of this verse is that Śrī Kṛṣṇa is the supreme predominator and enjoyer, who eternally manifests His influence through His diverse potencies.

Tātparya

Śrī Kṛṣṇa's pastimes are of two types: manifest and unmanifest. The *vṛndāvana-līlā* that are exhibited to the eyes of ordinary people are called manifest pastimes, and the pastimes that are not visible to material eyes are called unmanifest pastimes. In Goloka, the unmanifest pastimes are perpetually occurring. When Śrī Kṛṣṇa so desires, those unmanifest pastimes become visible to material eyes in Gokula. At such times they are called manifest pastimes.

In *Kṛṣṇa-sandarbha* Śrīla Jīva Gosvāmipāda has said: "*aprakaṭa-līlātaḥ prasūtiḥ prakaṭa-līlāyām abhivyaktiḥ* – the manifest pastimes are a revelation of the unmanifest pastimes." Furthermore, it is stated in *Kṛṣṇa-sandarbha*: "*śrī vṛndāvanasya prakāśa-viśeṣo golokatvam, tatra prāpañcika-loka-prakaṭa-līlā-vakāśatvenāvabhāsamānaṁ prakāśo goloka iti samarthanīyam* – the pastimes of Goloka remain in an unmanifest state in the special manifestation of Goloka within this material universe, called Vṛndāvana. Those pastimes are manifested whenever there is an opportunity." Therefore, Śrī Rūpa Gosvāmipāda has reconciled this subject in his *Laghu-bhāgavatāmṛta* (5.498):

yat tu goloka-nāma syāt
tac ca gokula-vaibhavam
tādātmya-vaibhavatvaṁ ca
tasya tan-mahimonnateḥ

The higher aspect of the greatness of Gokula is its non-difference from Goloka. Thus Goloka is simply the greatness or *vaibhava* of Gokula.

Although Śrī Kṛṣṇa's pastimes are not always manifest in Gokula, they are eternally manifest in Goloka-dhāma.

This mystery is such that Goloka and Vṛndāvana (Gokula) are both one and the same *tattva*; there is no difference between them. One is above, in the spiritual realm, and the other manifests or appears below, in the material world. However, from the angle of vision of one special conception, just as Gokula is in Mathurā-maṇḍala, Vṛndāvana is also present in Goloka. According to this specialized deliberation, Goloka is considered to be only the external manifestation of Vṛndāvana. There is sameness between these two abodes from the perspective of *līlā*, in which case a difference is seen only in regard to manifest and unmanifest pastimes. Śrī Kṛṣṇa's *līlā* is eternally manifest in Goloka.

Yet, from the point of view of differentiation, one will observe that the pastimes of Goloka are integrated with a reverential mood, whereas the pastimes of Vṛndāvana are integrated with pure human-like sweetness. That is why Goloka has been called the *vaibhava* or greatness of Gokula.

The unmanifest pastimes of this Goloka that are revealed to the conditioned soul are of two types. The purport is that there are two types of process adopted by practicing devotees in order to realize these pastimes. One is *mantramayī-upāsanā* and the other *svārasikī-upāsanā*. These will now be explained.

Śrī Jīva Gosvāmī has stated: "*tat tad ekatara sthānādi*; *niyata-sthitika evaṁ tat-tan-mantra-dhyānamayaḥ*; *mantramayī-*

upāsanā is the process in which any one particular pastime, which is situated in one location, is being contemplated continuously by means of a *mantra*, and the worship of that pastime is being accomplished by this method." The pastimes in which various types of spontaneous playful revelry are strung together of their own accord in an uninterrupted succession extending over several locations are called *svārasikī* or *svābhāvikī*, meaning "natural."

This verse explains both *mantramayī-upāsanā* and *svārasikī-upāsanā*. The first meaning (indicating *mantramayī-upāsanā*) is as follows. In the *līlā* indicated by eighteen syllables, the bases of the *mantra*, which are arranged in different places, manifest only one particular *līlā* of Kṛṣṇa. For example: *klīṁ kṛṣṇāya govindāya gopījana-vallabhāya svāhā*. This *mantra* has six limbs made of the following components: (1) *kṛṣṇāya*, (2) *govindāya*, (3) *gopījana*, (4) *vallabhāya*, (5) *svā* and (6) *hā*. The *mantra* is formed when these six parts are arranged in sequence one after the other.

The six-pointed *mahā-yantra* is as follows. The *kāma-bīja*, *klīṁ*, is situated in the middle of the diagram as the pivot. If one draws the *yantra* in this way and meditates on the transcendental *tattva*, knowledge of reality arises in the heart, as it did for Mahārāja Candradhvaja. The *Gautamīya-tantra* gives the following instruction: "*svā-śabdena ca kṣetrajño heti cit-prakṛtiḥ parā* – the word *svā* indicates the individual *jīvātmā*, who is the knower of his own field of activities, and *hā* indicates the spiritual dominated potency, the eternal nature of the *jīva*."

According to *Śrī Hari-bhakti-vilāsa* (1.87): "*uttarād govindāyety asmāt surabhiṁ gojātim. tad-uttarād gopījanety asmād vidyāś caturdaśa. tad-uttarād vallabha* – the word *govindāya* after the word *klīṁ* indicates Śrī Kṛṣṇa, who is known as Govinda because He tends the *surabhī* cows and nurtures their pleasure. After that, the word *gopījana* indicates the society of Vraja *gopīs*, who are the embodiments of the fourteen types of knowledge of Śrī Kṛṣṇa's internal potency. Then the word *vallabhāya* indicates that Śrī Kṛṣṇa, the lover of those *gopīs*, is the paramour hero of Vraja." When worship is performed by *mantra* through meanings such as these, realization awakens of a *līlā* occuring in one location. This is the purpose of *mantropāsanā*. The general meaning is that those who cherish the exclusive aspiration to enter into Kṛṣṇa's transcendental pastimes will engage in Kṛṣṇa's service in accordance with their own *svarūpa* by incessantly cultivating their particular relationship with Him, which gives rise to *bhakti-rasa*.

The living entity's relationship with Kṛṣṇa is established when realized knowledge of the following six *svarūpas* arises: (1) Kṛṣṇa's *svarūpa* (intrinsic form and nature), (2) the *svarūpa* of His transcendental pleasure pastimes, (3) the *svarūpa* of His associates, the *gopīs*, (4) the *svarūpa* of unconditional surrender of the self to Kṛṣṇa, following in the wake of the *gopīs*, (5) the *svarūpa* of the pure soul in full spiritual cognizance and (6) the *svarūpa* of service to Kṛṣṇa. The happiness of service to Bhagavān is the only relishable mellow. It is accomplished by an unwavering conviction in the process of *bhakti*, whose very nature is such that the soul becomes established in the following relationship: "The ultimate shelter is the Supreme Enjoyer, Śrī Kṛṣṇa, and I am the predominated or enjoyed principle in the form of a maidservant of Śrī Rādhā." This is the essential purport of the verse.

In the stage of *sādhana*, when *bhakti* is initiated by the material senses, the practicing devotee realizes the type of pastime in Goloka or Gokula that is the object of meditation by *mantra* (*mantropāsanā-dhyānamayī-līlā*). In the stage of perfection, the perfect devotee realizes the pastimes of Goloka or Gokula in their feature of totally uninhibited revelry. This is the condition of affairs in Goloka or Gokula; it will be revealed gradually.

The expression *jyotī-rūpeṇa manunā* in verse 3 indicates that the transcendental meaning may be illuminated or realized in the *mantra*. Having integrated pure *kṛṣṇa-prema* in the form of transcendental amorous love in this *mantra*, the practicing devotee who goes on rendering service becomes situated in the form of a perfect associate of Śrī Kṛṣṇa, and realizes the astonishing mellows of the greatest blissful love (*premānanda-mahānanda-rasa*). This type of eternal *līlā* is always radiant in Goloka.

The shape of the transcendental Gokula resembles a fully blossomed lotus flower, whose central pericarp has a six-pointed shape. Within this lies the embodiment of the purport of the eighteen-syllable *mantra*, namely *śrī rādhā-kṛṣṇa-tattva*, surrounded by Their direct bodily expansions, the attendant *gopīs* who are manifested by the internal potency. Here Śrī Rādhā-Kṛṣṇa Yugala are the full manifestation of the seed of the *mantra*. It is stated in the *Uttara-gopāla-tāpanī Upaniṣad* (13):

tasmād oṁkāra-sambhūto
gopālo viśva-sambhavaḥ
klīm-oṁkārasya caikatvaṁ
paṭhyate brahma-vādibhiḥ

> *Oṁkāra*, the sacred syllable *oṁ*, is the perfect and complete truth, the combination of potency and the possessor of potency, Gopāla, from whom the entire universe has arisen. Those who know the Absolute Truth, Brahman, regard *oṁkāra* and *klīṁ* as synonyms.

Consequently, *oṁkāra* is Gopāla and *klīṁ* is also *oṁkāra*. Therefore *kāma-bīja* indicates *rādhā-kṛṣṇa-tattva*.

Verse 5

चतुरस्रं तत्परितः श्वेतद्वीपाख्यमद्भुतम् ।
चतुरस्रं चतुर्मूर्त्तेश्चतुर्द्धाम चतुष्कृतम् ॥
चर्तुर्भिः पुरुषार्थैश्च चतुर्भिर्हेतुभिर्वृतम् ।
शूलैर्दशभिरानद्धमूर्द्धाधो दिग्विदिक्ष्वपि ॥
अष्टभिर्निधिभिर्जुष्टमष्टभिः सिद्धिभिस्तथा ।
मनुरूपैश्च दशभिर्दिक्पालैः परितो वृतम् ॥
श्यामैर्गौरैश्च रक्तैश्च शुक्लैश्च पार्षदर्षभैः ।
शोभितं शक्तिभिस्ताभिरद्भुताभिः समन्ततः ॥५॥

catur-asraṁ tat-paritaḥ
śvetadvīpākhyam adbhutam
catur-asraṁ catur-mūrteś
catur-dhāma catuṣ-kṛtam

caturbhiḥ puruṣārthaiś ca
caturbhir hetubhir vṛtam
śūlair daśabhir ānaddham
ūrddhādho dig-vidikṣv api

aṣṭabhir nidhibhir juṣṭam
aṣṭabhiḥ siddhibhis tathā
manu-rūpaiś ca daśabhir
dik-pālaiḥ parito vṛtam

śyāmair gauraiś ca raktaiś ca
śuklaiś ca pārṣadarṣabhaiḥ
śobhitaṁ śaktibhis tābhir
adbhutābhiḥ samantataḥ

Anvaya

tat-paritaḥ – surrounding Gokula; *adbhutam* – is an astonishing; *catur-asram* – quadrangle; *śvetadvīpa-ākhyam* – named Śvetadvīpa; *catur-asram* – having four corners; *catuḥ-kṛtam* – it is divided into four parts; *catuḥ-dhāma* – which are the four abodes; *catuḥ-mūrteḥ* – of the four deities: Vāsudeva, Saṅkarṣaṇa, Pradyumna and Aniruddha; *caturbhiḥ puruṣa-arthaiḥ* – with the four attainments of human life, namely religiosity, economic development, sense gratification and liberation; *ca vṛtam caturbhiḥ hetubhiḥ* – and endowed with the four Vedas: *Ṛg, Sāma, Yajuḥ* and *Atharva*, which are of the nature of *mantra*; *ānaddham api* – and (that abode) is held; *dik-vidikṣu* – in all directions: east, west, north, south, north-east, north-west, south-east and south-west; *ūrddha-adhaḥ* – above and below; *śūlaiḥ daśabhiḥ* – by ten spears; *juṣṭam* – it is surrounded (in the eight directions); *aṣṭabhiḥ nidhibhiḥ* – with the eight jewels: *mahāpadma, padma, śaṅkha, makara, kacchapa, mukunda, kunda* and *nīla*; *aṣṭabhiḥ siddhibhiḥ tathā* – and with the eight perfections: *aṇimā, laghimā, mahimā, garimā, īśitva, vaśitva, prāpti* and *prākāmya*; *paritaḥ* – it is surrounded; *vṛtam* – and protected; *daśabhiḥ dik-pālaiḥ* – by the ten protectors of the directions (headed by Indra), who are of the nature of *mantra*; *śobhitam* – (that abode of Śvetadvīpa) is beautified; *pārṣada-ṛṣabhaiḥ* – by the Lord's exalted associates; *śyāmaiḥ* – whose bodily hues are bluish black; *gauraiḥ ca* – and golden; *raktaiḥ ca* – and red; *śuklaiḥ ca* – and white; *samantataḥ* – and who are accompanied; *tābhiḥ adbhutābhiḥ śaktibhiḥ* – by their astonishing potencies (headed by Vimalā).

Translation

The identity of Gokula's surrounding area is being presented. In the four directions beyond Gokula lies a wonderful, four-cornered place called Śvetadvīpa. Śvetadvīpa is divided into four sections in the four directions, and each section is the abode of one of the presiding deities: Vāsudeva, Saṅkarṣaṇa, Pradyumna and

Aniruddha. These four abodes are adorned with the four objectives of life, namely religiosity, economic development, sense gratification and liberation, and the causes of those four objectives, namely the four Vedas (*Ṛg*, *Yajur*, *Sāma* and *Atharva*), which are composed of *mantras*. They are surrounded in eight directions and above and below by ten lances. The eight directions are ornamented with the eight jewels known as *mahāpadma*, *padma*, *śaṅkha*, *makara*, *kacchapa*, *mukunda*, *kunda* and *nīla*. Ten guardians in the form of *mantras* are present in the ten directions, which are all beautified by blackish, golden, red and white associates of Bhagavān, along with the host of wondrous potencies headed by Vimalā.

Ṭīkā translation

After the description of Gokula, its surrounding area is now being described in four verses. Beyond Gokula lies an exceedingly miraculous, four-cornered abode called Śvetadvīpa. Although only Śvetadvīpa is mentioned here, one should also understand it to be Goloka. Actually, Śvetadvīpa is also a term for Gokula. All places are within that region known as Śvetadvīpa or Gokula. The employment of yet another special nomenclature indicates that all locations are included within its jurisdiction. The interior region is Vṛndāvana. Different names such as Śvetadvīpa, Goloka, Gokula, Vṛndāvana, Vraja and so on are used because of the different meanings carried by the various names. This Śvetadvīpa which is the outer covering of Goloka is different from the Śvetadvīpa situated in Gokula,[11] which will be described separately. Vṛndāvana-dhāma is within the quadrilateral realm.

[11] The Śvetadvīpa within Gokula is that place where Śrī Śacīnandana Gaurahari manifests His eternal pastimes, and is manifest in this world as Śrīdhāma Navadvīpa.

For example, it is stated in the *Svāyambhuva-āgama*: "*dhyāyet tatra viśuddhātmā idaṁ sarvaṁ krameṇaiva* – the *sādhaka* whose heart is pure will meditate on all of the following one after another." Later, it is further stated: "*vṛndāvanaṁ kusumitaṁ nānā-vṛkṣair vihaṅgamaiḥ saṁsmaret* – one should meditate by remembering Śrī Vṛndāvana with its charming groves (*kuñjas*) and many varieties of trees. The trees are covered in fragrant, flowering vines and resound with the sweet singing of birds."

Similarly, in the prayers of the personified Vedas to Śrī Bhagavān in the *Vāmana Purāṇa*, we find the following statement:

ānanda-rūpam iti yad
vidanti hi purā vidaḥ
tad-rūpaṁ darśayāsmākaṁ
yadi deyo varo hi naḥ

śrutvaitad darśayām āsa
gokulaṁ prakṛteḥ param
kevalānubhavānanda-
mātram akṣaram adhvagam
yatra vṛndāvanaṁ nāma
vanaṁ kāma-dughair drumaiḥ

"O Bhagavān, if You want to bestow a benediction upon us, then kindly grant us the boon that we may see the divine abode that the enlightened sages call *ānandamaya-dhāma*." Upon hearing this, Bhagavān blessed them with *darśana* of His supreme abode, Gokula, which is beyond the influence of material nature, known only by realization, and indestructible and absolute. In that supreme abode is a charming forest called Vṛndāvana, which is adorned with desire trees that completely fulfill all the desires of the devotees.

Beyond this Vṛndāvana is a four-cornered area divided into four sections, which are the individual abodes of the four forms known as *catur-vyūha*: Śrī Vāsudeva, Saṅkarṣaṇa, Pradyumna and Aniruddha. However, They are situated in aircraft above because They are performing pastimes that manifest Their divine opulence. Here *hetu* (the causes) indicates that They reign splendidly with *dharma*, *artha*, *kāma* and *mokṣa*, and that They are decorated with the guardians of the ten directions, headed by Indra, who are present in the form of their respective *mantras*. The four Vedas – *Ṛg*, *Sāma*, *Yajur* and *Atharva* – are also gracefully present in personified forms. That the Vedas have individual embodiments is confirmed by *Śrīmad-Bhāgavatam*, wherein it is stated that the personified Vedas offered prayers to Śrī Kṛṣṇa.

In that abode Śrī Hari is resplendent with His sixteen potencies, headed by Vimalā-devī, as stated in *Laghu-bhāgavatāmṛta* (3.129):

śrīr bhūḥ kīrtir ilā līlā
kāntir vidheti saptakam
vimalādhā navehyetā
mukhyāḥ ṣoḍaśa-śaktayaḥ

The sixteen potencies are as follows: (1) Śrī, (2) Bhū, (3) Līlā, (4) Kānti, (5) Kīrti, (6) Tuṣṭi, (7) Gī, (8) Puṣṭi, (9) Satyā, (10) Jñānājñānā, (11) Jayā Utkarṣiṇī, (12) Vimalā, (13) Yogamāyā, (14) Prahvī, (15) Īśānā and (16) Anugraha.

Thus this planet is also called Goloka-dhāma. The following description can be found in *Śrīmad-Bhāgavatam*:

nandas tv atīndriyaṁ dṛṣṭvā
loka-pāla-mahodayam
kṛṣṇe ca sannatiṁ teṣāṁ
jñātibhyo vismito 'bravīt

te tv autsukya-dhiyo rājan
matvā gopās tam īśvaram
api naḥ svagatiṁ sūkṣmām
upādhāsyad adhīśvaram

iti svānāṁ sa bhagavān
vijñāyākhila-dṛk svayam
saṅkalpa-siddhaye teṣāṁ
kṛpayaitad acintayat

jano vai loka etasminn
avidyā-kāma-karmabhiḥ
uccāvacāsu gatiṣu
na veda svāṁ gatiṁ bhraman

iti sañcintya bhagavān
mahā-kāruṇiko hariḥ
darśayām āsa lokaṁ svaṁ
gopānāṁ tamasaḥ param

satyaṁ jñānam anantaṁ yad
brahma-jyotiḥ sanātanam
yad dhi paśyanti munayo
guṇāpāye samāhitāḥ

te tu brahma-hradaṁ nītāḥ
magnāḥ kṛṣṇena coddhṛtāḥ
dadṛśur brahmaṇo lokaṁ
yatrākrūro 'dhyagāt purā

nandādayas tu taṁ dṛṣṭvā
paramānanda-nivṛtāḥ
kṛṣṇaṁ ca tatra cchandobhiḥ
stūyamānaṁ su-vismitāḥ

Śrīmad-Bhāgavatam (10.28.10–17)

When Nanda Mahārāja returned to Vraja from Varuṇaloka, he told his cowherd family and friends what had happened there. Hearing this incredible and astonishing account of Śrī Kṛṣṇa's greatness, they became extremely curious and amazed, and began to consider whether Śrī Kṛṣṇa could actually be the supreme controller, Parameśvara.[12] They began to request Him to show them His incomprehensible transcendental abode.

Then Svayam Bhagavān, who sees everything, understood the desire of the cowherds and, out of compassion, He began to contemplate the fulfillment of their aspiration: "Conditioned souls take birth in higher and lower species such as demigods and animals as a result of the selfish material pursuits they perform out of ignorance. All these Vrajavāsīs are My nearest and dearest family members. Although they have descended to this material world, they consider themselves to be the same as the conditioned souls because they are totally absorbed in My sweet human-like pastimes. They are oblivious to their actual position." Pondering in this way, the immensely compassionate Bhagavān Śrī Kṛṣṇa granted the *gopas* a vision of His own realm, which is situated beyond the material nature.

This realm of Bhagavān is transcendental, immeasurable, real, self-effulgent, eternal and the embodiment of Brahman. Even the great sages who have attained a state of consciousness that is free from the three modes of material nature can see that place only in trance. Śrī Kṛṣṇa took the *gopas* to the place called Brahma-hrada, where Akrūra also had *darśana* of that supreme abode after immersing himself in the water. They saw that Śrī Kṛṣṇa was also there, and that the Vedas personified were offering prayers to

[12] This is the explanation of Śrīla Jīva Gosvāmī: the Vrajavāsīs considered how Śrī Kṛṣṇa could possibly be the supreme controller, Parameśvara. A different explanation is given by Śrīla Viśvanātha Cakravartī Ṭhākura, who explains that the Vrajavāsīs never even for a moment considered that Śrī Kṛṣṇa could possibly be Bhagavān, the Supreme Personality who is full in six opulences. The Vrajavāsīs' knowledge of Kṛṣṇa's opulence remains covered at all times by the predominating mood of sweetness.

How is it possible for such an apparent difference between these great *ācāryas*? Śrīla Jīva Gosvāmī explains in the verse *svecchayā likhitaṁ kiñcit* that he wrote certain things for unqualified persons. Those things he did not reveal were later revealed by Śrīla Viśvanātha Cakravartī Ṭhākura, who always gave respect to the opinion of Śrīla Jīva Gosvāmī.

Him. That *loka* was ultra-subtle, beyond mundane sense perception, and unintelligible to worldly thought processes. Upon seeing it, they were both utterly amazed and overwhelmed with joy.

In this narration, the word *atīndriya* means "that which has never been seen before." The word *svagatim* means "His own abode," which is thoroughly incomprehensible. Śrī Kṛṣṇa granted a vision of that otherwise incomprehensible realm. Why did He grant them *darśana* of this abode? Because the Vrajavāsīs are His nearest and dearest family members.

sālokya-sārṣṭi-sāmīpya-
sārūpyaikatvam apy uta
dīyamānaṁ na gṛhṇanti
vinā mat-sevanaṁ janāḥ

Śrīmad-Bhāgavatam (3.29.13)

Without service to Me, My devotees will not accept the forms of liberation known as *sālokya* (living on the same planet as the Lord), *sārṣṭi* (having similar opulence to the Lord), *sāmīpya* (always being near to the Lord) and *sārūpya* (having a similar form to the Lord) – what to speak of impersonal liberation – even if they are offered to them.

Just as the word *janāḥ* in the above verse is understood to mean *nija-jana* (His own people), similarly the word *jana* in the previously quoted verse of *Śrīmad-Bhāgavatam* (10.28.13) also indicates *nija-jana*. It would be inconsistent to accept the word to refer to anyone else. Above all others, Śrī Kṛṣṇa considers the residents of Vraja to be His kith and kin, and He has personally confirmed this fact (*Śrīmad-Bhāgavatam* 10.25.18):

tasmān mac-charaṇaṁ goṣṭhaṁ
man-nāthaṁ mat-parigraham
gopāye svātma-yogena
so 'yaṁ me vrata āhitaḥ

> This community of cowherds is under My shelter. I am the patron of these Vrajavāsīs. I personally use My own power and prowess to protect those whom I have accepted as My closest family members, intimate relatives and bosom friends. This is My steadfast vow.

Śrī Kṛṣṇa further considers, "Simply due to ignorance, the living entities in this universe, which is composed of five gross elements, attain various destinations in higher and lower species, such as demigods and animals. The Vrajavāsīs consider themselves to be in the same category, and thus they could not understand their own situation. They have forgotten their own constitutional status. Their knowledge of My opulence has become concealed because of their absorption in My unique, sweet human-like pastimes."

This is also illustrated in *Śrīmad-Bhāgavatam* (10.11.58):

iti nandādayo gopāḥ
kṛṣṇa-rāma-kathāṁ mudā
kurvanto ramamāṇāś ca
nāvindan bhava-vedanām

> Nanda Mahārāja and all the Vrajavāsīs always used to enjoy talking about Kṛṣṇa and Balarāma. By doing so, they would become so overwhelmed with bliss that they never felt the distress of material existence.

Material qualities such as ignorance and self-centered fruitive activities could never touch the Vrajavāsīs, for the influence of ignorance is only exerted upon the conditioned *jīvas* who are indifferent to Kṛṣṇa, not upon the personal associates of Bhagavān.

From the expression *gopānāṁ svaṁ lokam* in *Śrīmad-Bhāgavatam* (10.28.14),[13] it is clear that Śrī Kṛṣṇa had granted the

[13] See p. 61 (*darśayām āsa lokaṁ svaṁ gopānām*).

Vrajavāsīs a vision of His divine abode, Goloka, which is beyond the illusory material nature in all respects. That abode is the manifest expression of the internal potency, which is indivisible and self-effulgent, and the eternally true embodiment of infinite existence, consciousness and bliss. Although it is extremely difficult to see this abode, Śrī Kṛṣṇa mercifully granted them a vision of it.

It is a matter of sheer wonderment to have such a *darśana* of Goloka while being in Vṛndāvana-dhāma on this Earth. How was it possible? In answer to this question, it has been said that Śrī Kṛṣṇa had taken the Vrajavāsīs headed by Nanda Mahārāja to Brahma-hrada, otherwise known as Akrūra-tīrtha, and instructed them to immerse themselves in Brahma-hrada. They dipped under the water once. Then, on Śrī Kṛṣṇa's request, they dipped under again several times, and each time Śrī Kṛṣṇa granted them *darśana* of a different *loka*. In the end He granted them a vision of Brahma-dhāma, His greatest transcendental abode, Goloka.

It is also stated in *Śrīmad-Bhāgavatam* (2.5.39): "*mūrdhabhiḥ satyalokas tu brahmalokaḥ sanātanaḥ* – above the head of Satyaloka lies the eternal Brahmaloka."

Here one may raise the question, "Other sections of Vaikuṇṭha are also called Brahmaloka, so which Brahmaloka is this one?" In response to this it is said, "In Brahma-hrada, Akrūra had a vision of the Brahmaloka that is the highest abode of Goloka.[14] Śrī Kṛṣṇa had granted the *darśana* of His supreme abode there especially to indicate the glories of that holy place of pilgrimage."

Śrīla Viśvanātha Cakravartipāda has expressed the following opinion in his commentary on the previously mentioned verses of *Śrīmad-Bhāgavatam* (10.28.10–17): "In order to make the Vrajavāsīs realize the superexcellent sweetness of the eternal

[14] Here is an example of different names being used to indicate Goloka: Brahma-dhāma refers to Goloka in this case. In other contexts, Brahma-dhāma may refer to the abode of impersonal liberation, or to Vaikuṇṭha.

abode of Vṛndāvana, the most compassionate Śrī Kṛṣṇa first showed them the realm of impersonal liberation, Brahmaloka. Then He granted them a vision of Vaikuṇṭhaloka, which is superior to that Brahmaloka. Finally, He granted them *darśana* of the superlative abode, Goloka-dhāma. In other words, Śrī Kṛṣṇa submerged those Vrajavāsīs in impersonal liberation by immersing them in Brahma-hrada, and from there He lifted them up to have *darśana* of the spiritual abode, Vaikuṇṭha-dhāma, by His inconceivable potency."

In this way, the immensely merciful master of all saved His devotees from the dire calamity of impersonal liberation,[15] and made them taste the happiness of Vaikuṇṭha. The feeling of loving happiness in Vaikuṇṭha is superior to the happiness derived from the impersonal Brahman, which is completely devoid of love. Furthermore, the love-laden happiness of Goloka surpasses even the happiness of Vaikuṇṭha.

taṁ vaikuṇṭha-lokaṁ dṛṣtvā tu paramānanda-nivṛtāḥ
vaikuṇṭhīya-golokasya vṛndāvanasya vṛndāvana-sādharmyaṁ
darśanād iti bhāvaḥ

Those Vrajavāsīs saw Vaikuṇṭhaloka and felt the highest bliss, because the Vaikuṇṭha planet of which they had *darśana* was actually the Goloka of the Vaikuṇṭha realm or spiritual sky. This seems to be the same as Vṛndāvana, due to the features that they have in common, but they are not one and the same place. A millionaire becomes severely aggrieved upon losing his wealth, and overjoyed if he somehow retrieves it again. Similarly, the

[15] Here, one may ask, "How is it that Nanda Mahārāja and the other Vrajavāsīs, who are all eternally liberated personalities, needed to be rescued from the calamity of impersonal liberation?" The answer is that the Vrajavāsīs felt great distress upon seeing the situation of impersonal liberation, and the greatly merciful Śrī Kṛṣṇa rescued them from their distress. For pure devotees, the condition of impersonal liberation is considered hellish (*kaivalyaṁ narakāyate*).

Vrajavāsīs were restless in Brahmaloka and Vaikuṇṭhaloka, because they were unable to see their Śrī Kṛṣṇa, whose face is like a lotus flower, and to whom they offer *ārati* with the lamp of their lives millions of times over. Calling out, "Where, oh where, is our darling Kṛṣṇa?" they were becoming increasingly anxious. However, when they came to Goloka, they did see Kṛṣṇa there. "*Aho*!" they exclaimed, "There's Kṛṣṇa!" They began to approach Him, but what they saw when they drew nearer to Him took them by surprise. "*Aho*! What kind of place have we come to? There are radiant, divine beings here offering reverent hymns to Kṛṣṇa. They look just like our old acquaintances, but we cannot call to mind exactly who they are. We also feel hesitant to inquire from them. The most surprising thing is that Kṛṣṇa, who is sitting in their midst, is not expressing His mood of childhood as He did before. Even upon seeing His father and elder relatives, He is not coming to us and putting His arms around our necks. And what's more, we are also hesitant to go to Him and take Him in our laps. Why is He not feeling any hunger and thirst today? How will His mother live without feeding Him?"

When Śrī Kṛṣṇa saw their reactions, His pastime potency inspired Yogamāyā to lift the depressed Vrajavāsīs up from that realm of Goloka and deliver them back to Vṛndāvana (*Śrīmad-Bhāgavatam* 10.28.16–17).

Furthermore, it is stated in the *Harivaṁśa*, in the narration concerning Indra (2.19.29):

svargād ūrdhvaṁ brahmaloko
brahmarṣi-gaṇa-sevitaḥ
tatra somagatiś caiva
jyotiṣāṁ ca mahātmanām

nighnatopadravān gavām... etc.

> In the celestial sphere above Svarga lies the world called Brahmaloka, which is attended by the sages known as *brahmarṣis*. That place is the destination of Candra and the powerful *mahātmās*. Above that region lies the planet of the cows, Goloka, which is protected by perfected personalities. That great, all-pervading realm is situated in a vast sky. Your (Śrī Kṛṣṇa's) radiant refuge is considered to lie even above that. Although we inquired from Pitāmaha Brahmājī about this radiant refuge, we are still incapable of knowing it. Personalities who are endowed with qualities such as control of the mind and senses, and who are dedicated to pious activities, attain Svargaloka. The adherents of impersonal knowledge, who are incessantly engaged in the austerities associated with the impersonal feature of the Absolute Truth, attain Brahmaloka. However, it is extremely difficult to ascend to the planet of the cows, Goloka. O almighty Śrī Kṛṣṇa, O self-manifest and equipoised Lord, You are capable of accomplishing anything. When this world was in a crisis, You upheld it and relieved the cows from their calamity.

In this context, if we take the meaning of "calamity" in the general sense, it would be unreasonable to interpret Brahmaloka as the planet that lies above Svargaloka. After deep deliberation, it must be understood that the Brahmaloka described in this quotation is in every way transcendental to the three mundane planetary systems. The moon has no access to that realm, what to speak of the other celestial bodies that are all situated beneath Dhruvaloka. Furthermore, the phrase *sādhyāḥ pālayanti* indicates that this Brahmaloka is protected by perfected personalities (*sādhyas*). However, this is also unreasonable because the *sādhyas* are included within the species of demigods. The *sādhyas* cannot even protect Svargaloka, so how can they protect Goloka? From every angle this interpretation is impossible.

This passage continues, "The aforementioned planet, which is also famous by the name of Surabhīloka, is all-pervading." This statement also seems to be inappropriate. Just as Śrī Bhagavān's form is all-pervading by the power of His inconceivable energy, similarly His planet is also all-pervading. This is not possible for any planet other than the planet of Bhagavān. Here in the statement of Indra, *pṛcchanto 'pi*, the word *api* has been used to indicate extreme astonishment: "*Aho*! How amazing it is that, although we inquired about this subject from Pitāmaha Brahmājī, we still cannot understand it." Surabhīloka is said to be within the universe, and hence it is neither fully transcendental, nor can it be the topmost planet. Therefore the Surabhīloka in this world is distinct from Goloka, which is transcendental to everything material, being the superexcellent form of Śrī Bhagavān's planet. In the *Mokṣa-dharma-nārāṇanīya-upākhyāna*, Śrī Bhagavān Himself states:

evaṁ bahu-vidhai rūpaiś
carāmīha vasundharām
brahma-lokaṁ ca kaunteya
golokaṁ ca sanātanam

O son of Kuntī! I wander upon this Earth in many forms. In addition to this, I also roam perpetually in the eternal abodes, Brahmaloka and Goloka Vṛndāvana.

Therefore the verse *svargād ūrdhvaṁ brahma-lokaḥ, nighnatopadravān gavām* is properly understood as follows. The word *svargāt* in this verse refers to Goloka Vṛndāvana. In the Second Canto of *Śrīmad-Bhāgavatam*, Bhūrloka, Bhuvarloka and Svargaloka are described as the lotus feet, the navel and the head, respectively, of the imaginary universal form. From Svarga to Satyaloka there are five planetary systems: Svarga, Mahar, Janas, Tapas and Satya. Above these five planetary systems is the chief Svarga, or in other words the spiritual Brahmaloka, the embodiment of eternity, knowledge and bliss that lies beyond the insentient material energy. The term Brahmaloka is used to indicate the planet of Bhagavān. It is also stated in the Second Canto of *Śrīmad-Bhāgavatam* that the eternal Brahmaloka lies above the head of Satyaloka, the topmost planet within this material world. Therefore the correct interpretation of the term Brahmaloka in this context is "the eternal and primeval Vaikuṇṭhaloka." It is not a material place within this created universe.

This is confirmed in the *śruti.* This Brahmaloka is also known as Ātmaloka, the eternal planet of Bhagavān. It is served by the *brahmarṣis* including Brahmājī, the personified Vedas, the *ṛṣis* headed by Nārada, Śrī Garuḍa, and the Lord's other associates headed by Viṣvaksena. This description of the personalities who are eternally sheltered there acts as an indication of the qualifications required to go to that realm. The Soma who resides there is not the moon; rather, this Soma refers to Śrī Śiva. This place is his desired destination, because Śrī Śiva himself states in the *Rudra-gīta* of the Fourth Canto, "That person who performs his *dharma* unflinchingly for one hundred births attains the position of Brahmā. Those who have performed even more pious activities can attain my position, the position of Śiva. But a living entity born in an ordinary family who renders service to Bhagavān even for a very short time becomes a Vaiṣṇava and attains the supreme abode that I desire to attain after giving up this position of Śiva."

The word *jyotiṣām* in the previously quoted verse from the *Harivaṁśa* refers to that Brahman into which persons desire to merge. This Brahmaloka is extremely difficult to attain, even for liberated saints who have realized Brahman. That abode is only attained by great souls such as the four Kumāras headed by Sanaka, as well as other *jñānīs* who have attained *prema-bhakti*, all of whom render devotional service to Bhagavān with an utter disregard for impersonal liberation. For example, it is stated in *Śrīmad-Bhāgavatam* (6.14.5):

muktānām api siddhānāṁ
nārāyaṇa-parāyaṇaḥ
sudurlabhaḥ praśāntātmā
koṭiṣv api mahā-mune

O great sage, one among many millions of liberated persons may attain perfection, and among many perfected beings, one may become fully devoted to Nārāyaṇa; and among billions of such personalities, one who is fully peaceful and self-satisfied is extremely rare.

Bhagavān has also stated in *Bhagavad-gītā* (6.47):

yoginām api sarveṣāṁ
mad-gatenāntarātmanā
śraddhāvān bhajate yo māṁ
sa me yuktatamo mataḥ

Amongst all *yogīs*, the best is he who is fully dedicated to Me, Śrī Vāsudeva, and who serves Me with great faith. This is My definite opinion.

Herein we find described the greatness of those devotees who render loving service with immovable faith. The word *mahat* (in the verse from the *Harivaṁśa*) refers to those personalities who are possessed of the highest *prema*. Only they attain Goloka.

Above Brahmaloka is *gavāṁ loka*, in other words Goloka-dhāma. It is said that this planet is served by *sādhyas*. Here *sādhya* refers to the original forms upon which the forms of the demigods within the material world are based. They are eternal associates of Śrī Kṛṣṇa who serve in Goloka in the capacity of guardians of the directions.

It is also confirmed in the *śruti* that this excellent place is known as Svargaloka, and that it is the residence of all the *sādhyas* and *devatās*. In this case, Svargaloka refers to Goloka-dhāma, where all the original forms of the demigods reside and render service to Bhagavān Śrī Kṛṣṇa. It does not refer to the mundane Svargaloka where Indra and other demigods reside.

In the *Uttara-khaṇḍa* of the *Padma Purāṇa*, in a description of Mahā-Vaikuṇṭha Goloka-dhāma, it is stated that this supremely glorious Goloka-dhāma is the residence of the eternal *devatās*, *viśvedevas* and *sādhyas*, who have immense beauty, and whose sight invokes auspiciousness.

In Brahmājī's prayers in the Tenth Canto of *Śrīmad-Bhāgavatam* (10.14.34), we find that he also hankers to take birth in Gokula: *tad-bhūri-bhāgyam iha janma kim apy aṭavyāṁ yad gokule 'pi*. Great devotees of the caliber of four-headed Brahmā also take birth there as immobile trees or creepers, and pray to receive the foot-dust of the *gopas* and *gopīs*. Therefore Goloka-dhāma is famous for being superior to all other abodes. Just as Bhagavān Nārāyaṇa exists everwhere, Goloka-dhāma is also all-pervading, for it simultaneously pervades all material and spiritual universes. It is also mentioned in *śāstra* that the attainment of Goloka is the final destination among the progressive stages of liberation.

It is described in the Second Canto that Brahmā, who sits upon a lotus flower, saw Vaikuṇṭhaloka. Similarly the Vrajavāsīs also saw Goloka in which opulence predominates. This Goloka-dhāma is great; indeed, it is a form of Bhagavān, as stated in *śruti*, *mahāntaṁ vibhum ātmānam*.

This deliberation arises because several terms – such as *mahākāśa*, *brahma* and *paravyoma* – have been used in descriptions of Goloka. For example, Goloka has been described as *mahākāśa* (the great sky) in the *Vedānta-sūtra* code *ākāśas tal-liṅgāt*.

The phrase *tad-gataḥ* indicates the attainment of one's spiritual form, and consequently the attainment of this supreme abode. For example, Ajāmila also attained Vaikuṇṭha after being awarded his spiritual form. The significance is that Bhagavān's names, form, qualities, pastimes and abode are all transcendental. Consequently, upon attaining one's *svarūpa*, one also attains Bhagavān's abode.

In Goloka-dhāma, which shines victoriously far above all other planets, Śrī Kṛṣṇa sports in the form of Govinda. The place wherein Śrī Kṛṣṇa revels in His pleasure pastimes in the form of Govinda is by no means ordinary; it is *tapomayī*. The word *tapaḥ* (austerity) should be accepted in the sense of boundless and indivisible opulence. The same interpretation of the word *tapaḥ* is found in the commentary on *Śrī Viṣṇu-sahasra-nāma-stotram* in relation to the phrase *paramaṁ yo mahat-tapaḥ*. The *śruti* statement *satayo 'tapyata* pertains to Parameśvara. Its meaning is, "That Parameśvara has manifested *aiśvarya*." Therefore Goloka is extremely difficult to attain, even for Brahmā.

This planet has been described in various places as Brahmaloka, Vaikuṇṭha, Mahā-Nārāyaṇaloka, Paravyoma, Mahākāśa and so on, which are all originally names only for Goloka. Just as the attainment of Brahmaloka is possible only for a person whose mind is perfectly controlled, similarly only a *premamaya-bhakta* (one who worships Śrī Viṣṇu – meaning Śrī Kṛṣṇa – with undivided attention) can know this planet Goloka. *Śruti* also confirms this: *yasya jñānamayaṁ tapaḥ*. Here the word Brahmaloka means Vaikuṇṭha, the word *parā* means "transcendental to material nature," and *gavām* refers to all the residents of Vraja including the trees, vines, cows, cowherds and *gopīs*. Moreover, *nighnatopadravān gavām* means that Kṛṣṇa dispels all the miseries of the residents of Vraja. What are their miseries? They are described in the *Yugala-gīta* of *Śrīmad-Bhāgavatam* (10.35.25) by the *gopīs* in their mood of separation:

"*mocayan vraja-gavāṁ dina-tāpam* – our dearmost Śyāmasundara is returning to drive away the intolerable affliction of separation that all the residents of Vraja have suffered throughout the day in His absence." This is the meaning of His dispelling the calamities that befall the Vrajavāsīs. The Vrajavāsis' affection for Śrī Kṛṣṇa is natural. One who is inspired by their loving moods must practice *sādhana* continuously in order to attain an emotional attachment just like theirs. Only then can this extremely rare loving attachment that is found in Vraja be attained. Thus, such a destination is extraordinarily uncommon.

After the description of Goloka, now in the phrase beginning with *sa tu*, there is an explanation of the non-difference between Goloka and Gokula: "He protected the Vrajavāsīs by holding up the mountain Govardhana." The same version is found in *Śrī Nārāyaṇīyopākhyāna* of *Mokṣa-dharma*, wherein Śrī Bhagavān personally states, "O son of Kuntī, I wander throughout the universe in many forms. I roam throughout Brahmaloka, eternal Goloka, and also in Śrīdhāma Vṛndāvana Gokula." It is also stated in the *Mṛtyuñjaya-tantra*: "According to His own independent desire, He established Vaikuṇṭha from the Mahākāśa (spiritual sky) upon the surface of the Earth in the form of Gokula, and made successful very great festivals such as the *rāsa-līlā* with the *gopīs*. This type of festival is the very heart of *bhakti*, and it bestows pure transcendental love upon the faithful."

Nārada-pañcarātra contains the following description in the history of Vijaya: "In Goloka-dhāma, which exists above all other abodes, the incomparable supremely blissful hero known as Govinda delights in the abode of Gokula." This is also confirmed in the *Ṛg Veda* (1.154.6) as follows:

tā vāṁ vāstūny uśmasi gamadhyai
yatra gāvo bhūri-śṛṅgā ayāsaḥ
atrāha tad urugāyasya kṛṣṇaḥ
paramaṁ padam avabhāti bhūri

In the first line the word *tāḥ* means "all," *vām* means "of Rāma and Kṛṣṇa," *vāstūni* means "the pastime places of Gokula," *gamadhyai* means "to attain," and *uśmasi* means "we desire." What is the nature of those *līlā-sthalīs*? Very excellent and beautiful horned cows are found there. Here the word *bhūri* not only means that the cows have very excellent horns; it also means that they are endowed with great prosperity. These cows, which are endowed with all auspicious symptoms, are *kāma-dhenus*, who are capable of satisfying all desires of all people. The word *ayāsaḥ* found here is defined in the *Amara-koṣa* as meaning "auspiciousness," and *devāsa* as meaning "you are." Thus Goloka is renowned in Bhū-maṇḍala, in Vaikuṇṭha and in the Vedas. This Goloka-dhāma is in many ways as famous and as transcendental to the material nature as the much-famed Śrī Bhagavān.

In the *śruti*, the *mādhyandinīya* portion of the *Yajur Veda* mentions: "*dhāmāny uśmasīti iti viṣṇoḥ paramaṁ padam avabhāti bhūri* – we desire to attain that Goloka-dhāma, which is the *svarūpa* of Śrī Viṣṇu's supreme abode." In addition there are many other statements from the *śāstra* that establish the same essential conclusion.

Tātparya

The supreme abode, Gokula, is the prominent seat or shelter of *prema-bhakti*. Therefore all the places of the manifestation of Vraja in the material world (Bhauma-Vraja), such as Rādhā-kuṇḍa, Govardhana and the Yamunā, are gracefully present there. Besides this, the complete opulence of Vaikuṇṭha expands to the fullest extent in all directions. The original quadruple pastime expansion called *ādi-catur-vyūha* (Vāsudeva, Saṅkarṣaṇa, Pradyumna and Aniruddha) and other such manifestations are present there in their appropriate situations. This *catur-vyūha* is partially manifest as the *catur-vyūha* of Vaikuṇṭha, who in turn manifests the unlimited realm of Vaikuṇṭha. The liberation attained in Vaikuṇṭha, and the three objectives attained in the material world – namely religiosity, economic development and sense gratification – are also appropriately situated in Gokula (Goloka) in their original root forms. The Vedas are present there in their personified forms as well, and are deeply absorbed in singing about the qualities of the master of Gokula.

The endeavors of those who try to attain that Goloka-dhāma solely by their own contemplation and meditation, without attaining the favor of Śrī Kṛṣṇa, are utterly futile. This is because it is surrounded on all sides by ten formidable spears to check anyone from entering. These ten spears bestow hopelessness on those desiring to enter illegally. Proud persons who attempt to go to that topmost planet by means of the paths of *yoga* and *jñāna* are also pierced by those spears, and are forced to return defeated. *Nirvāṇa* is worthy of a position in Brahma-dhāma (the destination of impersonal liberation), but not in Goloka. This impersonal liberation has been called the spears (*śūla*) which form the outer covering of Goloka. The meaning of the word *śūla* comes from *triśūla*, or trident. *Triśūla* is comprised of the three material qualities and also the three divisions of time: past, present and future.

In this way, whatever aspirations the *aṣṭāṅga-yogīs* and the monistic *brahma-jñānīs* hold for progress toward Goloka are cut to shreds on the tridents situated in the ten directions, and they fall into the ditch of unmitigated dejection. When those traveling in the direction of Goloka along the path of *bhakti* in the mood of opulence make some progress on their journey, they see the eight perfections of mystic *yoga* headed by *aṇimā-siddhi*, and the treasures headed by *mahāpadma*, and they become attracted to them. Thus, they stop in Vaikuṇṭha, which is of the nature of an outer covering of Śrī Goloka. Those whose intelligence is even less refined are defeated by the guardians of the ten directions who exist in the form of *mantras*, and return again to the seven planetary systems within the material universe.

Therefore, Goloka-dhāma is an incomprehensible and impenetrable realm, which is easily accessible only through pure *prema-bhakti*. The preacher of *yuga-dharma*, who is the sum total of all *avatāras* of Bhagavān, remains there eternally in order to bestow mercy upon the devotees who arrive there after traversing the path of *śuddha-prema-bhakti*. There He is surrounded by eternal associates in accordance with His complexion, mood and other specific features. That *dhāma* in Gokula (the inner region of Goloka), called Śvetadvīpa, is His abode.[16]

For this reason, Śrīla Vṛndāvana dāsa Ṭhākura, who is the incarnation of Vyāsa, has described Śvetadvīpa thus: "*śvetadvīpa nāma, navadvīpa grāma* – the pastimes of Navadvīpa-dhāma, which are supplementary to *gokula-līlā*, are eternally present in the center of that Śvetadvīpa." Therefore Navadvīpa-maṇḍala, Vraja-maṇḍala and Goloka are one undivided reality. They are perceived in a variety of forms only because they are illuminated by an unlimited number of special ecstatic sentiments arising from the variegated nature of *prema*.

[16] Śvetadvīpa has been mentioned previously as the outer perimeter of Goloka-dhāma. In other words, Śvetadvīpa is sometimes taken to mean the outer manifestation of Goloka that is predominated by a mood of opulence. In this case, however, Śvetadvīpa refers to an area within the inner region called Gokula. This Śvetadvīpa described here is manifest in this world in the form of Navadvīpa.

There is yet another confidential truth that is understood directly only by the most realized *premi-bhaktas*, through the mercy of Śrī Kṛṣṇa. In the mundane world there is a sequence of upper and lower planetary systems totaling fourteen in all. The householders who are dedicated to prescribed duties performed for the sake of fulfilling material desires transmigrate within the three planetary systems Bhūr, Bhuvar and Svar. Peaceful personalities who are fixed in their great vows of celibacy, austerity and truthfulness are elevated to the spheres of Maharloka, Janaloka, Tapoloka and up as far as Satyaloka, by engaging in their duties without any desire to enjoy the fruit of their activities. In the highest part of that planetary system is the planet of the four-headed Brahmā, and above that lies the Vaikuṇṭhaloka of Kṣīrodakaśāyī Viṣṇu. The *paramahaṁsa sannyāsīs* and the demons killed by Bhagavān Śrī Hari cross beyond the Virajā; that is, they cross beyond the fourteen planetary systems of this mortal world and attain monistic liberation by immersing the individual existence of their selves in the light of Brahma-dhāma.

The *jñāni-bhaktas*, who are fond of Bhagavān's supreme opulence, the *śuddha-bhaktas*, *premi-bhaktas*, *premapara-bhaktas* and *premātura-bhaktas* attain positions in Vaikuṇṭha, which is the transcendental abode of Nārāyaṇa also known as Paravyoma.[17] The only devotees who attain Goloka-dhāma are those who are absorbed in Śrī Kṛṣṇa's supremely sweet, human-like feature, following the mood prevalent in Vraja. By the influence of His inconceivable potency, such devotees who are fully intent on entering these sweet, human-like pastimes are situated in different positions corresponding to the gradations found between the individual *rasas*.

[17] In this connection, Mathurā and Dvārakā are considered to be included within the abode of Nārāyaṇa.

The devotees who exclusively follow the pure and transcendental mood of Vraja make their residences in Kṛṣṇaloka, while those who exclusively follow the mood of Navadvīpa make their residences in Gauraloka. The devotees who are equally dedicated to the *bhāvas* of Vraja-dhāma and Navadvīpa-dhāma take up residence simultaneously in both Kṛṣṇaloka and Gauraloka, and attain the happiness of divine loving service in both places at once. Therefore, Śrī Jīva Gosvāmī has stated in *Śrī Gopāla-campū*:

yasya khalu lokasya golokas tathā go-gopāvāsa-rūpasya śvetadvīpatayā cānanya-spṛṣṭaḥ parama-śuddhatā-samudbuddha-svarūpasya tādṛśa-jñānamaya-katipaya-mātra-prameya-pātratayā tat-tat-paramatā matā, parama-golokaḥ paramaḥ śvetadvīpa iti.

That supreme planet is called Goloka because it is the residence of the cows (*go*) and the cowherds (*gopa*). This is the prominent location of the *rāsa-līlā*, which is Śrī Kṛṣṇa's very self. That topmost realm is also known as Śvetadvīpa in the form of the primary place for relishing the *rasa* of several varieties of spiritual sentiments, which are of exactly the same sort of inconceivable nature. It is an exceptionally pure manifestation, for it is untouched by associates possessed of other types of *bhāva*. Thus, these two *svarūpas* of Parama-Goloka and Parama-Śvetadvīpa exist in the undivided form of Goloka-dhāma.

The fundamental purport of this statement is that, even after tasting His own pastimes in the form of *vraja-līlā*, Kṛṣṇa had not attained the happiness derived from relishing *rasa* completely. Therefore, Vrajendra-nandana Śrī Kṛṣṇa accepted the internal mood and golden luster of Śrī Rādhikā, who is the supermost abode of *kṛṣṇa-rasa*. The compartment (*prakoṣṭha*) of Goloka where He eternally manifests the pastime of completely tasting *rasa* to the superlative degree is called Śvetadvīpa. The special *bhāva* mentioned here has been described thus:

śrī-rādhāyāḥ praṇaya-mahimā kīdṛśo vānayaivā-
svādyo yenādbhuta-madhurimā kīdṛśo vā madīyaḥ
saukhyaṁ cāsyā mad-anubhavataḥ kīdṛśaṁ veti lobhāt
tad-bhāvāḍhyaḥ samajani śacī-garbha-sindhau harīnduḥ

Śrī Caitanya-caritāmṛta (*Ādi-līlā* 1.6)

"How great is the deeply intense love (*praṇaya*) of Śrī Rādhā? What is the nature of My astonishing sweetness, which She alone relishes? And what special kind of happiness does She experience on tasting My sweetness?" A greed to taste these three things arose within the heart of Śrī Kṛṣṇa, and to fulfill that intense desire, He took birth from the womb of Śrī Śacīmātā like the moon appearing from the ocean.

Thus, the profound intention hidden within the aforementioned *Gopāla-campū* verse of Śrī Jīva Gosvāmī has been illuminated in the above verse. In the Vedas it has also been stated:

"rahasyaṁ te vadiṣyāmi" – jāhnavī-tīre navadvīpe golokākhye dhāmni govindo dvi-bhujo gauraḥ sarvātmā mahāpuruṣo mahātmā mahāyogī triguṇātītaḥ sattva-svarūpo bhaktiṁ loke kāśyatīti. tad ete ślokā bhavanti – eko devaḥ sarva-rūpī mahātmā gaura-rakta-śyāmala-śveta-rūpaś caitanyātma. sa vai caitanya-śaktir bhaktākāro bhaktido bhakti-vedyaḥ

Listen! I am about to disclose a deep mystery to you. In that Navadvīpa-dhāma, also known as Goloka, on the bank of the Jāhnavī River, Gaura-Govinda, the two-handed embodiment of pure existence, manifests pure *bhakti* for the sake of delivering the living entities who are ensnared in the chain of repeated birth and death. He is all-pervading and beyond the influence of the three modes of nature. He is the Supreme Personality, the best *yogī* and the greatest *ātmā*. That one divinity, the embodiment of all divine forms, the Supreme Soul, appears as the golden, red, black and white *yuga-avatāras*. He is the complete consciousness, and He is endowed with spiritual potency. He appears in the form of a devotee, He bestows *bhakti* and He is understood only through *bhakti*.

There is much scriptural evidence that establishes the non-difference of Śrī Gauracandra (Śrī Caitanya Mahāprabhu) and Śrī Kṛṣṇacandra, e.g. *āsan varṇās trayaḥ, kṛṣṇa-varṇaṁ tviṣākṛṣṇam, yadā paśyaḥ paśyate rukma-varṇam* and *mahān prabhur vai.* In His eternal form as Śrī Gaurahari in Navadvīpa, He is absorbed in tasting the *rasa* of Rādhā and Kṛṣṇa's Goloka pastimes. This has been certified by the Vedic *mantras* cited on the previous page. Just as by the influence of Yogamāyā the original form of Śrī Kṛṣṇa takes birth in the earthly Gokula and performs pastimes of infancy, boyhood and adolescence, so the original form of Śrī Gaura is similarly endowed with such pastimes in the earthly Navadvīpa, beginning with His birth from the womb of Śrī Śacīmātā. This fundamental truth is an axiomatic principle realized by the faculty of pure transcendental cognition. It is not a figment of the imagination, or a contemplation induced by the illusory energy.

Verse 6

एवं ज्योतिर्मयो देवः सदानन्दः परात्परः ।
आत्मारामस्य तस्यास्ति प्रकृत्या न समागमः ॥६॥

evaṁ jyotir-mayo devaḥ
sad-ānandaḥ parāt paraḥ
ātmārāmasya tasyāsti
prakṛtyā na samāgamaḥ

Anvaya

evam – thus (existing in great opulence); *devaḥ* – Śrī Govinda, the controller of Gokula; *jyotir-mayaḥ* – the effulgent Supreme Controller; *sad-ānandaḥ* – who is the original form of eternal bliss; *parāt paraḥ* – who is greater than any other lord and controller; *ātma-ārāmasya tasya* – delights with His internal potency; *na asti samāgamaḥ* – and has no meeting; *prakṛtyā* – with His external potency.

Translation

Thus it is seen that Bhagavān Gokuleśvara is the self-effulgent worshipable personality, the Supreme Absolute Truth and the embodiment of eternal bliss. He is absorbed in amorous pastimes with His internal potency in His own eternal abode, and He has no direct connection with the dull material nature.

Ṭīkā translation

Now we will explain the deep intentions of Brahmājī in uttering this verse. Just as *mantras* such as *Puruṣa-sūkta* in the Vedas have defined Bhagavān Śrī Kṛṣṇa as being one with the universal form, similarly the creator, Viṣṇu, is described here in the verse beginning *evam* as being non-different from Bhagavān Śrī Kṛṣṇa, the presiding deity of Goloka.

The word *deva* indicates Śrī Govindadeva, the eternally self-effulgent presiding deity of Goloka. He is called *deva* because He is ever absorbed in pastimes, which are of two types: pastimes in which His transcendental opulence is predominant, and pastimes in which His transcendental sweetness is predominant. Śrī Mahā-Viṣṇu's pastime of creating the cosmos, from which all moving and non-moving living entities in the universe have sprung forth, is a manifestation of only one-fourth of Bhagavān's opulence.

The expression *sad-ānanda* indicates the *sac-cid-ānanda svarūpa* of Bhagavān, who exists as the *puruṣa* in His eternal form of bliss. The inherent constitutional nature of the *puruṣa* is the state of being the predominating male enjoyer. According to the statement of *śruti*: "*vijñānam ānandaṁ brahma* – Brahman is the origin of knowledge and bliss." Here Brahman has been referred to by the use of a noun that is neither masculine nor feminine, but neuter. Since Bhagavān is the Supreme Personality engaged in pastimes, why would He give up His form as enjoyer and become an impersonal entity, devoid of masculinity? He is self-satisfied, and takes pleasure in His own *ātmā*; He does not have to depend upon anyone else. Therefore He is impartial and independently capable of accomplishing everything. Nevertheless, He is eternally busy in pastimes with His own pleasure potency. He never touches the inert material nature, nor does He have any connection with it. For example, in *Śrīmad-Bhāgavatam* (2.9.10) it is stated: "*na yatra māyā kim utāpare* – *māyā* cannot enter that region."

> The material modes of passion and ignorance, or even goodness mixed with passion and ignorance, are not found in that Vaikuṇṭha-dhāma. There, only pure goodness is eternally present. In that realm, there is no influence of time, what to speak of

qualities such as attachment and aversion. The illusory nature, which is the cause of worldly happiness and distress, cannot even enter that place. It is inhabited forever by the associates of Bhagavān, who is praised by both demigods and demons.

Tātparya

The one supreme transcendental potency or internal potency of Gokuleśvara Śrī Kṛṣṇa has manifested the pastimes of Goloka, or Gokula. By the mercy of this divine potency, the living entities who are manifestations of the marginal potency can also enter into those pastimes. Mahā-Vaikuṇṭha is the covering of Goloka.[18] Its extreme outer border is Brahma-dhāma, and beyond Brahma-dhāma lies the Virajā River. The inferior external energy, which is the shadow of the spiritual potency, is situated on the other side of that Virajā River. Therefore, the illusory energy (*māyā*) cannot attain the direct association of the supremely pure *sac-cid-ānanda-svarūpa* of Śrī Kṛṣṇa. To say nothing of associating with Him, she even feels ashamed to come within His sight.

[18] Here, Mahā-Vaikuṇṭha refers to the supremely opulent abode of Nārāyaṇa.

Verse 7

माययाऽरममाणस्य न वियोगस्तया सह ।
आत्मना रमया रेमे त्यक्तकालं सिसृक्षया ॥७॥

māyayāramamāṇasya
na viyogas tayā saha
ātmanā ramayā reme
tyakta-kālaṁ sisṛkṣayā

Anvaya

aramamāṇasya – (although) not enjoying directly; *māyayā* – with His external potency; *na viyogaḥ* – He is not fully detached; *tayā saha* – from her; *ātmanā ramayā reme* – He enjoys with His own internal potency Ramā-śakti; *sisṛkṣayā* – (but) on account of His desire to create the universes made of the five gross elements; *tyakta-kālam* – He enjoys with her in a secondary form by means of His glance by which His time-potency becomes enacted.

Translation

Mahā-Viṣṇu never consorts with the external energy (*māyā*). Still, it cannot be said that *māyā* is entirely separated or divorced from that aspect of the supreme reality. Mahā-Viṣṇu consorts with His own personal potency, Ramā-devī. Whenever He desires to create the universe, Bhagavān activates His time potency, and casts His glance toward the inert material energy.

Ṭīkā translation

Creating the universe is not the duty of Svayam Bhagavān, but the responsibility of the expansion of His expansion in the form of the *puruṣa-avatāra*. In this task, the relationship of the *puruṣa-avatāra* with the inert material energy is not direct, but indirect. Bhagavān's direct relationship is with His personal energy, Ramā-devī. The external potency is not permanently manifest, because she enters into the *puruṣa-avatāra* at the time of the cosmic annihilation. The *puruṣa-avatāra* causes *māyā* to perform her duties of creation and so on by inspiring her through the agency of His time potency. That is the only contact He has with her; He has no direct contact with *māyā* in this operation. The contact is only indirect, as confirmed in *Śrīmad-Bhāgavatam* (10.85.31): "*yasyāṁśāṁśāṁśa-bhāgena* – the creation, maintenance and destruction of the mundane universe is accomplished by the *puruṣa-avatāra*, who is an expansion of an expansion of His expansion."

A doubt may arise in this connection: The living entities become attached to *māyā*, so does Bhagavān also become engrossed in *māyā* in the same way, and cease to be the Lord? To resolve this doubt, it is said: "*ātmanā ramayā reme* – Bhagavān consorts with His own personal, intrinsic potency, Ramā-devī." Therefore, Bhagavān is neither attached to *māyā*, nor subject to its control, unlike the living entities who are bound by the results of their *karma*. He is served by the external potency in the external quarter, and by the intrinsic, internal potency Śrī Ramā-devī in the internal realm. This is the purport of the verse in question.

It is also stated in the prayers of Brahmā found in *Śrīmad-Bhāgavatam* (3.9.23): "*eṣa prapanna-varado ramayātma-śaktyā yad yat kariṣyati gṛhīta-guṇāvatāraḥ* – O Bhagavān, You bestow benedictions upon the living entities who are unconditionally surrendered to You. In order to manifest varieties of pastimes in the universe composed of five gross elements, You descend along with Your internal potency."

This is also supported by Śrī Arjuna's statement in *Śrīmad-Bhāgavatam* (1.7.23): "*māyāṁ vyūdasya cic-chaktyā kaivalye sthita ātmani* – O Bhagavān, You are the transcendental controller and enjoyer, You are beyond the material nature, and You are the master of existence. Therefore You are immutable; that is, You are not attached to *māyā*. You keep the external potency far distant by the influence of Your intrinsic, internal potency, and You remain situated exclusively in Your own intrinsic nature."

If this conclusion is accepted, then how does creation take place without being activated by Him? In answer to this question it is said, *sisṛkṣayā*: when Bhagavān desires to create, He activates His time potency, through which He agitates the material nature. Material existence takes place by the influence of this time potency, which is the light of Bhagavān's bodily luster.

The constitutional nature of time has been described thus: "*prabhāvaṁ pauruṣaṁ prāhuḥ kālam eke yato bhayam* – all remain in a state of fear of this *puruṣa's* influence in the form of time." One can find a detailed analysis of this in *Śrīmad-Bhāgavatam* (3.5.23):

kāla-vṛttyā tu māyāyāṁ
guṇamayyām adhokṣajaḥ
puruṣeṇātma-bhūtena
vīryam ādhatta vīryavān

Bhagavān Viṣṇu is the *puruṣa*, who is beyond material sense perception and who is replete with spiritual potency. By His time potency, He agitates the material energy, which consists of the modes of material nature, and then sows the seed of the cause of creation in *māyā* through the medium of His partial manifestation.

The purport of this verse is that the first *puruṣa-avatāra* of Adhokṣaja Bhagavān is Kāraṇodakaśāyī Mahā-Viṣṇu, who glances toward *māyā* from a distance. By the influence of this glance, Bhagavān impregnates *māyā* with potency in the form of *jīva-śakti*, which is a semblance of the transcendental potency (*cit-śakti*). The living entities who, as a result of fruitive activities performed in ignorance, had merged into the unmanifest material nature at the time of the cosmic annihilation, are sent again into the field of fruitive activities at the time of creation and made to enter *māyā*.

The universe appears as a result of the combination of *māyā-śakti* and *jīva-śakti*. Furthermore, *śāstra* confirms that although *jīva-śakti*, who is the knower of the field of his own activities, is superior to the material energy, he is subordinate to *māyā* on account of his entering into *māyā*. In this context the word *puruṣa* indicates one who glances toward the predominated material nature. This is how the *puruṣa* has impregnated the unmanifest material nature with seed-potency in the form of the living entities.

Tātparya

Bhagavān Śrī Kṛṣṇa has no direct connection with the illusory potency; His contact with *māyā* is only indirect. In His form of Kāraṇodakaśāyī Mahā-Viṣṇu, the *puruṣa-avatāra*, He glances toward *māyā*. This form is a plenary portion of Mahā-Saṅkarṣaṇa, who resides in the seat of pastimes known as Vaikuṇṭha. Even in this act of glancing He has no association with *māyā* because, by His desire, Ramā-devī, the *cit-śakti*, carries out the function of His glance as His inseparable potency. The external potency renders service to the personal expansion of Bhagavān as He sports with Ramā-devī, so she acts in the capacity of Ramā-devī's maidservant. The function of time is simply Ramā-devī's power of cause and effect. In other words, only *kāla-puruṣa*, the personified time factor, unites with the inert material energy, with the result that the universe composed of five elements emerges. Thus that *kāla-puruṣa*, or the influence by which the cosmic creation, maintenance and destruction take place, is the wish of Bhagavān.

Verse 8

नियतिः सा रमादेवी तत्प्रिया तद्वशं तदा ।
तल्लिङ्गं भगवान् शम्भुर्ज्योतिरूपः सनातनः ॥
या योनिः सापराशक्तिः कामोबीजं महद्धरेः ॥८॥

niyatiḥ sā ramā devī
tat-priyā tad-vaśaṁ tadā
tal-liṅgaṁ bhagavān śambhur
jyoti-rūpaḥ sanātanaḥ
yā yoniḥ sāparā-śaktiḥ
kāmo bījaṁ mahad dhareḥ

Anvaya

sā ramā – that Ramā-devī (with whom Mahā-Viṣṇu enjoys); *devī* – is the Lord's self-effulgent potency; *tat-priyā* – she is dear to Him; *niyatiḥ* – is born of His *svarūpa*; *tad-vaśam* – and is fully submissive to Him; *tadā* – then (at the time of creation); *jyoti-rūpaḥ sanātanaḥ* – the personified reflection of His eternal effulgence; *bhagavān śambhuḥ* – appears as the renowned Bhagavān Śambhu; *tat-liṅgam* – the generative capacity (Śambhu's localized representation) of that same first *puruṣa*, Kāraṇodakaśāyī Viṣṇu. He is a plenary portion of Saṅkarṣaṇa who in turn is a plenary portion of Śrī Kṛṣṇa; *sā yā aparā śaktiḥ* – (similarly) she who is the inferior potency of Mahā-Viṣṇu, and the semblance of Yogamāyā; *yoniḥ* – becomes the womb (for universal generation); *kāmaḥ* – Mahā-Viṣṇu has a desire for universal creation, as a result of which His glance falls upon His illusory potency; *bījam hareḥ* – and on account of the seed of Hari (bestowed upon *māyā*); *mahat* – the *mahat-tattva* arises (which is the combined form of the living entities and the five gross elements, the result of the action performed by His personified glance).

Translation

[Now the way in which Bhagavān indirectly comes in contact with *māyā* is being described.]

The spiritual potency in the form of Ramā-devī, who is dear to Bhagavān, is Destiny. That goddess is always controlled by the Supreme Lord and is always dedicated to His service. At the onset of creation, the effulgence of Mahā-Viṣṇu, who is the expansion of Śrī Kṛṣṇa's plenary portion, is manifest in the form of Śambhu. That Śambhu is called the *liṅga* of Bhagavān, meaning the manifest symbol of His generative capacity, and appears for the purpose of preparing the cosmic manifestation of the material universes. The *liṅga* in the form of Śambhu is a reflection of the eternal light or effulgence. The feminine receptive potency is manifest from Ramā-devī or Destiny. That potency which gives birth to the material creation is the inferior energy called *māyā*, whose intrinsic form is the *yoni*, the womb of universal creation. The union of the *yoni* and *liṅga* is the reflection of the Supreme Lord Śrī Hari's desire seed, in the form of the unmanifested material energy (*mahat-tattva*).

Ṭīkā translation

Who is Ramā-devī? The one-and-a-half *ślokas* beginning with *niyatiḥ* are being spoken in answer to this question. She is constitutionally the spiritual potency, and she is called *niyati* because she is eternally present within the *svarūpa* of Svayam Bhagavān, and because she remains *niyamita* (regulated in her activities) by Svayam Bhagavān. Thus, she is Bhagavān's submissive and beloved consort. It is stated in *Śrīmad-Bhāgavatam* (12.11.20): "*anapāyinī bhagavatī śrīḥ sākṣād-ātmano hareḥ* – she is directly

Bhagavatī Śrī Lakṣmī-devī, who is the internal, inseparable potency of Śrī Hari." The *śakti* of Śrī Hari is inseparable because she is directly of His intrinsic nature. That is to say, just as Śrī Hari is the embodiment of transcendental consciousness, similarly His internal potency, being non-different from Him, is the feminine aspect of the embodiment of transcendental consciousness. Here the word *sākṣāt* (directly) indicates that she is not the *śakti* who is ashamed to be in the path of Śrī Hari's vision. That *śakti* is the illusory potency, who bewilders the living entities who are averse to Bhagavān. Bhagavatī Lakṣmī-devī has also been called *anapāyinī* (imperishable or inseparable) in the *Viṣṇu Purāṇa*:

nityaiva sā jagan-mātā
viṣṇo śrīr anapāyinī
yathā sarva-gato viṣṇus
tathaiveyaṁ dvijottama

O best of the twice-born, the mother of the universe, Lakṣmī-devī, is Bhagavān Viṣṇu's eternal *anapāyinī-śakti*. Just as Viṣṇu is all pervading, similarly His *śakti* is also present everywhere.

Whenever the master of the universe, the God of gods, Janārdana, descends to this world, His internal potency Bhagavatī Lakṣmī-devī also descends along with Him in appropriate forms, such as those of goddesses or human beings, corresponding to the forms of Śrī Hari.

In some scriptures it is mentioned that Śivajī's potency is the cause of the creation. Such statements should be reconciled as follows. Just as the universe has been considered the *svarūpa* of Bhagavān in descriptions of the universal form, similarly Śivajī's potency has been referred to as the cause of the universe in the context of considering her to be a limb of Bhagavān.

According to the *Viṣṇu Purāṇa*, the entire universe is a semblance of the transcendental radiance of Bhagavān's plenary portion, i.e. it is the symbol (*liṅga*) of the unmanifest *puruṣa*. The plenary portion that is indicated by this symbol is the plenary portion that creates the total material energy, and He is called Śambhu. The word *liṅga* should be interpreted to mean symbol or form.

Bhagavān's first incarnation for creating this world, in whom the material universe is situated, who takes a rounded form, and who is the shelter and benefactor of unlimited living entities, is called *śiva-liṅga*, or Śambhu.

The phrase *anyas tu tad-āvirbhāva-viśeṣa* means, "The other form of Śiva is called Sadāśiva. He is a manifestation of Bhagavān for a specific purpose, and thus He is *viṣṇu-tattva*. He is supremely benevolent."

However, the form of Śiva described as *śivaḥ śakti-yuktaḥ śaśvat tri-liṅgo guṇa-saṁvṛtaḥ* is not *viṣṇu-tattva*. The Śiva who is united with the illusory potency remains covered by three types of false ego, namely goodness, passion and ignorance. This Śiva will be described ahead in verse 45, *kṣīraṁ yathā dadhi-vikāra-viśeṣa-yogāt*. It should be understood that the portion functioning as the womb of creation is the inferior potency. In other words, it is that unmanifested area of *māyā* that acts as the receptacle for Bhagavān's impregnation of potency in the form of innumerable living entities. This is also called *pradhāna*.

The purport of this analysis is that Bhagavān glanced toward *māyā* to create the cosmic existence. As a result of this glance, Ramā-devī as material nature (that is, her shadow) gave birth to progeny in the form of the twenty-four elements of creation, beginning with the total material energy (*mahat-tattva*).

In this verse 8, the unmanifested material energy has been called the desire-seed of Śrī Hari, whose desire to glance in the direction of *māyā* for the purpose of creation is called *kāma*. Then Bhagavān impregnated the material nature with His seed in the form of the instrumental causes of creation, namely the *jīva-śakti* and the *mahat-tattva*. This is the sense in which the word *mahat* has been used.

A description found in *śruti* states: "*so 'kāmayata* – at the beginning of creation, Bhagavān manifested the desire to beget the entire population." According to *Śrīmad-Bhāgavatam* (3.5.26), the statement beginning with *kāla-vṛttyā* confirms that Bhagavān impregnated the conscious spiritual *jīva-śakti* into the actively manifesting area of material nature consisting of the three modes of material nature, which was in a state of being agitated by the time potency. As a result, that manifestation of the predominated material nature gave birth to the vast *mahat-tattva*.

Tātparya

Saṅkarṣaṇa is a personal expansion (*aṁśa*) of Śrī Kṛṣṇa. Being imbued with a desire to create, He is inclined to manifest the universe of five elements. As He reclines in the Causal Ocean in the form of the first *puruṣa-avatāra*, He casts toward *māyā* a glance that is the instrumental cause of the creation. The semblance of its reflected light is *śambhu-liṅga*, the generative capacity, which unites with the shadow of *ramā-śakti* in the form of the universal womb of Māyā-devī. At that time, the semblance of the desire-seed in the form of the aggregate unmanifest elements (*mahat-tattva*) emerges and becomes absorbed in the task of creation. The first awakening of the desire-seed created by Mahā-Viṣṇu is called *hiraṇyamaya-mahat-tattva* (the golden form of the aggregate elements), which is the mental principle of readiness for cosmic creation. There is an extremely confidential consideration here: the desire of the *puruṣa* engages in the act of creation after accepting the aspects of the instrumental cause and the ingredient cause. Here *māyā*, the female receptive potency, acts as the instrumental cause, while Śambhu, the male generative capacity, acts as the ingredient cause (*upādāna*). The *puruṣa*, who acts according to His own sweet will, is Mahā-Viṣṇu. The ingredient principle (*pradhāna*) is the ingredient cause (*upādāna*). The receptive principle (*prakṛti*) is *māyā*. The creator of the material universe and the cause of the union of the other two principles is Śrī Kṛṣṇa's partial expansion, the *puruṣa*, or the principle of desire. These three (*pradhāna*, *prakṛti* and *puruṣa*) constitute the agents of creation.

The desire-seed of Goloka is a purely transcendental reality, whereas the desire-seed of the material world is a manifestation of potencies such as time, which are included within the shadow of the spiritual potency. Although the transcendental desire-seed mentioned previously is the original principle of which *māyā* is the reflection, the purely transcendental reality is far removed from *māyā*. The second desire-seed is the illusory reflection of that original transcendental desire-seed. *Śambhu-tattva* is elaborately described ahead in verses 10 and 15.

Verse 9

लिङ्गयोन्यात्मिका जाता इमा माहेश्वरी प्रजाः ॥९॥

liṅga-yony-ātmikā jātā
imā māheśvarī-prajāḥ

Anvaya

liṅga-yoni-ātmikā – through the combination of *liṅga*, who is *puruṣa-śakti* as well as *upādāna-kāraṇa*, with *yoni*, who is *strī-śakti* as well as *nimitta-kāraṇa*; *imāḥ māheśvarī-prajāḥ* – all the universal progeny including gods, mankind, animals, etc. through the great powers of *māyā*; *jātāḥ* – have been born.

Translation

All progeny such as humans and demigods, along with their respective worlds, have issued forth from this combination of the generative capacity in the form of *liṅga*, and the universal womb of material nature, called *yoni*.

Ṭīkā translation

Whatever details have been narrated in *śāstras* such as *śaiva* and *tantra* about Śiva's creation of progeny are not authentic; rather they have been spoken independently out of ignorance. Actually, Mahā-maheśvara refers exclusively to Śrī Kṛṣṇa. Thus the fundamental purport of *māheśvarī-prajāḥ* is that all progeny have originally emerged from the *māyā* of the Supreme Controller, Śrī Kṛṣṇa. It is in this context that the expression has been used in the current verse.

Tātparya

Bhagavān's divine opulence consists of the entirety of His majestic influence. Out of that entirety, the opulence of Vaikuṇṭha and Goloka constitutes three-fourths of His majestic influence, wherein there is no lamentation, death or fear. The remaining one-fourth is the opulence of *māyā*, and consists of the entire population of living entities, such as human beings and demigods, along with all their planets in the mundane universes. All these substances have issued forth from the union of the ingredient cause and the instrumental cause, that is *liṅga* and *yoni*. Whatever facts have been accumulated to date through material science are all characterized by this type of union. All inert material objects such as trees, creepers, worms and insects have been produced from the combination of *puruṣa* and *prakṛti*, the generative masculine principle and the receptive feminine principle.

There is a particularly profound point worthy of consideration in this regard. Although the Sanskrit words *liṅga* and *yoni*, generally indicating the male and female generative organs, seem somewhat crude, these terms are extremely useful for defining elementary principles in scientific literature, and also for illuminating matters of confidential significance. Indecency is an external conception related to social formality. However, science and transcendental science cannot destroy the true substance by depending on social formality. Thus, in order to understand the desire-seed related to the material potency, which is the original principle of the inanimate universe, the use of these words is unavoidable. However, one should simply interpret *liṅga* and *yoni* as referring to the active potency of the predominating agent (*puruṣa-śakti*), and the active potency of the predominated function (*strī-śakti*).

Verse 10

शक्तिमान् पुरुषः सोऽयं लिङ्गरूपी महेश्वरः ।
तस्मिन्नाविरभूल्लिङ्गे महाविष्णुर्जगत्पतिः ॥१० ॥

śaktimān puruṣaḥ so 'yaṁ
liṅga-rūpī maheśvaraḥ
tasminn āvirabhūl liṅge
mahā-viṣṇur jagat-patiḥ

Anvaya

mahā-viṣṇuḥ – the first of the *puruṣa-avatāras*, who is known as Mahā-Viṣṇu or Kāraṇodakaśāyī, which means one who lies within the Causal Ocean (*kāraṇa-udaka*); *jagat-patiḥ* – the supreme master and Supersoul of all the universes; *āvirabhūt* – appeared (by means of His glance); *tasmin liṅge* – within that form; *liṅga-rūpī maheśvaraḥ* – Bhagavān Śambhu, whose personal form is represented by the localized symbol of *liṅga* (His generative capacity); *śaktimān* – connected with His illusory potency, who furnishes the universal ingredients; *saḥ ayam puruṣaḥ* – is factually non-different from that same Mahā-Viṣṇu (who performs the function of ingredient cause through that Śambhu).

Translation

The controller of all, the original agent, who has been indicated by the word *maheśvara*, is the potent male (*puruṣa*). For the purpose of creation, He is manifest in the form of the original male generative capacity (*liṅga*). He who is called Mahā-Viṣṇu, the Lord of the cosmos, also appears in that combination of the active and receptive principles of creation by His expansion in the form of His glance.

Ṭīkā translation

This verse has been spoken to clarify the previous verse. The unmanifest form mentioned previously now emerges in its manifest form for the purpose of creation. How does it emerge? The partial expansion of a partial expansion of Bhagavān, called the original potent male principle, Maheśvara, creates the material universe. Everything in the world of *māyā* – such as false ego, intelligence, mind, the five gross elements, the five sense objects and the unmanifest aggregate of the material energy – is the manifest representation of the unmanifest form of Bhagavān. The self-sufficient Mahā-Viṣṇu, who is the Lord of all living entities and all spiritual and material worlds, is the origin (*aṁśī*) of Maheśvara, who appears in a manifest form as the *liṅga* or original male generative capacity.

It is also stated in the commentary on *Laghu-bhāgavatāmṛta*:

so 'yaṁ śaktimān puruṣaḥ
liṅga-rūpī maheśvaro bhavati
tasmin liṅge jagat-patir
mahā-viṣṇur āvirabhūt

That Supreme Personality, the possessor of all potencies, Mahā-Viṣṇu, takes the form of Maheśvara as the *liṅga* or original generative capacity, and then enters within it as the Lord of the mundane universes.

Tātparya

Śrī Nārāyaṇa, Śrī Kṛṣṇa's personal expansion, who is non-different from Him, reigns gracefully in the Vaikuṇṭha realm of the spiritual sky, wherein transcendental opulence predominates. The Mahā-Saṅkarṣaṇa of His quadruple expansion is also a partial expansion of Śrī Baladeva, Śrī Kṛṣṇa's first pastime expansion. By the influence of the inconceivable potency, that Mahā-Saṅkarṣaṇa in the form of His partial expansion Kāraṇodakaśāyī Mahā-Viṣṇu eternally reposes in Virajā, which is the borderline between the conscious and unconscious realms. From there He glances toward *māyā*, which is the remotely situated shadow of the spiritual potency. The semblance of that transcendental glance is Śambhu, the lord of *pradhāna*, which is replete with the potential material ingredients. Śambhu, in the form of Rudra, unites with *māyā*, the instrumental cause. However, he cannot do anything without the influence of the direct spiritual might of Śrī Kṛṣṇa in the form of Mahā-Viṣṇu. Therefore the unmanifest material energy (*mahat-tattva*) emerges only when the active endeavors of *māyā* (i.e. *śiva-śakti*) and the primordial material ingredients (*pradhāna*) are sanctioned by Saṅkarṣaṇa, who is Śrī Kṛṣṇa's personal expansion, and Mahā-Viṣṇu, who is Saṅkarṣaṇa's personal expansion and the first *puruṣa-avatāra*.

Only when Mahā-Viṣṇu is favorable does *śiva-śakti* gradually create the element of false ego, the five gross elements beginning with space, the five sense objects and the material senses of the *jīvas*, who are particles of the rays of Mahā-Viṣṇu's effulgence. An elaborate analysis of this aspect will be presented in the coming verses.

Verse 11

सहस्रशीर्षा पुरुषः सहस्राक्षः सहस्रपात् ।
सहस्रबाहुर्विश्वात्मा सहस्रांशः सहस्रसूः ॥११॥

sahasra-śīrṣā puruṣaḥ
sahasrākṣaḥ sahasra-pāt
sahasra-bāhur viśvātmā
sahasrāṁśaḥ sahasra-sūḥ

Anvaya

puruṣaḥ – Mahā-Viṣṇu, the master of the universe; *sahasra-śīrṣā* – has thousands of heads; *sahasra-akṣaḥ* – thousands of eyes; *sahasra-pāt* – thousands of feet; *sahasra-bāhuḥ* – thousands of arms; *viśva-ātmā* – He pervades the whole universe as the Supersoul; *sahasra-aṁśaḥ* – thousands of *avatāra* expansions; *sahasra-sūḥ* – and generates many thousands of living beings.

Translation

That master of the universe, Mahā-Viṣṇu, possesses thousands upon thousands of heads, thousands upon thousands of eyes, thousands upon thousands of arms, and thousands upon thousands of incarnations and plenary expansions. He is the Self of the cosmos, and He alone creates thousands upon thousands of living entities.

Ṭīkā translation

The form of Mahā-Viṣṇu is being described thus in the current verse beginning with the words *sahasra-śīrṣā*. He whose innumerable incarnations appear in thousands upon thousands of plenary portions is called *sahasrāṁśa*. Similarly, He who creates thousands upon thousands of living entities is called *sahasra-sūḥ*. Here the word *sahasra* (one thousand) has been used to indicate an uncountable number. It is evident that the word *sahasra* is used throughout the scriptures to convey the sense of "innumerable."

Furthermore, in describing the intrinsic form and nature of Mahā-Viṣṇu, it is stated in *Śrīmad-Bhāgavatam* (2.6.42): "The first *avatāra* of Bhagavān, the Lord of the spiritual realm, is the *puruṣa* who lies down in the Causal Ocean and casts His glance upon material nature. The following are all substances related to Parameśvara: His activities, such as the creation of time and acquired nature; material nature, which is composed of cause and effect; the unmanifest stage of material nature (*mahat-tattva*); the gross elements; false ego; the aggregate of the modes of material nature beginning with the mode of goodness manifested as various forms of life; hellish planets such as Pātālaloka; the aggregate of living entities; Garbhodakaśāyī Viṣṇu; moving and non-moving entities; and individual bodies."

In the commentary to this verse, it is stated that the gigantic *puruṣa*, who instigates the activities of material nature and who has thousands of heads and so on, has been called the original *avatāra* who assumes a pastime form. His activities include creation of the time factor, acquired nature and other elements of the material creation. Thus, the original *puruṣa-avatāra* creates, maintains and destroys within Himself and by Himself, at the beginning of every lifetime of Brahmā. Although He is one, He is manifest in many forms through His illusory energy. This universe, consisting of factual existence and the non-factual or temporary existence of cause and effect, is situated within Him alone. Therefore, all these phenomena have been called substances related to Him.

Tātparya

Mahā-Viṣṇu, who is praised throughout the Vedas, is replete with unlimited transcendental senses, and is characterized by endless power. That *puruṣa* is the origin of all incarnations.[19]

[19] All the incarnations within the material world come from Mahā-Viṣṇu. Śrī Kṛṣṇa is Himself the source of all other expansions and incarnations, including Mahā-Viṣṇu.

Verse 12

नारायणः स भगवानापस्तस्मात् सनातनात् ।
आविरासीत् कारणार्णो निधिः संकर्षणात्मकः ॥
योगनिद्रां गतस्तस्मिन् सहस्रांशः स्वयं महान् ॥१२॥

nārāyaṇaḥ sa bhagavān
āpas tasmāt sanātanāt
āvirāsīt kāraṇārṇo
nidhiḥ saṅkarṣaṇātmakaḥ
yoga-nidrāṁ gatas tasmin
sahasrāṁśaḥ svayaṁ mahān

Anvaya

saḥ bhagavān – that very Mahā-Viṣṇu Bhagavān, the first of the *puruṣa-avatāras*; *nārāyaṇaḥ* – is renowned in the illusory universe by the name Nārāyaṇa; *saṅkarṣaṇa-ātmakaḥ* – and is originally manifested from Mūla-Saṅkarṣaṇa in Goloka, via His expansion named Mahā-Saṇkarṣaṇa in the Vaikuṇṭha planets, which are situated within the spiritual sky; *tasmāt sanātanāt* – from that eternal Lord; *kāraṇārṇaḥ nidhiḥ āpaḥ* – the vast waters of the Causal Ocean; *āviḥ āsīt* – become manifest; *gataḥ* – (then) entering; *yoga-nidrām* – into *samādhi* upon the bliss of His own intrinsic form and nature; *tasmin* – upon those waters; *svayam mahān* – and that Supreme Personality of Godhead; *sahasra-aṁśaḥ* – accepts many thousands of expansions as His *avatāras.*

Translation

This Mahā-Viṣṇu is celebrated within the world of *māyā* by the name "Nārāyaṇa." The water of the Causal Ocean has emanated from this eternal *puruṣa*. He is Bhagavān, the supreme predominator, possessed of thousands of

plenary portions, although He is Himself a plenary portion of the Saṅkarṣaṇa of Paravyoma. The eternal *puruṣa* takes shelter of mystic slumber and lies down in the vast waters of Virajā.

Ṭīkā translation

This Mahā-Viṣṇu reclines in the causal waters. He is called the first *puruṣa-avatāra*, and this particular verse is about Him, from whom the water of the Causal Ocean has emanated. He is called Nārāyaṇa because He lies down in this water (*nāra* means "water," and *ayana* means "shelter" or "resting place"). He is a partial *avatāra* of Mahā-Saṅkarṣaṇa in Vaikuṇṭha. The Saṅkarṣaṇa in the chamber of Goloka, who was described earlier, is Mūla-Saṅkarṣaṇa, His plenary portion in the second quadruple expansion in Vaikuṇṭha is called Mahā-Saṅkarṣaṇa, and Kāraṇodakaśāyī Mahā-Viṣṇu is an expansion of this Mahā-Saṅkarṣaṇa. It is His pastime to create the Causal Ocean and lie down in it in mystic slumber, which is a state of trance induced by His own intrinsic, ecstatic nature (*svarūpānanda-samādhi*). It is stated in the *Viṣṇu Purāṇa* (1.4.6):

āpo nārā iti proktā
āpo vai nara-sūnavaḥ
tasya tā ayanaṁ pūrvaṁ
tena nārāyaṇaḥ smṛtaḥ

Āpa means *nāra*, which in turn is understood to mean both water and the living entity (*jīva*). Because Bhagavān is the supreme shelter of both, He is called Nārāyaṇa.

Tātparya

Bhagavān's *samādhi* in the form of absorption in His own pleasure potency is called *yoga-nidrā*. Ramā-devī, who was mentioned previously, is herself Yogamāyā in the form of *yoga-nidrā*.

Verse 13

तद्रोमबिल – जालेषु बीजं संकर्षणस्य च ।
हैमान्यण्डानि जातानि महाभूतावृतानि तु ॥१३॥

tad-roma-bila-jāleṣu
bījaṁ saṅkarṣaṇasya ca
haimāny aṇḍāni jātāni
mahā-bhūtāvṛtāni tu

Anvaya

bījam saṅkarṣaṇasya – the seeds made of *mahā-tattva* (from which the five gross material elements manifest) along with the *jīvas*, which are generated from Mahā-Viṣṇu (the expansion of Saṅkarṣaṇa) and implanted within the illusory potency, and which have not yet developed into the subtle primordial forms of the material creation; *tat-roma-bila-jāleṣu* – they remain within His skin-pores; *haimāni aṇḍāni* – in the form of (countless) golden eggs; *mahā-bhūta-āvṛtāni ca* – and covered by the five gross elements; *tu jātāni* – are indeed born.

Translation

The transcendental seeds of Saṅkarṣaṇa emerge in the form of countless golden eggs from the pores of the skin of Mahā-Viṣṇu as He reclines in the Causal Ocean. All those eggs remain covered by the great material elements.

Ṭīkā translation

Innumerable universes are born from Mahā-Viṣṇu as He lies in the Causal Ocean. This point is analyzed in the present verse. That *puruṣa* is a manifestation of Saṅkarṣaṇa. All the seeds, in the form of the unmanifest material energy, along with the aforementioned living entities who were contained in the material nature, first attain the state of the subtle primordial forms of the elements. After transforming into the twenty-four elements of creation,[20] they manifest in the form of golden eggs within the skin-pores of the *puruṣa*. All these golden eggs remain covered by the gross elements in their unmixed state.

In *Śrīmad-Bhāgavatam* (10.14.11), Śrī Brahmā has also stated:

> *kvedṛg-vidhāvigaṇitāṇḍa-parāṇu-caryā*
> *vātādhva-roma-vivarasya ca te mahitvam*:

> O Bhagavān, within the sphere of the universe composed of material energy, the unmanifest material energy, false ego, space, air, fire, water and earth, where am I, Brahmā, carrying this body, which measures seven spans of my own hand? And where are You, that personality within whose skin-pores innumerable universes are drifting like infinitesimal dust particles seen in the sun-rays entering through a window?

Furthermore, it is stated in *Śrīmad-Bhāgavatam* (3.11.40–41), *vikāraiḥ sahito yuktaiḥ koṭiśo hy aṇḍa-rāśayaḥ*:

> This universe is assembled by the combination of the eightfold material nature, in the form of *prakṛti*, the unmanifest aggregate of material elements, false ego and the five sense objects, as well as sixteen transformations in the form of the eleven senses and the five great elements. Its inner portion extends over 5,000,000,000 *yojanas* (40,000,000,000 miles), and its outer portion consists of the seven coverings beginning with earth, each extending ten

[20] The twenty-four elements of creation are as follows: five gross elements (earth, water, fire, air and space); five sense objects (form, taste, fragrance, sound and touch); the five knowledge-acquiring senses (eyes, ears, nose, tongue and skin); the five working senses (speech, hands, legs, rectum and genitals); and the three subtle senses (mind, intelligence and false ego). Along with the unmanifest material energy and the living entities, all these elements were contained within the illusory material nature in the form of the seeds of Mahā-Saṅkarṣaṇa, the presiding deity of the twenty-four elements of creation.

times further than the previous one. There are millions upon billions of universes that extend even further than this universe. Nevertheless, millions and billions of such universes are situated like tiny atomic particles within each of the skin-pores of Mahā-Viṣṇu. Learned persons describe the nature of Mahā-Viṣṇu in this way. That Kāraṇodakaśāyī Viṣṇu is the cause of all the universes.

TĀTPARYA

The first *puruṣa-avatāra*, who lies in the Causal Ocean, is so colossal that the seeds of endless billions of universes are born in the pores of His skin. Those universes are only an imitation of the unlimited abodes of the spiritual world. As long as they remain within the body of the *puruṣa-avatāra*, they exist like golden eggs in the form of a semblance of transcendence. However, by the will of Mahā-Viṣṇu, they remain covered by the subtle aspects of the gross elements that have arisen from the instrumental cause and ingredient cause of the illusory energy. These golden eggs manifest along with the breathing of the *puruṣa*, and when they enter the unlimited chamber of the illusory energy, they are expanded by the unmixed five gross material elements.

Verse 14

प्रत्यण्डमेवमेकांशादेकांशाद् विशति स्वयम् ।
सहस्रमूर्धा विश्वात्मा महाविष्णुः सनातनः ॥१४॥

praty-aṇḍam evam ekāṁśād
ekāṁśād viśati svayam
sahasra-mūrdhā viśvātmā
mahā-viṣṇuḥ sanātanaḥ

Anvaya

evam – thereafter; *sanātanaḥ* – the eternal; *viśvātmā* – all-pervasive; *mahā-viṣṇuḥ* – Mahā-Viṣṇu; *sahasra-mūrdhā* – who has thousands of heads; *svayam* – personally; *viśati* – enters; *praty-aṇḍam* – each egg; *eka-aṁśāt eka-aṁśāt* – by means of His respective expansions.

Translation

This Mahā-Viṣṇu entered into every individual universe as His individual plenary portions, each of which is complete with all His mystic opulences. In other words, within each universe Mahā-Viṣṇu assumes the form of the universal soul with thousands upon thousands of heads.

Ṭīkā translation

Mahā-Viṣṇu then enters into those billions of universes in separate individual forms of Viṣṇu, who are called Garbhodakaśāyī Viṣṇu. The meaning of *ekāṁśād ekāṁśāt* is that an individual plenary portion of Mahā-Viṣṇu enters each womb-like universe.

TĀTPARYA

The Mahā-Viṣṇu who lies down in the Causal Ocean is a plenary portion of Mahā-Saṅkarṣaṇa. In the form of His individual plenary portions, He personally enters into each of the universes that are manifested from Him. Every one of those plenary portions is directly Viṣṇu, and they are similar to Mahā-Viṣṇu in every respect. Each Garbhodakaśāyī Viṣṇu is the aggregate feature of all forms of the indwelling witness.

Verse 15

वामाङ्गादसृजद्विष्णुं दक्षिणाङ्गात् प्रजापतिम् ।
ज्योतिर्लिङ्गमयं शम्भुं कूर्चदेशादवासृजत् ॥१५॥

vāmāṅgād asṛjad viṣṇuṁ
dakṣiṇāṅgāt prajāpatim
jyotir-liṅga-mayaṁ śambhuṁ
kūrca-deśād avāsṛjat

Anvaya

vāma-aṅgāt – from the left side of Kāraṇodakaśāyī Mahā-Viṣṇu; *asṛjat* – He created; *viṣṇum* – Śrī Viṣṇu; *dakṣiṇa-aṅgāt* – from His right side; *prajā-patim* – (He created) the primal progenitor known as Hiraṇyagarbha; *kūrca-deśāt* – from the center of His eyebrows; *avāsṛjat* – He created; *śambhum* - His expansion of Śambhu; *jyotiḥ-liṅga-mayam* – in the form of an effulgent *liṅga* (male symbol of generative capacity).

Translation

That Mahā-Viṣṇu created Viṣṇu from His left side, Prajāpati from His right side, and Śambhu in the form of an effulgent *liṅga* from between His eyebrows.

Ṭīkā translation

What did Śrī Mahā-Viṣṇu do next? In answer to this question it is stated, *vāmāṅgāt*: "He manifested Viṣṇu from His left side, Prajāpati from His right side and Śambhu from between His eyebrows." Brahmā is the creator, Viṣṇu is the maintainer and Maheśa is the destroyer of all the universes. The form of Śrī Viṣṇu in each universe directs His own expansions in the form of

Brahmā and Śiva, and as a result of this impetus, Brahmā is absorbed in the task of creation, and Maheśa is absorbed in the task of annihilation. In this context one should understand the term *prajāpati* (primal progenitor) to mean Hiraṇyagarbha-Garbhodakaśāyī Viṣṇu. In some places the four-headed Brahmā has also been referred to as the *prajāpati*, but in this context *prajāpati* does not refer to Brahmā with four faces. This Hiraṇyagarbha-puruṣa creates the predominating deities within the shell of each universe. Viṣṇu and Śambhu are also the maintainer and destroyer respectively of their universes.

Śambhu has emanated from the area between the eyebrows of Mahā-Viṣṇu. The place of Mahā-Viṣnu is the water covering, which is considered to be His residence.

Tātparya

Kṣīrodakaśāyī Viṣṇu is the indwelling witness of the individual living entity, whereas Garbhodakaśāyī Viṣṇu is the indwelling witness of the aggregate of living entities. The primal progenitor is Hiraṇyagarbha, the expansion of Bhagavān, and he is different from the four-headed Brahmā. This Hiraṇyagarbha is the seed principle of each of the Brahmās in all the unlimited universes. *Jyotir-liṅga-mayaṁ śambhum* refers to the Śambhu who is the immensely qualified manifestation of the fundamental principle of procreation in the form of the original male generative capacity (*liṅga*). Śrī Viṣṇu is Mahā-Viṣṇu's personal expansion, and is therefore in the category of the Supreme Īśvara. Prajāpati and Śambhu are both Mahā-Viṣṇu's separated expansions, and are thus demigods who have been invested with special authority. Since His potency resides in His left side, it is from the transcendental potency of pure spiritual existence in Mahā-Viṣṇu's left limb that Viṣṇu emerges. Thus Viṣṇu appears from the pure spiritual existence of Bhagavān.

As Īśvara, Viṣṇu is the Supersoul (Paramātmā) or indwelling witness of every living entity. In the Vedas He has been called "the thumb-sized predominator." He is the maintainer. Those who perform fruitive activities worship Him as Yajñeśvara Nārāyaṇa, the Lord of sacrifice, while the *yogīs* desire to attain the state of trance by meditating upon Him.

Verse 16

अहंकारात्मकं विश्वं तस्मादेतद्व्यजायत ॥१६॥

ahaṅkārātmakaṁ viśvaṁ
tasmād etad vyajāyata

Anvaya

tasmāt – from Śambhu; *etad viśvam* – this universe; *vyajāyata* – became; *ahaṅkāra-ātmakam* – imbued with the nature of false ego.

Translation

The world of false ego has been born from Śambhu. This is his function in relation to the living entities.

Ṭīkā translation

Another function of Śambhu is being described here. He is called the original form of false ego because this world of false ego was born from him. Thus Śambhu is the presiding deity of false ego. For example, it is stated in *Śrīmad-Bhāgavatam* (3.26.24):

> The unmanifest aggregate material energy originates from Bhagavān's spiritual potency, and it transforms into three types of false ego, which were imbued with the potency for activity at the time of creation. The mind, the senses and the life airs are born from these three modifications of false ego, namely false ego in goodness, false ego in passion and false ego in the mode of ignorance.

Therefore Śambhu is called the presiding deity of all false ego. Learned authorities have also called him Anantadeva. He is also the cause of matter, the senses and the mind.

Tātparya

The original form of pure existence in its transcendental constitutional state has no sense of self-conception separate from the Supreme Person Bhagavān. The symbol of separate self-conception, or the separate existence that emerges in this material world, is exemplified by the male generative capacity. This is a mundane reflection of the original pure spiritual existence. This *liṅga*, the emblem of the male generative capacity, is Ādi-Śambhu. He unites with the receptive principle, which is a transformation of Ramā-devī in the form of the *yoni* or womb of material existence. At this time, Śambhu is the material cause by dint of supplying the raw material substances for creation. When each universe is manifest from the gradual evolution of this state of existence, the *rudra* or destructive principle emerges from the existence of Śambhu. Although born from between the eyebrows of the *puruṣa-avatāra* Mahā-Viṣṇu, Śambhu remains as the epitome of false ego in all conditions.

An unlimited number of atomic conscious particles emerge from the spiritual rays of Paramātmā as the aggregate of the living entities. When they identify themselves as the servants of Bhagavān, they are of Vaikuṇṭha, and have no relationship with the world of *māyā*. When the living entity forgets this pure identity, he desires to become the enjoyer of *māyā*, and the false ego principle of Śambhu then enters his existence and produces within him the self-conception of being a separate enjoyer. Therefore, Śambhu alone is the principle underlying the world of false ego and the identification of the living entities with their material bodies.

Verse 17

अथ तैस्त्रिविधैर्वेशैर्लीलामुद्वहतः किल ।
योगनिद्रा भगवती तस्य श्रीरिव सङ्गता ॥१७॥

atha tais tri-vidhair veśair
līlām udvahataḥ kila
yoga-nidrā bhagavatī
tasya śrīr iva saṅgatā

Anvaya

atha – thus (after *mahā-puruṣa* Kāraṇodakaśāyī entered each universe in the form of Bhagavān Garbhodakaśāyī Viṣṇu); *kila udvahataḥ tasya* – He indeed carried out; *līlām* – His pastime, i.e. the duty of creation, maintenance and destruction in each universe; *taiḥ* – through these; *tri-vidhaiḥ* – three kinds; *veśaiḥ* – of dresses, i.e. His expansions of Prajāpati, Viṣṇu and Śambhu; *śrīḥ iva saṅgatā* – just as a plenary portion of the intrinsic, personal potency meets with Kāraṇodakaśāyī Viṣṇu; *tasya* – similarly Garbhodakaśāyī Viṣṇu also meets; *yoga-nidrā* – mystic slumber, another plenary portion of the same *śakti*; *bhagavatī* – who is replete with all opulence, and who is an expansion of the mystic slumber aspect of the intrinsic, personal potency. (This is to indicate that Garbhodakaśāyī Viṣṇu also reposes in mystic slumber.)

Translation

Thereafter, *mahā-puruṣa* Bhagavān, having entered the universe in the forms of Prajāpati, Viṣṇu and Śambhu, performs His pastime of maintenance, creation and dissolution, which occurs within the inert material energy. Since this pastime is so insignificant, He associates with Bhagavatī Yoganidrā, who is the personification of

mystical absorption in His own intrinsic bliss, and the partial manifestation of the spiritual potency.

Ṭīkā translation

The current verse describes the *līlā* of the Brahmā, Viṣṇu and Maheśa who have entered the material universe. Bhagavān Viṣṇu performs the tasks of creating, maintaining and annihilating the material world by entering the universe in the three forms, Brahmā, Viṣṇu and Maheśa. Here, *yoganidrā bhagavatī tasya śrīr iva saṅgatā* indicates that, because Brahmā and Śambhu have a self-conception of being separate from the essential reality of Bhagavān, they sport with their respective aspects of the inferior potency, namely Sāvitrī and Umā, who are the shadow forms of the transcendental potency. However, Bhagavān Viṣṇu associates (sleeps) with Bhagavatī Mahā-Yoganidrā, who, being the partial manifestation of Ramā-devī or Śrī Lakṣmī, is the personification of mystical absorption in His own intrinsic bliss. The expression *śrīr iva* means that this Ramā-devī is an expansion of the original Lakṣmī-devī who reigns in Vaikuṇṭha.

Tātparya

Since Brahmā and Śambu are both separated personal expansions, and since they have a self-conception of being separate from the essential reality of Bhagavān, they sport with their respective aspects of the inferior potency, Sāvitrī and Umā, who are the shadow forms of the transcendental potency. Only Bhagavān Viṣṇu is the husband of the personal transcendental potency, Ramā or Lakṣmī.

Verse 18

सिसृक्षायां ततो नाभेस्तस्य पद्मं विनिर्ययौ ।
तन्नालं हेमनलिनं ब्रह्मणो लोकमद्भुतम् ॥१८॥

sisṛkṣāyāṁ tato nābhes
tasya padmaṁ viniryayau
tan nālaṁ hema-nalinaṁ
brahmaṇo lokam adbhutam

Anvaya

tataḥ – therafter; *tasya* – when Garbhodakaśāyī Viṣṇu; *sisṛkṣāyām* – desired to create; *nābheḥ* – from His lotus navel; *hema-nalinam padmam* – a lotus flower appearing to be made of gold; *viniryayau* – was manifest; *tan-nālam* – within the stem of that lotus; *adbhutam* – was the astonishing; *lokam* – world of fourteen planetary systems; *brahmaṇaḥ* – for the creation of Brahmā.

Translation

When Garbhodakaśāyī Viṣṇu desired to create, from His navel emerged a golden lotus flower, from which the creator, Brahmā, appeared. Complete with its stem, this wonderful golden lotus flower is the residence of Brahmā and is known as Brahmaloka or Satyaloka.

Ṭīkā translation

This golden lotus flower, complete with its stem, is the birthplace and resting-place of Brahmājī. It is therefore called Brahmaloka.

Tātparya

In this context, the word *svarṇa* (golden) indicates the semblance of transcendence.

Verse 19

तत्त्वानि पूर्व्वरूढ़ानि कारणानि परस्परम् ।
समवायाप्रयोगाच्च विभिन्नानि पृथक् पृथक् ॥
चिच्छक्त्या सज्जमानोऽथ भगवानादिपूरुषः ।
योजयन् मायया देवो योगनिद्रामकल्पयत् ॥१९॥

tattvāni pūrva-rūḍhāni
kāraṇāni parasparam
samavāyāprayogāc ca
vibhinnāni pṛthak pṛthak

cic-chaktyā sajjamāno 'tha
bhagavān ādi-pūruṣaḥ
yojayan māyayā devo
yoganidrām akalpayat

Anvaya

pūrva-rūḍhāni – the primevally established; *tattvāni* – essential principles of gross matter (described in verse 16); *kāraṇāni* – of universal causality, i.e. before the interaction of the five gross elements, when they were in a subtle, unmixed state; *samavāya aprayogāt* – because of not coming together in the unified form of five elements; *ca parasparam pṛthak pṛthak* – those elements were mutually distinct from one another; *vibhinnāni* – and separate; *bhagavān ādi-pūruṣaḥ* – Kāraṇodakaśāyī Mahā-Viṣṇu, the original Personality of Godhead, replete with all opulence; *devaḥ* – who was engaged in pleasure pastimes; *sajjamānaḥ* – associating; *cit-śaktyā* – with His spiritual potency; *yojayan* – He engaged; *māyayā* – with His illusory potency, consisting of the distinct principles of matter (thus they were transformed into a combined form and created countless gross material universes); *atha* – thereafter; *akalpayat yoga-nidrām* – He enjoyed with His spiritual potency by taking shelter of His pastime potency. (In other words, He reposed upon His bed of Ananta.)

Translation

Before the creation of the five gross elements, the fundamental elements existed in their natural condition in separate, individual forms, because the process of combining them had not been applied. The primeval personality, Bhagavān Mahā-Viṣṇu, acted through the illusory potency by associating with His own transcendental potency. Uniting those separate elements by systematic combination, He created the material world. After accomplishing the task of creation in this way, He became absorbed in mystic slumber, the form of union with His own transcendental potency.

Ṭīkā translation

The method of creation by Kāraṇodakaśāyī Viṣṇu has been described in the Third Canto of *Śrīmad-Bhāgavatam*. In order to describe the act of creation as the awakening of the universal form, who is the embodiment of the aggregate of countless living entities, it is being explained more elaborately here. The primeval personality, Bhagavān Kāraṇodakaśāyī, accomplished the creation of the universe by amalgamating the previously unmixed five gross elements through the influence of His own spiritual potency reflected in the form of the illusory energy. Then the Supreme Person, who is inclined to perform pastimes, not being ambitious to carry out the duty of creation, became engrossed in mystic slumber with His transcendental potency, Ramā-devī.

etāny asaṁhatya yadā
mahad-ādīni sapta vai
kāla-karma-guṇopeto
jagad-ādi rūpāviśat

Śrīmad-Bhāgavatam (3.26.50)

The cause of the universe, Bhagavān, being endowed with time, activity and the modes of material nature, entered this universe when the seven essential realities – that is, the whole aggregate material energy, false ego and the five gross elements – were in their unmixed state.

Thereby, all the substances became agitated and mixed together. Then, from this mixture was born an unconscious egg, from which the universal form was manifested. This egg-like object is enclosed by *pradhāna* (the seed principle of creation) and *prakṛti* (material nature) and covered in layers of the elements beginning with water,[21] each layer being ten times greater than the previous one.

Thus the Supreme Divinity, who was resting in the water within the embryonic universe, arose and, giving up His neutrality, He began to manifest many kinds of variegatedness within the universal egg. Thus, the mouth, the voice and fire were manifest from that egg, and the nose, the life air and the sense of smell emerged in the same way. Then the two eyes emerged, along with Sūrya, the presiding deity of the eyes. The ear also emerged and from the ear, the sense of hearing was manifest. After that His skin, pores, tears, genitals, legs, hands, feet and other bodily parts were manifest.

All the demigods, being the presiding deities of the senses, entered into that gigantic form, but the universal form did not

[21] According to *Śrīmad-Bhāgavatam*, the coverings of the material universes begin with earth. Here, the Causal Ocean itself, within which Mahā-Viṣṇu lies in mystic slumber, is counted as the first covering.

wake up. When, despite the presence of faculties such as mind, intelligence and ego, the universal form still did not awaken, the Supersoul, who is the presiding deity of consciousness, finally entered the heart from the consciousness. At that time the universal form arose within the water. Therefore, no one is capable of awakening the universal form as He lies submerged beneath the waters except for the *kṣetrajña-puruṣa*, the personality who is the knower of all fields, and who is the presiding deity of the life air, senses, mind, intelligence and consciousness.

In this way, after combining all the essential realities, Bhagavān woke up the universal form for the purpose of creation. Thereafter, since He is indifferent and free from ambition, after engaging in all these activities, He accepted the state of mystic slumber.

Tātparya

In *Bhagavad-gītā* (9.10) it is stated *mayādhyakṣeṇa prakṛtiḥ sūyate sa-carācaram.* The purport is that before the creation, Māyā-devī, the shadow of the transcendental potency, was inactive, and the substances of her ingredient aspect also existed separately in a state of non-amalgamation. By the desire of Kṛṣṇa – that is, by the influence of Mahā-Viṣṇu – when the instrumental and ingredient aspects of *māyā* were combined, an effect emerged in the form of the cosmic manifestation. When this was accomplished, Bhagavān again became engrossed in His transcendental potency of mystic slumber. The word *yogamāyā* (pastime potency) or *yoga-nidrā* (mystic slumber) should be understood to mean the natural or inherent illumination of the transcendental potency. However, its shadow, the illusory potency, is by nature inert and full of darkness.

When Kṛṣṇa wants to make some illumination in the object composed of insentient inertia, He combines (*yoga*) the influence of His own transcendental potency with the inactive shadow potency (*māyā*), thereby accomplishing the aforementioned task of cosmic creation. This is called *yogamāyā*, in which there are two types of experience, namely the Vaikuṇṭha experience and the insentient material experience. Śrī Kṛṣṇa, His plenary portions, and the pure living entities who are His separated expansions realize the Vaikuṇṭha experience, whereas the bound living entities realize the insentient material experience. The covering of spiritual realization in the experience of the conditioned souls has been called *yoga-nidrā*. This is also the influence of Bhagavān's potency. There will be a more elaborate analysis of this principle later in the text.

Verse 20

योजयित्वा तु तान्येव प्रविवेश स्वयं गुहाम् ।
गुहां प्रविष्टे तस्मिंस्तु जीवात्मा प्रतिबुध्यते ॥२०॥

yojayitvā tu tāny eva
praviveśa svayaṁ guhām
guhāṁ praviṣṭe tasmiṁs tu
jīvātmā pratibudhyate

Anvaya

tāni yojayitvā tu eva – having mixed (the separate gross principles of material nature in their collective form and creating unlimited billions of illusory material universes); *svayam* – He personally; *praviveśa* – entered; *guhām* – those cavities, i.e. entered within the universes as the universal form and in the form of the aggregate of living entities (Hiraṇyagarbha Prajāpati); *praviṣṭe tu* – when He had indeed entered; *tasmin guhām* – within those caves; *jīvātmā* – the universal form and the aggregate living entities; *pratibudhyate* – awoke from their sleep after the period of universal dissolution.

Translation

When Bhagavān mixed together the individual essential realities, He manifested unlimited numbers of material universes. After that He personally entered into His hidden abode, the innermost region of each universe. At that time, all the living entities woke up from the sleeping condition in which they had passed the duration of the cosmic dissolution.

Ṭīkā translation

Now there is a description of Bhagavān's third type of procedure. After combining the individual gross essential realities, Bhagavān accepted mystic slumber. In between the activity of amalgamating the essential realities and accepting mystic slumber, He entered His hidden abode, the body of the universal form. Then, all the living entities who had been sleeping during the cosmic dissolution woke up; that is, they immediately became absorbed in enjoyment and activities in accordance with their past impressions.

Tātparya

The term "hidden abode" assumes a variety of connotations in numerous places throughout *śāstra*. In some places the unmanifest pastimes have been called "hidden abode." In other places "hidden abode" refers to the location of the indwelling witness. In many instances the inner chamber of every *jīva's* heart has been called "hidden abode." In essence, the term "hidden abode" is used to indicate any place that is imperceptible to the common man. In the previous creation, countless living entities were absorbed into the bodily limbs of Śrī Hari at the time of the cosmic annihilation at the end of Brahmājī's lifespan. These living entities again became manifest within the creation according to their previous fruitive desires.

Verse 21

स नित्यो नित्यसम्बन्धः प्रकृतिश्च परैव सा ॥२१॥

sa nityo nitya-sambandhaḥ
prakṛtiś ca paraiva sā

Anvaya

saḥ nityaḥ – He is that same eternal person (who for limitless time pervades the innumerable aggregate of the potency that manifests the living entities); *ca eva* – and indeed; *sā parā prakṛtiḥ* – Bhagavān's superior potency known as the marginal potency (the aggregate of the living entities); *nitya-sambandhaḥ* – (there is) an eternal relationship between the two.

Translation

The living entities are eternal, and they have an eternal relationship with Bhagavān that extends throughout time, with neither beginning nor end. By constitution they are intrinsically His superior potency.

Ṭīkā translation

The constitutional position of the living entities is being described in this half *śloka* beginning with the words *sa nityaḥ*. The word *nitya* (eternal) indicates that the living entity exists throughout beginningless and endless time. The living entity has an intimate and inseparable eternal relationship with Bhagavān, called *samavāya-sambandha*. The living entities have an eternal relationship with Bhagavān, just as the rays of the sun are always related to the sun. This has been explained in the *Nārada-pañcarātra*:

yat taṭasthantu cid-rūpaṁ
saṁvedāt tu vinirgatam
rañjitaṁ guṇa-rāgeṇa
sa jīva iti kathyate

The entity who is constituted of the marginal potency, who has been manifested from the knowledge aspect of transcendence, but who is colored by the influence of *māyā's* qualities of goodness, passion and ignorance, is called the living entity (*jīva*).

It has also been stated in *Bhagavad-gītā* (15.7): "*mamaivāṁśo jīva-loke, jīva-bhūtaḥ sanātanaḥ* – the living entity is My part and parcel. He exists eternally as an individual living entity, and is therefore eternal by nature." Thus the living entity is called superior energy. *Prakṛti* means that the living entity is a reflection of the image of Bhagavān, who is manifest as the indwelling witness, the Supersoul. In the form of the knower of the body, the living entity has attained a state like one of the Lord's predominated potencies. Therefore it is also stated in *Bhagavad-gītā* (7.5): "*prakṛtiṁ viddhi me parām, jīva-bhūtām* – the living entity is My superior potency."

The eternal intrinsic nature of the living entity is also established by the *Śvetāśvatara Upaniṣad* (4.6): *dvā suparṇa-sayujā sakhāyā*; there, the individual *jīvātmā* and Paramātmā have been compared to two birds sitting on a branch of the same *pīpala* tree.

Tātparya

Just as the relationship beween the sun and its rays is eternal, similarly the living entities have an eternal relationship with Bhagavān, the transcendental sun. Since the living entities are particles of the rays of Bhagavān, they are not temporary like material substances, and His spiritual qualities are also partially present in them. Therefore, by his intrinsic nature, the living entity is knowledge, the knower, the possessor of ego, the enjoyer, the thinker and the doer. Śrī Kṛṣṇa is unlimited, omniscient and omnipotent.

The living entity is Bhagavān's eternal servant, and Bhagavān is the *jīva's* eternal master. The living entities are also eligible for exchanging transcendental loving mellows with Bhagavān. From the *Bhagavad-gītā* statement *apareyam itas tv anyāṁ prakṛtiṁ viddhi me parām*, it is understood that the living entity is Śrī Kṛṣṇa's superior potency. All the qualities of the pure *jīvātmā* are beyond the eight components of the inferior energy, beginning with false ego. Thus, although the potency that comprises the living entities is insignificant, being composed of tiny spiritual particles, it is still superior to *māyā*. This potency is also known as the marginal potency. The word "marginal" (*taṭasthā*) indicates that it is situated on the marginal line between the material energy and the eternal reality of spiritual existence. The living entity is liable to come under the control of *māyā* because of his infinitesimal nature. The living entities who have been conditioned from time immemorial suffer the distress of material existence, and repeatedly rotate in the cycle of birth and death. However, when the living entity submits and remains under the control of Śrī Kṛṣṇa, the master of *māyā*, he can never fall under the control of *māyā*.

Verse 22

एवं सर्वात्मसम्बन्धं नाभ्यां पद्मं हरेरभूत् ।
तत्र ब्रह्माभवद्भूयश्चतुर्वेदी चतुर्मुखः ॥२२॥

evaṁ sarvātma-sambandhaṁ
nābhyāṁ padmaṁ harer abhūt
tatra brahmābhavad bhūyaś
catur-vedī catur-mukhaḥ

Anvaya

evam – thus (when the first *puruṣa-avatāra* Kāraṇodakaśāyī Viṣṇu entered within the universe through the form of Garbhodakaśāyī Viṣṇu, the second *puruṣa-avatāra*); *nābhyām* – within the navel; *hareḥ* – of Garbhodakaśāyī Viṣṇu; *padmam* – a lotus flower; *abhūt* – arose; *sarva-ātma-sambandham* – which had the form of the abode for the collective living entities (i.e. it contained the fourteen planetary systems within it. It was the source of Hiraṇyagarbha Brahmā, who had the bodily self-conception of the personified aggregate *jīvātmās*); *tatra bhūyaḥ* – then later (within this lotus); *brahmā* – Brahmā; *catur-mukhaḥ* – the four-headed; *catur-vedī* – knower of the four Vedas; *abhavat* – was born.

Translation

The lotus flower that emerged from the area of Śrī Viṣṇu's navel contained the collective bodily conception of all living entities. The four-headed Brahmā, who is the knower of the four Vedas, was manifested from that lotus.

Ṭīkā translation

Then the lotus flower that was the resting place of all living entities emerged from the *puruṣa* who had entered His hidden abode. Thereafter Hiraṇyagarbha Brahmā, the possessor of the collective bodily identification, manifested. After that, four-headed Brahmā, the knower of the four Vedas, emerged as the embodiment of enjoyment from Hiraṇyagarbha. The four-headed Brahmā appeared from the lotus that came from the area of Śrī Hari's navel, and whose flower and stem are the resting place of the fourteen planetary systems. Here, "embodiment of enjoyment" means that Brahmā's present four-headed body is a repository of material enjoyment, made according to the impressions of desires to enjoy the fruits of his actions from the previous creation. Because of his previous impressions, he desired to create the material world as soon as he appeared.

Tātparya

This lotus flower, which is the resting place of the aggregate of the living entities, was manifested from the *puruṣa* who had entered His hidden abode, namely the egg-shaped universe. Four-headed Brahmā, who is the embodiment of enjoyment, took birth from Hiraṇyagarbha Brahmā, the personification of the collective bodily conception. Four-headed Brahmā is known as a delegated authority. Just as Brahmā is understood to be a delegated authority, it is similarly understood that he is a part and parcel of Kṛṣṇa in the category of His separated expansions.

Verse 23

सञ्जातो भगवच्छक्त्या तत्कालं किल चोदितः ।
सिसृक्षायां मतिं चक्रे पूर्व संस्कारसंस्कृतम् ॥
ददर्श केवलं ध्वान्तं नान्यत् किमपि सर्वतः ॥२३॥

sañjāto bhagavac-chaktyā
tat-kālaṁ kila coditaḥ
sisṛkṣāyāṁ matiṁ cakre
pūrva-saṁskāra-saṁskṛtam
dadarśa kevalaṁ dhvāntaṁ
nānyat kim api sarvataḥ

Anvaya

sañjātaḥ – when Caturmukha Brahmā was born; *coditaḥ* – being inspired; *bhagavat-śaktyā* – by the potency of Śrī Bhagavān; *tat-kālaṁ kila* – at that very moment; *pūrva-saṁskāra-saṁskṛtam* – in accordance with the impressions he had undergone in his previous birth; *matim cakre* – he absorbed his mind; *sisṛkṣāyām* – in matters concerning his duties of creation; *sarvataḥ* – on all sides; *dadarśa* – he perceived; *kevalam dhvāntam* – only darkness; *na anyat* – nothing else; *kim api* – at all.

Translation

After manifesting from the lotus flower, Brahmājī, who is empowered by Bhagavān's potency, absorbed his mind in the subject of creation according to his previous impressions. However, he saw nothing but darkness in all four directions.

Ṭīkā translation

Now the activities of four-headed Brahmā are being described in this verse beginning with *sañjātaḥ*. First of all Brahmājī wanted to create the material world. However, he saw nothing but darkness all around.

Furthermore, we find the following description in *Śrīmad-Bhāgavatam*. When Brahmā appeared from the lotus flower, he began to situate himself in its pericarp, but he could not see anything because of the dense darkness. Brahmājī wanted to see by casting his glance in four directions at once, and in so doing, he manifested four faces in the four directions.

At that time, when the cosmos had been dissolved and the vast waters were agitated into whirlpools by the force of the wind, Brahmā, the original demigod, was situated in the lotus flower that had emerged from the water. However, he could neither factually understand the situation of the world nor of his own self. Being seated on the upper surface of the lotus flower, he began to consider, "Who am I? What is the origin of this unique lotus flower within the water? How did it appear? There must definitely be something below it, and this lotus flower must also be situated upon some supporting base."

Deliberating in this way, Brahmājī entered the path formed by the hollow within the middle of the lotus stem. Still, despite approaching the base of the lotus stem, namely Nārāyaṇa's navel, he was incapable of understanding anything, even after making extensive research. Retiring from his investigation with his ambition unfulfilled, Brahmājī returned once more to his sitting-place on top of the lotus flower. There he sat in a posture for meditation, and by controlling his breathing he gradually concentrated his consciousness by introspection.

Tātparya

Due to Brahmājī's previous impressions, he had a desire to create. Every living entity acquires a particular nature in accordance with his previous impressions and, in accordance with his nature, different types of endeavors appeal to his heart. This is called *adṛṣṭa* (unseen) because it is the fruit of action performed in previous lives. In Brahmājī's heart was the desire to create just as he had done in the previous creation. Similarly, certain qualified living entities may also attain the position of Brahmā.

Verse 24

उवाच पुरतस्तस्मै तस्य दिव्या सरस्वती ।
काम कृष्णाय गोविन्द-ङे गोपीजन इत्यपि ॥
वल्लभाय प्रिया वह्नेर्मन्त्रं ते दास्यति प्रियम् ॥२४॥

uvāca puratas tasmai
tasya divyā sarasvatī
kāma kṛṣṇāya govinda-
ṅe gopījana ity api
vallabhāya priyā vahner
mantraṁ te dāsyati priyam

Anvaya

divyā sarasvatī – divine Sarasvatī; *uvāca* – then spoke a message; *tasya* – from Bhagavān; *tasmai* – to Brahmā (who was looking in the darkness); *purataḥ* – in his presence; *kāma-kṛṣṇāya* – *klīṁ kṛṣṇāya* (*kāma* indicating the seed of the mantra, *klīṁ*); *govinda-ṅe* – *govindāya*, unto Govinda (*ṅe* indicates the dative declension, meaning "unto"); *api* – also; *gopījana-vallabhāya iti* – unto the beloved of the *gopīs*; *priyā vahneḥ* – she who is dear (*priyā*) to fire (*vahni*) i.e. *svāhā*; thus the eighteen-syllable *mantra*, *klīṁ kṛṣṇāya govindāya gopījana-vallabhāya svāhā*; *mantram* – this *mantra*; *dāsyati* – will bestow; *te priyam* – your most cherished desire.

Translation

Śrī Bhagavān's transcendental Sarasvatī spoke to Brahmājī as he was looking at the darkness in all directions. "O Brahmā, *klīṁ kṛṣṇāya govindāya gopījana-vallabhāya svāhā*. This *mantra* will fulfill your cherished desires."

Ṭīkā translation

Why did Divya Sarasvatī give this rare and precious *kṛṣṇa-mantra* to Brahmājī so easily? It was only possible by the mercy of Bhagavān. And why was such unexpected mercy suddenly available? It should be understood that Brahmājī had worshiped Bhagavān in his previous life. This mercy of Bhagavān is being described in this verse. Everything else described here is self-evident.

Tātparya

The eighteen-syllable *kṛṣṇa-mantra*, prefixed by the *kāma-bīja klīṁ*, is the highest of all *mantras*, and it has two functions. One is to attract the pure living entities toward the supremely attractive master of Gokula and beloved of the *gopīs*, Śrī Kṛṣṇa. This is the highest attainment of the living entity's transcendental pursuit. When the *sādhaka* is free from material desires, he attains the fruit of this perfect *prema*. However, in the case of the *sādhaka* who has material desires, this superlative *mantra* only fulfills those cherished desires. In regard to spiritual matters, the *kāma-bīja* is situated within the lotus flower of Goloka. In regard to mundane affairs, it is the reflection of the *kāma-bīja* that bestows the fulfillment of all types of worldly aspirations.

The eighteen-syllable mantra

The Divine Couple, Śrī Śrī Rādhā-Govinda, who are full of unlimited sweetness, are seated splendidly upon a throne of jewels, surrounded by thousands upon thousands of cowherd maidens, at the foot of a desire tree upon a thousand-petaled lotus flower in the *yoga-pīṭha* in the transcendental abode of Śrī Vṛndāvana. The supreme method for attaining the loving service of Their divine lotus feet is embodied in the monarch of all *mantras* (*mantra-rāja*), the eighteen-syllable *mantra*. This *mantra-rāja* is divided into five parts.[22]

The first syllable *klīṁ* is the seed, or *kāma-bīja*. Joined together with this seed, the *mantra* is *klīṁ kṛṣṇāya govindāya gopījana-vallabhāya svāhā*. The *mantra* is called a *ṣaḍ-aṅga ṣaṭ-padī mantra*, meaning that its six words (*pada*) comprise its six limbs (*aṅga*). The six words are (1) *kṛṣṇāya*, (2) *govindāya*, (3) *gopījana*, (4) *vallabhāya*, (5) *svā* and (6) *hā*. The *mantra* is formed by arranging the words in this order. *Klīṁ* is the original one-syllable seed (*kāma-bīja*), whose meaning has been expressed as follows in the *Gautamīya-tantra* and in the Upaniṣads. "Śrī Bhagavān created the universe by the *kāma-bīja*, *klīṁ*. In this *kāma-bīja*, the letters *k*, *l*, *ī*, the sign of the half moon and the dot (*bindu*) above it have given rise to the elements water, earth, fire, air and space respectively." Therefore this *mantra*, whose heart is the *kāma-bīja*, is the root cause of all living beings.

Those on the path of *rāgānuga-bhakti* interpret the meaning as follows:

[22] According to the *Gopāla-tāpanī Upaniṣad*, the eighteen-syllable *mantra* is divided into five parts. Here in *Brahma-saṁhitā* it is divided into six parts.

(1) *Klīṁ*: The letter *k* indicates the very form of eternity, knowledge and bliss, the Supreme Person, Śrī Kṛṣṇa. The letter *l* signifies the highest bliss in the ocean of happiness born from the love of Śrī Śrī Rādhā-Kṛṣṇa. The letter *ī* indicates Vṛndāvaneśvarī, the supreme potency, Śrī Rādhā. The sign of the half-moon and the *bindu*, which together form the ending *ṁ* (ँ), signify the supremely ecstatic sweetness derived from the mutual kissing of Śrī Śrī Rādhā-Kṛṣṇa.

The *kāma-bīja klīṁ* is the intrinsic form and nature of Śrī Kṛṣṇa. For example, it is stated in the *Sanat-kumāra-saṁhitā*, "O Nārada, this *kāma-bīja* is not something that is only made of letters; it is the very embodiment of Śrī Kṛṣṇa's divine transcendental form, because each one of its component letters is one of Śrī Kṛṣṇa's limbs. One should understand the letter *k* (क) to be Śrī Kṛṣṇa's head, specifically the crown of His head, His forehead, His two eyebrows, His nose, His two eyes and His ears. The letter *l* (ल) embodies His cheeks, the upper portion of the cheeks, His chin, neck, throat and His fingernails. The half-moon (˘) is His chest, His belly, the sides of His body, His navel and His waist. One should understand the *bindu* (˙) to be His thighs, His knees, His calves, the center of His knees, the backs of His heels, His feet, the lower part of His thighs, His toes and His toenails."

Furthermore, it is stated, "O Nārada, this *kāma-bīja*, composed of five letters, indicates five flower arrows: *k* (क) indicates a budding mango blossom (*āmra-mañjarī*), *l* (ल) is an *aśoka* blossom, *ī* (ी) is a jasmine flower (*mallikā*), the half-moon (˘) is a *mādhavī* flower, and the *bindu* (˙) is a *maulaśrī* flower. These five types of flowers are the five flower arrows."

(2) *Kṛṣṇāya*: In the *Gopāla-tāpanī Upaniṣad* it is stated: "*pāpa-karṣaṇo hi kṛṣṇaḥ* – Kṛṣṇa is He who completely takes away all *pāpa*." Here *pāpa* means "all kinds of sins and offenses." Moreover, He even vanquishes the offenses of the demons.

Therefore, the etymology of the word *kṛṣṇa* indicates that Śrī Kṛṣṇa destroys all the offenses of everyone.

That very Kṛṣṇa is Parabrahma and the form of eternity, knowledge and bliss. In this connection, it is stated in the *Gautamīya-tantra*: "*kṛṣṇa eva paraṁ brahma sac-cid-ānanda-vigrahaḥ* – Śrī Kṛṣṇa is the Supreme Absolute Truth, Parabrahma, and His form consists of eternality, cognizance and bliss."

Also, in *Brahma-saṁhitā* it is stated: "*īśvaraḥ paramaḥ kṛṣṇaḥ sac-cid-ānanda-vigrahaḥ* – Śrī Kṛṣṇa is the supreme controller, and His form is eternal, full of knowledge and full of bliss." This has been explained earlier in the text.

In the *Mahābhārata* (*Udyoga-parva* 71.4) it is stated:

kṛṣir bhū-vācakaḥ śabdo
ṇaś ca nirvṛti-vācakaḥ
tayor aikyaṁ paraṁ brahma
kṛṣṇa ity abhidhīyate

Śrī Kṛṣṇa attracts the hearts of all moving and stationary living beings throughout the three worlds by the exceptional sweetness of His flute-playing, His form, His pastimes and His qualities. Therefore, this Supreme Brahman, Śrī Kṛṣṇa, is the supreme and only object of our worship.

(3) *Govindāya*: The following description is found in the *Gopāla-tāpanī Upaniṣad*: "*go-bhūmi-veda-veditā govindaḥ* – Govinda is He who pleases the senses, the Earth and the Vedas, and who nourishes all, thereby increasing their bliss." Although the word *go* has many meanings, three of them are: (a) the cows (*prasiddha-paśu-jāti-viśeṣa*), (b) the world and (c) the Vedas.

The phrase *paśu-jāti-viśeṣa* indicates the cows in Śrī Nanda-Gokula. Śrī Kṛṣṇa is complete in His unparalleled opulence and sweetness, yet He is surrounded by cows, and in that simple village setting He is absorbed in playing according to His own independent will. He abides splendidly in Śrī Nanda-Gokula in His beautiful form, which has the color of a fresh raincloud, stealing the hearts of the residents of Vraja, and expanding His exquisitely endearing pastimes there. The whole world and all the Vedas loudly sing of the sweetness of those pastimes. Thus Śrī Kṛṣṇa, the moon of Gokula in cowherd boy attire, who is celebrated throughout the world and the Vedas, is addressed as Govinda.

(4) *Gopījana*: It is stated in the *Gopāla-tāpanī Upaniṣad*: "*gopījanāvidyā-kalā – gopījana* means *āvidyā-kalā* in the form of the *gopīs*." Here the word *āvidyā* is formed from *ā* (complete) and *vidyā* (knowledge). Thus *āvidyā* refers to the best knowledge of all, namely the potency to attract Śrī Kṛṣṇa. The word *kalā* means the embodiment of *prema-bhakti*. Therefore one should understand *gopījana* to indicate those *gopīs* who are the very embodiment of that *prema-bhakti* that is itself the power to attract Śrī Kṛṣṇa, who is only controlled by this type of *prema-bhakti*. The *prema* of *mādhurya-rasa* reigns splendidly above all, having conquered the *prema* of the mellows of servitorship, friendship and parenthood.

Here, *gopījana* can also be interpreted in another way. The word *gopī* is derived from the verbal root *gup*, which means "to protect or to maintain." Śrī Kṛṣṇa's special potency that bestows *prema* upon the devotees and nourishes and protects them is called *gopī*, or the pleasure potency (*hlādinī-śakti*), and Śrī Rādhā is the original embodiment of the pleasure potency. Therefore, the word *gopī* indicates the embodiment of the pleasure potency, the aggregate of the predominated principle, namely Śrī Rādhikā, the beautiful daughter of Vṛṣabhānu-rāja.

In the statement *gopī tu prakṛtī rādhā janas tad-aṁśa-maṇḍalaḥ*, *gopī* means the predominated principle, Śrī Rādhā; and *jana* means the circle of Her plenary expansions, or those who are expansions of Her personal form (*kāya-vyūha-rūpā*), the *sakhīs* such as Śrī Lalitā and Viśākhā.

(5) *Vallabhāya*: The word *vallabha* means "one who stimulates" or "a lover." He who stimulates the *gopīs* through His endearing pastimes, or the most excellent hero who enjoys the sweetest amorous sports with the *gopīs*, is called Gopījana-vallabha. Thus, Gopījana-vallabha is the dearest life-breath of Śrī Rādhā, who is always accompanied by Her friends, such as Śrī Lalitā and Viśākhā.

Śrī Kṛṣṇa, the son of Nanda Mahārāja, is chief among those who are expert in tasting transcendental mellows. He is splendidly situated in Vṛndāvana, surrounded by His beautiful, lotus-eyed, adolescent beloveds, the *gopīs*. In the company of Śrī Rādhikā, He manifests as Madana-mohana, the form that infatuates the mind of Cupid. However, He is only Madana-mohana when He is alongside Śrī Rādhikā, the crown-jewel of the *gopīs*. "*Rādhā saṅge yadā bhāti tadā madana-mohanaḥ* – He shines attractively in the presence of Śrī Rādhikā, surrounded by the circle of cowherd girls. He is therefore eternally called Madana-mohana." Śrī Kṛṣṇa, who as Govinda is the attractor of Cupid (Madana-mohana), is Gopījana-vallabha.

The expression *gopījana-vallabha* is therefore properly interpreted to mean Śrī Madana-mohana, who is the form eternally embraced by Śrī Rādhā (*rādhāliṅgita-vigraha*). Since *gopījana-vallabha* evidently refers to the Divine Couple, Śrī Rādhā-Kṛṣṇa Yugala, the eighteen-syllable and ten-syllable *yugala-mantras* are each called the most excellent monarch of transcendental invocations.

(5 and 6) *Svāhā*: It is stated in the *Gopāla-tāpanī Upaniṣad* that the word *svāhā* means *tan-māyā ca* (meaning "and His energy"). Thus *svāhā* is understood as Śrī Kṛṣṇa's *māyā*, or Śrī Yogamāyā. Yogamāyā is the spiritual potency that manifests from Gopījana-vallabha Śrī Kṛṣṇa's intrinsic nature, and she offers the devotees unto the lotus feet of Śrī Kṛṣṇa. Hence the appropriate

meaning of the word *svāhā* is "she by whose help one's *ātmā* is absolutely and irrevocably offered" (*svāhayātma-samarpaṇam iti*). By uttering or remembering the word *svāhā*, the devotees accomplish totally unconditional self-surrender. Therefore one should recite or remember the word *svāhā* with this specific contemplation. This is the method of completely selfless dedication unto Śrī Rādhā-Kṛṣṇa Yugala.

Verse 25

तपस्त्वं तप एतेन तव सिद्धिर्भविष्यति ॥२५॥

tapas tvaṁ tapa etena
tava siddhir bhaviṣyati

Anvaya

tvam – you*; tapa tapaḥ* – must perform austerity; *etena* – by chanting this *mantra*; *tava* – your; *siddhiḥ* – desired perfection; *bhaviṣyati* – will be achieved.

Translation

O Brahmā, perform austerity by this *mantra*. Thus your cherished desire will be fulfilled.

Ṭīkā translation

In this half *śloka* beginning with the words *tapas tvam*, instruction is being given on how austerity should be performed; that is, by the aforementioned method. According to the Third Canto of *Śrīmad-Bhāgavatam*, Brahmājī heard the sixteenth and twenty-first consonants of the alphabet, namely *ta* and *pa*, combined to make the word *tapa*. Upon hearing this, he began to meditate on Bhagavān with one-pointed attention. At that time, by the mercy of Bhagavān, he heard the supreme monarch of *mantras*, the *kṛṣṇa-mantra*, spoken by the transcendental Sarasvatī. Goddess Sarasvatī said, "O Brahmā, perform austerity by repeating this *mantra* with the utmost diligence. Thus all your heart's desires will be fulfilled."

Tātparya

The purport of this verse and its commentary are clear.

Verse 26

अथ तेपे स सुचिरं प्रीणन् गोविन्दमव्ययम् ।
श्वेतद्वीपपतिं कृष्णं गोलोकस्थं परात्परम् ॥
प्रकृत्या गुणरूपिण्या रूपिण्या पर्य्युपासितम् ।
सहस्त्रदलसम्पन्ने कोटि किञ्जल्कबृंहिते ॥
भूमिश्चिन्तामणि स्तत्र कर्णिकारे महासने ।
समासीनं चिदानन्दं ज्योतिरूपं सनातनम् ॥
शब्दब्रह्ममयं वेणुं वादयन्तं मुखाम्बुजे ।
विलासिनीगणवृतं स्वैः स्वैरंशैरभिष्टुतम् ॥२६॥

atha tepe sa suciraṁ
prīṇan govindam avyayam
śvetadvīpa-patiṁ kṛṣṇaṁ
goloka-sthaṁ parāt param

prakṛtyā guṇa-rūpiṇyā
rūpiṇyā paryupāsitam
sahasra-dala-sampanne
koṭi-kiñjalka-bṛṁhite

bhūmiś cintāmaṇis tatra
karṇikāre mahāsane
samāsīnaṁ cid-ānandaṁ
jyoti-rūpaṁ sanātanam

śabda-brahma-mayaṁ veṇuṁ
vādayantaṁ mukhāmbuje
vilāsinī-gaṇa-vṛtaṁ
svaiḥ svair aṁśair abhiṣṭutam

Anvaya

atha – then (after hearing that divine message); *saḥ* – Brahmājī; *tepe* – performed austerities; *su-ciram* – for a very long time; *prīṇan* – for the purpose of pleasing; *kṛṣṇam govindam* – Śrī Kṛṣṇa, who is known as Govinda; *avyayam* – whose form is immutable; *śveta-dvīpa-patim* – who is the master of Śvetadvīpa; *parāt param* – the supreme transcendence; *go-loka-stham* – and who is situated within the planet of the cows; *paryupāsitam* – (then in Brahmā's trance he saw that from outside Śrī Kṛṣṇa's abode) He was being offered worship; *rūpiṇyā* – by the beautiful; *prakṛtyā* – material nature personified; *guṇa-rūpiṇyā* – whose form comprises the three modes of material nature (*guṇas*), namely goodness, passion and ignorance; *tatra* – there (He saw); *bhūmiḥ* – a land; *cintā-maṇiḥ* – composed of wish-fulfilling gems; *karṇikāre* – within the pericarp; *sahasra-dala-sampanne* – of a thousand-petaled lotus; *koṭi-kiñjalka-bṛṁhite* – filled with millions of saffron filaments; *mahā-āsane* – and upon a great throne; *samāsīnam* – comfortably seated; *sanātanam* – was the eternal; *jyoti-rūpam* – effulgent form; *cid-ānandam* – of cognizance and bliss; *mukha-ambuje* – upon His lotus mouth; *vādayantam* – He was playing; *veṇum* – His flute; *śabda-brahma-mayam* – which is imbued with the sound of the Vedic hymns; *āvṛtam* – He was surrounded; *vilāsinī-gaṇa* – by a group of *gopīs* who engaged in pleasure-pastimes with Him; *abhiṣṭutam* – He was offered praise; *svaiḥ svaiḥ* – by His respective; *aṁśaiḥ* – plenary portions.

Translation

After hearing this divine message, Brahmājī engaged in austerities for a very long time in order to please Govinda, Śrī Kṛṣṇa, the Lord of Śvetadvīpa, who is situated in Goloka Vṛndāvana. Brahmā's meditation was as follows: "In that land, which is made of transcendental desire-fulfilling gems, there is a lotus with thousands of petals and millions of filaments. In the center or pericarp there is a great sitting-place or throne, upon which is seated Śrī

Kṛṣṇa, the eternal form of effulgent cognizance and bliss. With His lotus lips He is playing the flute, whose sound contains all the Vedic hymns, and He is surrounded by *gopīs* engaged in pleasure-pastimes with Him. He is attended by His own plenary portions who are pastime expansions, and who are engaged in offering praise to Him. From outside Śrī Kṛṣṇa's abode, *māyā*, who takes the form of the three material modes of ignorance, passion and goodness, is also worshiping Him."

Ṭīkā translation

After Brahmā had performed *japa* of the aforementioned *mantra* on account of his specific desire to create, he recited the following hymn to worship Śrī Govindadeva as He gracefully reclines in the holy sanctuary of Gokula. In these four *ślokas* beginning with the words *atha tepe*, Brahmājī describes the nature of Govindadeva, the master of Goloka, whom he was worshiping. In that astonishing vision, Brahmājī saw that the personified illusory energy, who embodies the three qualities of material nature, also performed worship of the all-worshipable Bhagavān Śrī Govindadeva through meditation from outside His abode. She did not come directly in Śrī Kṛṣṇa's presence, because she felt very ashamed, considering herself an offender for punishing the rebellious living entities (*Śrīmad-Bhāgavatam* 2.7.47): "*yogābhimukhe māyā vilajjamānā satī pṛṣṭha-deśam upaiti* – the extremely chaste *māyā* remains far behind Bhagavān, and offers Him worship through meditation."

It is also stated in *Śrīmad-Bhāgavatam* (10.87.28): "*balim udvahanti samadanty ajayā nimiṣaḥ* – the demigods and material nature herself offer tribute to You." In this verse it is stated that the demigods are also external functionaries of the material creation, and they remain outside Śrī Bhagavān's planet, together with the illusory potency. As the lords of small kingdoms offer oblations to their emperor, so the demigods also offer their oblations of *pūjā* to Govinda. What to speak of others, even the great demigods must certainly remain situated in their separate worlds.

The word *aṁśaiḥ* (meaning "by the plenary portions") in this verse indicates the direct expansions of the personal form of Bhagavān who are situated in Goloka. These associates also perform worship of Śrī Govindadeva. Brahmājī engaged in austerities for a long time in order to please the imperishable Lord Śrī Kṛṣṇa, who is known as Govinda, and who is the supreme transcendence and the master of Śvetadvīpa. To please Śrī Kṛṣṇa, His external potency also performed worship of Him by meditation, not directly before Him but remaining far away, outside of His abode.

What is the nature of her meditation? Herein it is specifically described: "The land in Goloka is made of desire-fulfilling gems. In that place is a thousand-petaled lotus, the beauty of which is enhanced by millions of saffron filaments. Śrī Govindadeva, whose effulgent form is composed of eternity, knowledge and bliss, is seated upon the pericarp of that lotus, which takes the form of a throne. With His lotus lips He plays a flute, whose sound manifests the Vedic hymns. He is surrounded by His dearmost beloved *gopīs*, and He is glorified by His associates, who also reside in Goloka." Such a meditation is capable of bestowing all blessings.

One who achieves a human birth but does not worship Śrī Bhagavān certainly lives in vain. Bewildered by *māyā*, he becomes her slave and wanders through the 8,400,000 species, being devoured by the threefold miseries. For a specific discussion on this topic, see *Śrīmad-Bhāgavatam* (3.15.25).

Tātparya

Although the subject matter of this meditation is transcendental, the illusory potency is still situated in the material mode of passion. She is the personification of the material modes of goodness, passion and ignorance, and, as the embodiment of Bhagavān's inferior potency, she has many forms, such as Durgā. Herein she is meditating on Bhagavān Śrī Kṛṣṇa as the object of her worship.

When a person desires to acquire a material object, Māyā-devī certainly becomes his worshipable deity. If he does not worship Māyā-devī, then he should perform *pūjā* of Śrī Kṛṣṇa, and by this means he will attain the fulfillment of all his desires. This is also confirmed in *Śrīmad-Bhāgavatam* (2.3.10):

akāmaḥ sarva-kāmo vā
mokṣa-kāma udāra-dhīḥ
tīvreṇa bhakti-yogena
yajeta puruṣaṁ param

> Whether one is desireless, or desires sense enjoyment or liberation, one who is intelligent should worship the Supreme Person through intense and unalloyed cultivation of *bhakti-yoga.*

This means that the various demigods and demigoddesses are expansions of Śrī Bhagavān's opulences, and they bestow their respective boons. However, an intelligent person should give up worshiping them, and should engage in undeviating *bhakti* to Bhagavān Śrī Hari, who is fully capable of bestowing all boons.

In accordance with this principle, Brahmājī meditated upon the Supreme Personality, who performs pastimes in Goloka and who is the worshipable deity of Māyā-devī. Pure *bhakti* means *niṣkāma-bhakti,* i.e. *bhakti* that is free from any other desire, whereas the *bhakti* of Brahmā and other demigods is mixed with desire (*sakāma*). Within *sakāma* there also exists a type of *bhakti* called *niṣkāma*, and this is elaborately described in five *ślokas* at the end of this book. These concluding verses describe the practice of *sādhana-bhakti* through the processes of hearing, chanting, remembering and so on with knowledge of one's eternal relationship with Kṛṣṇa (*sambandha-jñāna*). Until one attains the perfectional stage of *svarūpa-siddhi*, this *sādhana-bhakti* is an easily accessible facility for the soul bound in illusion.

Verse 27

अथ वेणुनिनादस्य त्रयीमूर्त्तिमयी गतिः ।
स्फुरन्ती प्रविवेशाशु मुखाब्जानि स्वयम्भुवः ॥
गायत्रीं गायतस्तस्मादधिगत्य सरोजजः ।
संस्कृतश्चादिगुरुणा द्विजतामगमत्ततः ॥२७॥

atha veṇu-ninādasya
trayī-mūrti-mayī gatiḥ
sphurantī praviveśāśu
mukhābjāni svayambhuvaḥ

gāyatrīṁ gāyatas tasmād
adhigatya sarojajaḥ
saṁskṛtaś cādi-guruṇā
dvijatām agamat tataḥ

Anvaya

atha – then (after Brahmā had performed penance for a long time); *sphurantī* – the brilliant melody, i.e. the *kāma-gāyatrī mantra* that was articulated on Śrī Kṛṣṇa's flute; *trayī-mūrtimayī gatiḥ* – which was imbued with the three Vedas; *veṇu-ninādasya* – of the vibration of Śrī Kṛṣṇa's bamboo flute; *āśu* – swiftly; *praviveśa* – entered; *mukha-abjāni* – the ears of the four lotus faces; *svayambhuvaḥ* – of the self-born Brahmā; *adhigatya* – having thus received Gāyatrī; *tasmāt* – from Śrī Kṛṣṇa; *saroja-jaḥ* – that lotus-born Brahmā; *gāyatrīm gāyataḥ* – through chanting that Gāyatrī; *saṁskṛtaḥ* – became fully trained and enlightened; *ādi-guruṇā* – by the original preceptor, Śrī Kṛṣṇa; *tataḥ* – and thereby; *agamat* – he achieved; *dvijatvam* – twice-born status.

Translation

Then the mother of all Vedic hymns, Gāyatrī (which emanated as the sound of Śrī Kṛṣṇa's flute), along with the means for receiving and transmitting it, entered the lotus faces of Brahmā through his eight earholes, and Brahmā achieved realization of the *kāma-gāyatrī mantra*. The lotus-born Brahmā was thus initiated by the flute-song of Bhagavān Śrī Kṛṣṇa, the original *guru*, and by that reformation he attained twice-born status.

Ṭīkā translation

The *sādhaka* first becomes trained and purified through the process of becoming twice-born as described in this verse, and afterwards, through *mantra-sādhana* he attains *darśana* of the presiding deity of the *mantra*. For example, Dhruva Mahārāja left his home at the age of five years to worship Śrī Bhagavān, although he had no knowledge of the procedure for His worship. Bhagavān, who dwells in the hearts of all, sent Devarṣi Nārada to him, and when Śrī Nārada clearly saw Dhruva's firm determination, he bestowed *dīkṣā-mantra* upon him on the bank of the Yamunā at Mathurā, and told him, "Go to Madhuvana and perform *bhajana* of Śrī Bhagavān there. He will give you His *darśana* very soon." As a result of performing severe *sādhana* in accordance with Nārada's instructions, Dhruva received the Lord's *darśana* within six months. As illustrated in this history, the acceptance of *dīkṣā* is absolutely necessary in order to perform the *sādhana* and *bhajana* for realizing Śrī Bhagavān.

Brahmājī also became fully accomplished after undergoing the process of purification by becoming twice-born, just as Dhruva did. This process is described by the two *ślokas* beginning with the words *atha veṇu-ninādasya*. It is clearly stated in the second *śloka* that Gāyatrī is the mother of the Vedas. *Tan-mayī gatiḥ* means that the *mantra*, together with the traditions for receiving, practicing and transmitting it, entered within his lotus faces by way of his eight earholes. In this way Brahmā received the reformatory process of initiation by means of *gāyatrī-mantra* from the original *guru* Śrī Kṛṣṇa, and attained the status of a twice-born *brāhmaṇa*.

Tātparya

The nature of the sound of Śrī Kṛṣṇa's flute is specifically eternity, knowledge and bliss, and therefore all of the Vedas exist in their perfect form within that sound. *Gāyatrī* is a Vedic meter, and in brief it can be said to contain a meditation and a prayer. Among all the *gāyatrīs*, *kāma-gāyatrī* is the best because, unlike any other *gāyatrī*, the prayer and meditation within it are fully imbued with transcendental pleasure-pastimes.

The *gāyatrī* that is chanted after the eighteen-syllable *gopāla-mantra* is known as *kāma-gāyatrī*. It is as follows: *klīṁ kāma-devāya vidmahe puṣpa-bāṇāya dhīmahi tan no 'naṅgaḥ pracodayāt*. Within this *gāyatrī*, after a fully complete meditation on Śrī Gopījana-vallabha, the transcendental Cupid is invoked by a prayer to attain entrance into His pastimes. Nowhere can one find a more excellent example of *rasika* poetry concerning the transcendental world, through which the *sādhaka* can take shelter of the abode of *prema*. At the moment this very *gāyatrī* entered the ears of Brahmājī, he became qualified as a *brāhmaṇa* and began to sing it. It should be properly understood that whichever fortunate *jīva* receives this *mantra* factually attains spiritual rebirth. There are two types of second birth. One is automatically attained by entrance into the transcendental world. The second, which is for those conditioned by gross matter in this illusory material existence, is the acceptance of the reformatory process called second birth according to the customs pertaining to one's lineage and personal nature. The *jīva* who attains second birth in the first way is in every way sublime and superexcellent in comparison to the *jīva* who undergoes second birth by the second process. This is because the purpose of undergoing *dīkṣā*, enlightenment concerning spiritual topics, is to attain spiritual birth, and the consequent attainment of the transcendental realm is the ultimate glory of the *jīva*. This is the ultimate benefit, which makes the life of a *jīva* successful.

Verse 28

त्रय्या प्रबुद्धोऽथ विधिर्विज्ञात तत्त्वसागरः ।
तुष्टाव वेदसारेण स्तोत्रेणानेन केशवम् ॥२८॥

trayyā prabuddho 'tha vidhir
vijñāta-tattva-sāgaraḥ
tuṣṭāva veda-sāreṇa
stotreṇānena keśavam

Anvaya

atha – thereafter; *trayyā* – through taking shelter of *gāyatrī-mantra*, the essence of all the Vedas; *vidhiḥ* – Brahmā; *prabuddhaḥ* – (became) fully enlightened; *vijñāta-tattva-sāgaraḥ* – and an ocean of realized truths, that is to say he comprehended the *svarūpa* of Śrī Bhagavān; *tuṣṭāva* – he pleased; *keśavam* – Śrī Kṛṣṇa (who has beautiful hair); *anena stotreṇa* – by (composing) the (following) hymn.

Translation

By remembrance of that *gāyatrī-mantra*, which is the essence of all the Vedas, Brahmājī became fully enlightened with the ocean of realized truths, and with that essence of Vedic knowledge he offered the following hymn to Śrī Kṛṣṇa, who is known as Keśava.

Ṭīkā translation

Following the mood of verse 26, Brahmājī performed *ārādhana* (worship) by means of the *kāma-gāyatrī kṛṣṇa-mantra* for a very long time. After that long period, Bhagavān Śrī Kṛṣṇa, who is supremely full of compassion, manifested all the truths and conclusions of the Vedas and other scriptures within the heart of

Brahmājī. Then Brahmā began to offer prayers that were born from the essence of the Vedas. Whatever else has been said in this *śloka* is clear.

The word *keśava* is derived as follows: *keśa* means "all the parts" or the expansion of all the various energies. One who manifests these parts (*aṁśas*) and energies is called Keśava. Also, *ka* means Brahmā, and *īśa* means Śaṅkara, so the one who manifests both Brahmā and Śaṅkara is called Keśava. There is one more hidden meaning: *keśān vayati saṁskarotīti keśavaḥ.* Śrī Kṛṣṇa is called Keśava because He arranges the hair (*keśa*) of His dearmost *gopīs.*

Tātparya

By remembering the *kāma-gāyatrī*, Brahmājī achieved some degree of realization that "I am the eternal maidservant of Kṛṣṇa." The conception of being a maidservant of Kṛṣṇa is such a deep and confidential mystery that it was not fully realized by Brahmā, but his ability to distinguish between spirit (*cit*) and dull matter (*acit*) was so developed that the ocean of truths such as *kṛṣṇa-tattva, kṛṣṇa-śakti-tattva, māyā-tattva, bhakti-tattva*[23] and so on were fully manifest within his heart. All Vedic knowledge was thus revealed to Brahmā, and with the essence of the Vedas he offered this prayer known as *Śrī Brahma-saṁhitā* to Śrī Kṛṣṇa. In this prayer all the conclusions of Vaiṣṇava philosophy are present, as if the ocean were condensed into a waterpot. For this reason, Śrī Caitanya Mahāprabhu taught this to His own devotees, and all intelligent readers should therefore make every endeavor to recite and taste the moods of this *Brahma-saṁhitā* every day.

[23] *Kṛṣṇa-tattva* – truths concerning the nature of Bhagavān Śrī Kṛṣṇa; *kṛṣṇa-śakti-tattva* – truths concerning the various energies of Kṛṣṇa; *māyā-tattva* – truths concerning the illusory energy of Kṛṣṇa; *bhakti-tattva* – truths concerning the nature and development of *bhakti*, devotional service to Kṛṣṇa.

Verse 29

चिन्तामणिप्रकरसद्मसु कल्पवृक्ष-
लक्षावृतेषु सुरभीरभिपालयन्तम् ।
लक्ष्मीसहस्रशतसम्भ्रमसेव्यमानं
गोविन्दमादिपुरुषं तमहं भजामि ॥२९॥

cintāmaṇi-prakara-sadmasu kalpa-vṛkṣa-
lakṣāvṛteṣu surabhīr abhipālayantam
lakṣmī-sahasra-śata-sambhrama-sevyamānaṁ
govindam ādi-puruṣaṁ tam ahaṁ bhajāmi

Anvaya

aham bhajāmi – I perform *bhajana*; *tam* – of that; *ādi-puruṣam govindam* – primeval person, Śrī Govinda; *abhipālayantam* – who is tending with great care; *surabhīḥ* – the wish-fulfilling cows; *āvṛteṣu* – amidst; *lakṣa* – hundreds of thousands; *kalpa-vṛkṣa* – of wish-fulfilling trees; *sevyamānam* – He is served; *sambhrama* – with special care and attention; *lakṣmī-sahasra-śata* – by hundreds of thousands of goddesses of fortune, i.e. the *gopīs*, who are all Mahā-Lakṣmīs; *sadmasu* – in abodes; *prakara* – constructed; *cintāmaṇi* – from wish-fulfilling gems.

Translation

The transcendental realm is eternally adorned by millions of wish-fulfilling trees, by pavilions made of desire-fulfilling jewels and by innumerable wish-fulfilling cows. There, thousands upon thousands of Lakṣmīs, or *gopīs*, are rendering services to the Supreme Personality with great affection. I worship that original Supreme Personality, Śrī Govinda.

ṬĪKĀ TRANSLATION

Beginning with this verse 29, Brahmājī praises the primeval personality, Śrī Govinda, with thirty-one verses describing the glories of His name, form, qualities, pastimes, opulence, sweetness, transcendental abode and so on.

The pastimes of Śrī Kṛṣṇa are endless, and among them His daily pastimes are also innumerable. Those pastimes are called *aṣṭa-kālīya-līlā*, the pastimes performed throughout the eight periods of the day and night. In these pastimes, Śrī Kṛṣṇa's associates who have taken shelter of the transcendental mellows of parenthood, friendship and amorous love simultaneously relish the pastimes of Śrī Kṛṣṇa's infancy, childhood and adolescence respectively according to their own moods. Śrī Kṛṣṇa's *svarūpa* is that of an eternal adolescent, a fresh youth, the best of dancers, dressed in the attire of a cowherd boy with a flute in His hands (*nava-kiśora-naṭavara, gopa-veśa veṇukara*). This is His eternal and original *svarūpa*, which every devotee realizes according to his own transcendental sentiment.

In *śāstra* we find that His worship is of two kinds. One type is *svārasikī* and the other *mantramayī-upāsanā*, and they are understood as follows. The pastimes of Śrī Kṛṣṇa in various places in Goloka Vṛndāvana are of many types; therefore, the worship that is performed through the limbs of *bhakti*, such as remembering, hearing and chanting about those pastimes, is called *svārasikī-upāsanā*. The term *mantramayī-upāsanā* applies to the forms of hearing, contemplation and formal worship with auspicious articles, in which a *mantra* is employed in order to apply the consciousness to one particular pastime that occurs in one particular location in Śrī Kṛṣṇa's place of pastimes. In this method of worship, there is meditation upon only one of Kṛṣṇa's pastimes in one place, and therefore it has been called *mantramayī-upāsanā*.

Śrī Kṛṣṇa has unlimited pastimes, such as the pastimes of Vāsudeva, Saṅkarṣaṇa and other expansions in the realm of transcendental opulence; the pastimes of the *puruṣa-avatāra* Kāraṇodakaśāyī Mahā-Viṣṇu; the pastimes of the occasional incarnations such as Matsya and Kūrma; the pastimes of the presiding deities of the material modes such as Brahmā and Śiva; the pastimes of the empowered incarnations such as Pṛthu and Vyāsa; the pastimes of Paramātmā, who is endowed with attributes (*saviśeṣa*); and the pastimes of the formless undifferentiated Brahman, which is devoid of specific attributes.[24] First of all, Brahmājī has praised the supermost of all pastimes of the unlimitedly sportive Bhagavān, namely Śrī Kṛṣṇa's pastimes in Gokula Vṛndāvana. This is the object of his soul's deepest yearning.

The place of pastimes that are the object of *mantramayī-upāsanā*, which are situated in one particular place, as well as the settings of innumerable pastimes (such as the *rāsa-līlā*) that occur in many different locations and are the object of *svārasikī-upāsanā*, are both present in Goloka. Nevertheless, in this first verse beginning *cintāmaṇi-prakara-sadmasu*, Brahmājī prays by describing the superior meditation on *svārasikī-līlās* that occur in the central, most prominent seat of pastimes (*yoga-pīṭha*).

What kinds of pastimes occur there? *Surabhīr abhipālayantam*: Śrī Kṛṣṇa takes the cows from the village to the forest to graze on very green, soft grass. He makes them drink and take bath in lakes such as Pāvana-sarovara, and then again He brings them back to the cowsheds. In this way He protects and nourishes

[24] What are the pastimes of the formless undifferentiated Brahman? This Brahman is the effulgence of the personal form of Govinda, and pervades the entire cosmic manifestation, as described in *Bhagavad-gītā* (14.27): "*brahmaṇo hi pratiṣṭhāham* – I am the basis of that formless and undifferentiated Brahman."

them with much affection. Sometimes, in a solitary place, He also engages in exceptionally confidential pastimes. What are those astonishing, secret activities? *Lakṣmī-sahasra-śata*: I render service to the primeval personality who, in a pavilion made of desire-fulfilling gems which is completely hidden among countless surrounding desire-trees, is intimately served with elation by unlimited numbers of beautiful *vraja-gopīs*. The word *lakṣmī* should be understood to mean charming cowherd girls.

TĀTPARYA

Here the word *cintāmaṇi* indicates transcendental, desire-fulfilling jewels. Just as the illusory potency has created the mundane world from the five inert gross elements, similarly the spiritual potency has produced the spiritual world from a transcendental substance, namely *cintāmaṇi*. Furthermore, the *cintāmaṇi* jewels used as the materials in the construction of Bhagavān's chambers in Goloka are infinitely more rare and resourceful than ordinary touchstone. Whenever one milks the ordinary wish-fulfilling cows of the heavenly planets (*kāmadhenus*), they give ordinary milk. However, an ocean of milk, which is actually a transcendental current of *prema*, is constantly cascading from the udders of the wish-fulfilling cows of Goloka to allay the hunger and thirst of the *jīvas* engaged in pure *bhakti*. In this verse the words *lakṣa-lakṣa* and *sahasra-śata* indicate an infinite or uncountable number. The word *sambhrama*, meaning "with veneration," is used to indicate "saturated with unconditional love." One should understand the word *lakṣmī* to refer to the beautiful cowherd maidens. The words *ādi-puruṣa* indicate that Śrī Govindadeva is the origin of all existence, though He Himself, being eternal, has no origin.

VIVṚTI

Śrī Brahmā has glorified Śrī Kṛṣṇa with this *śloka* beginning with the words *cintāmaṇi-prakara-sadmasu*. In this verse he has expressed profound moods of immense longing. Regarding the most effective *sādhana* for a *sādhaka-bhakta*, there are two methods, each appropriate to the *sādhaka* in different stages. One is *mantramayī-upāsanā*, which entails contemplating one specific pastime situated in one place. The other is the method of *svārasikī*, which entails contemplation on all the pastimes collectively. In this prayer, Brahmājī has first of all described the subject of the superior meditation, *svārasikī-līlā*.

Brahmājī has also offered similar prayers in the *Gopāla-tāpanī Upaniṣad* (1.37):

namo vijñāna-rūpāya
paramānanda-rūpiṇe
kṛṣṇāya gopīnāthāya
govindāya namo namaḥ

O Bhagavān, You are the foundation of that realized knowledge, by whose power all things are illuminated. You are the original reservoir of all pleasure, and You attract all and bestow joy upon all. O Gopīnātha! O Govinda! I offer my *praṇāma* unto You again and again.

Furthermore:

O Prabhu, Your two eyes expand like the petals of a lotus flower, and a garland of forest flowers hangs down gracefully from Your neck. O Govinda, the creation of the universe has sprung up from the lotus of Your navel, and You maintain the life-breath of all the *gopīs*. May You accept my obeisances unto You.

barhāpīḍābhirāmāya
rāmāyākuṇṭha-medhase
rāmā-mānasa haṁsāya
govindāya namo namaḥ

Gopāla-tāpanī Upaniṣad (1.39)

O Bhagavān, Your head is decorated with a crown bedecked with peacock feathers. You delight the hearts of all, and there is no anxiety at all within You. You are the embodiment of immeasurable knowledge. You are the king of swans, who always plays upon the lake of the *gopīs'* hearts. Therefore, O Govinda, may You kindly accept my *praṇāma* at Your lotus feet.

veṇu-vādana-śīlāya
gopālāyāhi-mardane
kālindī-kūla-lolāya
lola-kuṇḍala-dhāriṇe

Gopāla-tāpanī Upaniṣad (1.41)

O Śrī Kṛṣṇa, You frolic eternally in the forest of Vṛndāvana, and at every moment You attract the devotees by playing sweetly upon Your flute. You are the guardian of the Vedas, Mother Earth and the cows. Your splendid presence in the form of a cowherd boy, protecting the land, cowherd boys, *gopīs* and cows is eternal. You give life to all the *gopas* and *gopīs* by vanquishing wicked demons such as Kāliya, Agha and Baka. O Yamunā-taṭa-bihārī, You engage in delightful revelry on the banks of the River Yamunā. Your dangling earrings swing to and fro. O Govinda, may You kindly accept my humble obeisances.

In this way Brahmājī has offered prayers while immersed in the waves of a variety of wonderful *bhāvas.*

When the lotus-eyed Śrī Kṛṣṇa, surrounded by all His friends, leaves the cowherd village and enters the forest to tend the cows, He increases the bliss of the residents of Vraja, especially the *vraja-gopīs*, and steals their hearts, minds and life-breath. The unprecedented aura of His cowherd-boy attire and His attractive, dark, fresh raincloud complexion seems to expand in all directions. As a blue sapphire fills its surroundings with its brilliant luster, similarly Śyāmasundara's radiant hue makes the entire forest of Vṛndāvana azure.

In the arbors of Vṛndāvana forest, the trees, which are covered with flowering vines, observe a grand festival to welcome Śrī Kṛṣṇa. Immediately upon His return to the forest, the friendly creatures and birds become submerged in the highest bliss of *prema*. On the pretext of dripping streams of honey, all the trees weep tears of joy. They experience *bhāvas* such as horripilation by sprouting new thorns.

Brahmājī saw such love-laden trees of Vṛndāvana as desire-trees (*kalpa-vṛkṣa*); therefore, to indicate that thousands upon thousands of such desire-trees adorn the transcendental forest of Vṛndāvana, he has said, *kalpa-vṛkṣa-lakṣāvṛteṣu*. Countless bowers of desire-trees stand as the concentrated embodiments of eternal, conscious and euphoric *rasa*, fulfilling all the desires of those who take shelter of them. Their different colors are astonishing, and their various shapes cause one to be struck with wonder. They produce exquisite fruits, flowers and tender buds (*mañjarīs*) that perfume the forest with amazing fragrances. For the sake of facilitating Śrī Rādhā-Kṛṣṇa's loving affairs, the bowers of Vṛndāvana's desire-trees are manifest in many varieties. Some are the highest transformation of the essence of nectar; some appear to be artistically fashioned from transcendental butter; and some hold intoxicating condensed nectar in their branches. There are also some that have a brilliant white appearance – one type resembles crystal, while others are like camphor.

Another idea is conveyed by the words *kalpa-vṛkṣa-lakṣāvṛteṣu*: the trees, which are covered with flowering vines, are animate and possessed of ecstatic emotions. Śrīla Prabodhānanda Sarasvatī has also stated: "*he mādhavī-madhurāṅga-taruṇa-tamāla* – O young *tamāla* tree, in the empire of the Vṛndāvana forest, Rājya-lakṣmī, the empress in the form of the flowering *mādhavī* vine, has enveloped you from head to toe, and thus she is enhancing the exceptionally enchanting beauty of your trunk, branches, twigs and other features. All directions of Śrī Vṛndāvana are fully permeated by your fragrance, and all the burning distress of the people of this world is relieved by the cooling shade of your fame."

The trees of Vṛndāvana are studded with horripilation in the form of newly-sprouted shoots, due to their intense transcendental affection (*anurāga*) for Śrī Rādhā-Kṛṣṇa. On the pretext of dropping honey, they rain down streams of tears. When the gentle breezes blow, the trees strike comical poses by moving their leaves, and they begin to perform a transcendental dance in the bliss of *prema*. When the trees appear to bring forth a profusion of blossoming flowers, they are actually bursting out laughing. The desire-trees also perfectly sing the praises of Śrī Rādhā-Mādhava through the chirping of the birds residing in their branches. By bending down due to the burden of so many fruits, they offer *praṇāma* to the lotus feet of Śrī Rādhā-Kṛṣṇa. May the bowers of Śrī Vṛndāvana confer the supreme transcendental bliss upon us all.

Thus all the trees and creepers of Vṛndāvana are desire-trees and desire-creepers. They cannot be compared with ordinary desire-trees and vines that fulfill the worldly desires of mortal beings in the spheres of religiosity, economic development and sense gratification. By taking shelter of these transcendental desire-trees and desire-creepers, all material ambitions and desires are dispelled from the heart, which becomes completely filled with the mood of divine service to Śrī Rādhā-Mādhava. These trees and creepers bestow *prema* for the Divine Couple upon those who are under Their shelter, thus allowing such surrendered souls to become supremely fortunate.

In this regard Śrīla Prabodhānanda Sarasvatīpāda has commented:

yā rādhāyā vara-tanu-natety ukti-mātreṇa nṛtyed
gāyety uktyā madhukara rutair vijña-gānaṁ tanoti
krandety uktyā visṛjati madhutphullitā syād dhaseti
proktā śliṣya-drumam iti girā sasvaje dhṛṣṭa-gucchā

Śrī Vṛndāvana-mahimāmṛta (5.37)

When Śrī Rādhā says to those creepers of Vraja, "O beautiful-limbed ones, you should dance," they begin to dance by moving their leaves. When She says, "Now sing," they begin to sing by means of the humming of bumblebees. When She says, "Now weep," they at once shower streams of honey, and when She says, "Now smile," they immediately burst into bloom. On hearing Śrī Rādhā say, "Embrace this tree," they become utterly overjoyed, and wind around the tree.

Sometimes Vṛṣabhānu-nandinī Śrī Rādhā conceals Herself in a *kuñja* (bower) during a game of hide-and-seek. Śyāmasundara then tries to find Her by taking help from the creepers, who enable Him to discover Her by hinting at Her whereabouts through the trembling of their newly sprouted foliage. In this way, wherever the confidential pastimes of Śrī Rādhā-Mādhava take place in the *kuñjas* and hidden bowers, all the residents of Vraja are forever immersed in the waves of the topmost bliss of *prema*. I render service to the primeval personality, Śrī Govinda, who resides eternally in that supreme abode of Vṛndāvana.

Verse 30

वेणुं क्वणन्तमरविन्ददलायताक्षं
वर्हावतंसमसिताम्बुदसुन्दराङ्गम् ।
कन्दर्पकोटिकमनीयविशेषशोभं
गोविन्दमादिपुरुषं तमहं भजामि ॥३०॥

veṇuṁ kvaṇantam aravinda-dalāyatākṣaṁ
barhāvataṁsam asitāmbuda-sundarāṅgam
kandarpa-koṭi-kamanīya-viśeṣa-śobhaṁ
govindam ādi-puruṣaṁ tam ahaṁ bhajāmi

Anvaya

aham bhajāmi – I perform *bhajana*; *tam* – to that; *ādi-puruṣam govindam* – the primeval person, Śrī Govinda; *kvaṇantam* – who is vibrating; *veṇum* – His flute; *akṣam* – whose blooming eyes; *āyata* – are extended; *aravinda-dala* – like the petals of a lotus; *avataṁsam* – who has a crest; *barha* – of peacock feathers; *sundara-aṅgam* – whose beautiful body; *asita-ambu* – has the hue of black clouds, i.e. thunder-clouds; *viśeṣa-śobham* – and whose unique loveliness; *kamanīya* – enchants the hearts; *koṭi* – of millions; *kandarpa* – of Cupids.

Translation

I worship the primeval personality, Śrī Govinda, who is absorbed in playing upon His flute, whose long eyes expand and bloom like lotus flowers, whose headdress is adorned with peacock feathers, and whose unique bodily complexion, which resembles the luster of a dark blue raincloud, bewilders the minds of millions of Cupids.

Ṭīkā translation

Later in this devotional scripture there are descriptions such as: "*kathā gānaṁ nāṭyaṁ gamanam api* – in that abode even natural speech is melodious song, coming and going is a dance, and the flute is the intimate female companion." In accordance with these descriptions, the previous verse has also described the abode of desire-fulfilling gems as the extraordinary setting of the *svārasikī-līlā* in Goloka. Now these two verses (30–31), beginning with the words *veṇuṁ kvaṇantam*, describe the second place of pastimes, wherein the *mantra-upāsanāmayī-līlā*, the subject of this detailed meditation, takes place. The *mantra-upāsanāmayī-līlā* is situated in one place, without the singing, dancing and so on included in *svārasikī-līlā*. I worship Śrī Govindadeva, the primeval personality, who is absorbed in playing a sweet, stirring melody on His flute, who glances softly with His two elongated eyes, which resemble the expanded, soft petals of a lotus flower, who wears a crown of peacock feathers upon His head, whose bodily complexion is like a fresh raincloud, and whose radiant limbs reproach the beauty of millions of Kandarpas (Cupids).

Tātparya

In this verse, the incomparable beauty of Śrī Kṛṣṇa, the transcendental lover of Vṛndāvana, is being described. Śrī Kṛṣṇa is the supreme conscious entity, whose body has a fully spiritual *svarūpa*. In describing Kṛṣṇa's *svarūpa*, one may compare it with charming aspects of the mundane world, but this simply indicates the general direction of the factual substance, in accordance with the logic known as *śākhā-candra-nyāya*, "pointing to the moon through the branches of a tree." Kṛṣṇa is absorbed in playing upon His flute, which steals the consciousness of all living entities when they come in contact with its delightful melody.

Just as the quality of softness is present in the petals of a lotus flower, similarly His transcendental glance, which removes pain from the hearts of all, is full of tenderness and compassion. The sympathetic glances from His lotus eyes expand the unlimited beauty of His moonlike face. The elegance of Kṛṣṇa's headdress, decorated with peacock feathers, enhances His sublime transcendental countenance. Just as a dark blue raincloud is a soothing sight for the eyes, similarly Śrī Kṛṣṇa's transcendental bluish complexion is a joy to behold. Moreover, if one could multiply a millionfold the attractive qualities present in Cupid, the resultant creation would still become madly infatuated upon seeing Śrī Kṛṣṇa's enchanting *svarūpa.*

Verse 31

आलोलचन्द्रक–लसद्वनमाल्यवंशी–
रत्नाङ्गदं प्रणयकेलिकलाविलासम् ।
श्यामं त्रिभङ्गललितं नियतप्रकाशं
गोविन्दमादिपुरुषं तमहं भजामि ॥३१॥

ālola-candraka-lasad-vanamālya-vaṁśī-
ratnāṅgadaṁ praṇaya-keli-kalā-vilāsam
śyāmaṁ tri-bhaṅga-lalitaṁ niyata-prakāśaṁ
govindam ādi-puruṣaṁ tam ahaṁ bhajāmi

Anvaya

aham bhajāmi – I perform *bhajana*; *tam* – of that; *ādi-puruṣam govindam* – original person, Śrī Govinda; *ālola-candraka-lasad-vanamālya* – who is beautified by an effulgent garland of forest flowers and peacock feathers, which swings to and fro; *vaṁśī* – who holds a flute; *ratna-aṅgadam* – and whose arms are bedecked with jeweled bangles; *kalā-vilāsam* – He is most expert in the sixty-four pastime-arts; *praṇaya-keli* – of affectionate loving affairs; *śyāmam* – His complexion is bluish like the thundercloud of the rainy season; *tri-bhaṅga-lalitam* – and whose graceful, threefold-bending form; *niyata-prakāśam* – is eternally manifest.

Translation

I worship the original personality, Śrī Govinda, around whose neck a garland of forest flowers and peacock feathers swings gently, whose lotus hands hold a captivating flute, whose arms are decorated with jeweled ornaments, who is always madly absorbed in intimate loving pastimes, and whose eternal natural

aspect is His graceful, threefold-bending Śyāmasundara form.

Ṭīkā translation

Here *praṇaya-keli-vilāsa*, games full of intimate loving pastimes, indicates that Śrī Kṛṣṇa is the crest-jewel of experts in the art of laughter and joking, and that His pastime is to revel in that skillfulness. In the *Amara-koṣa* Sanskrit dictionary, the word *keli* is defined as "humorous behavior" (*dravakeli-parihāsāḥ*).

Tātparya

In verse 29, beginning *cintāmaṇi-prakara*, Govinda's transcendental abode and name have been described. Then His eternal spiritual form has been depicted in verse 30 beginning *veṇuṁ kvaṇantam*. Now, in this verse we find an account of His playful pastimes, which are complete with sixty-four qualities. Insofar as it is possible to describe transcendental affairs, one should understand that all activities pertaining to the amorous mellow (*mādhurya-rasa*) have been included in the phrase *praṇaya-keli-vilāsa*.

Vivṛti

In the verse beginning *cintāmaṇi-prakara*, Brahmājī has described the method of meditation on many types of Śrī Kṛṣṇa's pastimes (*svārasikī-upāsanāmayī*), and in the verse beginning *veṇuṁ kvaṇantam*, he has described meditation on one pastime situated in one location (*mantramayī-upāsanā*). Now in this verse, Brahmājī gives another example of meditating on *mantramayī-upāsanā* pastimes, of which there are many examples in *śāstra*.

On another occasion Brahmājī has stated:

sat-puṇḍarīka-nayanaṁ
meghābhaṁ vaidyutāmbaram
dvibhujaṁ mauna-mudrāḍhyaṁ
vanamālinam īśvaram

Gopāla-tāpanī Upaniṣad (*dhyāna* 1)

I remember this very form of Govinda, the Lord of all lords, whose eyes are extremely beautiful and soft like an immaculate lotus; whose *śyāma*-colored bodily luster resembles the hue of a fresh raincloud; who gives relief to the hearts of the distressed; who is eternally full of unique effulgence (that is to say, His form is self-luminous, or His yellow upper cloth is like a fixed flash of lightning); who has two arms, so that with one hand He can deliver the *jīvas* who are averse to Him, and with the other He can give them *prema*; who is eternally situated in one mellow and one form (*jñāna-mudrā*);[25] who is decorated with a garland of forest flowers (*vanamālā*); who is hiding from the view of others; and who is tasting a special *rasa* in a solitary place with one particular *gopī*.

In this verse, an alternative meaning of *jñāna-mudrā* is "who, by playing His phenomenally *rasa*-laden flute-song, is absorbed in *rasa* and therefore remains silent, unable to speak." In the word *vanamālā*, *vana* also implies that He is staying in a solitary place, while the verbal root *māla* means "illumination." In other words, it refers to one who is revealed in the close company of His beloveds in a lonely place, and who is busy in pastimes with those *gopīs* who surround Him.

Furthermore, Brahmājī has also stated (*Gopāla-tāpanī Upaniṣad, dhyāna* 2):

gopa-gopī-gavāvītaṁ
sura-druma-talāśritam
divyālaṅkaraṇopetaṁ
ratna-paṅkaja-madhyagam

[25] *Jñāna-mudrā* normally refers to a finger position indicating knowledge – this is also exhibited when Śrī Kṛṣṇa plays His flute.

I meditate upon Śrī Kṛṣṇa, who is surrounded by *gopas*, *gopīs* and cows, who keeps Himself hidden (*gopa*), or who is in the company of His *gopa* friends such as Śrīdāmā. (The word *gopī* refers to His mother, or to the *gopīs* headed by Śrī Rādhā. The word *go* means Veda or the cows such as Kapilā, who have all taken shelter of Him.) *Sura-druma-talāśrita* means that Śrī Kṛṣṇa is the subject matter established by the Vedas, or that He is standing beneath a desire tree. He is decorated with divine ornaments, and possesses opulences such as wealth, strength, fame, beauty, knowledge and renunciation. He is seated like a jewel in the lotus of those hearts that are perfectly pure; in other words, He reposes upon a lotus beneath a desire tree in Vṛndāvana.

Similarly:

dīvyad-vṛndāraṇya-kalpa-drumādhaḥ-
śrīmad-ratnāgāra-siṁhāsana-sthau
śrī-śrī-rādhā-śrīla-govinda-devau
preṣṭhālībhiḥ sevyamānau smarāmi

Śrī Caitanya-caritāmṛta (*Ādi-līlā* 1.16)

I absorb my mind in remembering Śrī Śrī Rādhā-Govindadeva, who are gracefully seated upon a throne in a temple of jewels beneath a desire tree in the self-effulgent, enchanting forest of Vṛndāvana. They are surrounded by the *priya-sakhīs*, who are rendering loving services to Them.

Śrī Rūpa has given a similar description:

mahendra-maṇi-mañjula-dyuti-maranda-kunda-smitaḥ
sphurat-puraṭa-ketakī-kusuma-ramya-paṭṭāmbaraḥ
srag-ullasad-uraḥ-sthalaḥ kvaṇita-veṇur atrāvrajan
vrajād agha-haro haraty ahaha naḥ sakhīnāṁ manaḥ

Bhakti-rasāmṛta-sindhu (3.3.4)

Kṛṣṇa's bodily complexion is more beautiful than a brilliant blue sapphire, and the *kunda* flower of His radiant smile shines on His lips. His upper garment resembles a fully blossomed golden *ketakī* flower, and His chest, which is adorned with a garland of forest flowers, is captivating. That very Śrī Hari, who plays upon His flute in Vraja, is stealing our hearts.

Verse 32

अङ्गानि यस्य सकलेन्द्रियवृत्तिमन्ति
पश्यन्ति पान्ति कलयन्ति चिरं जगन्ति ।
आनन्दचिन्मयसदुज्ज्वलविग्रहस्य
गोविन्दमादिपुरुषं तमहं भजामि ॥३२॥

aṅgāni yasya sakalendriya-vṛttimanti
paśyanti pānti kalayanti ciraṁ jaganti
ānanda-cinmaya-sad-ujjvala-vigrahasya
govindam ādi-puruṣaṁ tam ahaṁ bhajāmi

Anvaya

aham bhajāmi – I perform *bhajana*; *tam* – of that; *ādi-puruṣam govindam* – original person, Śrī Govinda; *yasya vigrahasya* – whose body; *ānanda-cinmaya-sat* – is imbued with eternity, cognizance and bliss; *ujjvala* – and is extraordinarily brilliant; *aṅgāni* – His limbs; *vṛtti-manti* – can perform the functions; *sakala-indriya* – of all His senses; *paśyanti* – He beholds; *pānti* – maintains; *kalayanti* – and regulates; *ciram* – eternally; *jaganti* – the infinite universes.

Translation

I worship that original personality, Śrī Govinda. His divine form is composed of eternity, cognizance and bliss, and is therefore exceptionally effulgent. Each and every limb or sense of His transcendental body is inherently endowed with all the functions of all the other senses. He eternally sees, maintains and regulates an infinite number of universes, both spiritual and mundane.

Ṭīkā translation

Brahmājī has described both types of *līlā* of Govinda, the original personality. Now, in four verses beginning with the verse *aṅgāni yasya*, he will explain the influence of Śrī Kṛṣṇa's inconceivable potency. His hands and feet also have the power to see, while His eyes, besides having the capacity to see, can also perform all other functions such as protecting, nourishing and so on. Similarly, each one of His senses is capable of performing the activities of all the other senses. Therefore, it is stated in *śruti*: "*sarvataḥ pāṇi-pādaṁ tat sarvato 'kṣi-śiro-mukham* – His hands and feet are everywhere, and His eyes, heads and mouths are on all sides." The word *jaganti* indicates that He manifests His own *svarūpa* among His pastime associates simultaneously according to their individual *bhāvas*, and that He personally tastes the miraculous *rasa* of those associates through His own limbs and senses. All this can only be accomplished through the unique influence of His divine, transcendental form.

Tātparya

There is an abysmal doubt in the minds of persons who are completely bound in mundane knowledge, due to having no experience of transcendental *rasa*. Such persons think that the scholars of ancient times have concocted the fundamental reality of Kṛṣṇa (*kṛṣṇa-tattva*) by the power of their imagination, based on their experience of the mundane world. In order to dispel this doubt, which originates from the platform of material attachment and offenses, Brahmājī has clearly shown the difference, according to philosophical principles, between the conscious spiritual substance (*cit*) and the unconscious material substance (*acit*).

In this verse and the following three consecutive verses, Brahmājī has made a diligent endeavor to make us understand that the pastimes of Śrī Kṛṣṇa are not the imagination of a fertile mind, but rather they are experienced in the stage of pure trance that is beyond the reach of the material mental faculty.

Here the intention of Brahmājī is to establish that the transcendental form of Śrī Kṛṣṇa is composed of eternal existence, knowledge and bliss, whereas all the phenomena of the material world are inanimate and composed of ignorance. Despite these two being categorically distinct from each other, the spiritual affair is factually the original root principle, and therefore variety and specific distinctions must necessarily exist there eternally. Thus it is confirmed that Kṛṣṇa's form, name, qualities, abode and pastimes are transcendental, and only those whose consciousness is pure and free from all connections with mundane delusion are eligible to taste such pastimes.

All the following are comprised of the transcendental substance: (1) Śrī Kṛṣṇa's personal form, (2) the spiritual realm and (3) the arena of pastimes, which is made of transcendental wish-fulfilling gems and which is illuminated by the spiritual potency. Just as the illusory potency is the shadow of the transcendental potency, similarly the fascinating variety generated through the inert material energy is also nothing but the crude reflection or shadow of the fascinating variety that is manifest in the transcendental realm. It is for this reason that all types of material phenomena are dull and composed of the mode of darkness.

In conclusion, the spiritual world is the substance and the material world is its insubstantial shadow. The varieties experienced in the material world allude to the appearance of the variety that exists eternally in the transcendental world. Although there seems to be a similarity between the diversity found in both realms, they are categorically distinct from each other.

Lifelessness is the defect of the dull material realm, where everything comes into existence, develops and produces byproducts, and is finally destroyed. Thus, even the apparent happiness of this world is temporary and full of distress. However, the transcendental world has no such defects. The wonderful varieties of that realm are pure, conscious, eternal and completely devoid of any material defect. There is no difference between Kṛṣṇa and His body, whereas the body of the conditioned soul in this world is different from his *ātmā*, for they are entirely separate substances. In the spiritual *svarūpa*, there is no difference between the body and the embodied, the individual limb and the entire body, the nature and the possessor of that nature. However, in conditioned souls all these aspects are totally distinct. Although Kṛṣṇa is the possessor and source of His limbs, each and every limb is fully Kṛṣṇa Himself, because all of His transcendental functions are included in any particular limb. Therefore He is the indivisible, complete and perfect transcendental principle.

The individual living entity and Kṛṣṇa are the same in that they are both inherently conscious. The difference between them is that the aggregate of all divine qualities is eternally present in the living entity only to a minute extent, whereas those divine attributes are present in Kṛṣṇa to the full extent. Even when the *jīva* attains his pure constitutional form, those qualities will only be manifest to a minute degree in his pure *svarūpa*. When by Kṛṣṇa's mercy the potencies of cognizance and pleasure (*cit* and *hlādinī*) gradually make their appearance in the heart of the *jīva*, he attains a perfect state similar to that of the Supreme Personality. Still, some special qualities remain unique to Śrī Kṛṣṇacandra, and He is therefore the worshipable deity for everyone.

The four qualities that are only found in Kṛṣṇa are the unparalleled sweetness of His form (*rūpa-mādhurī*), qualities (*guṇa-mādhurī*), flute-song (*veṇu-mādhurī*) and pastimes (*līlā-mādhurī*). These four unique, personal characteristics pertain exclusively to Śrī Kṛṣṇa, and are not to be found even in Nārāyaṇa, the Lord of Paravyoma, in the *puruṣa-avatāra* Kāraṇodakasāyī Mahā-Viṣṇu, or in any other expansion of Bhagavān. If these qualities are not present even in demigods such as Mahādeva, how will it be possible for any ordinary *jīva* to possess them?

Verse 33

अद्वैतमच्युतमनादिमनन्तरूप–
माद्यं पुराणपुरुषं नवयौवनञ्च ।
वेदेषु दुर्लभमदुर्लभमात्मभक्तौ
गोविन्दमादिपुरुषं तमहं भजामि ॥३३॥

advaitam acyutam anādim ananta-rūpam
ādyaṁ purāṇa-puruṣaṁ nava-yauvanaṁ ca
vedeṣu durlabham adurlabham ātma-bhaktau
govindam ādi-puruṣaṁ tam ahaṁ bhajāmi

Anvaya

aham bhajāmi – I perform *bhajana*; *tam* – of that; *ādi-puruṣam govindam* – primeval person, Śrī Govinda; *advaitam* – who has no second; *acyutam* – who is infallible; *anādim* – who is beginningless; *ananta-rūpam* – who possesses limitless forms; *ādyam* – who is the origin; *purāṇa-puruṣam* – who is the primeval person; *nava-yauvanam ca* – yet is ever-youthful; *vedeṣu durlabham* – whose *tattva* is difficult to determine through study of the Vedas; *adurlabham* – but is understood without difficulty; *ātma-bhaktau* – by His own devotional service.

Translation

Although He is non-dual, infallible, beginningless, possessed of unlimited forms and the oldest of all, nevertheless He is a beautiful person with everlasting, fresh youthfulness. Although He is incomprehensible through study of the Vedas, He is easily attained by spontaneous devotion of the soul (*śuddha-prema*). I worship that original personality, Śrī Govinda.

Ṭīkā translation

In the three verses beginning with this verse 33, Brahmājī confirms that Śrī Bhagavān is possessed of extraordinary and unique characteristics. Extremely learned personalities who are fully conversant with all philosophical principles say that the Supreme Absolute Truth is non-dual knowledge. He is the shelter of the impersonal effulgence known as Brahman and of the all-pervading Supersoul known as Paramātmā. The Vedas refer to Him as one without a second (*ekam eva advitīyam*), for no one is equal to or greater than Him. He has no material senses and He is not bound by the results of His activities. That supreme, transcendental reality is the fully independent, singular, non-dual, transcendental enjoyer, Bhagavān Śrī Kṛṣṇa.

In regard to His being one without a second, it has been stated:

svayaṁ tv asāmyātiśayas tryadhīśaḥ
svārājya-lakṣmy-āpta-samasta-kāmaḥ
baliṁ haradbhiś cira-loka-pālaiḥ
kirīṭa-koṭy-eḍita-pāda-pīṭhaḥ

Śrīmad-Bhāgavatam (3.2.21)

Śrī Kṛṣṇa, the original form of Bhagavān, is the master of three potencies (*sandhinī*, *saṁvit* and *hlādinī*). No one is equal to or greater than Him. He is completely self-satisfied in His own intrinsic form of supreme, transcendental bliss. All the demigods such as Indra, Candra, Kuvera, Varuṇa, Brahmā and Śiva, and all the countless guardians of the world, such as the *puruṣa-avatāras*, offer various kinds of worship, presentations and obeisances, and they keep their heads, which are decorated with millions of crowns, at His lotus feet.

vismāpanaṁ svasya ca saubhagarddheḥ
paraṁ padaṁ bhūṣaṇa-bhūṣaṇāṅgam

Śrīmad-Bhāgavatam (3.2.12)

> His pastimes are wonderful for everyone, even for those who are proud of their own opulence, including the Lord Himself in His form as the Lord of Vaikuṇṭha. Thus Śrī Kṛṣṇa's transcendental body is the ornament of all ornaments.

From this verse it is understood that, in order to show the influence of His Yogamāyā, Bhagavān manifests His own form of eternity, knowledge and bliss in this world, which is composed of five gross elements. This form of Kṛṣṇa, which is just suitable for performing pastimes resembling the activities of ordinary mortal humans, is so beautiful and enchanting that even Kṛṣṇa Himself is thoroughly astonished upon seeing it. This *svarūpa* is the ultimate limit of extremely great fortune, and it is so beautiful that it beautifies the ornaments with which it is adorned. In other words, it is transcendental to all material comparisons.

Acyuta refers to one who never deviates from His own form, nature and occupation. In the *Kāśī-khaṇḍa* it has been stated: "*ato 'cyuto 'khile loke sa ekaḥ sarvago 'vyayaḥ* – His devotees do not fall down even at the time of the cosmic annihilation. Therefore, in all the worlds, only the all-pervading personality Śrī Kṛṣṇa has been called Acyuta." Śrī Akrūra has also spoken about the subject of Acyuta-Kṛṣṇa in his prayers:

> *Aho*! Today Kaṁsa has bestowed great mercy upon me, by which all inauspiciousness in my life has been vanquished. The lotus feet of Bhagavān Śrī Kṛṣṇa have descended upon the surface of the Earth. Now my human birth has become successful, because today I will be able to bow down directly to those lotus feet, although they are the highest object of meditation for *yogīs*. In ancient times great liberated personalities such as Ambarīṣa, having attained just one glimpse of the radiance emanating from the nails of those lotus feet, have crossed over the insurmountable ocean of birth and death. *Aho*! The demigods headed by Brahmā and Śiva are possessed of all opulence, yet they never tire of worshiping those lotus feet, which the supremely fortunate Lakṣmī-devī worships

incessantly, because they bestow all good fortune. Those lotus feet are also worshiped by the devotees and sages, because they bestow the ultimate success of life. And because they are an ocean of mercy, Śrī Kṛṣṇa's cowherd boyfriends serve them with newer and newer feelings of deep love when He sports in the forest at the time of cow grazing. Those very same lotus feet are colored by the vermillion *kuṅkuma* powder from the breasts of the *gopīs*, who are full of the highest spontaneous love for Kṛṣṇa (*mahābhāva*).

Similarly, in describing the glories of those lotus feet, Śrī Uddhavajī has said:

yā vai śriyārcitam ajādibhir āpta-kāmair
yogeśvarair api yad ātmani rāsa-goṣṭhyām
kṛṣṇasya tad bhagavataś caraṇāravindaṁ
nyastaṁ staneṣu vijahuḥ parirabhya tāpam

Śrīmad-Bhāgavatam (10.47.62)

The lotus feet of Śrī Kṛṣṇa are served by Lakṣmī-devī, the goddess of fortune, and are worshiped in the heart by the self-satisfied masters of mystic *yoga* headed by Brahmājī. Yet at the time of the *rāsa-līlā*, the *gopīs* of Vṛndāvana relieved the burning of their hearts by directly embracing those lotus feet to their breasts.

The glories of Śrī Kṛṣṇa's lotus feet have been described in this way throughout the scriptures.

Similarly, Śrī Kṛṣṇa's transcendental abode is also beyond this world, beyond the illusory energy and beyond the three modes of material nature. For instance, Bhagavān gave Nanda Mahārāja and all the Vrajavāsīs a vision of the spiritual abode of Vaikuṇṭha, which is transcendental to material nature. That abode is supramundane, composed of conscious spiritual energy, indivisible, real, self-luminous, eternal and the embodiment of truth. The great sages who have attained a state beyond the three modes of material nature are incapable of seeing the abode of Kṛṣṇa even in their pure trance. On seeing the personified Vedas offering reverent prayers to Śrī Kṛṣṇa in that world, Nanda and the Vrajavāsīs were utterly astonished.

Śrī Jīva Gosvāmipāda has explained the meaning of *advaita* and *acyuta* in this verse recited by Brahmājī, and now he comments on the word *anādi*. In the discussion regarding *sāṅkhya* found in *Śrīmad-Bhāgavatam* (11.24.27), the verse *kālo māyāmaye jīve* states that Śrī Kṛṣṇa is the origin of that which has no origin. He remains present in one *svarūpa* throughout the creation, maintenance and annihilation. Even at the time that Brahmā and Śaṅkara cease to exist, Bhagavān alone remains present. Although the universe is eventually destroyed, He remains absorbed in His eternal pastimes with His eternal associates in His eternal abode. Therefore, there is never a time when He is not present.

In *Śrīmad-Bhāgavatam* (11.24.22–27), the annihilation has been described thus: "At the time of the cosmic annihilation, the mortal bodies of the living entities enter into grains, grains enter into seeds, seeds into the earth, earth into fragrance, fragrance into water, water into the sense-object taste, taste into fire, fire into form, form into air, air into touch, touch into space, and space into the sense-object sound. All the senses enter their respective presiding demigods, the demigods enter into the controlling mind, mind enters into false ego, sound enters the tamasic phase of false ego, all the three modes of false ego enter into the *mahat-tattva*, the *mahat-tattva* enters into the modes of material nature, the modes of material nature enter into the predominated principle (*prakṛti*), the predominated principle (*prakṛti*) enters into time, time enters into Bhagavān who is the controller of *māyā*, and finally enters into Me. However, My *svarūpa*, which is the cause of creation, maintenance and annihilation, is never absent at any time."

Śrī Kṛṣṇa has also been described as the oldest person in the following way: *ekas tvam ātmā puruṣaḥ purāṇaḥ*. Brahmājī said, "O Bhagavān, You are the only truth, because You are Paramātmā, and You are separate from this world of misleading appearances. You are the root cause of the creation, maintenance and annihilation of the universe. You are the oldest person, and You are eternal, perfect, complete and unchanging. You are the embodiment of nectar, composed of eternal bliss, and free from all mundane designations and the qualities of the illusory energy. You are pure, endless, indivisible and non-dual."

The Yadu wives of Mathurā said (*Śrīmad-Bhāgavatam* 10.44.13):

gūḍhaḥ purāṇa-puruṣo vana-citra-mālyah

> This Kṛṣṇa is the eternal and primeval personality, whose lotus feet are worshiped by Brahmā, Śaṅkara and Lakṣmī-devī. "*Avyaktaṁ vyaktim āpannaṁ manyante mām abuddhayaḥ* – You are unknown to ignorant people who harbor the misconception that the formless, undifferentiated, unmanifest Brahman has manifested separately by the knowledge function of the illusory potency, and has descended to this world in Nanda-bhavana in the form of Śrī Kṛṣṇa." Therefore You are confidential. Your original form is decorated with a wonderful garland of forest flowers, and You perform many varieties of pleasing pastimes while playing on Your flute and grazing cows along with Baladeva.

This is the meaning of primeval personality (*purāṇa-puruṣa*).It has also been mentioned in the *śruti* that Śrī Kṛṣṇa's ever-fresh adolescent form is the eternal form in which He is forever situated. Although He is the oldest, He is eternally young.

It is stated in *Śrīmad-Bhāgavatam* (10.44.14):

gopyas tapaḥ kim acaran yad amuṣya rūpaṁ
lāvaṇya-sāram asamordhvam ananya-siddham
dṛgbhiḥ pibanty anusavābhinavaṁ durāpam
ekānta-dhāma yaśasaḥ śriya aiśvarasya

Aho! What kind of austerities did the *gopīs* perform to be able to constantly drink the unequaled and unsurpassed sweetness of His bodily beauty, which is newer and newer at every moment? The *gopīs* directly see with their own eyes the very rare and ever-fresh loveliness of Śrī Kṛṣṇa's form, which is the essence of all luster, and is the unrivaled, exclusive reservoir of independently perfect fame, beauty and opulence. When He begins to laugh, the *makara*-shaped ornaments adorning His two charming ears cast sparkling reflections that play with astonishing beauty upon His two cheeks. With His form and qualities He attracts the hearts, minds and lives of all pure devotees.

In *Śrīmad-Bhāgavatam* (1.16.26–30) Śrī Kṛṣṇa's qualities are described thus:

satyaṁ śaucaṁ dayā kṣāntis
tyāgaḥ santoṣa ārjavam
śamo damas tapaḥ sāmyaṁ
titikṣoparatiḥ śrutam

jñānaṁ viraktir aiśvaryaṁ
śauryaṁ tejo balaṁ smṛtiḥ
svātantryaṁ kauśalaṁ kāntir
dhairyaṁ mārdavam eva ca

prāgalbhyaṁ praśrayaḥ śīlaṁ
saha ojo balaṁ bhagaḥ
gāmbhīryaṁ sthairyam āstikyaṁ
kīrtir māno 'nahaṅkṛtiḥ

ete cānye ca bhagavan
nityā yatra mahā-guṇāḥ
prārthyā mahattvam icchadbhir
na viyanti sma karhicit

tenāhaṁ guṇa-pātreṇa
śrī-nivāsena sāmpratam
śocāmi rahitaṁ lokaṁ
pāpmanā kalinekṣitam

Bhagavān Śrī Hari has unlimited qualities, some of which are being described here simply to afford us a glance in the direction of His excellence. (1) His words are true. (2) He is pure. (3) He is unable to tolerate the distress of others. (4) He protects those who are unconditionally surrendered to Him. (5) He is the friend of the devotees. (6) His consciousness is equipoised even when there is cause to be angry. (7) He is generous. (8) He naturally feels satisfied. (9) He is simple-hearted. (10) His activities are auspicious for everyone because He is the well-wisher of all. (11) His mind is steady and not prone to attachment and aversion. (12) He is firmly avowed toward favorable subjects. (13) He controls the external senses. (14) When He descends and performs pastimes as a *kṣatriya* or a member of any other caste, He adheres responsibly to the appropriate principles of religious conduct. (15) He is equally disposed to friends and enemies. (16) He tolerates great offenses committed against Him. (17) He is indifferent to things that are ordinarily most desirable. (18) He abides by the injunctions of the scriptures. (19) He possesses five types of knowledge, namely that which pertains to direct sense perception of gross phenomena (*pratyakṣa*), to Svarga (*parokṣa*), to the unmanifest, formless Brahman (*aparokṣa*), to Vaikuṇṭha (*adhokṣaja*) and to Goloka Vṛndāvana (*aprākṛta*). (20) He is intelligent. (21) He is grateful for services rendered by others. (22) He is an expert judge of time, place and persons, and He acts accordingly. (23) He is omniscient. (24) He is self-realized. (25) He is the controller of all opulence. (26) He is enthusiastic in battle. (27) He is influential.

(28) He can subdue others by His influence. (29) He is expert in quickly accomplishing that which is ordinarily impossible. (30) He can ascertain what kind of duty should be performed in any particular situation. (31) His mind is never agitated. (32) He is not dependent on others. (33) He is expert in all activities. (34) He can accomplish many activities at the same time. (35) He is expert in all arts. (36) His limbs are beautiful. (37) His color, taste, fragrance, touch and sound are beautiful. (38) His adolescence is beautiful. (39) He is attractive to all women. (40) He is patient. (41) His heart melts with *prema*. (42) He is controlled only by love. (43) His bold speech is remarkably witty. (44) He is an eloquent speaker. (45) He is gentle. (46) He is bashful when He thinks someone has detected His amorous affairs, or when others glorify Him. (47) He offers appropriate respect to all. (48) His words are sweet and pleasing. (49) His natural disposition is charming. (50) He is partial to the *sādhus*. (51) He is sharp-witted. (52) His knowledge-acquiring senses are acute. (53) His working senses are dexterous. (54) He is the abode of all enjoyment. (55) He is always happy. (56) He possesses all opulence. (57) It is very difficult to understand His intentions. (58) He is immovable. (59) He sees through the eyes of scripture. (60) He is famous for His sterling qualities. (61) He is the object of love and attachment for everyone. (62) He is worshipable for everyone. (63) He is devoid of pride, despite being worshiped by everyone. (64) He is possessed of brahminical qualities. (65) All mystic powers are under His control. (66) He is the concentrated embodiment of eternal existence, consciousness and bliss. (67) Some qualities, such as satisfaction, are also found in devotees, *karmīs*, *jñānīs* and *yogīs*. However, all such qualities are present only in a common way, whereas in Bhagavān they are fully present to the ultimate extent. Therefore all these qualities are transcendental, fully spiritual and inherent in His very nature. (69) Śrī Kṛṣṇa's qualities, pastimes, associates, transcendental abode, devotees and paraphernalia are all eternal, supramundane and complete. Therefore the qualities that the ordinary living entities cannot possibly possess are all present only in Bhagavān. For example: (70) His avowed intention becomes reality. (71) He is

> the controller of *māyā*. (72) He is situated in pure goodness (*viśuddha-sattva*). (73) He is the maintainer of the universe. (74) He awards salvation to the enemies killed by Him. (75) He attracts even the self-satisfied liberated souls. (76) He is served by the demigods such as Brahmā and Śiva. (77) He is equipped with unlimited, inconceivable potency. (78) His beauty is eternally increasing in freshness at every moment. (79) He is the predominating deity of *māyā* in the form of the *puruṣa-avatāra*. (80) He is the creator, maintainer and destroyer of the universes. (81) He is the source of all incarnations. (82) Unlimited universes are situated in the pores of His skin. (83) He is complete with the aggregate of all inconceivable energies in His forms such as Vāsudeva and Nārāyaṇa. (84) In His original form as Śrī Kṛṣṇa He can bestow *mukti* and even *bhakti* upon His enemies. (85) His form is so sweet that it astonishes even Himself. (86) Unlimited qualities are eternally present in Bhagavān, such as bestowing boundless joy upon an unconscious substance in His proximity.

This type of description is found in both Brahmājī's meditation on one pastime in a single location (*mantramayī-upāsanā*), and also in his broader meditation. In the *Gopāla-tāpanī Upaniṣad* it has been stated: "*gopa-veśam abbhrābhaṁ taruṇaṁ kalpa-drumāśritam* – Śrī Kṛṣṇa, who is dressed as a cowherd boy, whose divine luster resembles the hue of a raincloud, who is a fresh youth and who is seated at the foot of a desire tree, has been called Gopāla." Here the word *taruṇa* indicates His ever-youthful personal form, which is the storehouse of elegance and beauty.

By the phrase *vedeṣu durlabham* in this verse 33, Brahmājī has explained that Śrī Kṛṣṇa is very difficult to comprehend even for the personified Vedas, what to speak of the adherents of Vedic paths such as *karmīs*, *jñānīs* and *yogīs*. This is confirmed in the statement of Śrī Uddhava (*Śrīmad-Bhāgavatam* 10.47.61): "The *śrutis* have become exhausted by continually searching for the lotus feet of Mukunda, and they are still searching to this very day for those lotus feet, which the *gopīs* of Vṛndāvana have already attained."

Similarly, Brahmājī also stated (*Śrīmad-Bhāgavatam* 10.14.34): "*adyāpi yat pada-rajaḥ śruti-mṛgyam eva* – motivated by an intense greed to attain the dust of His lotus feet, the *śrutis* are still performing austerities to this very day."

Although Yaśodā-nandana Śrī Kṛṣṇa is inaccessible to the *karmīs* and *yogīs*, He is easily accessible through the love of His devotees: "*bhaktyāham ekayā grāhyaḥ* – He is attained only through devotion."

In this regard Bhagavān has also said (*Śrīmad-Bhāgavatam* 11.14.21): "O Uddhava, *bhakti* is the powerful method of attaining Me. I am completely controlled by that devotion, but I am never controlled by *yoga*, philosophical deliberation, adherence to religious principles, meticulous study of the Vedas, austerities, giving charity, nor by any other method. I am the Supersoul in everyone's heart, and I am easily attained by the *sādhus* alone, not by anyone else. This is because they have unadulterated and undivided devotion, which is born of their unflinching faith in Me. This type of exclusive devotion has the power to purify even a member of the caste of dog-eaters. However, all qualities such as truthfulness, mercy, observing silence, following scriptural injunctions, austerities and the cultivation of knowledge definitely cannot purify the heart of a human being who is devoid of *bhakti* unto Me."

Brahmājī has declared (*Śrīmad-Bhāgavatam* 10.14.5): "*pureha bhūman bahavo 'pi yoginaḥ* – O indivisible one! O Acyuta! There were many *yogīs* in this world in ancient times who, being unable to attain success in the path of *yoga*, began to perform their worldly and religious duties as an offering unto Your lotus feet. As a result of this, they began to practice *bhakti* in the form of hearing and chanting the narrations of Your glories. Thus they realized the essential reality of the self without any extraneous endeavor, and without difficulty they attained the excellent destination of becoming Your associates."

TĀTPARYA

The word *advaita* denotes the non-dual, undivided principle; He remains undivided, although the radiance of His limbs comprises the endless *brahmajyoti*, and the Supreme Lord in the form of Paramātmā in countless millions of expansions is His partial manifestation. *Acyuta* means that He remains full and complete, although there are billions of incarnations who are His personal expansions, and although unlimited millions of living entities emanate from Him as His separated expansions. Although He exhibits the pastime of being born, He actually Has no beginning. Although He winds up His manifest pastimes in this world, He is endless. Although He is without a beginning, He also has an origin, because He performs pastimes such as being born in His *prakaṭa-līlā*. Although he is the primordial personality, He is also the embodiment of fresh youthfulness. The purport is that although all kinds of contradictory qualities co-exist within Him, all compatible qualities as well as mutually incompatible qualities are reconciled by His inconceivable potency. This is the nature of transcendence and its distinction from mundane material characteristics.

Śrī Kṛṣṇa's utterly enchanting, threefold-bending personal form as Śyāmasundara is eternally in the bud of youth. It is beyond the confines of time and space and the mundane defects of the illusory energy. He exists splendidly in the transcendental, spiritual abode, where time is in the pure present, devoid of past and future. In the material world, there is a distinction between substances and their qualities. This distinction allows material substances to sometimes take on various qualities, and to sometimes become bereft of particular qualities, but this distinction is absent from the transcendental realm. Therefore, the qualities of the inert universe are all simultaneously present, reconciled, harmonious and purposeful in the transcendental world, although they seem to be mutually contradictory in the estimation of intelligence that is covered by the experience of *māyā's* time, place and person. How can the living entity under the influence of the illusory energy realize the spiritual existence when he has no comparable experience?

The conditioned soul's knowledge is always polluted by the defects of material time and space, and therefore he is helpless in the matter of renouncing his mundane conception. If the conditioned soul is incapable of understanding the spiritual substance by the faculty of knowledge, then by which faculty can one realize the specific nature of the aforementioned pure spiritual substance? In answer to this question, Brahmājī has said, "Transcendental affairs are incomprehensible even for the Vedas, for the Vedas are based on sound, which is material. Thus they cannot give us direct experience of the supramundane Goloka. Only when the Vedas are infused with the transcendental knowledge potency (*saṁvit-śakti*) can they say something about transcendental affairs."

However, when that knowledge potency, combined with the essence of the transcendental pleasure potency (*hlādinī-śakti*), is manifest in the living entities in the form of *bhakti*, then realization of the essential reality of Goloka becomes possible. The bliss function of *bhakti* is endless and unlimited, and is by nature full of pure transcendental knowledge. When knowledge attains oneness with the function of *bhakti* – that is to say, when it does not express an identity separate from *bhakti* – at that time it bestows perception of the essential reality of Goloka.

Verse 34

पन्थास्तु कोटिशतवत्सरसंप्रगम्यो
वायोरथापि मनसो मुनिपुङ्गवानाम् ।
सोऽप्यस्ति यत्प्रपदसीम्न्यविचिन्त्यतत्त्वे
गोविन्दमादिपुरुषं तमहं भजामि ॥३४॥

panthās tu koṭi-śata-vatsara-sampragamyo
vāyor athāpi manaso muni-puṅgavānām
so 'py asti yat-prapada-sīmny avicintya-tattve
govindam ādi-puruṣaṁ tam ahaṁ bhajāmi

Anvaya

aham bhajāmi – I perform *bhajana*; *tam* – of that; *ādi-puruṣam govindam* – original person, Śrī Govinda; *tu* – indeed; *atha api* – even; *panthāḥ* – the paths; *vāyoḥ* – of controlling the breathing process; *manasaḥ* – and mental speculation (*neti neti* – "not that, not that"); *sampragamyaḥ* – practiced; *muni-puṅgavānām* – by powerful sages; *koṭi-śata* – for hundreds of millions; *vatsara* – of years; *asti* – is (only capable of approaching); *saḥ api* – (that non-differentiated divine light, or *brahmajyoti*), which is nothing but; *sīmni* – the tip; *yat-prapada* – of the toenails; *avicintya-tattve* – of that inconceivable Absolute Truth.

Translation

Some *yogīs*, desiring to attain the Supreme Absolute Truth, who lies beyond the realm of contemplation, follow the path of strictly regulating the breathing process. The prominent sages who advocate the philosophy of the formless absolute follow the path of philosophical discussion to ascertain the formless, impersonal Brahman by the process of gradually eliminating the unreal. After

pursuing these paths for hundreds of millions of years, they may reach only as far as the tips of the toes of His lotus feet. I worship that original personality, Śrī Govinda.

Ṭīkā translation

The advocates of the impersonal conception may, after performing rigorous *sādhana* for billions of years, reach only as far as the tips of the toes of Śrī Kṛṣṇa's lotus feet. The purport is that at best they can only achieve perception of the light emanating from His divine lotus feet from very far away. It is absolutely impossible for them to see Śrī Govinda being served by His associates in Gokula.

How will it be possible for *jñānīs* and *yogīs* to have *darśana* of Śrī Govinda being served by His associates in Gokula, when it is astonishing even for *premi-bhaktas* such as Śrī Nārada? Such *jñānīs* and *yogīs* cannot even enter that place. In *Śrīmad-Bhāgavatam* (10.69.2) it has been stated:

citraṁ bataitad ekena
vapuṣā yugapat pṛthak
gṛheṣu dvy-aṣṭa-sāhasraṁ
striya eka udāvahat

On one occasion, the spectacle that Devarṣi Nārada beheld when he went to Dvārakā filled him with wonder. Bhagavān Śrī Kṛṣṇa was marrying sixteen thousand beautiful young ladies in separate ceremonies, which were being conducted in sixteen thousand different royal palaces simultaneously. In one place He was accepting the hand of the bride; in another He was offering oblations in the fire sacrifice; somewhere else, where the knot had already been tied, He was circumambulating the fire; and in all the other places He was engaged in many different aspects of the marriage ritual. Upon seeing this, even the omniscient Śrī Nārada was astonished.

It is also stated in the *Gopāla-tāpanī Upaniṣad* (21):

> *eko vaśī sarvagaḥ kṛṣṇa īdyaḥ*
> *eko 'pi san bahudhā yo vibhāti*

Śrī Kṛṣṇa is the one supreme controller of all controllers, and He is all-pervading. Although He is one, by the influence of His inconceivable potency He manifests as incarnations who are His personal expansions; as the living entities, who are His separated subjective portions; and as innumerable associates, who are His bodily expansions. He is the incomparable and unsurpassed reality.

In *Śrīmad-Bhāgavatam* (3.33.3) it is stated: "*ātmeśvaro 'tarkya-sahasra-śaktiḥ* – Bhagavān alone is the soul of all. He is the controller of all, being equipped with unlimited, inconceivable powers that defy mundane reasoning."

In the *Skanda Purāṇa* and the *Mahābhārata* (*Bhīṣma-parva* 5.22), it is stated: "*acintyāḥ khalu ye bhāvāḥ na tāṁs tarkeṇa yojayet* – the substances and moods that lie beyond material nature have been called inconceivable. They are absolutely incomprehensible to the power of human intelligence, which is limited and full of material defects."

Similarly, we find this statement in the *Vedānta-sūtra* (2.1.11): "*tarkāpratiṣṭhānāt* – logic is not the basis for understanding anything." This is because any conclusion established by logic today will be refuted tomorrow by another person with a new logic. Therefore the *Vedānta-sūtra* also states (2.1.27): "*śrutes tu śabda-mūlatvāt* – you should understand the inconceivable, supreme personal Absolute Truth only through the statements of *śruti*, because they are the teachings of Bhagavān." The statements of the Vedas are the fundamental evidence because they are free from the four defects of mistakes, illusion, defective perception and the desire to cheat others. They are reliable statements received through the system of *guru-paramparā*. The inconceivable Absolute Truth can be known only by this preceptorial succession. In this regard, the commentary on *Vedānta-sūtra* reasons that, just as the influence of a gemstone, a *mantra* or a potent medicinal herb is beyond the comprehension of the intelligence of the common man, so are the inherent powers of the Absolute Transcendence. The supernatural substance can only be known by the uncommon and divine power of undivided, pure *bhakti*.

Tātparya

Only one who is tasting the transcendental mellows of pure *bhakti* is considered to have attained the lotus feet of Śrī Govinda. The practitioners of *aṣṭāṅga-yoga* may absorb themselves in trance, and the greatest philosophers of the doctrine of monism may deliberate on matter and spirit, eliminating and rejecting all material phenomena one by one for millions of years. In the end they may both attain the state of merging into the formless, impersonal, spiritual radiance. This spiritual radiance, which is situated outside the transcendental abode, is nothing more than the reflected effulgence emanating from the small toenails of the lotus feet of Śrī Govindadeva in Goloka. It cannot even be considered to be the reflected effulgence of Śrī Govinda's lotus feet.

Actually, the processes of merging into the Absolute and dissolving the self in Brahman are both situated in the boundary area between the spiritual and material worlds. Unless one crosses beyond these two conceptions, one cannot realize the fascinating varieties of the served, the servant and the service in the transcendental world. The conditions of merging into the Absolute and dissolving the self in Brahman are not genuine happiness. They only mark the cessation of distressful experiences arising from a connection with the illusory energy. Although the absence of distress can be called happiness to a certain extent, it is meager and insignificant. Merely dispelling the suffering condition of material existence is not sufficient; the statement "*ātyantika-duḥkha-nivṛtti* – the ultimate goal of life is to end distress" is not correct. The ultimate attainment of the living entity is to be situated in his pure, transcendental, constitutional position of devotional service to Bhagavān. This condition can only be achieved by the mercy of *bhakti*, which is inherently transcendental. It is never available by following a tasteless and troublesome path that is completely devoid of *rasa*.

Verse 35

एकोऽप्यसौ रचयितुं जगदण्डकोटिं
यच्छक्तिरस्ति जगदण्डचया यदन्तः ।
अण्डान्तरस्थपरमाणुचयान्तरस्थं
गोविन्दमादिपुरुषं तमहं भजामि ॥३५॥

eko 'py asau racayituṁ jagad-aṇḍa-koṭiṁ
yac-chaktir asti jagad-aṇḍa-cayā yad-antaḥ
aṇḍāntara-stha-paramāṇu-cayāntara-stham
govindam ādi-puruṣaṁ tam ahaṁ bhajāmi

Anvaya

aham bhajāmi – I perform *bhajana*; *tam* – of that; *ādi-puruṣam govindam* – original person, Śrī Govinda; *api* – although; *asau asti* – He exists; *ekaḥ* – as a single, absolute reality; *yat-śaktiḥ* – by His self-sufficient potency; *racayitum* – in creating; *koṭim* – the tens of milllions; *jagad-aṇḍa* – of universes; *yad-antaḥ* – through His entrance; *cayāḥ* – within the host; *jagad-aṇḍa* – of universes; *antara-stha* – He becomes situated; *aṇḍa* – (simultaneously) in each universe; *antara-stham* – and within; *cayā* – each of the host; *paramāṇu* – of atoms.

Translation

Potency and the possessor of potency are one undifferentiated principle. The potency by which billions of universes are created is situated inseparably within Bhagavān. All the universes are situated within Bhagavān, and by the influence of His inconceivable potency, Bhagavān is also fully present in every atom of all the universes. I worship that original personality, Śrī Govinda.

Ṭīkā translation

Although Śrī Kṛṣṇa is one, He creates everything, and pervades every atom in the creation. He is smaller than the smallest, and greater than the greatest. The following description of His inconceivable potency is found in *Śrīmad-Bhāgavatam* (10.13.46–55):

tāvat sarve vatsa-pālāḥ
paśyato 'jasya tat-kṣaṇāt
vyadṛśyanta ghanaśyāmāḥ
pīta-kauśeya-vāsasaḥ

The influence of His inconceivable potency is such that, although Kṛṣṇa is one, He assumed the form of innumerable calves and cowherd boys, as Brahmā looked on again and again. All those forms became *śyāma*-colored, like fresh rainclouds, and all were attired in yellow upper garments. All the forms were resplendent with four arms that held the conch, disk, mace and lotus flower. Their heads were adorned with crowns, their ears with earrings, their chests with necklaces and their necks with garlands of forest flowers. All of them looked beautiful with a clockwise curl of hair on their right breast, three lines marking their throats and the Kaustubha-jewel ornamenting their necks. They had bracelets on their wrists, ankle-bells on their feet, belts on their waists and rings on their fingers. Each form was decorated from head to toe with a garland of fresh young *tulasī* leaves, which had been offered by some immensely pious personalities, and they were all fulfilling the hearts' desires of all their devotees. The moving and non-moving living entities, from Brahmā down to insignificant pieces of straw, all assumed forms in which they performed varieties of worship by dancing, singing, playing musical instruments and offering different types of paraphernalia.

The expansions of Bhagavān were surrounded by the personified mystic powers headed by *aṇimā*, by the opulences headed by *māyā*, and by the twenty-four elements headed by the *mahat-tattva*. All the ingredients of the universe such as time, acquired nature, impressions, desires, fruitive activities and the three modes of material nature assumed personified forms, and Brahmā saw that they were all worshiping the expansions of Kṛṣṇa. Their conception of being independent from Him was completely dispelled by His glories.

Then, the cowherd boys, all the substances from unlimited numbers of universes, as well as the multitude of presiding deities in those universes, entered into Kṛṣṇa and again manifested from Him.

Then again, *jagad-aṇḍa-cayāḥ* – Brahmājī saw *that* Parabrahma from whom all the animate and inanimate worlds are manifest, along with His cows, calves and cowherd boys, which were all non-different from Him.

Although Bhagavān Śrī Kṛṣṇa possesses a distinctly human-like appearance, He has no outside or inside. He is smaller than the smallest, and greater than the greatest. He is all-pervading. He is not obstructed by past and future time. He is the cause and the effect of the universe. Since He is all-pervading, He is inside and outside the cosmic manifestation. The form of the universe is also Him, because cause and effect may be seen as non-different. He is unmanifest in the sense that He is beyond the range of material sense perception. He is praised by *śruti-mantras* such as *anor aṇīyān mahato mahīyān.* In *Gopāla-tāpanī Upaniṣad* (23), it is stated:

yo 'sau sarveṣu bhuteṣv āviśya bhūtāni vidadhāti sa vo hi svāmī bhavati. yo 'sau sarva-bhūtātmā gopāla eko devaḥ sarva-bhūteṣu gūḍhaḥ

Only Bhagavān Śrī Kṛṣṇa is Parabrahma. He is not only free from birth and decay, but is completely untouched by the six waves: hunger, thirst, aging, death, lamentation and bewilderment. He is eternally in one form, and free from deterioration. He is the center of the universe. He is tending wish-fulfilling cows in order to make them joyful. He is also present in all the Vedas, who are loudly proclaiming His glories. He remains within all moving and non-moving living entities, and He regulates them. Such is the nature of that cowherd boy, Govinda, who is the master of us all. Gopāla is the Soul and Self of all living entities. Although the Lord is one, He is hidden within all animate beings.

Thus the fact that the Absolute Truth is possessed of personal attributes is proven by evidence such as this.

Tātparya

The form and substance of the transcendental realm is entirely beyond the illusory material nature. Śrī Kṛṣṇa reigns supreme above even that superior nature. By His free will, He creates unlimited numbers of universes through the agency of His inconceivable potency. All the universes are a transformation of His potency. Still, His location remains transcendental, because all the spiritual and material worlds are situated within Him, and He is within them. Moreover, He is fully present within each and every atom of all the universes. The quality of being all-pervading is only one aspect of Śrī Kṛṣṇa's opulence, for He is also fully present everywhere in His form as Śrī Kṛṣṇa, which is neither gigantic nor minute, but of intermediate proportions like that of a human being. This is His supernatural, transcendental opulence. By this consideration, the principle of inconceivable distinction with non-distinction (*acintya-bhedābheda-tattva*) is established, and simultaneously all contaminating opinions such as Māyāvāda philosophy become unacceptable.

Verse 36

यद्भावभावितधियो मनुजास्तथैव
संप्राप्य रूपमहिमासनयानभूषाः ।
सूक्तैर्यमेव निगमप्रथितैः स्तुवन्ति
गोविन्दमादिपुरुषं तमहं भजामि ॥३६॥

yad-bhāva-bhāvita-dhiyo manujās tathaiva
samprāpya rūpa-mahimāsana-yāna-bhūṣāḥ
sūktair yam eva nigama-prathitaiḥ stuvanti
govindam ādi-puruṣaṁ tam ahaṁ bhajāmi

Anvaya

aham bhajāmi – I perform *bhajana*; *tam* – of that; *ādi-puruṣam govindam* – original Supreme Person, Śrī Govinda; *yad-bhāva-bhāvita-dhiyaḥ* – on account of being aborbed in ecstatic consciousness of Him; *manujāḥ* – men; *tathā eva* – in accordance with their respective moods and perfections;[26] *samprāpya* – attain; *rūpa-mahimā-āsana-yāna-bhūṣāḥ* – beautiful forms, glories, seats, conveyances and ornaments; *yam eva* – and whom; *stuvanti* – they sing His praises; *sūktaiḥ* – by chanting *mantras*; *nigama-prathitaiḥ* – renowned in the Vedas.

Translation

I worship the original personality, Śrī Govinda. Those human beings whose hearts are enthused with ecstatic devotion for Him attain their respective forms, seats, conveyances and ornaments, in accordance with their

[26] Those who are eligible for *śānta-rasa* attain the setting of peacefulness, *brahma-paramātma-dhāma*. Those who are eligible for *dāsya-rasa* attain the opulent abode of Vaikuṇṭha. Those who are eligible for pure *sakhya-*, *vātsalya-* or *mādhurya-rasa* attain Goloka-dhāma, which is above Vaikuṇṭha.

individual moods, and they glorify Him through the hymns renowned in the Vedas.

ṬĪKĀ TRANSLATION

It is true that Bhagavān Śrī Kṛṣṇa continually performs His playful loving pastimes with His own eternal associates. Now the verse *yad-bhāva-bhāvita-dhiyaḥ* uses the logic of inferential partial illustration (*kaimutikī-nyāya*)[27] to describe how generous and merciful He is to His practicing devotees in this world. The residents of Vraja render various types of intimate service to Śrī Kṛṣṇa by virtue of their intrinsic qualities that are similar to His, such as their disposition, age, playfulness, attire and so on. In this way they sport and enjoy along with Him. *Śāstras* such as the Vedas and Purāṇas give this account of their position being on the same level with Śrī Kṛṣṇa as His associates. Just as those eternal associates enjoy pastimes along with Śrī Kṛṣṇa, similarly the *sādhakas* under the guidance of those eternal associates follow their respective service moods, and taste the happiness of eternal service to Kṛṣṇa along with them. If one can attain Kṛṣṇa by constantly thinking of Him as one's enemy, then those who are devoted to Kṛṣṇa must definitely attain Him – how can there be any doubt about it?

vaireṇa yaṁ nṛpatayaḥ śiśupāla-śālva-
pauṇḍrādayo gati-vilāsa-vilokanādyaiḥ
dhyāyanta ākṛti-dhiyaḥ śayanāsanādau
tad-bhāvam āpur anurakta-dhiyāṁ punaḥ kim

Śrīmad-Bhāgavatam (11.5.48)

[27] The logic called *kaimutikī-nyāya* makes a point by partial illustration, saying, "Here is an example of how merciful Śrī Kṛṣṇa is: He awards salvation even to His enemies." Then it points by inference to the point to be established, saying *kim uta* (how much more): "How much more merciful must He be to His loving devotees?" In this example, Śrī Kṛṣṇa's mercy is illustrated.

Kings such as Śiśupāla, Pauṇḍraka and Śālva used to think about Śrī Kṛṣṇa in an inimical mood even while they were sleeping, eating and performing all their duties. If they attained nearness in the form of impersonal liberation simply by being absorbed in thoughts of His activities, movements, sporting and glancing, then those eminent personalities who are deeply attached to Śrī Kṛṣṇa must definitely attain equality with Him. What is the necessity of reassurance in this regard? Without doubt they will all attain perfection in their respective *bhāvas*.

Tātparya

From the perspective of transcendental mellows (*rasa*), there are five types of *bhāva* (mood) in *bhakti*: neutrality (*śānta*), servitorship (*dāsya*), friendship (*sakhya*), parenthood (*vātsalya*) and amorous love (*śṛṅgāra*). The devotee who adheres firmly to any one of these *bhāvas*, and meditates continually on the service of the appropriate form of Śrī Kṛṣṇa, eventually attains a position befitting his eligibility. According to his *rasa*, he attains a transcendental form, greatness, situation (i.e. place of service) and conveyance, as well as ornaments in the form of supramundane qualities that enhance his personal beauty. Those who are eligible for the mellow of neutral adoration (*śānta-rasa*) attain the setting of peacefulness, *brahma-paramātma-dhāma*. Those who are eligible for the mellow of servitorship attain the opulent abode of Vaikuṇṭha, while those who are eligible for the mellows of pure friendship, parenthood and service as a beloved attain Goloka-dhāma, which is above Vaikuṇṭha. In each of these locations, the devotees attain all the necessary elements and ingredients appropriate to their own *rasa*. They offer praise in accordance with the hymns mentioned in the Vedas, or else they engage in intimate services.

In some places the Vedas narrate Bhagavān's pastimes through the support of the transcendental potency. Through these indications, one can also find descriptions of the great, liberated devotees. For example, it has been stated in the *Padma Purāṇa*: "*māne 'syāpi vandanam, arcanaṁ kuñja-sevāyām* – the sulky reproaches of the *gopīs* are the limb of *bhakti* known as offering prayers, and service within the groves (*kuñjas*) of Vṛndāvana is called *arcana*."

Verse 37

आनन्दचिन्मयरसप्रतिभाविताभि –
स्ताभिर्य एव निजरूपतया कलाभिः ।
गोलोक एव निवसत्यखिलात्मभूतो
गोविन्दमादिपुरुषं तमहं भजामि ॥३७॥

ānanda-cinmaya-rasa-pratibhāvitābhis
tābhir ya eva nija-rūpatayā kalābhiḥ
goloka eva nivasaty akhilātma-bhūto
govindam ādi-puruṣaṁ tam ahaṁ bhajāmi

Anvaya

aham bhajāmi – I perform *bhajana*; *tam* – of that; *ādi-puruṣam govindam* – original Supreme Person, Śrī Govinda; *yaḥ* – who; *eva* – certainly; *nivasati* – resides; *goloke* – in Goloka-dhāma; *akhila-ātma-bhūtaḥ* – as the original complete intrinsic form; *pratibhāvitābhiḥ* – for all of His dear associates who act as His counterparts; *ānanda* – in enjoying transcendental, blissful; *cinmaya-rasa* – spiritual mellows; *eva nija-rūpatayā* – with none other than His own internal pleasure potency Śrī Rādhā, who has the *bhāva* of amorous *rasa*; *tābhiḥ kalābhiḥ* – together with the expansions of Śrī Rādhā's body (*kalās*), who act as Her *sakhīs*.

Translation

Śrī Govinda, who is all-pervading and who exists within the hearts of all, resides in His Goloka-dhāma along with Śrī Rādhā, who is the embodiment of His pleasure potency and the counterpart of His own spiritual form. She is the epitome of transcendental *rasa*, and is expert in sixty-four arts. They are also accompanied by the *sakhīs*, who

are expansions of Śrī Rādhā's own transcendental body, and who are infused with blissful, spiritual *rasa*. I worship that original personality, Śrī Govinda.

Ṭīkā translation

The *gopīs*, with whom Bhagavān Śrī Kṛṣṇa resides in that world, are Mahā-Lakṣmīs, original goddesses of fortune. In this context, what does it mean to say that those beloveds of Śrī Kṛṣṇa have the mood of complete unity with Him? To demonstrate the pre-eminence of the *gopīs*, Śrī Jīva Gosvāmipāda explains here that Śrī Kṛṣṇa only stays in that place where the *gopīs* live. This is the message loudly proclaimed by this verse. Consequently, the planet of the *gopīs* is called Goloka-dhāma.[28] To establish this conclusion, Brahmājī is revealing the unique distinction of those *gopīs* in the verse beginning *ānanda-cinmaya-rasa*. The residents of Goloka, such as Śrī Kṛṣṇa's bosom friends, His brother, close relatives, mother, father and other well-wishing superiors, are all the recipients of His extreme affection, and they are as dear to Him as His very self. Nevertheless, *nija-rūpatayā kalābhiḥ* means that the function of His own pleasure potency in the form of His beloved *gopīs* is non-different from His intrinsic form and nature. Thus the *gopīs* are manifestations of His personal potency, and they are embodiments of the most elevated amorous mellow. The purport is that they are naturally His beloveds because they are infused with the complete transcendental bliss. Therefore, the topmost excellence of the *gopīs* has been established by stating that Śrī Kṛṣṇa resides in Goloka with his beloveds, who are the direct embodiments of the transcendental, blissful mellow (*ānanda-cinmaya-rasa*).

[28] One meaning of the word *go* is *gopī*, therefore Goloka may also be understood to mean "the planet where the *gopīs* reside."

The *gopīs* and their unique distinction have been described by the word *prati-bhāvitābhiḥ*. The *gopīs* are infused by the most elevated and radiant mellow of amorous love (*ānanda-cinmaya-rasa*). "You reside always and forever with those *gopīs*" means that Śrī Kṛṣṇa has inspired them all with *prema-rasa*, and that the *gopīs* love Him with hearts totally saturated with that astonishing mellow of love. This is clearly stated by the word *prati*. For example, if it is said of someone, *praty-upakṛtaḥ saḥ*, it should be understood from the word *prati* that first he performed some beneficial work, and afterwards he attained the benefit. The word *pratibhāvita* should be accepted in the same way. Thus the meaning in this context becomes, "Just as Śrī Kṛṣṇa inspired the *gopīs* with the transcendental, blissful mellow (*ānanda-cinmaya-rasa*), the *gopīs* also caused Śrī Kṛṣṇa, who is absorbed in the most resplendent mellow, to drink that very *rasa*. In this way the *gopīs* also catered to His highest welfare."

Here the word *nija-rūpatayā* reveals an even more confidential meaning of the verse. Since the *gopīs* are the embodiments of Śrī Kṛṣṇa's pleasure potency, they are His parts, and are therefore non-different from Him. Hence, it is not possible for the *gopīs*, who are all Mahā-Lakṣmīs, to be the wives of others in the unmanifest pastimes of Goloka in the same way that they appear to be the wives of others in the manifest pastimes. In Goloka they are Śrī Kṛṣṇa's own beloved wives. Just as a wife is sometimes impelled by playful curiosity to arouse some special eagerness in her husband by using her veil to conceal her face, similarly Yogamāyā crafts the experience of paramourship in the manifest pastimes of Vṛndāvana[29] in order to intensify the feeling of eagerness.

[29] In Śrī Kṛṣṇa's manifest pastimes, there is an actual situation of paramourship wherein the *gopīs* are apparently married to others, but in the unmanifest pastimes of Goloka Vṛndāvana, only the self-conception of being married to others exists in order to nourish the mood of transcendental paramourship.

Goloka eva – Here the word *eva* emphasizes that in Goloka Śrī Kṛṣṇa resides eternally with the *gopīs* as His wives, and not as His paramours. The *Gautamīya-tantra* also confirms this in its explanation of the ten-syllable *mantra* for realization of the eternal unmanifest pastimes: "*aneka-janma-siddhānāṁ gopīnāṁ patir eva vā* – Śrī Kṛṣṇa is the husband of the *gopīs* who have attained perfection after many lifetimes." Therefore, the purport emphasized by the word *eva* after the word *goloke* is that in the Goloka pastimes, the *gopīs* are only related to Śrī Kṛṣṇa as His wives, and not in any other way.

Tātparya

Although the potency (*śakti*) and the possessor of the potency (*śaktimān*) are both one soul, by the action of the pleasure potency They exist eternally and separately in the forms of Śrī Rādhā and Śrī Kṛṣṇa.

The inconceivable amorous mellow is resplendent only in that *ānanda* as Śrī Rādhā, the personification of the pleasure potency, and Śrī Kṛṣṇa, the embodiment of the knowledge potency (*cit-svarūpa*). There are two types of cause (*vibhāva*) of this *rasa*, namely the support (*ālambana*), in whom the *rasa* appears, and the cause of awakening (*uddīpana*). The support aspect is also of two types, namely the object of *rasa* (*viṣaya*) and the abode of *rasa* (*aśraya*). Śrī Rādhikā and the *gopīs*, who are Her bodily manifestations, are the abode of *rasa*, and Śrī Kṛṣṇa is the object. That Kṛṣṇa is the Lord of Goloka, Govinda. The *gopīs* are fully infused with this *rasa* (*pratibhāvita āśraya*), and Śrī Kṛṣṇa performs His eternal pastimes in Goloka with them.

The expression *nija-rūpatayā* indicates that the functions of the pleasure potency are manifest in the form of different arts, of which there are sixty-four types: (1) *gīta* – the art of singing;

(2) *vādya* – the art of playing on musical instruments; (3) *nṛtya* – the art of dancing; (4) *nāṭya* – the art of theatricals; (5) *ālekhya* – the art of painting; (6) *viśeṣaka-cchedya* – the art of painting the face and body with colored unguents and cosmetics; (7) *taṇḍula-kusuma-balī-vikāra* – the art of preparing offerings from rice and flowers; (8) *puṣpāstaraṇa* – the art of making a covering of flowers for a bed; (9) *daśana-vasanāṅga-rāga* – the art of applying preparations for cleansing the teeth and clothes, and painting the body; (10) *maṇi-bhūmikā-karma* – the art of arranging jewels on the ground; (11) *śayyā-racana* – the art of arranging bed coverings; (12) *udaka-vādya* – the art of playing music on water; (13) *udaka-ghāta* – the art of splashing water; (14) *citra-yoga* – the art of applying an admixture of colors; (15) *mālya-grathana-vikalpa* – the art of weaving garlands together; (16) *śekharāpīḍa-yojana* – the art of setting the coronet on the head; (17) *nepathya-yoga* – the art of dressing backstage in the green room; (18) *karṇapātra-bhaṅga* – the art of decorating the part of the external ear that partly covers the ear-hole; (19) *sugandha-yukti* – the art of practical application of aromatics; (20) *bhūṣaṇa-yojana* – the art of applying or setting ornaments; (21) *aindra-jāla* – the art of jugglery; (22) *kaucumāra* – a kind of decorative art; (23) *hasta-lāghava* – the art of sleight of hand; (24) *citra-śākā-pūpa-bhakṣya-vikāra-kriyā* – the art of preparing varieties of salad, bread, cake and delicious food; (25) *pānaka-rasa-rāgāsava-yojana* – the art of preparing palatable drinks and tingeing draughts with red color; (26) *sūcī-vāya-karma* – the art of needlework and weaving; (27) *sūtra-krīḍā* – the art of playing with thread; (28) *prahelikā* – the art of making and solving riddles; (29) *pratimālā* – the art of reciting a verse-sequence as a trial of memory and skill; (30) *durvacaka-yoga* – the art of practicing language to which others find it difficult to respond; (31) *pustaka-vācana* – the art of reciting books;

(32) *nāṭikākhyāyikā-darśana* – the art of enacting short plays and anecdotes; (33) *kāvya-samasyā-pūraṇa* – the art of solving enigmatic verses; (34) *paṭṭikā-vetra-bāṇa-vikalpa* – the art of preparing shield, bow and arrows; (35) *tarku-karma* – the art of using a spindle to spin thread; (36) *takṣaṇa* – the art of carpentry; (37) *vāstu-vidyā* – the art of engineering; (38) *raupya-ratna-parīkṣā* – the art of testing silver and jewels; (39) *dhātu-vāda* – the art of metallurgy; (40) *maṇi-rāga-jñāna* – the art of tingeing jewels; (41) *ākara-jñāna* – the art of mineralogy; (42) *vṛkṣāyur-veda-yoga* – the art of practicing herbal medicine; (43) *meṣa-kukkuṭa-lāvaka-yuddha-vidhi* – the art of knowing the mode of fighting of lambs, cocks and birds; (44) *śuka-śārikā-pralāpana* – the art of maintaining or knowing conversation between male and female parrots; (45) *utsādana* – the art of healing or cleaning a person with perfumes; (46) *keśa-mārjana-kauśala* – the art of combing hair; (47) *akṣara-muṣṭikā-kathana* – the art of talking using letters and fingers; (48) *mlecchita-kutarka-vikalpa* – the art of fabricating barbaric or foreign sophistry; (49) *deśa-bhāṣā-jñāna* – the art of knowing provincial dialects; (50) *puṣpa-śakaṭikā-nirmiti-jñāna* – the art of preparing toy carts using flowers; (51) *yantra-mātṛkā* – the art of mechanics; (52) *dhāraṇa-mātṛkā* – the art of using amulets; (53) *saṁvācya* – the art of conversation; (54) *mānasī-kāvya-kriyā* – the art of composing verse mentally; (55) *kriyā-vikalpa* – the art of designing a literary work or a medical remedy; (56) *chalitaka-yoga* – the art of deception; (57) *abhidhāna-koṣa-cchando-jñāna* – the art of lexicography and the use of poetic meters; (58) *vastra-gopana* – the art of concealment of cloths; (59) *dyūta-viśeṣa* – the art of specific gambling; (60) *ākarṣa-krīḍā* – the art of playing with dice by using magnets; (61) *bālaka-krīḍanaka* – the art of using children's toys; (62) *vaināyikī vidyā* – the art of enforcing discipline; (63) *vaijayikī vidyā* – the art of gaining victory; and

(64) *vaitālikī vidyā* – the art of awakening one's master with music at dawn.

All these types of knowledge are embodied and eternally manifest in the form of the ingredients of *rasa* in Goloka-dhāma, and in the mundane universe they are beautifully manifest in the Vraja pastimes by the spiritual potency, Yogamāyā.

Therefore Śrīla Rūpa Gosvāmī has stated:

sadānantaiḥ prakāśaiḥ svair
līlābhiś ca sa dīvyati
tatraikena prakāśena
kadācij jagad antare
sahaiva sva-parivārair
janmādi kurute hariḥ

kṛṣṇa-bhāvānusāreṇa
līlākhyā śaktir eva sā
teṣāṁ parikarāṇāṁ ca
taṁ taṁ bhāvaṁ vibhāvayet

prapañca-gocaratvena
sā līlā prakaṭā smṛtā
anyās tv aprakaṭā bhānti
adṛśyas tad-agocarāḥ

tatra prakaṭa-līlāyām
eva syātāṁ gamāgamau
gokule mathurāyāṁ ca
dvārakāyāṁ ca śārṅginaḥ

yās tatra tatrāprakaṭās
tatra tatraiva santi tāḥ

Laghu-bhāgavatāmṛta (5.436–40)

Śrī Kṛṣṇa is eternally resplendent in Goloka with His display of unlimited pastimes. Sometimes He descends to this world and, along with His associates who appear with Him, manifests pastimes such as His birth and so on. In accordance with Śrī Kṛṣṇa's desire, the pastime potency also infuses His associates with their individual *bhāvas.* The pastimes that are perceived in the material world are collectively called the manifest pastimes, and the pastimes of Goloka that cannot be perceived in the material world, and that remain unmanifest to the world, are called unmanifest pastimes. In the manifest pastimes, Kṛṣṇa travels to and from Gokula, Mathurā and Dvārakā. However, the pastimes that are not manifested in these three places during Śrī Kṛṣṇa's pastimes on this Earth remain eternally manifest in the transcendental abodes such as Goloka Vṛndāvana. By these conclusive statements it is understood that there is no difference at all between the manifest and unmanifest pastimes.

Our honorable *ācārya-caraṇa* Śrī Jīva Gosvāmipāda has explained in his commentary on this verse of *Brahma-saṁhitā*, in his commentary on *Śrī Ujjvala-nīlamaṇi*, in *Kṛṣṇa-sandarbha* and in other places as well that Kṛṣṇa's manifest pastimes are arranged by Yogamāyā. Because of their connection with the illusory realm, they appear to have assimilated some mundane features that cannot exist in the intrinsic fundamental reality (*svarūpa-tattva*). Examples of such pastimes include killing the demons, associating with the wives of others, taking birth and so on. It is an established truth that the *gopīs* are extensions of Kṛṣṇa's personal intrinsic potency. Hence, since they are unquestionably His own consorts, how can there be any possibility of their being anyone else's wives? Still, we see that in the manifest pastimes the *gopīs* do appear to be the wives of others, but this is only an implicit conviction created by *māyā.*

There is a secret meaning in Śrī Jīva Gosvāmī's explanation, which, if brought to light, will automatically dispel all types of doubt. The revered Śrī Jīva Gosvāmī, the foremost follower of Śrīla Rūpa and Sanātana Gosvāmīs, is the *ācārya* of essential truth and reality (*tattva-ācārya*) of the Gauḍīya Vaiṣṇavas. Furthermore, he is Śrī Rādhā's confidential assistant in *kṛṣṇa-līlā*. Therefore, there is no secret truth that is unknown to him. Those who do not understand his profound intentions raise arguments for and against his ideas by presenting their own concocted interpretations.

According to Śrī Rūpa and Sanātana's vision, there is no difference between the manifest and the unmanifest pastimes. The only distinction is that one manifestation is beyond the material domain, and the other is seen within it. In the region beyond the mundane sphere, everything – the seer and the seen – is transcendentally pure. Fortunate people, on receiving the extraordinary mercy of Śrī Kṛṣṇa, relinquish all material connections and enter the spiritual domain. If during the performance of *sādhana* they attained perfection in savoring the extraordinary varieties of *rasa*, they can then see and take delight in all the supremely pure pastimes of Goloka. Such recipients of mercy are very rare.

On the other hand,[30] those who attain perfection in *bhakti*, and experience the nectar of spiritual *rasa* by Kṛṣṇa's mercy, witness the pastimes of Goloka in the pastimes of Gokula which are manifest in this world, even while remaining in the material universe. There are some gradations of qualification in both categories of *sādhaka*. As long as one has not attained *vastu-siddhi* (birth from the womb of a *gopī* in Kṛṣṇa's manifest pastimes), the influence of *māyā* maintains some restriction in one's vision of the Goloka pastimes. On the other hand, realization of one's *svarūpa* varies according to the level of one's attainment of *svarūpa-siddhi*. It must be accepted that a devotee's *darśana* of

[30] What is the difference between these two types of *sādhaka*? The first type makes very rapid progress by extraordinary mercy, galloping through the various stages due to giving up all material relationships and attachments, whereas the second makes progress in a more gradual manner.

Goloka will vary according to the degree that he has realized his intrinsic form and nature. *Jīvas* who are tightly bound by *māyā* have no spiritual vision. Some of them are trapped by the variegated charm of *māyā*, and some, having taken shelter of impersonal knowledge of the formless aspect of the Absolute, which is opposed to the reality of Bhagavān's personality, proceed toward the path of total destruction. Even after seeing Bhagavān's manifest pastimes, both types of bound *jīvas* view such pastimes as mundane activities, having no connection with the unmanifest pastimes. Thus, there is gradation in one's *darśana* of Goloka depending upon one's qualification.

There is a subtle point to note here. Just as Goloka is the completely pure, divine truth beyond the illusory realm, the Gokula which is manifest on this Earth is similarly always pure and uncontaminated, even though it appears in the material world by Bhagavān's knowledge potency, Yogamāyā. There is not even the slightest touch of material defect, degradation or imperfection in either the manifest or the unmanifest pastimes. Different people perceive the pastimes differently, depending on their qualification. Defect (contamination), foulness, designation, illusion, ignorance, impurity, falsity, loathsomeness and grossness are all perceived through the conditioned living entities' intelligence, false ego and eyes that have been dulled by the material nature. They do not belong to the object of their perception, Gokula. The more one is free from defects, the more one is granted vision of the transcendental truth. The truth is revealed in *śāstra*, but the purity of realization for those who deliberate on these *tattvas* will depend upon their qualifications.

According to the views of Śrī Rūpa and Śrī Sanātana, whatever pastimes are manifest in Bhauma-Gokula are also present in Goloka, also in their pure form without a tinge of *māyā*. That is why the mood of transcendental paramourship is also certainly present in some form or another in Goloka in its inconceivably pure state. All the manifestations created by Yogamāyā are immaculate. The transcendental mood that Yogamāyā creates of being the wife of someone other than Kṛṣṇa, or of being His paramour, is therefore based on the pure absolute reality. But what is this pure absolute reality? This should be discussed.

Śrīla Rūpa Gosvāmī writes (*Ujjvala-nīlamaṇi* 1.9–10, 2.21, 5.2):

pūrvokta-dhīrodattādi
caturbhedasya tasya tu
patiś copapatiś ceti
prabhedāv iha viśrutau

patiḥ sa kanyāyāḥ yaḥ
pāṇi-grāhako bhavet
rāgeṇollaṅghayan dharmaṁ
parakīyā-valārthinā

tadīya-prema-sarvasyaṁ
būdhair upapatiḥ smṛtaḥ
laghutvam atra yat proktaṁ
tat tu prākṛta-nāyake

na kṛṣṇe rasa-niryāsa – svādārtham avatāriṇi

tatra nāyikābheda-vicāraḥ,

"nāsau nāḍhye rase mukhye
yat paroḍhā nigadyate
tat tu syāt prākṛta-kṣudra-
nāyikādy-anusārataḥ."

After deep deliberation on these verses of *Ujjvala-nīlamaṇi*, Śrīla Jīva Gosvāmī establishes that the transcendental paramour mood, like the pastime of Kṛṣṇa's birth, is a divine delusion created by Yogamāyā. "*Tathāpi patiḥ pura-vanitānāṁ dvitīyo vraja-vanitānām* – it is understood that the mood of being married exists in Dvārakā, while the *vraja-sundarīs* have the transcendental paramour mood." According to the conclusions of Śrīla Rūpa and Sanātana Gosvāmīs, the delightfully deceptive pastimes are also accepted as the contrivance of Yogamāyā. Śrīla Jīva Gosvāmī has established that there is no difference between the pastimes of Goloka and Gokula, and it must be accepted that the original principle of all pastimes is manifest in Gokula.[31]

One who accepts the hand of a virgin girl according to the sacred rites of marriage is called a husband. And he who, being overcome by passion, violates conventional morality in order to win another's wife is called a paramour. Now, the religious obligation binding one within matrimonial regulation does not exist in Goloka. Even the concept of husbandhood within the bounds of matrimony does not exist there. Therefore the *gopīs*, who are Kṛṣṇa's own potency, cannot be married to any other person, and can never be the wives of other men. In that realm of Goloka it is not possible for the paramour (*parakīyā*) and married (*svakīyā*) conditions to exist separately from each other. In the manifest pastimes within the illusory realm, the strictures of marriage do exist, but Śrī Kṛṣṇa is beyond their jurisdiction. Therefore, the form of *dharma* (righteous prescription) found in the sweet realm of Vraja is a creation of Yogamāyā. Kṛṣṇa transgresses this *dharma* and enjoys the transcendental paramour mellow. Only a person with mundane vision in the material world will see this as a violation of the *dharma* created by Yogamāyā. In reality, there is no such degradation in Kṛṣṇa's pastimes.

[31] In this context, Gokula refers to the manifestation of the divine abode in this world rather than to the inner section of Goloka.

The paramour mellow is the very essence of all *rasas*, so a denial of its presence in Goloka would minimize that realm. It is not possible that the highest delight in *rasa* could be absent from the topmost abode of Goloka. Śrī Kṛṣṇa, who is the source of all incarnations, relishes this *rasa* in one way in Goloka and in another way in Gokula. Thus, even though there appears to be a transgression of *dharma* according to material vision, this truth must also exist in some form in Goloka.

"*Ātmārāmo 'py arīramat* (*Śrīmad-Bhāgavatam* 10.29.42) – Kṛṣṇa performed amorous pastimes, although He is self-satisfied (*ātmārāma*)." "*Ātmany avaruddha-sauratah* (*Śrīmad-Bhāgavatam* 10.33.25) – Śrī Kṛṣṇa, whose every desire comes to fruition, keeps in His heart the *hāva*, *bhāva* and other *anubhāvas* arising from His amorous diversions." "*Reme rameśo vraja-sundarībhir yathārbhakaḥ sva-pratibimba-vibhramaḥ* (*Śrīmad-Bhāgavatam* 10.33.16) – Bhagavān Śrī Kṛṣṇa, who gives pleasure to the supreme goddess of fortune Śrīmatī Rādhārāṇī, enjoyed with the beautiful Vraja maidens just as an innocent child plays with his reflection without undergoing any transformation."

It is understood from these statements of *śāstra* that Śrī Kṛṣṇa's constitutional nature is to be self-satisfied. In those spiritual planets predominated by opulence, He manifests His own potency as Lakṣmī, and consorts with her in the mellow of wedded conjugal love. There, with the sense of wedlock prevailing, *rasa* only goes up to the stage of servitorship (*dāsya*). But in Goloka, Kṛṣṇa manifests millions and millions of *gopīs* and enjoys with them continuously, oblivious to any sentiments of wedded love. In the *svakīyā* conception, *rasa* does not remain extremely inaccessible as in the *parakīyā* mood, where the obstacles to meeting make union all the more precious. Hence, from beginningless time, the *gopīs* are naturally imbued with an innate conception of being other men's wives. Śrī Kṛṣṇa therefore reciprocates with their mood, and naturally assumes the identity of their paramour, taking the help of His flute, which is His dearly beloved intimate companion, to accomplish the *rāsa* dance and other pastimes.

Goloka, which is eternally perfect and free from illusion, is the abode of divine rapture. Thus, the flow of *rasa* in the conception of paramourship finds its perfection there. Even the parental mellow is not found in Vaikuṇṭha because of the sense of awe and reverence there. However, in the fountainhead of ultimate sweetness, which is the Vraja situated in Goloka, there exists nothing but the original conception of this *rasa*. Nanda and Yaśodā are present there, but Śrī Kṛṣṇa's birth does not actually take place. In reality, parenthood does not exist in the absence of birth, so Nanda and Yaśodā only have the self-conception (*abhimāna*) of being parents. This is substantiated in the verse *jayati jana-nivāso devakī-janma-vādaḥ*. This *abhimāna* is eternal for the sake of perfect *rasa*.

By the same logic, there is no fault or transgression of scriptural prohibitions in the amorous mellow, since the *bhāvas* of being the wife of another and of being a paramour are simply eternal self-conceptions. When the essential reality of Goloka appears in manifest Vraja, both of these conceptions (being another's wife and paramourship) are seen in a tangible form by worldly vision. This is the only difference. In the mellow of parenthood, Nanda and Yaśodā's mood of being parents becomes apparent in a concrete way through birth and other pastimes; and in the amorous mellow, the idea of the Vraja maidens being the wives of others takes on a perceptible shape in the form of their marriages with Abhimanyu, Govardhana Malla and others. In reality there is no such thing as the *gopīs* having husbands, either in Gokula or in Goloka.

Śāstra therefore proclaims: "*na jātu vraja-devīnāṁ patibhiḥ saha saṅgamaḥ* – the *vraja-devīs* never had union with their husbands." Thus, Śrīla Rūpa Gosvāmī, the master of the truths of *rasa*, has written: "*patiś copapatiś ceti prabhedāv iha viśrutau* – in the resplendent mellow of amorous love, there are two types of heroes: husband and paramour." Śrīla Jīva Gosvāmī has written in his commentary on this *śloka*: "*patiḥ pura-vanitānāṁ dvitīyo vraja-vanitānām* – the hero of Dvārakā-purī's young women is called a husband, and in Vraja, the hero Śrī Kṛṣṇa is the paramour of the young women of Vraja."

This passage shows that Śrīla Jīva Gosvāmī has accepted Kṛṣṇa as the husband in Vaikuṇṭha and Dvārakā, and as the eternal paramour in Goloka-Gokula. The characteristics of a paramour are exhibited to their full extent in the Lord of Goloka-Gokula. Śrī Kṛṣṇa, who is completely self-satisfied, transgresses His natural state of self-satisfaction. The cause for this transgression is His intense passion to meet with the Vraja damsels, who are others' wives. The state of being another's wife is nothing but the eternal self-conception (*abhimāna*) of the *gopīs*. Even though the *gopīs* do not factually have real husbands, their transcendental paramour mood is fulfilled just by having the sentiment of being the wives of others. Therefore, transgressing the rules of *dharma* out of their intense attachment and all other such symptoms are eternally present in the arena of the super-excellent amorous mellow. In Bhauma-Vraja, this *bhāva* is partially visible in a tangible form to people with mundane vision.

Therefore, the simultaneous divergence and non-distinction between the transcendental mellows of wedlock and paramourship in Goloka is inconceivable by material intelligence. It can be said that there is no difference between them, and it can also be said that there is difference. Why? The essence of paramourship is loving enjoyment outside of the sanction of wedlock, and the essence of wedlock is abstention from unlawful connections. Therefore, Śrī Kṛṣṇa's loving enjoyment with *svarūpa-śakti* (His own personal potency) can also be understood as *svakīyā* by this definition.[32] Although these two, paramourship and wedlock, are one *rasa*, they exist eternally as its dual variations. Furthermore, although the form of *rasa* in Gokula is the same, mundane observers view it otherwise.

Śrī Govinda, the hero of Goloka, exhibits His qualities of being the *pati* (meaning "husband" or "shelter") of the *gopīs* as well as being their *upapati* (meaning "paramour"). Both qualities shine forth brilliantly in their pristine splendor, beyond all piety and impiety. These same characteristics also exist in the hero of Gokula, but with some diversity created by the agency of Yogamāyā. One may raise the following point: whatever Yogamāyā manifests is the Absolute Truth, so the sentiment of paramour love would similarly have to be accepted as absolutely true. To dispel this doubt, it is said that conviction in the paramour conception can exist in the relishing of *rasa*, and there is no fault in that, because it is not unfounded. However, whatever base convictions exist in mundane consciousness are faulty. They are not present in the pure, transcendental world.

Śrīla Jīva Gosvāmī has indeed given the correct, perfect philosophical conclusion, while the opposing conclusions are also inconceivably true. Simply arguing in vain about the conclusions of paramourship and wedlock is a fruitless exhibition of word jugglery. There is no possibility of any type of skepticism rising in the hearts of those who make a thorough and impartial study of the commentaries by Śrīla Jīva Gosvāmī and the "opposing

[32] The word *svakīyā* refers to a married relationship where there is a sense of propriety and proprietorship (*mamatā*): "This is my wife; this is my husband." Taken literally, it also means "one's own." Therefore it is not at all incorrect to describe Śrī Kṛṣṇa, the possessor of all potencies, as having a *svakīyā* relationship with the *gopīs*, who are His very own potency. The concept of proprietorship that exists between *sarva-śaktimān* Śrī Kṛṣṇa and the *gopīs* is far above and beyond any conception of mundane matrimony.

party." Whatever is spoken by pure Vaiṣṇavas is true and utterly free from any bias or party spirit, but there is a mystery surrounding their apparent verbal disagreements. Those whose intelligence is materialistic and lacks the spirit of devotion cannot fathom the deep secrets of the loving controversies between *śuddha* Vaiṣṇavas, and thus they wrongly conceive of such great personalities as philosophical adversaries. The great devotee Śrīla Cakravartipāda has wholeheartedly and with the utmost reverence supported the opinion that Śrī Sanātana Gosvāmī has given in his *Vaiṣṇava-toṣanī* commentary on the *śloka* from *Rāsa-pañcādhyāya* (*Śrīmad-Bhāgavatam* 10.33.35): "*gopīnāṁ tat-patīnāṁ ca* – the *gopīs* and their husbands."

When contemplating any opinion connected with the divine pastimes of Goloka and other transcendental realms, we should keep in mind the invaluable advice given by Śrīman Mahāprabhu and His followers, the Six Gosvāmīs. The Supreme Personality and Absolute Truth is never without form and attributes. Rather, He is full with variegated qualities and pleasurable engagements, which lie completely beyond the material plane.

The supremely relishable and splendid form of the mellows of transcendental service to Bhagavān, tasted through the four types of transcendentally variegated ingredients – *vibhāva*, *anubhāva*, *sāttvika* and *vyabhicārī*[33] – is eternally present in Goloka and Vaikuṇṭha. By the agency of Yogamāyā, this very *rasa* of Goloka manifests in the material realm as *vraja-rasa* for the benefit of the devotees. One should know that all the *rasas* seen in this Gokula must surely be found also in Goloka in their radiantly pure state. That is why the wonderful varieties of hero

[33] *Vibhāva* – causes for tasting *bhakti-rasa*; *anubhāva* – actions which display or reveal spiritual emotions situated within the heart; *sāttvika-bhāva* – symptoms of spiritual ecstasy arising exclusively from *viśuddha-sattva*; *vyabhicāri-bhāva* – transitory spiritual emotions.

and heroines (Kṛṣṇa and the *gopīs*), the diversity of *rasa* in them, and all the surroundings and paraphernalia of Gokula, including the land, rivers, mountain, residences, gateways, bowers (*kuñjas*), cows and so on, collectively exist in the same form in Goloka.

Only the worldly beliefs of those who are imbued with mundane intelligence are missing in Goloka. In the variegated pastimes of Vraja, different visions of Goloka are realized according to one's level of qualification. It is difficult to establish a fixed standard to determine which aspects of those varieties of visions are illusory and which are pure. A clear vision gradually arises within the heart as the eyes of devotion become cleansed through being anointed with the salve of *prema*. Therefore, there is no need to argue and counter-argue over this matter, because it will not elevate one's qualification. The truth of Goloka is filled with inconceivable *bhāva*, and any attempt to investigate this inconceivable reality by the mind would prove as unproductive as threshing empty husks. Hence, one should disregard the method of empirical knowledge, and strive for realization through the practice of unalloyed *bhakti*.

On the path of *bhakti*, it is crucial to renounce any subject matter whose acceptance would ultimately give rise to an impersonal impression. The pure paramour mellow described in the Goloka pastimes is free from all mundane conceptions, and is very rarely attained. Devotees on the path of *bhakti* following Kṛṣṇa's eternal associates in Goloka (*rāgānuga-bhakti*) should adopt this concept and perform *sādhana*. By doing so, they will realize this highly auspicious fundamental truth upon attaining perfection. When persons of gross worldly intellect endeavor for *bhakti* in the paramour mood, they generally end up engaging in immoral activity in the material sphere. Our *tattva-ācārya* Śrīla Jīva Gosvāmī took this into consideration and presented his line of thought out of great concern. The spirit of pure Vaiṣṇavism is to accept the essence of his statements. It is an offense to disregard the *ācārya* by attempting to establish another theory.

Verse 38

प्रेमाञ्जनच्छुरितभक्तिविलोचनेन
सन्तः सदैव हृदयेषु विलोकयन्ति ।
यं श्यामसुन्दरमचिन्त्यगुणस्वरूपं
गोविन्दमादिपुरुषं तमहं भजामि ॥३८॥

premāñjana-cchurita-bhakti-vilocanena
santaḥ sadaiva hṛdayeṣu vilokayanti
yaṁ śyāmasundaram acintya-guṇa-svarūpaṁ
govindam ādi-puruṣaṁ tam ahaṁ bhajāmi

Anvaya

aham bhajāmi – I perform *bhajana*; *tam* – of that; *ādi-puruṣam govindam* – original Supreme Person, Śrī Govinda; *yam* – whose; *svarūpam* – original form; *acintya-guṇa* – which is endowed with inconceivable transcendental qualities; *santaḥ* – exclusively devoted saints; *bhakti-vilocanena* – with eyes of devotion; *churita* – tinged; *prema-añjana* – with the salve of love; *eva vilokayanti* – certainly behold; *sadā* – at all times; *hṛdayeṣu* – within their purified hearts; *śyāmasundaram* – as beautiful Śyāma, the dark-hued prince of Vṛndāvana.

Translation

Saintly persons whose eyes of devotion are smeared with the salve of *prema* always behold Śrī Kṛṣṇa within their hearts as Śyāmasundara, the embodiment of inconceivable qualities. I worship that original personality, Govinda.

Ṭīkā translation

Although Śrī Kṛṣṇa's residence is in Goloka, and His qualities are inconceivable, He can nevertheless be seen by the eyes of devotion that are anointed with the black salve of unconditional love. Therefore not everyone realizes Him in the same way. His *darśana* is available according to the degree to which one has developed *prema*. Consequently, the depth of one's realization of Śrī Kṛṣṇa depends on how much one's *sādhana* is infused with *bhakti*. Therefore it is said (*Śrīmad-Bhāgavatam* 11.2.42): "*bhaktiḥ pareśānubhavo viraktiḥ* – realization of Bhagavān depends on the measure of one's *bhakti*." Furthermore, those whose hearts are filled with deep feelings of possessiveness can realize Śrī Kṛṣṇa all the more. Thus the level of perception of Śrī Kṛṣṇa's sweetness also depends on the intensity of *prema*.

Tātparya

The *śyāmasundara-svarūpa* is Śrī Kṛṣṇa's eternal form. It is personal and endowed with all qualities and attributes, and simultaneously impersonal and devoid of qualities and attributes. This is because all compatible and incompatible qualities are exquisitely reconciled within it. Saintly persons can see this form within their hearts in the trance of devotion.

The color of Śrī Kṛṣṇa's form as Śyāmasundara is not the blackish color of this world, but is the form that bestows eternal joy in that transcendental world. It cannot be perceived with material eyes. In *Śrīmad-Bhāgavatam* (1.7.4) it is stated: "*bhakti-yogena manasi, samyak praṇihite 'male, apaśyat puruṣaṁ pūrṇam* – by practice of *bhakti-yoga*, Vyāsadeva directly saw in trance within his purified heart the Supreme Personality in His complete and full manifestation." When we consider Śrīla Vyāsadeva's trance, we find that Śrī Kṛṣṇa's *svarūpa* is complete, and that He is the complete Personality of Godhead. He only appears in the heart that is enthused with *bhakti*. When Kṛṣṇa displayed His manifest pastimes in Vraja, devotees and non-devotees could see Him, but only the devotees could adore that Kṛṣṇa of Vraja as the greatest treasure of their hearts. This is because they were imbued with a loving disposition. Those whose hearts were devoid of *bhakti* could not realize His sweetness, even when they saw Him directly. Although devotees cannot see Him directly nowadays, they do see Śrī Kṛṣṇa within their love-laden hearts as He resides radiantly in Vraja-dhāma. The phrase "eyes of devotion" refers to the eyes of the *jīva's* pure transcendental form. Those eyes develop according to the advancement of one's *bhakti*, and in turn the pure vision of Śrī Kṛṣṇa's *svarūpa* is available proportionately.

When *sādhana-bhakti* attains the stage of *bhāva*, by Śrī Kṛṣṇa's mercy, the salve of *prema* is applied to the eyes of that *bhāva-bhakta*, and direct *darśana* is possible. This depends on the degree of one's devotion. The purport of this deliberation is that Śrī Kṛṣṇa's *svarūpa* as the very attractive threefold-bending Śyāmasundara – a fresh youth, the best of dancers, dressed as a cowherd boy and holding a flute (*nava-kiśora naṭavara gopa-veśa*) – is not an imaginary form. It is His trancendental constitutional form composed of eternal existence, consciousness and bliss. It can only be perceived directly with the eyes of *samādhi*, full absorption in spiritual trance.

Verse 39

रामादिमूर्त्तिषु कलानियमेन तिष्ठन्
नानावतारमकरोद्भुवनेषु किन्तु ।
कृष्णः स्वयं समभवत् परमः पुमान यो
गोविन्दमादिपुरुषं तमहं भजामि ॥३९॥

rāmādi-mūrtiṣu kalā-niyamena tiṣṭhan
nānāvatāram akarod bhuvaneṣu kintu
kṛṣṇaḥ svayaṁ samabhavat paramaḥ pumān yo
govindam ādi-puruṣaṁ tam ahaṁ bhajāmi

Anvaya

aham bhajāmi – I perform *bhajana*; *tam* – of that; *ādi-puruṣam govindam* – original Supreme Person, Śrī Govinda; *yaḥ* – who; *paramaḥ pumān* – is the Supreme Person; *kalā-niyamena* – through His forms of expanded plenary portions (*svāṁśa-kalā*); *akarot* – He performed; *nānā-avatāram* – many variegated descents as *avatāra*; *tiṣṭhan* – remaining; *bhuvaneṣu* – within the many material universes; *rāmādi-mūrtiṣu* – in the forms of Śrī Rāmacandra etc; *kintu* – however; *kṛṣṇaḥ* – as Śrī Kṛṣṇa; *svayam* – He Himself personally; *samabhavat* – descended accompanied by all of His subsidiary *avatāras* and potencies.

Translation

I worship the original personality, Govinda, who manifests Himself in the material world as Śrī Rāmacandra and many other incarnations who are His plenary portions and sub-portions, and who personally appears in the form of Śrī Kṛṣṇa.

Ṭīkā translation

It is explained in this verse beginning *rāmādi-mūrtiṣu* that Svayam Bhagavān Śrī Kṛṣṇa descends to this material world from time to time, sometimes personally and sometimes in the form of His plenary portions or sub-portions.

Śrī Kṛṣṇa, the supreme predominating enjoyer, manifests in the material world through His plenary expansions and partial expansions in forms such as Śrī Rāmacandra. Here the word *tiṣṭhan* implies that Śrī Rāma and the other *avatāras* are eternally manifest. Those *svarūpas* manifest in the creation from time to time for the welfare of the universe, and sometimes Śrī Kṛṣṇa descends personally. I perform *bhajana* of the *parama-puruṣa*, Śrī Govinda, who performs the aforementioned pastimes. For instance, in the Tenth Canto of *Śrīmad-Bhāgavatam*, the demigods have prayed:

matsyāśva-kacchapa-nṛsiṁha-varāha-haṁsa-
rājanya-vipra-vibudheṣu kṛtāvatāraḥ
tvaṁ pāsi nas tri-bhuvanaṁ ca yathādhuneśa
bhāraṁ bhuvo hara yadūttama vandanaṁ te

Śrīmad-Bhāgavatam (10.2.40)

O Bhagavān, previously You accepted incarnations as a fish, a horse, a tortoise, Narasiṁhadeva, a boar, a swan, Śrī Rāmacandra, Paraśurāma, Vipra Vāmana and various demigods to protect us and the entire world by Your mercy. Now please protect us again by diminishing the burden of Mother Earth. O Kṛṣṇa, best of the Yadus, we respectfully offer our obeisances unto You.

Tātparya

Avatāras such as Śrī Rāma, Nṛsiṁha and Varāha are called personal expansion *avatāras*. They all reside eternally in Their own *dhāmas* in Vaikuṇṭha along with Their associates, and whenever

Kṛṣṇa desires, They descend here for the welfare of the universe. All these incarnations descend to relieve the burden of the Earth, to chastise the miscreants, to establish religious principles for that age and to bestow auspiciousness upon the *jīvas*. However, whenever and wherever Bhagavān descends into this world of five material elements along with His *dhāma* and His associates, it is exclusively by His own sweet will. Similarly, Śrī Kṛṣṇa Caitanya Mahāprabhu, who is non-different from the Supreme Personality Śrī Kṛṣṇa, also appears in His original personal form (*svayaṁ-rūpa*). This is the confidential meaning of the verse.

Verse 40

यस्य प्रभा प्रभवतो जगदण्डकोटि –
कोटिष्वशेषवसुधादिविभूतिभिन्नम् ।
तद्ब्रह्म निष्कलमनन्तमशेषभूतं
गोविन्दमादिपुरुषं तमहं भजामि ॥४०॥

yasya prabhā prabhavato jagad-aṇḍa-koṭi-
koṭiṣv aśeṣa-vasudhādi vibhūti-bhinnam
tad brahma niṣkalam anantam aśeṣa-bhūtaṁ
govindam ādi-puruṣaṁ tam ahaṁ bhajāmi

Anvaya

aham bhajāmi – I perform *bhajana*; *tam* – of that; *ādi-puruṣam govindam* – original Supreme Person, Śrī Govinda; *yasya prabhā* – whose effulgence; *prabhavataḥ* – emanating from His effulgent form, which is replete with all potencies; *tat brahma* – is that divine light (Brahman); *niṣkalam* – which is free from all inebriety; *anantam* – without limitation; *aśeṣa-bhūtam* – and in complete existence (the Brahman that the Upaniṣads describe as impersonal and without qualities (*nirviśeṣa*) is constitutionally situated upon the spiritual form of Śrī Govinda, which has all transcendental qualities (*sa-viśeṣa*)); *aśeṣa-vasudhā-ādi-vibhūti-bhinnam* – and which is distinct from the unlimited opulences of the planets such as the Earth; *jagad-aṇḍa-koṭi-koṭiṣu* – within the millions and millions of universes.

Translation

I worship the original personality, Śrī Govinda. The non-differentiated, impersonal Brahman that has been described by the Upaniṣads has originated from the radiance of His limbs. That effulgence is distinct from the

majestic opulence of billions of worlds such as the Earth planet which comprise the mundane realm, and is perceived as the indivisible, unlimited, endless principle of truth.

Ṭīkā translation

The perfect completeness of Śrī Govinda, in the sense of His being the origin of all *avatāras*, has been established first. Now in this verse beginning *yasya prabhā prabhavato*, His completeness is being further established with regard to His *svarūpa*. Although Śrī Govinda and Brahman are one from the point of view of essential reality, Brahman, which is potency, is an adjective of the possessor of the potency, Śrī Govinda. This is because Śrī Govinda is *dharmī*, meaning that He possesses a nature by constitution, whereas the impersonal Brahman is His *dharma* (part of the nature that He possesses), and is thus only one aspect of His nature, namely His bodily effulgence. Therefore Śrī Govinda can be compared to the sun globe, and Brahman, which is devoid of transcendental variety, can be compared to the light that emanates from the sun. This idea is supported by this statement of the *Viṣṇu Purāṇa*: *śubhāśrayaḥ sacittasya sarvagasya tathātmanaḥ*. We have already explained this verse.

Śrīdhara Svāmī has also commented thus: Parabrahma is also the basis or shelter of Brahman. In *Bhagavad-gītā* (14.27) Svayam Bhagavān Śrī Kṛṣṇa has also said: "*brahmaṇo hi pratiṣṭhāham* – I am the sole foundation or shelter of Brahman." In *Śrīmad-Bhāgavatam* (11.16.37) Bhagavān has said while personally describing His own opulences: "I am earth, air, space, water, fire, the aggregate of material elements, transformation, *puruṣa* and the modes of goodness, passion and ignorance. I am also Parabrahma, situated beyond the material nature."

In the Eighth Canto, Śrī Matsya-deva has also stated:

madīyaṁ mahimānaṁ ca
paraṁ brahmeti śabditam
vetsyasy anugṛhītaṁ me
sampraśnair vivṛtaṁ hṛdi

Śrīmad-Bhāgavatam (8.24.38)

O Satyavrata Muni, you will be able to realize My glories from the word "Brahman," as revealed in your heart through our dialogue in the form of your questions and My answers.

In the commentary to this verse, it is stated, "O Muni, you have the desire to realize the intrinsic nature of Brahman, because you have associated with *sādhus* who are satisfied in the self. You will be successful in this by My mercy because this Brahman is My glory. It is part of My very nature, and it is all-pervading and devoid of attributes. Therefore, you will realize this impersonal Brahman only by My mercy, because Brahman is one of My aspects."

It is also stated in the story of Dhrūva in the Fourth Canto:

yā nirvṛtis tanu-bhṛtāṁ tava pāda-padma-
dhyānād bhavaj-jana-kathā-śravaṇena vā syāt
sā brahmaṇi sva-mahimany api nātha mā bhūt
kiṁ tv antakāsi-lulitāt patatāṁ vimānāt

Śrīmad-Bhāgavatam (4.9.10)

O Lord, the happiness of realizing Brahman does not contain even one particle of the bliss derived from meditating upon Your lotus feet, or hearing about Your pastimes in the company of Your dear devotees. Attaining the position of the demigods is even more insignificant, because when the celestial airships ascending to Svarga are slashed by the sword of time, the demigods fall down to the planet of death. Therefore, sages who are satisfied in the self also become attracted by the qualities of Bhagavān. The attributes of Śrī Hari are such that sages who are satisfied in the self engage in devotional service, their hearts being deeply attached to Bhagavān Urukrama. Perfect *sādhus* who have transcended the necessity to obey scriptural rules and regulations also engage in devotional service.

Thus, the bodily effulgence of Bhagavān Śrī Kṛṣṇa is called Brahman. It is endless and all-pervading. It is devoid of the narrations of pastimes, and it is by constitution uniformly non-distinct. Those who are specifically desirous of knowing this subject more elaborately may refer to *Śrī Bhāgavata-sandarbha*. There is no need to say more here.

Tātparya

The entire universe created by *māyā* is included within one-fourth of the creation of Śrī Govinda. The principle situated above this is the undifferentiated Brahman, which itself is only the light emanating from the external boundary of the transcendental cosmos which constitutes three-fourths of Śrī Govinda's creation. It is indivisible and thus one without a second (*ekam eva advitīyam*), endless and devoid of discernible features.

Verse 41

माया हि यस्य जगदण्डशतानि सूते
त्रैगुण्यतद्विषयवेदवितायमाना ।
सत्त्वावलम्बिपरसत्त्वविशुद्धसत्त्वं
गोविन्दमादिपुरुषं तमहं भजामि ॥४१॥

māyā hi yasya jagad-aṇḍa śatāni sūte
traiguṇya-tad-viṣaya-veda-vitāyamānā
sattvāvalambi-para-sattva-viśuddha-sattvaṁ
govindam ādi-puruṣaṁ tam ahaṁ bhajāmi

Anvaya

aham bhajāmi – I perform *bhajana*; *tam* – of that; *ādi-puruṣam govindam* – original Supreme Person, Śrī Govinda; *viśuddha-sattvam* – whose pure existence is free from any mixture of passion or ignorance; *para-sattva* – and upon whose supreme existence; *sattva-avalambi* – the material mode of goodness, which is mixed with passion and ignorance, is dependent; *hi* – indeed (it is He); *yasya* – whose; *māyā* – illusory potency; *sūte* – gives birth; *śatāni* – to hundreds; *jagad-aṇḍa* – of egg-like universes; *veda-vitāyamānā* – and who expands throughout the Vedas; *tad-viṣaya* – topics related to Govinda; *traiguṇya* – in terms of the three material binding qualities: goodness, passion and ignorance.

Translation

Māyā consists of the three material qualities of goodness, passion and ignorance, and is Bhagavān's inferior energy. She propagates the Vedic knowledge that pertains to the material universe. I worship the original personality Śrī Govinda, who is the shelter of that _māyā_, though His own existence is the embodiment of pure goodness untinged by passion and ignorance.

Ṭīkā translation

Brahmājī has described the glories of Bhagavān's *svarūpa*, and now in two verses he is presenting Bhagavān's glories relating to His material cosmic manifestation.

First he is describing the inconceivable activity of Bhagavān's external illusory potency, *māyā-śakti*, in creating the cosmic manifestation. Although Bhagavān causes the creation of unlimited mundane worlds through His external illusory potency, He personally remains absolutely untouched by that potency. He is eternally situated in transcendentally pure existence, which should be understood in the following way. Material nature has three qualities, namely the mode of goodness, the mode of passion and the mode of ignorance. Creation is conducted by the mode of passion, maintenance or temporary endurance is conducted by the mode of goodness mixed with passion, and destruction or devastation is conducted by the mode of ignorance. The mixture of these three qualities is called *prākṛta-sattva*, mundane existence. Existence that is not mixed with the three *guṇas*, and is beyond mundane existence, is called *śuddha-sattva*, pure existence. This pure existence is transcendental or supramundane, and it has also been called superior existence. Even superior to *śuddha-sattva* is the constitutional position of eternally remaining in one original and pristine condition. This is called *viśuddha-sattva*, perfectly pure existence. This perfectly pure existence is the function of the transcendental potency. Therefore the intrinsic nature of the worshipable form of Śrī Govinda is the state of perfectly pure existence. I perform *bhajana* of that Śrī Govinda.

In the *Viṣṇu Purāṇa* it has also been said:

sattvādayo na santīśe
yatra na prākṛtā guṇāḥ
sa śuddhaḥ sarva-śuddhebhyaḥ
pumān ādyaḥ prasīdatu

The three material qualities of goodness, passion and ignorance are not present in Bhagavān. He is completely free from the qualities of the illusory nature; that is, He is perfectly pure, and complete with all kinds of eternal supramundane qualities. Even among pure substances, the original personality is supremely pure. May He be pleased.

For specific inquiries on this subject, one can refer to *Śrī Bhāgavata-sandarbha.*

TĀTPARYA

Creation is conducted by the mode of passion, endurance by goodness mixed with passion, and destruction by ignorance. Existence mixed with the three modes of material nature has been called mundane existence (*prākṛta-sattva*). However, existence that is not mixed with passion and ignorance is called pure existence (*śuddha-sattva*). This supramundane and eternally present nature is superior existence. The intrinsic form and nature of Bhagavān, which exists permanently in that superior existence, is in the state of perfectly pure existence (*viśuddha-sattva*). It is beyond the illusory nature and the five elements of this world. It is free from material qualities and is composed of transcendental bliss (*cid-ānanda*). *Māyā* has propagated in this mundane world all the regulative Vedic knowledge that is related to the three modes of material nature.

Verse 42

आनन्दचिन्मयरसात्मतया मनःसु
यः प्राणिनां प्रतिफलन् स्मरतामुपेत्य ।
लीलायितेन भुवनानि जयत्यजस्रं
गोविन्दमादिपुरुषं तमहं भजामि ॥४२॥

ānanda-cinmaya-rasātmatayā manaḥsu
yaḥ prāṇināṁ pratiphalan smaratām upetya
līlāyitena bhuvanāni jayaty ajasraṁ
govindam ādi-puruṣaṁ tam ahaṁ bhajāmi

Anvaya

aham bhajāmi – I perform *bhajana*; *tam* – of that; *ādi-puruṣam govindam* – original Supreme Person, Śrī Govinda; *yaḥ* – who; *ātmatayā* – by the quality of His Being; *ānanda-cinmaya-rasa* – which is surcharged with the blissful mellows of the most resplendent amorous *prema*; *pratiphalan* – reflects His presence (in a partial form); *manaḥsu* – within the purified hearts; *prāṇinām* – of living beings; *smaratām upetya* – attaining the nature of a mind-enchanting Kāmadeva; *ajasram* – (He is) incessantly; *jayati* – victorious; *bhuvanāni* – over the universes; *līlāyitena* – by means of His *aṣṭa-kālīya-līlā* (eightfold daily pastimes).

Translation

When living entities remember Śrī Govinda, He is reflected in their pure hearts, appearing in His original form, which is surcharged with blissful transcendental mellows. This form is the embodiment of the most resplendent, transcendental amorous *rasa*, which churns the heart of the god of love, Cupid himself, although he

churns others' hearts. Through His pastimes, Śrī Govinda is ever victorious over the three worlds. I worship that original personality, Śrī Govinda.

Ṭīkā translation

Brahmājī has described Śrī Govindadeva's most brilliant and enchanting, love-laden nature. Now, in this verse, *ānanda-cinmaya-rasa*, he is explaining that an ardent greed to drink *vraja-rasa* appears in the hearts of sincere practitioners of *bhakti* when they associate with Vaiṣṇavas who know *tattva* and who are expert at tasting *rasa*, and when they hear their transcendental instructions. In accordance with those instructions, such genuine *sādhakas* constantly remember Śrī Kṛṣṇa's *manmatha-manmatha* form (which enchants the heart of Cupid, who agitates others' hearts) along with the names, beauty, qualities and pastimes related to it. At that time Śrī Kṛṣṇa is slightly reflected in their hearts in His form as the embodiment of the intensely amorous mellow. In this way He brings the three worlds under His direct control.

The salient point here is that He effortlessly conquers over the three worlds simply by slightly – even to an infinitesimal degree – reflecting His form that churns the heart of the all-enchanting Cupid. He achieves this simply by the remote semblance of His intrinsic form, nature and pastimes as the transcendental Cupid. Therefore Śrī Kṛṣṇa's *manmatha-manmatha* form has also been mentioned in the five chapters of *Śrīmad-Bhāgavatam* that relate the *rāsa-līlā* pastimes (10.32.2): *śākṣān manmatha-manmathaḥ*. The purport is that Śrī Kṛṣṇa is so attractive that His beauty crushes into fine powder the pride of Kāmadeva, who bewilders the whole universe. One should understand this fact by means of the example: "*cakṣuṣaś cakṣuḥ* – Kṛṣṇa is the eye of all eyes." Similarly Śrī Kṛṣṇa is the

Cupid of all Cupids. Therefore, although the Supreme Lord is the cause of Kāmadeva in the form of material lust, that Kāmadeva is thoroughly undesirable for the *jīvas* who are absorbed in lust. In the same way, although the material world is an external part of the Supreme Lord, it is thoroughly undesirable for the *sādhaka* to conceive of himself as the enjoyer of all the substances in the material world.

Tātparya

When fortunate *sādhakas* who are free from ulterior motives continually hear the pastimes of Bhagavān from the lips of devotees who are *rasika*, expert in relishing *bhagavad-rasa*, an intense greed awakens in their hearts to attain loving service in the wake of the eternal residents of Vraja. The only genuine practitioners of meditative remembrance in the process of *rāgānuga-bhakti* are those *sādhakas* who, in accordance with the good instructions of the *rasika* devotees, constantly remember the *manmatha-manmatha* form of Śrī Kṛṣṇa, and His names, beauty, qualities and pastimes in connection with *ujjvala-rasa*, the transcendental mellow of amorous love. That Śrī Kṛṣṇa, who is always engrossed in His playful antics, is manifest along with His abode in the hearts of the devotees who possess the aforementioned qualification. The *sādhaka* thus realizes the pastimes of that realm, which triumph in all respects over the sum total of all the opulence and sweetness of the entire material universe.

Verse 43

गोलोकनाम्नि निजधाम्नि तले च तस्य
देवी – महेश – हरि – धामसु तेषु तेषु ।
ते ते प्रभावनिचया विहिताश्च येन
गोविन्दमादिपुरुषं तमहं भजामि ॥४३॥

goloka-nāmni nija-dhāmni tale ca tasya
devī-maheśa-hari-dhāmasu teṣu teṣu
te te prabhāva-nicayā vihitāś ca yena
govindam ādi-puruṣaṁ tam ahaṁ bhajāmi

Anvaya

aham bhajāmi – I perform *bhajana*; *tam* – of that; *ādi-puruṣam govindam* – original Supreme Person, Śrī Govinda; *ca yena* – by whom; *nija-dhāmni* – (He who gracefully resides) in His own abode; *goloka-nāmni* – named Goloka (which is above all); *te te* – the respective; *prabhāva-nicayāḥ* – volumes of power; *vihitāḥ* – are apportioned; *teṣu teṣu* – in the respective; *devī-maheśa-hari-dhāmasu* – abodes of Vaikuṇṭhanātha-Hari, Maheśa Śiva and lastly Durgā-devī; *tale* – which are situated at the base; *tasya* – of His abode.

Translation

Devī-dhāma, the material world, consists of fourteen planetary systems. Above this lies Maheśa-dhāma, above that Hari-dhāma, and above all lies Goloka, the abode of Svayam Bhagavān Śrī Govinda. I worship the original personality Govinda, who regulates the characteristic influence pertaining to each individual abode.

Ṭīkā translation

Brahmājī has described the glories of Śrī Kṛṣṇa in relation to the material world, and he is now illuminating the glories of Śrī Kṛṣṇa's own abode in this verse beginning *goloka nāmni.* The locations of the *dhāmas* – Devī, Maheśa and so on – have been presented in ascending order in this verse. In describing how each abode, beginning from Devī-dhāma, is situated one above the other, Brahmājī defines the *svarūpa* of Śrī Kṛṣṇa's own planet, Goloka-dhāma, as existing splendidly in the supermost position. The meaning behind Goloka being the highest of all is that it encompasses all other *dhāmas*; it is all-pervading.

There is no difference between that Goloka and the Vṛndāvana manifest on the surface of this Earth. The non-different nature of these two has been described earlier. For instance, in the *Harivaṁśa* it is stated, "The worshipers of Brahman attain Brahmaloka. However, Goloka, the planet of cows, is very rarely attained. Only the *sādhaka* who is thoroughly determined and sober can reach that abode, which is free from all kinds of calamities. Goloka is not easily accessible for everyone." These two *dhāmas* have been described as non-different by this and other statements cited previously.

In the expression *goloka eva nivasati* found in verse 37, the word *eva* has been used to convey the certainty of the statement "He resides in Goloka." The purport is that Vṛndāvana, which has twelve forests, is completely protected by Śrī Vṛndā-devī. Śrī Vṛndāvana-dhāma is the eternal abode of Śrī Hari, Bhagavān Śrī Kṛṣṇa, whose lotus feet are constantly served by all the prominent demigods, such as Brahmā and Rudra.

The unique distinction of this abode is that it is the place where the God of gods, Gadādhara Śrī Kṛṣṇa, eternally enjoys His playful pastimes with His beloved *gopīs.* Many varieties of pastimes take place there, such as the Setubandha *līlā*,[34] which destroys grievous sins. In each pastime-place, Śrī Kṛṣṇa establishes a *valabhī*[35] and He becomes overjoyed in sporting every day with His friends. He spends eternal time there, in order to enjoy such pastimes.

A similar description has been given in the *Gautamīya-tantra*, wherein Śrī Nārada inquired from Bhagavān, "O Viśāmpati, maintainer of all living beings, I want to know about Vṛndāvana with its twelve forests. If I am qualified to hear, kindly explain this subject to me."

Śrī Bhagavān replied:

idaṁ vṛndāvanaṁ nāma
mama dhāmaiva kevalam
atra ye paśavaḥ pakṣi-
mṛgāḥ kīṭā narādhamāḥ

nivasanti mayāviṣṭe
mṛtā yānti mamālayam
atra yā gopa-kanyāś ca
nivasanti mamālaye

gopinyas tā mayā nityaṁ
mama sevā-parāyaṇāḥ
pañca-yojanam evāsti
vanaṁ me deha-rūpakam

[34] The Setubandha *līlā* in Vṛndāvana takes place at Setubandha-kuṇḍa in Kāmyavana. When Śrī Kṛṣṇa claims to have been Rāma in His previous birth, Lalitā-devī challenges Him to prove His bravery by building a bridge of stones with the aid of monkeys. Kṛṣṇa calls the monkeys by His flute and immediately builds a bridge across the *kuṇḍa*.

[35] A *valabhī* is a wooden pole fixed in the ground for the purpose of certain games.

kālindīyaṁ suṣumnākhyā
paramāmṛta-vāhinī
tejomayam idaṁ ramyam
adṛśyaṁ carma-cakṣuṣā

> This Vṛndāvana is exclusively My abode. All who reside here, whether they are birds, animals, worms, insects or the lowest of human beings, attain My eternal abode at the time of death because they are always absorbed in Me. All the daughters of the cowherds attain union with Me and are fully absorbed in My service. This Vṛndāvana, measuring five *yojanas*, is My body. Kālindī, the flowing current of transcendental nectar, is My *suṣumnā nāḍi.*[36] All demigods and other types of living entities reside here in a subtle form, and I am the embodiment of all the demigods. I never leave Vṛndāvana, although I appear and disappear from time to time. This *dhāma* is full of effulgence and charm. It cannot be perceived with the material eyes.

The subject of this unique Vṛndāvana-dhāma, with its eternally existing *kadamba* trees and other features, has been mentioned in Purāṇas such as the *Varāha Purāṇa.* The unmanifest Vṛndāvana-dhāma can only be seen by transcendental eyes, or by the eyes of *prema.* By such eyes one can also have *darśana* of Goloka while one is in the earthly Vṛndāvana; this is a special characteristic of the manifestation of Vṛndāvana on this Earth. Therefore it is said, "One can see Gokula in Goloka, and Goloka in Gokula." When Bhagavān Śrī Kṛṣṇa appears in the visible earthly Vṛndāvana along with His associates, that appearance is called *avatāra.* At that time, so many fascinating pastimes – meeting, separation and meeting again, and all the activities of paramour lovers – are clearly evident in order to nourish the varieties of *rasa.* Just as those pastimes are present in the earthly

36 *Suṣumnā nāḍī*: The yoga system gives this name to the prominent channel along the spine, without which one cannot function.

manifestation of Vṛndāvana, they are also going on in the manifestation that is beyond this world. An account of this fact can be found by a perusal of the scriptures such as *kalpa*, *tantra*, *yāmala*, *saṁhitā* and *pañcarātra*. These special characteristics should be understood from the various *śāstras*.

For example, it is stated in *Śrīmad-Bhāgavatam* (10.90.48):

jayati jana-nivāso devakī-janma-vādo
yadu-vara-pariṣat svair dorbhir asyann adharmam
sthira-cara-vṛjina-ghnaḥ su-smita-śrī-mukhena
vraja-pura-vanitānāṁ vardhayan kāma-devam

Śrī Kṛṣṇa resides in everyone's heart as the Supersoul. (Or: He lives among His own near and dear relatives, the *gopas* or Yādavas. Or: He is present in the heart of every *jīva* and He is the shelter of all.) It is only a rumor that He was born from the womb of Devakī; actually He has no birth. He is served by the best of the Yadu dynasty. (Or: He is the honorable chairman in the assembly of the Yādavas.) Although He can accomplish anything simply by His desire, by the strength of His own arms (or: by the strength of His arms in the form of His associates like Bhīma and Arjuna), He destroys the demons who oppose the principles of religion. He takes away the pain of the endless chain of birth and death from all moving and non-moving living entities. (Or: He takes away the pain of separation that all moving and non-moving living entities in Vraja-purī feel in His absence.) He increases the transcendental desire of all the young *gopīs* of Vraja-purī (or: of all the ladies of Mathurā-purī, Dvārakā-purī and Vraja-purī) by His smiling lotus face. May that Śrī Kṛṣṇa be ever victorious.

Furthermore, in the *Nirvāṇa-khaṇḍa* of the *Padma Purāṇa*, in the conversation between Śrī Bhagavān and Śrī Vyāsa, it is stated:

paśya tvaṁ darśayiṣyāmi...gopa-bālakaiḥ

Bhagavān said, "O Vyāsa, I am bestowing upon you the vision of My original form, which is hidden even from the Vedas. Behold this transcendental form." After seeing Bhagavān's *svarūpa*, Śrī

Vyāsadeva said, "O King, I have seen that Supreme Personality Śrī Kṛṣṇa, whose dark blue complexion resembles a fresh raincloud. He is surrounded by cowherd damsels (*gopa-kanyā*), and He is laughing with the cowherd boys."

The word *kanyā* (in the second verse quoted on page 243) indicates the particular distinction of the *gopīs*, namely that although they are mature youths, they have not attained womanhood. Or, although they are fully in love with Śrī Kṛṣṇa, they are still innocent girls who have not blossomed into fertility. By saying that they have not attained adulthood, it is to be understood that they are eternal adolescents (*nitya-kiśorī*). Thus by referring to them as *kanyā*, the idea that the *gopīs* are similar to other women has been demolished.

The same conception has been presented in the Fourth Chapter of the *Gautamīya-tantra* wherein it is stated: "*atha vṛndāvanaṁ dhyāyet* – then one may meditate on Vṛndāvana." After this there is a description of how to meditate on Vṛndāvana. "The entire cowherd community, including millions of *gopa-kanyās*, cows and calves, have descended from Svarga (Goloka-dhāma) and are beautifying the whole of Vṛndāvana. In that charming forest of Vṛndāvana, thousands upon thousands of *gopīs* with long eyes like blooming lotuses perform worship (*arcana* and *pūjā*) of the *guru* of the three worlds, Śrī Hari, with the flowers of their *bhāvas*."

Similarly, in the same scripture, it has been said in relation to the appropriate conduct of all those who aspire to have *darśana* of Śrī Kṛṣṇa or who have had His *darśana*:

ahar-niśaṁ japen mantraṁ
mantrī niyata-mānasaḥ
sa paśyati na sandeho
gopa-rūpa-dharaṁ harim

The *sādhaka* should chant *japa* of the *kṛṣṇa-mantra* day and night with constant, single-minded attention. That devotee definitely receives *darśana* of Śrī Kṛṣṇa in His cowherd boy dress. There is no doubt about it.

Furthermore, it is mentioned elsewhere in the *Gautamīya-tantra*: "*vṛndāvane vased dhīmān yāvat kṛṣṇasya darśanam* – highly intelligent persons always see Śrī Kṛṣṇa for as long as they reside in Vṛndāvana."

In the section concerning the eighteen-syllable *mantra* in the *Trailokya-sammohana-tantra*, it is stated, "Whoever performs the *sādhana* of this *mantra* will definitely behold Śrī Kṛṣṇa's cowherd boy form."

Therefore in the *Gopāla-tāpanī Upaniṣad* (27) one can find the following statement by Brahmājī beginning with *tad u hovāca*: "My dear child, when I was in the first part of my vast duration of life, I meditated on and offered prayers to Śrī Kṛṣṇa. At that time, when a *brāhmī-niśā* (4.32 billion years) had passed, He appeared in my heart in His cowherd boy dress."

Although Śrī Kṛṣṇa has been described as the Supreme Controller, the Supreme Brahman, the Supreme Personality and so on, in a few places He has been described as an *avatāra* of Śrī Kṣīrodakaśāyī Viṣṇu. This kind of description has been given only because the partial incarnations are within Him. Therefore it is not necessary to elaborate upon this point any further. A detailed exposition has been given in *Śrī Kṛṣṇa-sandarbha.*

After thus describing the glories of Bhagavān in relation to the material world, Brahmājī is now describing the glories of Bhagavān's own personal abode in this verse 43 beginning *goloka nāmni.* Śrī Goloka-dhāma exists splendidly above all other planets, but Brahmājī, the grandfather of the material planetary systems, resides in Brahmaloka, which is within Devī-dhāma. Consequently, he is describing the glories of Bhagavān existing in the different worlds from bottom to top. This sequence is exactly opposite to the factual order, in which Śrī Goloka is topmost, followed by Vaikuṇṭhaloka, then Maheśaloka, and finally Devīloka. The glories of Bhagavān are manifest in those worlds to varying degrees corresponding to their lower and higher positions. The supermost position and omnipresence of Goloka-dhāma is established everywhere in *śāstra*. If it is suggested that Śrī Vṛndāvana is situated within Devī-dhāma, one may reply that it cannot be so. Even though Vṛndāvana appears to be situated on the Earth planet, this perception is possible only by the influence of Yogamāyā; factually, Śrī Vṛndāvana-Gokula-dhāma is non-different from Śrī Goloka. We have already presented scriptural evidence to show that these two *dhāmas* are non-different. In the *Harivaṁśa* (*Viṣṇu-parva*, chapter 19), the following account has been given:

gavām eva tu goloko
durārohā hi sā gatiḥ
sa tu lokas tvayā kṛṣṇa
sīdamānaḥ kṛtātmanā
dhṛto dhṛtimatā vīra
nighnatopadravān gavām

O Kṛṣṇa, O Vīra, O calm and steadfast Supreme Person, You are capable of achieving anything. When the planet called Vṛndāvana was distressed, You remembered it and delivered the whole of Gokula, the cows and *gopīs* from all calamities.

This statement supports the idea that Goloka and Vṛndāvana are non-different. The use of the word *eva* in the phrase *goloka eva nivasati* in verse 37 expresses the non-difference of Goloka and Vṛndāvana. This non-difference is indicated by descriptions in the *śāstras* which state that Śrī Kṛṣṇa eternally resides in the place called Vṛndāvana that is manifest in Bhūloka (planet Earth). For example, in the *Ādi-Varāha Purāṇa* it is stated: *vṛndāvanaṁ dvādaśakaṁ...sevitam.*

Tātparya

Śrī Goloka-dhāma exists splendidly above all other worlds. Brahmājī is looking up in the direction of Goloka from his own position in Brahmaloka or Satyaloka, which is within Devī-dhāma, and he is describing the glories of Bhagavān that are present first of all in Devī-dhāma, and above that Maheśa-dhāma and so on. In this material world, which is called Devī-dhāma, there are seven upper planetary systems, namely Bhūḥ, Bhuvaḥ, Svaḥ, Mahaḥ, Janaḥ, Tapaḥ and Satya, and seven lower planetary systems, namely Atala, Vitala, Sutala, Talātala, Rasātala, Mahātala and Pātāla. Thus there are fourteen planetary systems within Devī-dhāma.

Above Devī-dhāma lies Śiva's abode, in which one part is in darkness and the other part is illuminated. The dark portion is celebrated by the name of Mahākāla-dhāma, and the light portion is renowned by the name of Sadāśivaloka. Hari-dhāma or the Vaikuṇṭhaloka in the spiritual world is situated above that Sadāśivaloka.

Influence (*prabhāva*) is present in Devī-dhāma as *māyā's* majestic opulence, and in Śiva-dhāma as the grandeur of time, the aggregate of material elements, and the semblance of a plenary portion of Bhagavān who manifests in the form of Śambhu via the transforming agent of the minuteness aspect of the marginal potency (this is described in detail in verse 45). However, in Hari-dhāma Vaikuṇṭha there is the influence of transcendental opulence, while the influence of the supreme sweetness that usurps all opulence is wonderfully present in Goloka. The original personality, Govindadeva, directly or indirectly ordains all these influences, and regulates them in the various abodes.

Verse 44

सृष्टि – स्थिति – प्रलय – साधनशक्तिरेका
छायेव यस्य भुवनानि बिभर्त्ति दुर्गा ।
इच्छानुरूपमपि यस्य च चेष्टते सा
गोविन्दमादिपुरुष तमहं भजामि ॥४४॥

sṛṣṭi-sthiti-pralaya-sādhana-śaktir ekā
chāyeva yasya bhuvanāni bibharti durgā
icchānurūpam api yasya ca ceṣṭate sā
govindam ādi-puruṣaṁ tam ahaṁ bhajāmi

Anvaya

aham bhajāmi – I perform *bhajana*; *tam* – of that; *ādi-puruṣam govindam* – original Supreme Person, Śrī Govinda; *yasya* – whose; *śaktiḥ* – potency; *durgā* – Durgā-devī; *iva chāyā* – who is like a shadow (of His transcendental potency); *bibharti* – nurtures; *bhuvanāni* – all the planetary systems; *ca* – and; *api ceṣṭate* – she also acts (thus); *yasya icchā-anurūpam* – in accordance with His will; *ekā* – she alone; *sādhana* – executes; *sṛṣṭi-sthiti-pralaya* – the duties of creation, sustenance and dissolution.

Translation

The shadow of the transcendental potency is that great potency who creates, maintains and annihilates the material universe. She is worshiped throughout the world as Durgā. I worship the original personality, Śrī Govinda, in accordance with whose desire Durgā conducts her every endeavor.

Ṭīkā translation

In the previous *śloka*, Brahmājī has described Devī-dhāma, Maheśa-dhāma and Hari-dhāma, as well as Goloka-dhāma, which is situated above all of them. Now the respective shelters of all those *dhāmas*, that is their presiding deities, are being described in five consecutive *ślokas* beginning with this present verse 44. The presiding deity of the fourteen planetary systems within the mundane realm is Durgā, of whom the personified Vedas speak as follows:

tvam akaraṇaḥ sva-rāḍ akhila-kāraka-śakti-dharas
tava balim udvahanti samadanty ajayānimiṣāḥ
varṣa-bhujo 'khila-kṣiti-pater iva viśva-sṛjo
vidadhati yatra ye tv adhikṛtā bhavataś cakitāḥ

Śrīmad-Bhāgavatam (10.87.28)

O Prabhu, although You are the independent controller, and have no connection with the material senses, the entire ability of all living beings to function with their working senses is conducted by You. O Śrī Govinda, Master of Goloka, the presiding deities headed by Durgā-devī and Maheśa present all the offerings of their *pūjā* unto Your illustrious lotus feet, just as the presiding lords of separate kingdoms accept the gifts presented by their respective subjects and in turn present them to the emperor. As everyone executes their prescribed work in accordance with their respective qualifications out of fear of You, similarly Durgā-devī surrenders the offerings made in her worship to Your lotus feet, although she is the presiding deity of her abode.

Tātparya

The specific attributes of Devī-dhāma have already been described, and now the presiding deity of that abode is being described in the current *śloka*. The place from which Brahmājī is offering his prayers to the Lord of Goloka is the universe composed of fourteen planetary systems known as Devī-dhāma, and its presiding deity is Durgā, whose ten arms represent the tenfold fruitive activities. She is known as Siṁha-vāhinī, because she rides upon a lion as an expression of her heroic prowess. As the subduer of sins, she is known as Mahiṣāsura-mardinī, because she tramples down the demon Mahiṣa, who is sin personified. She is the mother of two sons, Kārttika and Gaṇeśa, who represent beauty and success, and she is situated in the middle of her associates, Lakṣmī and Sarasvatī, who are, respectively, material opulence and material knowledge personified. In order to subdue sin, she holds twenty kinds of weapons, which comprise the ways of righteousness defined in the Vedas. Because her beauty is all-devouring time, she is Sarpa-śobhinī, adorned with a serpent. Thus Durgājī is distinguished by possessing all these forms.

The name Durgā means prison. This refers to the confinement of the *jīvas* born from the marginal potency (*taṭastha-śakti*) who, due to their aversion to Śrī Kṛṣṇa, are confined within the dungeon of the gross material elements. These bound *jīvas* are punished by being crushed in the wheel of fruitive activities. Only to fulfill Śrī Govindadeva's desire, Durgā continuously performs this task as the method to purify the living entities who are averse to Him. The living entities turn their attention within when, by good fortune and the influence of the association of enlightened devotees, they give up their indifference to Kṛṣṇa. Then, again in accordance with the desires of Śrī Govinda, Durgā brings about their liberation. Therefore, one should try to attain the genuine, non-deceptive favor of the prison warden Durgā by pleasing her through one's mood of introspection and attentiveness to Bhagavān. One should understand that, if one begs from Devī benedictions such as wealth, followers, sons, family members and freedom from ill health, her kindness in fulfilling such boons is deceptive. Durgā manifests the ten varieties of knowledge (*daśa-mahāvidyā*) so that the bewildered *jīvas* in the mundane realm can pursue mundane knowledge.

The living entity is a minute spiritual particle, but due to the defect of being indifferent to Kṛṣṇa he becomes agitated by the attraction of *māyā*. As soon as the living entity is thus agitated, Durgā dresses him in a gross material body, which can be compared to a convict's prison clothes. The gross material body is composed of the five gross elements, the five sense-objects and the eleven senses. When the *jīva* is thus attired, Durgā places him in the cycle of fruitive work, wherein he tastes material experiences such as happiness and distress in heaven and hell. In addition to this gross body, she also endows him with a subtle body composed of mind, intelligence and false ego. When the *jīva* gives up one gross body, he carries the subtle body with him to the next gross body. The subtle body, composed of ignorant and sinful desires, cannot be discarded until the *jīva* attains liberation. After ridding himself of the subtle body, the *jīva* bathes in the Virajā River and goes to Hari-dhāma. Durgā-devī performs all these duties in accordance with Śrī Govinda's desire.

vilajjamānayā yasya
sthātum īkṣa-pathe 'muyā
vimohitā vikatthante
mamāham iti durdhiyaḥ

Śrīmad-Bhāgavatam (2.5.13)

The illusory energy of the Lord cannot take precedence, being ashamed of her position, but those who are bewildered by her always talk nonsense, being absorbed in thoughts of "I" and "mine."

In *Śrīmad-Bhāgavatam* it is also said that Durgā's relationship is with the *jīvas* who have turned away from Kṛṣṇa. The Durgā-devī who is worshiped in the mundane world is the shadow aspect of Durgā, whereas the Durgā who takes the form of the covering of Śrī Bhagavān's abode in the form of *mantra* is a pure, spiritual maidservant of Kṛṣṇa, and the shadow aspect of Durgā performs her duties in the mundane world as the servant of the Durgā in the spiritual world. In this connection one may study the commentary on the third verse of *Śrī Brahma-saṁhitā*.

Verse 45

क्षीरं यथा दधि विकारविशेषयोगात्
सञ्जायते न हि ततः पृथगस्ति हेतोः ।
यः शम्भुतामपि तथा समुपैति कार्याद्
गोविन्दमादिपुरुषं तमहं भजामि ॥४५॥

kṣīraṁ yathā dadhi vikāra-viśeṣa-yogāt
sañjāyate na hi tataḥ pṛthag asti hetoḥ
yaḥ śambhutām api tathā samupaiti kāryād
govindam ādi-puruṣaṁ tam ahaṁ bhajāmi

Anvaya

aham bhajāmi – I perform *bhajana*; *tam* – of that; *ādi-puruṣam govindam* – original Supreme Person, Śrī Govinda; *yaḥ* – who; *upaiti* – takes on; *śambhutām* – the state of Śambhu; *kāryāt* – on account of performing a special duty; *yathā tathā* – in the same way that; *kṣīram* – milk; *sañjāyate* – becomes; *dadhi* – yogurt; *vikāra-viśeṣa-yogāt* – through contact with a transforming agent; *asti* – is; *hi* – certainly; *na* – not; *pṛthak* – different; *tataḥ* – than; *hetoḥ* – its cause (milk).

Translation

Śrī Govindadeva attains the condition of being Śambhu for the sake of performing a specific function, just as milk is transformed into yogurt by contact with a particular transforming agent, although yogurt is not a different substance, independent of milk, which is its cause. I worship that original personality, Śrī Govinda.

Ṭīkā translation

The next subject, in ascending order, is Maheśvara Śiva, whose *svarūpa* is being defined in this verse beginning *kṣīraṁ yathā*. Just as milk is transformed into yogurt by contact with a transforming agent, Śrī Govinda similarly accepts the form of Śambhu in order to accomplish a specific purpose. The example of yogurt is given in order to convey the idea of cause and effect. Here the transformation aspect of the analogy is not applicable, for this example has not been given to convey the idea of transformation. The reason for this is that Śrī Govindadeva is a reality who cannot be transformed, so it is not possible for Him to undergo any kind of distortion. A wish-fulfilling gem manifests many things according to one's desire, yet its constitutional nature remains untransformed; the desired articles are manifest by the influence of its inconceivable potency. Similarly, although Bhagavān Śrī Govinda manifests in the form of the instrumental cause Śambhu, His *svarūpa* remains unchanged.

As stated in *śruti*:

eko ha vai puruṣo nārāyaṇa āsīn na brahmā na ca śaṅkaraḥ
sa munir bhūtvā samacintayat
tata ete vyajāyanta viśvo hiraṇyagarbho 'gnir
varuṇa-rudrendrās tathā
sa brahmaṇā sṛjati rudreṇa nāśayati ity ādi

Before the creation only the Supreme Person Bhagavān Nārāyaṇa existed. At that time neither Brahmā nor even Śaṅkara was there. Bhagavān, taking the form of a sage, began to contemplate the means for bringing about the creation of the universe, which then took place through Hiraṇyagarbha; Agni, Varuṇa, Rudra, Indra and the other demigods also became manifest. Furthermore, Bhagavān takes the form of Brahmā to create, and the form of Rudra to destroy, but Śrī Hari Himself, who is the intrinsic form of supreme bliss, is completely devoid of the influences of creation and dissolution. He performs the duties of cosmic creation, maintenance and destruction in the forms of the *guṇa-avatāras*. His quality of being Śambhu occurs by his acceptance of material modes, such as the mode of ignorance.

For example, it is stated in *Śrīmad-Bhāgavatam* (10.88.5):

harir hi nirguṇaḥ sākṣāt
puruṣaḥ prakṛteḥ paraḥ
śiva-śakti-yutaḥ śaśvat
tri-liṅgo guṇa-saṁvṛtaḥ

Śrī Hari, who is transcendental to material nature and free from mundane qualities, is directly the Supreme Personality of Godhead. However, Śiva is simultaneously possessed of three types of false ego, namely goodness, passion and ignorance, and he is always connected with the illusory potency. Therefore, a *jīva* can only become transcendental to the material modes by the performance of *śrī hari-bhajana*.

To further clarify this point, this verse 45 specifically states *vikāra-viśeṣa-yogāt*. Śiva is fully in contact with the external illusory potency, which is subject to transformation. For this reason *śiva-tattva* is sometimes described as being different from Śrī Hari, and sometimes as being non-different. To resolve the difference between them, it is stated herein that Śiva is not an independent controller or cause separate from the cause of all causes, Śrī Hari. His dominion or aspect as controller is subordinate to the dominion of the Absolute Truth, Śrī Hari.

As it is stated in the *Ṛg Veda*, "Thus, hereafter it should be known that the one Nārāyaṇa is indeed eternal. Brahmā is Nārāyaṇa, Śiva is Nārāyaṇa, Indra is Nārāyaṇa, time is Nārāyaṇa and the ten directions are also Nārāyaṇa. Nārāyaṇa is below, Nārāyaṇa is above, Nārāyaṇa is within, Nārāyaṇa is without and whatever exists in this universe is also nothing but Nārāyaṇa."

In the Second Canto of *Śrīmad-Bhāgavatam* Brahmājī has stated, "I create by the inspiration of Bhagavān, Śrī Śiva also destroys in subordination to Him, and Śrī Hari Himself, equipped with His three potencies, also performs the function of maintenance through the agency of His *puruṣa-avatāras.*" In this way Bhagavān accomplishes the creation, destruction and maintenance of the universes through His three potencies, namely goodness, passion and ignorance.

Tātparya

The current verse beginning *kṣīraṁ yathā* is an analysis of the *svarūpa* of Śambhu, the previously mentioned presiding deity of Maheśa-dhāma. Actually Śambhu is not a separate lord, independent of Śrī Kṛṣṇa, and those who think that he is are offensive to Bhagavān. Śambhu's status as a lord is subordinate to and dependent upon Śrī Govinda's overlordship. Thus they are factually non-different realities. The example of that non-difference is that as milk is transformed into yogurt by contact with a specific transforming agent, similarly by union with a special transforming agent, the Supreme Lord takes on a separate form, which is dependent on Him; this separate form has no independence.

In this case, the special transforming agent is constituted of a mixture of *māyā's* aspect of the mode of ignorance, the non-plenitude or minuteness aspect of the marginal potency, and a slight degree of the combined knowledge (*saṁvit*) and bliss (*hlādinī*) aspects of the transcendental potency. The effulgent subordinate controller in the form of Śambhu *liṅga*, being united with this special transforming agent, is constitutionally the semblance of an expansion of the Supreme Godhead. He is the Sadāśiva from whom Rudradeva is manifest. Śrī Govinda is manifest in the form of Śambhu as *guṇa-avatāra*, in order to arrange the ingredient materials for creation, to annihilate certain *asuras* for the purpose of universal maintenance, and to execute all functions of destruction. This Śambhu is a separated expansion imbued with the mood of a plenary expansion, and he is also known as *kāla-puruṣa*, the personified time factor. In this regard a body of evidence has been cited in Śrīla Jīva Gosvāmī's commentary.

In *Śrīmad-Bhāgavatam* (12.13.16) it is stated: "*vaisnavānāṁ yathā śambhuḥ* – of all Vaiṣṇavas, Śambhu is the greatest." The purport of such statements is that Śambhu meets together with Durgā-devī and performs his function through his own time-potency in accordance with Śrī Govinda's desire. Many *śāstras* headed by the *tantras* give instruction to follow the principles of righteous conduct in accordance with the level of eligibility of the respective *jīvas*. These principles are compared to a ladder with steps that eventually lead to the attainment of *bhakti*. Furthermore, in accord with Govinda's desire, Śambhu maintains and protects pure devotional service by preaching Māyāvāda philosophy and imaginary supplementary scriptures (*āgamas*).[37] The fifty qualities of the *jīvas* are present in abundance in Śambhu, and five more great qualities not attainable by ordinary living entities are partially manifest in him. Thus, one cannot say that Śambhu is a *jīva*. Although his nature is that of a separated expansion, he is still a lord and controller (*iśvara*).

[37] How did Śambhu in the form of Ācārya Śaṅkara protect pure *bhakti* by preaching Māyāvāda philosophy, which is opposed to *bhakti*? By propagating the Māyāvāda doctrine, Śaṅkarācārya supplanted voidism and re-established a system which accepts the authority of the Vedas. Also, by focusing the living entities who are not inclined toward *bhakti* on the concept of "I am God," he turned them away from deep-seated envy of Vaiṣṇavas.

Verse 46

दीपार्च्चिरेव हि दशान्तरमभ्युपेत्य
दीपायते विवृतहेतुसमानधर्मा ।
यस्तादृगेव हि च विष्णुतया विभाति
गोविन्दमादिपुरुषं तमहं भजामि ॥४६॥

dīpārcir eva hi daśāntaram abhyupetya
dīpāyate vivṛta-hetu-samāna-dharmā
yas tādṛg eva hi ca viṣṇutayā vibhāti
govindam ādi-puruṣaṁ tam ahaṁ bhajāmi

Anvaya

dīpa-arciḥ eva hi – just as the flame of a lamp; *abhyupetya* – having been brought; *daśā-antaram* – to another lamp; *dīpāyate* – causes illumination; *vivṛta* – which is displayed; *samāna-dharmā* – in the same nature; *hetu* – as the original lamp; *aham bhajāmi* – I perform *bhajana*; *tam* – of that; *ādi-puruṣam govindam* – original Supreme Person, Śrī Govinda; *yaḥ vibhāti* – who illuminates; *viṣṇutayā* – through His Viṣṇu expansions; *tādṛk eva hi* – in exactly the same way.

Translation

I worship the original personality, Śrī Govinda. Just as when the flame of one lamp is transmitted to another lamp, the second lamp illuminates in the same manner as the original flame, although it exists separately, so does Govinda accept the form of Mahā-Viṣṇu reclining on the Causal Ocean. That Mahā-Viṣṇu is the source of all the Viṣṇu expansions and incarnations in this world.

Ṭīkā translation

Following the sequence given in verse 43, after the discussion of the *guṇa-avatāra* Maheśa, in order to further clarify the unique *svarūpa* of Śrī Hari, this *śloka* beginning *dīpārcir eva* is spoken to describe the position of the *guṇa-avatāra* Śrī Viṣṇu.

As one lamp can be used to light many other lamps, which can all shine in the same way as the original lamp, similarly Kāraṇodakaśāyī Mahā-Viṣṇu is the portion of a portion of Śrī Govinda; Garbhodakaśāyī Viṣṇu is an expansion of Mahā-Viṣṇu; and Kṣīrodakaśāyī Viṣṇu is in turn an expansion of Garbhodakaśāyī Viṣṇu. Although the light emanating from a large lamp is transmitted to a succession of lamps via a small flame, the lights are all as pure and bright as that of the original one. From the point of view of light, they are all equal. However, since the pastime of Śambhu is to be the presiding deity of the mode of ignorance, he can be compared to the flame in a sooty lamp that is filled with smoke, rather than a flame from a cleanly burning lamp. Thus, he is not of the same nature as Śrī Govinda. Mahā-Viṣṇu is a specific expansion of an expansion of Śrī Govinda. This will be discussed elaborately in the coming verses.

Tātparya

In the verse under discussion, the presiding deity of Hari-dhāma, who is named variously as Hari, Nārāyaṇa, Viṣṇu, etc., is being described as a plenary expansion. The Lord of Vaikuṇṭha, Śrī Nārāyaṇa, is the pastime form of Śrī Kṛṣṇa. His expansion is the first of the *puruṣa-avatāras*, Kāraṇodakaśāyī Mahā-Viṣṇu, who in turn expands as the second *puruṣa-avatāra*, Garbhodakaśāyī Viṣṇu, who further expands as the third *puruṣa-avatāra*, Kṣīrodakaśāyī Viṣṇu. The word "Viṣṇu" indicates "He who is known by His all-pervasiveness, which extends across all situations and conditions." Although He descends to the mundane universe, he remains omnipresent and in every way transcendental to the influence of the illusory potency. In this verse the nature of pastime expansions is being described by defining the nature of Kṣīrodakaśāyī Viṣṇu. *Viṣṇu-tattva*, the presiding deity of the material mode of goodness, is distinguished from *śambhu-tattva* by the latter's intermingling with the qualities of *māyā*. The purport is that Viṣṇu also possesses Śrī Govinda's intrinsic nature. Both have the quality of having a purely transcendental *svarūpa*. Because Viṣṇu is manifest from Śrī Govinda, He has the same constitutional nature as Śrī Govinda, that is to say, *viṣṇu-tattva* is completely pure and transcendental to *māyā*. The mundane mode of goodness present in the material energy composed of the three material modes is mixed with passion and ignorance; thus it is called impure goodness.

Brahmā is endowed with the potency of a personal expansion, but is a separated expansion mixed with the mode of passion, while Śambhu, who also has the potency of a personal expansion, is a separated expansion mixed with the material mode of ignorance. Since both principles are separated expansions mixed with the material modes of passion and ignorance respectively, they are extremely unconscious, or insentient. For this reason, they have been cast very far away from the original form (*svayaṁ-rūpa*), and from the expanded forms of the Divinity (*tad-ekātma-rūpa*). However, although Viṣṇu, the presiding deity of the material mode of goodness, is situated within the material mode of goodness, He is an expansion of Śrī Kṛṣṇa whose nature is in unalloyed pure goodness, and He is also situated in unalloyed pure goodness beyond the qualities of *māyā*. Therefore Viṣṇu, being fully the Supreme Controller and a pastime expansion, is not in contact with *māyā*; rather, He is the Lord of *māyā*.

Viṣṇu is aware that he is Śrī Govinda's personal expansion. Śrī Govinda's complete opulence, which consists of sixty qualities, is fully displayed in His pastime form, Śrī Nārāyaṇa. Brahmā and Śiva are mixed with the modes of material nature, and thus they are not unalloyed principles like Viṣṇu, although they are presiding deities of the material modes. Śrī Nārāyaṇa appears in the form of Kāraṇodakaśāyī Mahā-Viṣṇu, Mahā-Viṣṇu appears in the form of Garbhodakaśāyī, who in turn appears as Kṣīrodakaśāyī. Such appearances are examples of Viṣṇu's all-pervading nature. One whose individual *svarūpa* is manifest everywhere is called *cariṣṇu.* Viṣṇu is the only supreme controller; apart from Him the two other presiding deities of the material modes, as well as all of the demigods, are principles of subordinate authority. Garbhodakaśāyī Viṣṇu and Kṣīrodakaśāyī Viṣṇu, as well as the personal expansions such as Rāma, are manifest from Mahā-Viṣṇu, who is also a pastime form. Śrī Govinda is likened to the original great flame from whom the pastime expansion Kāraṇodakaśāyī Mahā-Viṣṇu is expanded. All personal expansions are likened to separately situated flames transmitted from the original. All such personal expansions shine brilliantly and forever through the agency of Śrī Govinda's transcendental potency.

Verse 47

यः कारणार्णवजले भजति स्म योग –
निद्रामनन्तजगदण्डसरोमकूपः ।
आधारशक्तिमवलम्ब्य परां स्वमूर्त्तिं
गोविन्दमादिपुरुषं तमहं भजामि ॥४७॥

yaḥ kāraṇārṇava-jale bhajati sma yoga-
nidrām ananta-jagad-aṇḍa-sa-roma-kūpaḥ
ādhāra-śaktim avalambya parāṁ sva-mūrtiṁ
govindam ādi-puruṣaṁ tam ahaṁ bhajāmi

Anvaya

aham bhajāmi – I perform *bhajana*; *tam* – of that; *ādi-puruṣam govindam* – original Supreme Person, Śrī Govinda; *yaḥ* – who; *bhajati sma* – enjoys; *yoga-nidrām* – mystic slumber (of His personal intrinsic potency); *jale* – in the water; *kāraṇa-arṇava* – of the Causal Ocean; *sa-roma-kūpaḥ* – within His hair follicles; *ananta-jagad-aṇḍa* – (are) the limitless universes; *avalambya* – reposing upon; *parām* – the most excellent; *sva-mūrtim* – His own personal form (His expansion named Ananta); *ādhāra-śaktim* – who is the embodiment of His all-accommodating potency.

Translation

I worship that original personality, Śrī Govinda. Having assumed His own most excellent form, Śeṣa, the embodiment of the all-accommodating potency, He enjoys mystic slumber while reclining in the Causal Ocean with innumerable universes within every hair-pore of His skin.

Ṭīkā translation

Now the principle of Kāraṇodakaśāyī Viṣṇu is being described. Unlimited millions of universes are situated in each of the hair-pores of His skin; when He exhales, countless universes are released, and they enter into Him again along with His inhalation. This Mahā-Viṣṇu rests within the causal water. The word *sa*, meaning "with," in the phrase *sa-roma-kūpaḥ* is an exception to grammatical formulae, and is thus considered to be acceptable due to its use by authoritative *ṛṣis*. Bhagavān Śeṣa (Anantadeva) is His own great personal form imbued with His all-accommodating potency. Reposing upon Śeṣa, who takes the form of His bed, the Lord enjoys with Yogamāyā.

Tātparya

In this verse the *tattva* of Anantadeva, taking the form of Mahā-Viṣṇu's bed, is described. Anantadeva is the bed on which Mahā-Viṣṇu reposes. This *avatāra* of Bhagavān named Śeṣa is in the category of a servant of Śrī Kṛṣṇa.

Verse 48

यस्यैकनिश्वसितकालमथावलम्ब्य
जीवन्ति लोमबिलजा जगदण्डनाथाः ।
विष्णुर्महान् स इह यस्य कलाविशेषो
गोविन्दमादिपुरुषं तमहं भजामि ॥४८॥

yasyaika-niśvasita-kālam athāvalambya
jīvanti loma-bilajā jagad-aṇḍa-nāthāḥ
viṣṇur mahān sa iha yasya kalā-viśeṣo
govindam ādi-puruṣaṁ tam ahaṁ bhajāmi

Anvaya

atha – thereafter; *aham bhajāmi* – I perform *bhajana*; *tam* – of that; *ādi-puruṣam govindam* – original Supreme Person, Śrī Govinda; *yasya* – whose; *kalā-viśeśaḥ* – special plenary portion; *saḥ mahān viṣṇuḥ* – (is) Mahā-Viṣṇu; *jagad-aṇḍa-nāthāḥ* – the lords of the material universes, Brahmā, Viṣṇu and Śiva; *avalambya* – taking shelter (of Him); *loma-bila-jāḥ* – become manifest within His hair-pores; *jīvanti* – they live; *iha* – in their respective universes; *yasya eka-niśvasita-kālam* – for the time-period of His one breath.

Translation

The lords of the universes, such as Brahmā, who emanate from the hair-pores of Mahā-Viṣṇu's skin, remain alive only for the duration of His one exhalation. I worship the original personality, Śrī Govinda, of whom Mahā-Viṣṇu is a portion of a portion.

ṬĪKĀ TRANSLATION

Mahā-Viṣṇu, who has been mentioned in the discussion of *avatāras*, is Śrī Govinda's *avatāra*, and is a portion of a plenary portion of His plenary portion. He is the protector of all the universes, and although He assists Garbhodakaśāyī Viṣṇu in the form of Mahā-Brahmā, or Hiraṇyagarbha Prajāpati,[38] Mahā-Viṣṇu is non-different from Garbhodakaśāyī Viṣṇu. His intrinsic nature is being defined in this verse. Headed by Brahmā, countless masters of the individual universes become manifest from the hair-pores of Mahā-Viṣṇu's skin, and remain alive only for the duration of one of His breaths. The purport is that Viṣṇu the maintainer, Brahmā the creator and Śiva the destroyer are manifest within this universe, and they remain situated in their respective jurisdictions of authority, absorbed in their prescribed duties. After that, they again enter Mahā-Viṣṇu at the time of His inhalation. That Mahā-Viṣṇu is a portion of a plenary portion of Śrī Govinda's plenary portion.

TĀTPARYA

The immense majestic opulence of *viṣṇu-tattva* has been illustrated in this verse.

38 Hiraṇyagarbha Prajāpati is the manifestation of Viṣṇu who is the original form of all Brahmās, and from whom the four-headed Brahmā is manifest. Hiraṇyagarbha is also known as Mahā-Brahmā, as described here.

Verse 49

भास्वान् यथाश्मशकलेषु निजेषु तेजः
स्वीयं कियत् प्रकटयत्यपि तद्वदत्र ।
ब्रह्मा य एष जगदण्डविधानकर्त्ता
गोविन्दमादिपुरुषं तमहं भजामि ॥४९॥

bhāsvān yathāśma-śakaleṣu nijeṣu tejaḥ
svīyaṁ kiyat prakaṭayaty api tadvad atra
brahmā ya eṣa jagad-aṇḍa-vidhāna-kartā
govindam ādi-puruṣaṁ tam ahaṁ bhajāmi

Anvaya

aham bhajāmi – I perform *bhajana*; *tam* – of that; *ādi-puruṣam govindam* – original Supreme Person, Śrī Govinda; *yathā* – just as; *bhāsvān* – the sun; *prakaṭayati* – manifests; *kiyat* – a certain portion; *svīyam* – of his own; *tejaḥ* – potency; *aśma-śakaleṣu nijeṣu* – within its own gem-stones (which are celebrated by the sun's names such as *sūrya-kānta*, and enacts his duty of heating the worlds); *tadvad atra* – similarly in the business of creation within this universe, etc.; *api* – also; *eṣaḥ brahmā* – Lord Brahmā; *yaḥ* – who; *jagad-aṇḍa-vidhāna-kartā* – (is) the director of the universe (who is empowered by Govinda).

Translation

Just as the sun manifests his potency to a minute degree within jewels such as *sūrya-kānta*, and invests them with the power to burn, similarly Śrī Govinda also infuses His creative potency within the secondary creator of the universe, Brahmā. I worship that original personality, Śrī Govinda.

Ṭīkā translation

The demigods and demigoddesses are all under Śrī Kṛṣṇa's shelter; they are not independent. To illustrate this, the nature of Brahmā is being defined. It is established in this verse that Brahmā is an extremely pious living entity, and is thus categorically distinct from *bhagavat-tattva*. In the same way that the sun manifests some portion of its energy within gems such as *sūrya-kānta* and invests them with the power to burn, similarly Bhagavān bestows a minute degree of His creative potency upon Brahmā, the secondary universal creator, and causes the creation of the universe through his agency.

In this verse the word *api* indicates the functional aspect of the heating potency of the jewel. This heating potency does not belong to the jewel, because a jewel cannot reduce anything to ashes by itself; it can only burn up other things when a minute portion of the sun's rays has entered into it. Similarly, Bhagavān's potency becomes manifest within the *jīva-tattva* Brahmā, who becomes the agent for accomplishing the creation. Just as the function of burning belongs to the sun, similarly the function of creation belongs to Bhagavān; Brahmā is only an instrument in the matter. Bhagavān manifests His potency in a qualified *jīva*, and causes the creation to be accomplished through him.

Sometimes Bhagavān Himself becomes Brahmā, the creator within an individual universe. Alternatively, He performs the duties of creation and so on as Mahā-Brahmā, Hiraṇyagarbha. By inference it should also be accepted that He also becomes Mahā-Śiva; that is, Bhagavān sometimes takes the form of Mahā-Śiva and performs the duties of destruction Himself. Therefore, the ultimate performer of the universal creation, maintenance and destruction is Govinda Himself.

Although Māyā-devī Durgā is Kāraṇodakaśāyī Viṣṇu's potency of cause and effect, and Brahmā, Kṣīrodakaśāyī Viṣṇu and so on are *avatāras* of Garbhodakaśāyī Viṣṇu, still Bhagavān Śrī Kṛṣṇa is the original source of all the *avatāras.* He is the shelter for all, and all others are His dependents. Similarly, the forthcoming verses will also describe those who are beings under His shelter.

Tātparya

There are two kinds of Brahmā. In some *kalpas,* Bhagavān empowers a worthy living entity with His potency, and that *jīva* performs the duty of Brahmā. Occasionally, in some *kalpas* when there is no suitable *jīva* and the Brahmā of the previous *kalpa* has become liberated, Śrī Kṛṣṇa manifests Brahmā, the *avatāra* of the material mode of passion, by a portion of His potency.

Brahmā is superior to all of the ordinary living entities in terms of *tattva,* but it cannot be said that he is directly the Supreme Lord. Furthermore, it should be kept in mind that Śambhu, who has already been discussed, possesses the qualities of *īśvara* to a greater extent than Brahmā. The basic meaning is that the fifty qualities present in the *jīvas* are present to a greater extent in Brahmā, along with five other qualities that are partially present in Brahmā but absent from the *jīvas.* However, those fifty qualities and the five further qualities are present to an even greater extent in Śambhu.

Verse 50

यत्पादपल्लवयुगं विनिधाय कुम्भ –
द्वन्द्वे प्रणामसमये स गणाधिराजः ।
विघ्नान् विहन्तुमलमस्य जगत्त्रयस्य
गोविन्दमादिपुरुषं तमहं भजामि ॥५०॥

yat-pāda-pallava-yugaṁ vinidhāya kumbha-
dvandve praṇāma-samaye sa gaṇādhirājaḥ
vighnān vihantum alam asya jagat-trayasya
govindam ādi-puruṣaṁ tam ahaṁ bhajāmi

Anvaya

aham bhajāmi – I perform *bhajana*; *tam* – of that; *ādi-puruṣam govindam* – original Supreme Person, Śrī Govinda; *vinidhāya* – by placing; *yat-pāda-pallava-yugam* – His two delicate lotus feet; *kumbha-dvandve* – upon the pair of cranial mounds on his elephant head; *praṇāma-samaye* – at the time of offering obeisances; *saḥ gaṇa-adhirājaḥ* – that chief among the demigods; *vihantum alam* – is able to remove easily; *vighnān* – the obstacles (on the path of devotion); *asya jagat-trayasya* – of the three worlds.

Translation

In order to obtain the power required to remove all the obstacles within the three worlds, Gaṇeśa, the bestower of success, always holds the divine lotus feet of Śrī Govinda upon the pair of cranial mounds protruding from his elephant head. I worship that original personality, Śrī Govinda.

Ṭīkā translation

Most people consider Gaṇeśajī to be an original and independent lord, and they therefore worship him at the beginning of any undertaking for the removal of the mundane obstacles that impede their respective endeavors. This verse beginning with *yat-pāda-pallava* is being presented to resolve the issue of whether Gaṇeśa should be worshiped as the original Personality or not. Gaṇeśajī is the monarch of the populace, and he always holds Śrī Govinda's lotus feet upon the cranial mounds on his elephant head so that he can obtain the power to remove all obstacles within the realm of birth and death. Thus it is by Govinda's mercy that Gaṇeśajī bestows all success and removes the obstacles impeding those who bow down to him. Actually, Śrī Govinda is the original bestower of perfections and the remover of obstacles. As He alone is the original shelter of the universe, intelligent men take exclusive shelter of Him.

Moreover, to reinforce this conclusion, the following example is being presented from the conversation between Kapiladeva and Devahūti in *Śrīmad-Bhāgavatam*. Bhagavān Kapiladeva said:

yat-pāda-niḥsṛta-sarit-pravarodakena
tīrthena mūrdhy-adhikṛtena śivaḥ śivo 'bhūt
dhyātur manaḥ śamala-śaila-nisṛṣṭa-vajraṁ
dhyāyec ciraṁ bhagavataś caraṇāravindam

Śrīmad-Bhāgavatam (3.28.22)

Śivajī attained his intrinsic quality of auspiciousness by holding upon his head the pure water of the exalted river Bhāgavatī Gaṅgā, who springs from the foot-wash of Śrī Govinda. If one simply meditates upon those lotus feet, they vanquish all the inebrieties of his heart, just as a thunderbolt hurled at a mountain smashes it into tiny fragments. Therefore one should meditate incessantly upon the divine lotus feet of Bhagavān.

In conclusion, it may be said that all kinds of abilities and powers are attained by the mercy of His lotus feet, and without that mercy, everything becomes useless. Thus one should meditate upon Bhagavān Śrī Hari, who is all-auspicious.

Tātparya

Śrī Gaṇeśa is a special authority, who is empowered by Bhagavān to perform the duty of destroying the obstacles on the path of progress for the entire universe. He is certainly the object of worship for people possessed of the appropriate eligibility. Moreover, among all the demigods he is counted as one of the five worshipable forms of Brahman with attributes (*saguṇa-brahma*). Gaṇeśa is a demigod who has been empowered with authority by Bhagavān. All of his glories are manifest only by Śrī Govinda's mercy.

Verse 51

अग्निर्मही गगनमम्बु मरुद्दिशश्च
कालस्तथात्ममनसीति जगत्त्रयाणि ।
यस्माद्भवन्ति विभवन्ति विशन्ति यञ्च
गोविन्दमादिपुरुषं तमहं भजामि ॥५१॥

agnir mahī gaganam ambu marud diśaś ca
kālas tathātma-manasīti jagat-trayāṇi
yasmād bhavanti vibhavanti viśanti yaṁ ca
govindam ādi-puruṣaṁ tam ahaṁ bhajāmi

Anvaya

aham bhajāmi – I perform *bhajana*; *tam* – of that; *ādi-puruṣam govindam* – original Supreme Person, Śrī Govinda; *yasmāt* – from whom; *jagat-trayāṇi* – the three worlds (heavenly, middle and hellish planets); *iti* – which are composed of; *agniḥ* – fire; *mahī* – earth; *gaganam* – space; *ambu* – water; *marut* – air; *diśaḥ* – the (ten) directions; *kālaḥ* – time; *tathā* – as well as; *ātma-manasī ca* – soul and mind; *bhavanti* – emanate; *vibhavanti* – are maintained; *yam* – (and) into whom; *viśanti* – they enter.

Translation

The three worlds have been created from nine elements, namely earth, water, fire, air, space, the directions, time, the mind and soul. I worship the original personality, Śrī Govinda, from whom the elements have originated, in whom they are situated after their manifestation, and into whom they enter at the time of the cosmic annihilation.

Ṭīkā translation

Everything is clear.

Tātparya

The entire universe is composed of nothing but the five gross elements – earth, water, fire, air and space – plus the directions, time, the *jīvātmā*, and the mental principle allied with the conditioned soul's subtle body, which consists of mind, intelligence and false ego. Those following the path of fruitive activities offer sacrificial oblations into the fire. Such materialistic *jīvas* do not know anything more than the perceptible world of these nine essential realities. The *jñānīs* engaged in the cultivation of dry impersonal knowedge are searching for the self in the form of the state of self-satisfaction, and the living entity is himself that *ātmā*. The *sāṅkhya* philosophical system calls this world *prakṛti* and says that the *ātmā* or self is situated within it. In other words, the principles defined by all kinds of philosophers are included within the nine *tattvas*. Thus, Śrī Govinda is exclusively the original cause and repose of the creation, maintenance and annihilation of the sum total of these *tattvas*.

Verse 52

यच्चक्षुरेष सविता सकलग्रहाणां
राजा समस्तसुरमूर्त्तिरशेषतेजाः ।
यस्याज्ञया भ्रमति संभृतकालचक्रो
गोविन्दमादिपुरुषं तमहं भजामि ॥५२॥

yac-cakṣur eṣa savitā sakala-grahāṇāṁ
rājā samasta-sura-mūrtir aśeṣa-tejāḥ
yasyājñayā bhramati sambhṛta-kāla-cakro
govindam ādi-puruṣaṁ tam ahaṁ bhajāmi

Anvaya

aham bhajāmi – I perform *bhajana*; *tam* – of that; *ādi-puruṣam govindam* – original Supreme Person, Śrī Govinda; *eṣaḥ savitā* – Sūryadeva (the sungod); *yat-cakṣuḥ* – who functions as His eye (in other words he illuminates the entire universe, thereby providing the power of sight); *rājā* – (is) the king; *sakala-grahānām* – of all the planets; *samasta-sura-mūrtiḥ* – regulator of all the demigods; *aśeṣa-tejaḥ* – possessed of limitless potency; *yasya ājñayā* – on account of Govinda's order; *bhramati* – he travels; *sambhṛta* – sustaining; *kāla-cakraḥ* – the wheel of time.

Translation

Sūryadeva, the predominating deity of the sun, is the king of all the planets, and is likened to the eye of this world. I worship the original personality, Śrī Govinda, upon whose order the sun travels in his regular orbit, having mounted the wheel of time.

Ṭīkā translation

Some people say that Sūryadeva is the controller of all, and the original person. The actual nature of the sun-god is being analyzed in this *śloka* beginning *yac-cakṣuḥ*, in order to resolve this misconception. Factually, he is the king of all the planets, full of infinite effulgence, and he acts as the eye of the universe. He is a demigod who has been invested with special authority by Śrī Govinda; he is not an independent or separate god. Indeed, it is in accordance with Śrī Govinda's order that he mounts the wheel of time and always remains dedicated to his service. This has also been described in *Bhagavad-gītā* (15.12):

yad-āditya-gataṁ tejo
jagad bhāsayate 'khilam
yac-candramasi yac-cāgnau
tat-tejo viddhi māmakam

All the power in the sun that illuminates the whole universe is certainly only My power, and so is the power of the moon and of fire.

Similarly, in the *śruti* we find: "*bhīṣāsmād vātaḥ parvate bhīṣodeti sūryaḥ* – the wind blows out of fear of Me, and the sun shines out of fear of Me." Furthermore, it is stated in *Śrīmad-Bhāgavatam* (3.25.42):

mad-bhayād vāti vāto 'yaṁ
sūryas tapati mad-bhayāt
varṣatīndro dahaty agnir
mṛtyuś carati mad-bhayāt

The wind blows out of fear of Me, the sun shines out of fear of Me, Indra sends the rain out of fear of Me, fire incinerates out of fear of Me, and death continuously traverses back and forth throughout the world out of fear of Me.

The commentary on this verse explains Śrī Bhagavān's words as follows: "If any of them inflict any kind of difficulty whatsoever upon My devotee, I do not delay in withdrawing their authority."

na tatra sūryo bhāti na candra-tārakaṁ
nemo vidyuto bhānti kuto 'yam agniḥ
tam eva bhāntam anubhāti sarvaṁ
tasya bhāsā sarvam idaṁ vibhāti

Katha Upaniṣad (2.2.15)

Although the sun, moon, stars, lightning and fire illuminate everything, they cannot illuminate Bhagavān or His abode.

Descriptions such as this verse 52 of *Brahma-saṁhitā*, defining Sūrya as the eye of the universal form, are found in many places throughout the Vedas.

Tātparya

Many followers of the Vedas worship Sūryadeva and consider him to be Brahman. Sūryadeva has also been included among the five demigods who are worshiped according to the system of *pañcopāsanā*. Some people consider heat to be the original cause, and believe Sūryadeva to be the original personality, because he is the foundation of all heat and therefore the cause of the universe. Whatever opinion they may hold, the fact is that the sun is the presiding deity of only one solar system, empowered with the aggregate of all the material heat therein. Therefore, he is one demigod among the delegated authorities of the mundane world. He always remains absorbed in his service according to the order of Śrī Govinda.

Verse 53

धर्मोऽथ पापनिचयः श्रुतयस्तपांसि
ब्रह्मादिकीटपतगावधयश्च जीवाः ।
यद्दत्तमात्रविभवप्रकटप्रभावा
गोविन्दमादिपुरुषं तमहं भजामि ॥ ५३ ॥

dharmo 'tha pāpa-nicayaḥ śrutayas tapāṁsi
brahmādi-kīṭa-patagāvadhayaś ca jīvāḥ
yad-datta-mātra-vibhava-prakaṭa-prabhāvā
govindam ādi-puruṣaṁ tam ahaṁ bhajāmi

Anvaya

aham bhajāmi – I perform *bhajana*; *tam* – of that; *ādi-puruṣam govindam* – original Supreme Person, Śrī Govinda; *yat-datta-mātra-vibhava* – who merely by His power of endowment; *prakaṭa-prabhāvāḥ* – are manifest the respective potencies; *dharmaḥ* – of pious activities i.e. *varṇa-* and *āśrama-dharmas* as described in the Vedas; *atha* – and; *pāpa-nicayaḥ* – the multitude of sins; *śrutayaḥ* – the *Ṛg*, *Sāma*, *Yajur* and *Atharva Vedas*, as well as the Upaniṣads, which are the crest-jewels of the Vedas; *tapāṁsi* – the various austerities; *ca jīvāḥ* – and the living beings; *brahmā-ādi* – beginning from the great Brahmā; *avadhayaḥ* – down to; *kīṭa-pataga* – the insignificant birds and insects.

Translation

I worship that original personality, Śrī Govinda, whose power of endowment alone manifests the respective potencies in the principles of religious conduct, sinful activities, the Vedas, various austerities and all living entities from Brahmā down to the most insignificant insect.

Ṭīkā translation

What remains to be said on this topic? In this world of repeated birth and death, there are so many forms of religious conduct and sinful activities, as well as all the various living beings. All of these manifest their own potency or prowess, which are all bestowed by Bhagavān alone. Otherwise they have not the slightest independent capacity to show their own potency. It is also stated in *Bhagavad-gītā* (10.8):

ahaṁ sarvasya prabhavo
mattaḥ sarvaṁ pravartate

I am the source from which everything emanates, and I am also the inspiration for all things.

Tātparya

The principles of religious conduct (*dharma*) are those which have been prescribed in the Vedas as proper conduct for the welfare of human society. The twenty *dharma-śāstras* describe *varṇa-dharma* and *āśrama-dharma*. *Varṇa-dharma* means religious duties prescribed according to the various natures of priests and intellectuals (*brāhmaṇas*), warriors and administrators (*kṣatriyas*), farmers, traders and merchants (*vaiśyas*), and artisans and workers (*śūdras*). *Āśrama-dharma* means the duties that are suitable for the respective spiritual orders (*āśramas*) of those living as celibate students (*brahmacārīs*), householders (*gṛhasthas*), retired ascetics (*vānaprasthas*) and renounced mendicants (*sannyasīs*). These two forms of *dharma* (according to *varṇa* and *āśrama*) alone have been ascertained to be proper conduct for those in the human form of life. *Adharma* (irreligion), as indicated by the words *pāpa-nicayaḥ*, refers to all the various types of sin, including ignorance, which is the root of sin;

sinful desires; the five heinous sins;[39] serious crimes such as murder, rape, adultery, robbery and so on; and all other forms of illicit behavior. One should understand *śrutayaḥ* to mean the *Ṛg*, *Sāma*, *Yajur* and *Atharva Vedas*, along with the Upaniṣads, which are considered the head of the body of *śruti*. The word *tapāṁsi* refers to the many various types of difficult practices that are characteristically meant for *dharma*, religious progress. Many instructions have been written in the *dharma-śāstras* regarding such troublesome and painful practice. In many places the process of "five fires"[40] and other great austerities and penances are described. The eightfold yoga process and the pursuit of impersonal spiritual realization are included within the category of austerities. The word *jīvāḥ* refers to all the conditioned souls who are bound within this world on the wheel of fruitive activities.

The conditioned souls wander throughout 8,400,000 species of life. There are so many varieties of life such as demigods, demons, *rākṣasas*, human beings, *nāgas*, *kinnaras* and *gandharvas*. The soul takes on bodies in unlimited forms of life from Brahmā down to the most insignificant insect. As the *jīvas* wander through various species on the wheel of *karma*, they attain the various powers that are specific to each life-form. Some species exhibit great strength, while others possess uncommon intelligence and so on. But these specific powers are not manifest of their own accord. Śrī Govindadeva bestows His own power or prowess upon the various forms of life, and therefore they each manifest varying degrees of Govinda's potency or prowess.

[39] According to *Manu-smṛti*, the five heinous sins (*mahā-pātaka*) are killing a *brāhmaṇa*, drinking liquor, stealing, committing adultery with the wife of one's *guru*, and associating with those who engage in such great sins.

[40] In the austerity known as *pañca-tapa*, or "five fires," one sits in the midst of four fires during summer, with the blazing sun overhead counted as the fifth fire.

Verse 54

यस्त्विन्द्रगोपमथवेन्द्रमहो स्वकर्म
बन्धानुरूपफलभाजनमातनोति ।
कर्माणि निर्दहति किन्तु च भक्तिभाजां
गोविन्दमादिपुरुषं तमहं भजामि ॥५४॥

yas tv indragopam athavendram aho sva-karma-
bandhānurūpa-phala-bhājanam ātanoti
karmāṇi nirdahati kintu ca bhakti-bhājāṁ
govindam ādi-puruṣaṁ tam ahaṁ bhajāmi

Anvaya

aham bhajāmi – I perform *bhajana*; *tam* – of that; *ādi-puruṣam govindam* – original Supreme Person, Śrī Govinda; *yaḥ* – who (in a disinterested manner); *ātanoti* – makes; *indragopam* – the insignificant red insect named *indragopa*; *athavā* – as well as; *indram* – Indra, the king of the administrative demigods; *phala-bhājanam* – the recipient of the fruits; *anurūpa-bandha* – in accordance with the bondage; *sva-karma* – generated by their respective activities; *kintu ca* – however; *aho* – Oh how astonishing!; *bhakti-bhājām* – for those dedicated in *śuddha-bhakti*; *nirdahati* – He utterly consumes, i.e. nullifies; *karmāṇi* – the results generated from their activities performed in all of their previous lives.

Translation

Śrī Govinda impartially bestows the fruits of reaction upon all living entities who are wandering on the path of *karma*, from the insignificant *indragopa* insect to Indradeva, the monarch of the demigods, according to the bondage accrued from their respective individual actions.

However, it is wonderful that He completely burns to the roots the *karma* of those who are devoted to Him. I worship that original personality, Śrī Govinda.

Ṭīkā translation

As the fully independent controller of all controllers, Bhagavān Śrī Kṛṣṇa does whatever He considers to be appropriate, and no one can oppose Him even in the slightest way. Just as a cloud gives rain impartially, He is equally disposed to all. In keeping with this principle, Śrī Kṛṣṇa is also the impartial bestower of the fruits of action. From the tiny red *indragopa* insect that appears during the rainy season, up to Indra, the king of heaven, Śrī Kṛṣṇa bestows good and bad results upon everyone according to their good and bad activities. However, He burns down to the roots the *karma*, the fruits of *karma*, the desire for *karma* and even the ignorance of His exclusively one-pointed devotees who are attentively engaged in *bhakti*. This favoritism that He shows to His devotees is utterly astonishing.

The profound implication of saying that Śrī Kṛṣṇa regards everyone equally like a cloud is as follows. Just as a cloud rains down water in one place and not another, or rains down more in one place and less in another, and just as no one can control the rainfall, similarly, although Bhagavān sees everyone equally, He is totally independent in the matter of punishing or showing favor to anyone. This particular quality of Bhagavān is described in this verse beginning *yas tv indragopam*.

For example Svayam Bhagavān has said in *Bhagavad-gītā* (9.29):

samo 'haṁ sarva-bhūteṣu
na me dveṣyo 'sti na priyaḥ
ye bhajanti tu māṁ bhaktyā
mayi te teṣu cāpy aham

I am equally disposed to all living entities. No one is My enemy and no one is My friend. However, I consider those who render service to Me with devotion to be Mine, and I am theirs.

It is also stated in *Bhagavad-gītā* (9.22): "*ananyāś cintayanto mām* – I personally carry the necessities of My unalloyed devotees who are exclusively engaged in My service, and I always protect them."

Someone may say, "Bhagavān delivers His own devotees from material existence and bestows upon them the loving service of His lotus feet, but He never does this for the non-devotees, so He must be guilty of partiality arising from attachment and aversion." However, such partiality can never be found in Bhagavān merely because He is extremely caring and affectionate to His devotees (*bhakta-vatsala*). Being so kind to His devotees is one of His unique characteristics, and this quality is His ornament. There is no fault or partiality on His side.

For example, it is described in *Śrīmad-Bhāgavatam* (8.16.24): *tathāpi bhaktaṁ bhajate maheśvaraḥ.* Although all living entities have come from Bhagavān and Bhagavān is equally disposed to all of them, still He shows a special favoritism toward His devotees. Just as the devotee remains constantly attached to Bhagavān, so Bhagavān also remains constantly attached to His devotee. Just as the devotee binds Bhagavān with the rope of *prema* and keeps Him bound within his heart, similarly Bhagavān binds His devotees with the ropes of His sweet qualities.

visṛjati hṛdayaṁ na yasya sākṣād
dharir avaśābhihito 'py aghaugha-nāśaḥ
praṇaya-rasanayā dhṛtāṅghri-padmaḥ
sa bhavati bhāgavata-pradhāna uktaḥ

Śrīmad-Bhāgavatam (11.2.55)

If someone calls the name of Śrī Hari even accidentally, He never leaves their heart, but destroys the heaps of sins residing there. One who binds Śrī Hari's lotus feet in his heart with the ropes of intimate love (*praṇaya*) is known as the topmost devotee.

It has also been stated in the *Ādi Purāṇa*:

asmākaṁ guravo bhaktā
bhaktānāṁ guravo vayam
mad-bhaktā yatra gacchanti
tatra gacchāmi pārthiva

O King, the devotees are My *gurus*, and I am their *guru*. I go wherever My devotees go.

This conclusion is also supported by the following statement from *Śrīmad-Bhāgavatam* (1.16.16):

sārathya-pāraṣada-sevana-sakhya-dautya-
vīrāsanānugamana-stavana-praṇāmān
snigdheṣu pāṇḍuṣu jagat-praṇatiṁ ca viṣṇor
bhaktiṁ karoti nṛ-patiś caraṇāravinde

That Śrī Kṛṣṇa, to whom all the living beings in the universe offer *praṇāma*, would sometimes become a chariot driver for his dear devotees, the Paṇḍavas, and sometimes He would become the chairman of their council. He was their servant and friend. Sometimes He would take up a sword in His hand and guard their door at night like a doorkeeper. Following behind them, praying and offering His obeisances, Śrī Kṛṣṇa showed His qualities of loving affection for His devotees in such a way that when Mahārāja Parīkṣit heard all this in the form of songs from the mouths of the royal court bards, *bhakti* that was full of intense pangs of separation from the lotus feet of Śrī Kṛṣṇa awakened in his heart.

Similarly Akrūrajī said:

na tasya kaścid dayitaḥ suhṛttamo
na cāpriyo dveṣya upekṣya eva vā
tathāpi bhaktān bhajate yathā tathā
sura-drumo yadvad upāśrito 'rtha-daḥ

Śrīmad-Bhāgavatam (10.38.22)

Although no one is eligible to be Śrī Kṛṣṇa's dear bosom friend, His undesirable enemy, or the object of His neglect, still, just as one attains whatever one prays for from a desire-tree, in the same way one attains a particular fruit from Śrī Kṛṣṇa corresponding to one's *bhajana*.

Only those who take shelter of a *kalpa-vṛkṣa*, desire-tree, attain the benefit bestowed by it, not others. This is not partiality on the part of the desire-tree. Similarly, although there is a difference in the results attained by those who take shelter of Bhagavān and those who do not, this cannot be considered partiality. Furthermore, the speciality of Bhagavān is even greater than that of a desire-tree. For example, a desire-tree never becomes subordinate to one who takes its shelter, but Bhagavān becomes subordinate to His unconditionally surrendered devotees.

Bhagavān is impartial in all cases. This is illustrated by the following statements from *Śrīmad-Bhāgavatam* (6.17.22–23):

na tasya kaścid dayitaḥ pratīpo
na jñāti-bandhur na paro na ca svaḥ
samasya sarvatra nirañjanasya
sukhe na rāgaḥ kuta eva roṣaḥ

He is equally disposed to all living entities. No one is dear to Him, nor does He dislike anyone. He is detached, and therefore He has no affinity for the happiness derived from sense objects. Neither is He subject to aversion, which is simply the antithesis of sense gratification. In the course of bestowing the results of the *jīvas'* own fruitive activities, He gives happiness to one and distress to another, bondage to one and liberation to another. Still, He never exhibits any partiality arising from attachment or aversion.

tathāpi tac-chakti-visarga eṣāṁ
sukhāya duḥkhāya hitāhitāya

Although Bhagavān is the original performer of activities, He is not personally responsible for the *jīva's* happiness, distress, bondage and liberation.

By acting under the influence of the three qualities of material nature, the living entity creates his own sinfulness and piety, which in turn become the cause of his birth and death. Although this is the function of *māyā*, it is understood to be the activity of Bhagavān. One should not imagine that Bhagavān is partial in this, because each individual living entity tastes the results of his own activities. Although the light of the sun generally gives happiness to everyone, it gives distress to the owl and the night lotus. Nevertheless, one cannot attribute partiality to the sun. Similarly, through the agency of Bhagavān's *māyā*, the *jīva* attains a particular result according to his *karma*. Thus, there is no question of partiality in Bhagavān.

The general rule is that Bhagavān bestows upon the *jīvas* the fruit of their work, but although He is impartial in all cases, He shows His loving care to His devotees. This is not His personal partiality. It is well known that Bhagavān is *bhakta-vatsala*, but He never becomes *jñāni-vatsala* or *yogi-vatsala*. This has never happened. Moreover, He is also not affectionate to the devotees of demigods and demigoddesses. He is affectionate to His own devotees (*sva-bhakta-vatsala*). Therefore in *Brahma-sūtra* (2.1.36) it is stated: *upapadyate ca api upalabhyate ca*. Bhagavān's quality of being *bhakta-vatsala* is imbued with partiality in the form of favoritism. The protection of His devotees is the function of His *svarūpa-śakti*.

This partiality in favoritism to His devotees is found in the description of the qualities of Śrī Hari. Moreover, Bhagavān's quality of favoring His devotee is the ornament among all other qualities.

Thus in his commentary on this verse from *Śrī Brahma-saṁhitā*, Śrī Jīva Gosvāmipāda has presented another verse from *Bhagavad-gītā* (9.22):

ananyāś cintayanto māṁ
ye janāḥ paryupāsate
teṣāṁ nityābhiyuktānāṁ
yoga-kṣemaṁ vahāmy aham

In personally describing the speciality of His unalloyed devotees, Bhagavān said, "My devotees consider Me to be the exclusive goal of their lives. They are always absorbed in thoughts of Me with undivided attention; that is, they never take shelter of any other object of desire or serve any other worshipable deity. Unlimitedly auspicious qualifications appear in them. Taking shelter of My lotus feet, which are the essence of the nectar of astonishing pastimes, they engage in *bhajana* with one-pointed determination. Such devotees do not even remember how to maintain their lives in this world, so I personally maintain them by protecting them and by collecting their eatables and other necessities.

"The purport of saying the word *vahāmi* (I personally carry) and not *karomi* (I arrange) in this verse is that the responsibility for maintaining those unalloyed devotees falls upon Me, and I carry that responsibility just as a householder personally maintains and nourishes the members of his own family."

Bhagavān takes the responsibility of personally and directly taking care of His devotees by His own free will, whereas duties such as creation and so on are accomplished simply by His desiring them to take place. Therefore His devotees are not really a burden for Him. Just as a man feels happiness by taking care of a lover with whom he enjoys, similarly Bhagavān feels happiness in supporting and nourishing His devotees.

In this regard there is an example from *Vedānta-sūtra* (3.4.44): *svāminaḥ phala-śruter ity ātreyaḥ*. Does the detached devotee maintain his life in this world by his own efforts, or does he depend on the efforts of Parameśvara? In answer to this question, it is stated that the devotee does not want Bhagavān to have to do anything for him, so he makes some endeavor for his own maintenance.

Although Bhagavān personally maintains His devotees, when Ātreya Muni saw the final benediction (*phala-śruti*) given to the readers of the *Taittirīya Upaniṣad*, he said, "The worldly maintenance of the devotees is arranged by Sarveśvara Bhagavān. Just as fish, turtles and birds maintain their offspring by sight, meditation and touch respectively, similarly Bhagavān maintains His devotees."

"My kindness upon such unalloyed devotees is that I make them attain My transcendental abode. I do not do this for the worshipers of other *devatās*." *Viśeṣaṁ ca darśayati*: this *sūtra* indicates that Bhagavān causes those devotees who have no material desires, and who are acutely afflicted by the distress of separation from Him, to attain His abode very quickly because He is unable to tolerate any delay. This is Bhagavān's special arrangement.

The following verse is found in the *Varāha Purāṇa*:

nayāmi paramaṁ sthānam
arcir-ādi-gatiṁ vinā
garuḍa-skandham āropya
yatheccham anivāritaḥ

My devotees are indifferent to material circumstances. I lift them up onto the shoulders of Garuḍa and, bypassing all the intermediate realms, I bring them directly to My transcendental abode without any impediments, in accordance with their desire.

Therefore Bhagavān personally carries the necessities of His unalloyed devotees. This means that He does not arrange for them through any other agent. It is understood that this is no burden for Him; rather, it gives Him great happiness due to His affection for His unalloyed devotees, who are exceedingly dear to Him.

Tātparya

The supreme controller sees with equal vision. Exactly in accordance with the previous activities of the conditioned souls, He bestows the inclination for particular *karma* at a later date without the slightest partiality. However, He is especially kind to His devotees. He totally incinerates their desires for fruitive activities, their ignorance and all the results of their sinful and pious work. Although *karma* is beginningless (*anādi*), it is destructible.

The *karma* of those who engage in work with the hope of enjoying the fruits of their activities is permanent; it is never destroyed. Even the duties of the renounced order (*sannyāsa-dharma*) is one kind of *karma* befitting that *āśrama*. Simply following the duties of a renunciant is not pleasing to Śrī Kṛṣṇa because the desire for the fruit of liberation remains. Therefore *sannyāsīs* also attain the results of their activities. Even if they reach the final limit of desirelessness, they certainly attain the insignificant result of satisfaction in the self.

On the other hand, pure devotees continuously render service to Śrī Kṛṣṇa with a favorable mood, abandoning without exception all independent endeavors such as *jñāna* and *karma*. For these pure devotees, who are devoid of all desires except the desire for service, Śrī Kṛṣṇa completely incinerates their *karma*, the desire for *karma* and the root of *karma*, namely ignorance.

In light of His general neutrality, Śrī Kṛṣṇa's partiality to His devotees is a matter of sheer astonishment.

Verse 55

यं क्रोधकामसहजप्रणयादिभीति –
वात्सल्यमोहगुरुगौरवसेव्यभावैः ।
सञ्चिन्त्य तस्य सदृशीं तनुमापुरेते
गोविन्दमादिपुरुषं तमहं भजामि ॥५५॥

yaṁ krodha-kāma-sahaja-praṇayādi-bhīti-
vātsalya-moha-guru-gaurava-sevya-bhāvaiḥ
sañcintya tasya sadṛśīṁ tanum āpur ete
govindam ādi-puruṣaṁ tam ahaṁ bhajāmi

Anvaya

aham bhajāmi – I engage in *bhajana*; *tam* – of that; *ādi-puruṣam govindam* – original Supreme Person, Śrī Govinda; *yam* – whom; *sañcintya* – by full contemplation; *bhāvaiḥ* – through the moods; *krodha* – of anger (such as that shown by Śiśupāla toward Kṛṣṇa out of enmity); *kāma* – of lust felt by the *vraja-gopīs* etc., out of a desire to give Kṛṣṇa pleasure (in other words *mādhurya-rasa* or *prema*); *sahaja-praṇaya-ādi* – of *sakhya-bhāva*, the spontaneous affection of the cowherd friends (*sakhās*) such as Śrīdāmā, Subala, etc.; *bhīti* – of incessant terror felt by persons such as Kaṁsa, accompanied by the evil thought, "I shall be slain by Kṛṣṇa!"; *vātsalya* – of parental affection felt by persons headed by Śrī Nanda and Yaśodā; *moha* – of delusion felt by those of the Māyāvādī cult, i.e. a mood of total forgetfulness in the contemplation of *sāyujya-mukti* (liberation through merging one's identity with Śrī Kṛṣṇa's impersonal aspect of the non-differentiated divine light, known as *nirbheda-brahma*); *guru-gaurava* – of *śānta-bhāva*, wherein one contemplates Him as a great personage, worthy of respect; *sevya* – of *dāsya-bhāva*, the mood of servitude rendered by those who contemplate Śrī Kṛṣṇa as the sole object worthy of their service; *ete* – those persons; *āpuḥ* – attain; *sadṛśīm* – an appropriate; *tanum* – body; *tasya* – for His service.

Translation

Those who contemplate Him with feelings of lust, anger, the natural intimacy of friendship, fear, parental affection, bewilderment, reverence and servitude, attain bodies (suitable for associates of Bhagavān) with various degrees of beauty and qualities corresponding to their individual meditations. I worship that original personality, Govinda.

Ṭīkā translation

Svayam Bhagavān Śrī Kṛṣṇa is the only actual bestower of results; He bestows the appropriate fruits upon all. The results bestowed by others are perishable, but the fruit bestowed by Śrī Kṛṣṇa is never subject to destruction. Bhagavān is eternal, His devotees are eternal, and His *bhakti* and the fruit of *bhakti* are also eternal. Because pure devotees are full of deep attachment for Him, they are infinitely superior to the desireless *yogīs*. That Prabhu who bestows even upon His most antagonistic enemies a result that is supremely difficult for great *yogīs* to attain must necessarily, according to the logic of "inferential partial illustration" (*kaimutika-nyāya*), bestow the highest fruit of all upon His devotees who incessantly cultivate favorable activities and moods in His service. This is certainly not a point of controversy. What intelligent person could possibly give up such a highly generous Prabhu as Śrī Kṛṣṇa to worship any other demigod or demigoddess? Having stated this in the previous verse, Brahmājī completes the section characterized by the phrase, "I worship the original personality, Śrī Govindadeva," with this verse beginning *yaṁ krodha-kāma*.

Words such as *krodha* indicate fear and enmity, as well as anger. For example, when Bhagavān Śrī Kṛṣṇa's enemies such as Kaṁsa and Śiśupāla become absorbed in Him, even through moods that are unfavorable to *bhakti*, He bestows upon them a transcendental destination. *Aho*! Pūtanā was a man-eating demoness, accustomed to killing babies and drinking their blood, yet the most liberal and merciful Śrī Kṛṣṇa gave her a destination befitting a nurse-maid in Goloka because she had assumed the appearance of a mother. Vṛṣabhāsura and Keśī-daitya also attained destinations like the oxen that pull carts in Goloka Vraja. Śrī Kṛṣṇa also awarded a destination to the wicked Kālīya-nāga in Goloka Vraja, using him as a boat in His water-pastimes. Although many other *avatāras* of Bhagavān are bestowers of elevated destinations upon their enemies, they have given the demons killed by them destinations such as heavenly happiness and vast sensory enjoyment. However, they have not given destinations extending even up to the point of liberation, what to speak of elevation to Goloka.

Anger is the mood of an enemy. Natural intimacy is the mood of a friend. Lust refers to *śṛṅgāra*, the amorous mood, which is the sweetest of all. The affection of a mother and father for their child is called *vātsalya*. Reverence like that offered to one's *guru* is neutrality (*śānta-bhāva*). Servitude indicates *dāsya-bhāva*. Here the word *moha* implies the utter forgetfulness experienced due to a vision of Brahman; this is the *brahmamaya-bhāva* of the proponents of impersonal knowledge.

The purport of saying that those who contemplate Bhagavān attain bodies corresponding to their moods is that by becoming absorbed in these moods at the time of *sādhana*, when they achieve perfection, they attain bodies like the associates of Bhagavān according to their individual *bhāvas*, and they become absorbed in His service. Those who become absorbed in the transcendental subject through the mood of anger attain only a partial aspect of that transcendence in the form of impersonal liberation (*sāyujya-mukti*). Aside from that, those who have the sentiments of *śānta*, *dāsya*, *sakhya*, *vātsalya* and *śṛṅgāra* attain bodies appropriate for those individual *bhāvas*, with beauty and qualities corresponding to the extent of their attainment. In this regard, we find evidence in the statement of Śrī Vasudeva (*Śrīmad-Bhāgavatam* 10.3.41): "*adṛṣṭānyatamaṁ loke śīlaudārya-guṇaiḥ* – in my previous life I begged from You the benediction of having a son endowed with all qualities like You. However, You said, 'There is no one else endowed with qualities like Me. It can never be. Therefore I will personally appear as your son.'" From this it is concluded that no living entity can have all the transcendental qualities of Bhagavān. Thus the words *sadṛśīṁ tanum* indicate that one can attain a body suitable for an associate of Bhagavān, which is partially imbued with His transcendental qualities.

It has also been stated in *Brahma-sūtra*: "*jagad vyāpāra-varjam* – it is not possible for the *jīvas* to perform the task of creation, maintenance and destruction of the universe. It is only possible for Brahman. This ability of Bhagavān cannot possibly occur in the *jīva*." Śrī Nārada has also stated (*Śrīmad-Bhāgavatam* 1.6.29): "*prayujyamāne mayi tāṁ śuddhāṁ bhagavatīṁ tanum* – when my devotional service was mature, Bhagavān mercifully bestowed upon me my pure body as His associate. My previous body composed of the five gross material elements was cast aside and I went to the abode of Bhagavān in that transcendental body." The essence of this statement is that no one is identical with Bhagavān in all respects and no one can become so at any time.

In *Śrīmad-Bhāgavatam* (11.5.48) we find: "*vaireṇa yaṁ nṛpatayaḥ* – if kings such as Śiśupāla and Dantavakra attained

Bhagavān by the mood of enmity, then *anurakta-dhiyāṁ punaḥ kim* – what will be unattainable for the unalloyed *premi-bhaktas* through their powerful attachment for Him? What need is there to say that they most definitely attain Him?"

One can attain Śrī Kṛṣṇa by being absorbed in anger, hostility or envy, or also through the moods of *śānta*, *dāsya*, *sakhya*, *vātsalya* and *śṛṅgāra*. However, just as there is a difference between hostility and loving attachment, there is also a difference in the destinations attained through these respective moods. The *sādhakas* attain the positions of being different types of associates in accordance with the level of their *prema* or *anurāga* (deep attachment). The highest attainment is only achieved by those with the highest loving attachment. On the basis of this principle, it is established that there is no difference between the associates situated in Goloka and the associates who descend to Bhauma-Vṛndāvana. The two are non-different. This is also mentioned in *Śrīmad-Bhāgavatam*: "*nandādayas tu taṁ dṛṣtvā* – the Vrajavāsīs headed by Śrī Nanda saw the majesty of Goloka in Brahma-hrada and became joyfully amazed." The oneness of Goloka and Bhauma-Vṛndāvana has been established by this statement.

Tātparya

Bhakti is of two kinds: regulative (*vaidhī*) and spontaneous (*rāgānugā*). The first type of *bhakti* is based on the faith that arises to a small extent through the medium of *śāstra* and the instructions of one's *guru*, and it develops very slowly because of the confinement of observing the rules and regulations of scripture. That *bhakti* is transformed into *niṣṭhā*, *ruci*, *āsakti* and *bhāva* by the cultivation of activities in connection with Śrī Kṛṣṇa in the form of hearing, chanting and remembering in the association of *sādhus*. When *bhāva* arises, the *sādhaka-bhakta* can be the recipient of Śrī Kṛṣṇa's mercy. In this process there is a long delay before arriving at the stage of *bhāva*. This is called *vaidhī-bhakti*.

Rāgātmikā-bhakti gives results very quickly and attracts Śrī Kṛṣṇa, and therefore it is superior. What is its inherent nature? This particular verse describes the various forms in which it is perceived. The category of *rāgātmikā-bhakti* includes passive or neutral adoration (*śānta-bhāva*) characterized by *guru-gaurava* (reverence); *dāsya-bhāva* exemplified by *sevya-bhāva* (servitude); *sakhya-bhāva* (friendship) typified by *sahaja-praṇaya* (natural intimacy); *vātsalya-bhāva* (parental affection); and *mādhurya-bhāva* (amorous love) characterized by *kāma*. Anger (*krodha*), fear (*bhaya*) and delusion (*moha*), although spontaneous, are not included in the category of *bhakti*. Anger is seen in demons like Śiśupāla, fear in demons like Kaṁsa and delusion in the scholars of Māyāvāda philosophy. Although there is absorption in the spontaneous activities of anger, fear and the total forgetfulness of everything arising from the internal vision of the impersonal Brahman, they are still not considered to be *bhakti*, because they are not favorable to Śrī Kṛṣṇa.

Furthermore, when we consider *śānta*, *dāsya*, *sakhya*, *vātsalya* and *mādhurya*, spontaneous attachment (*rāga*) remains almost absent from *śānta-bhāva* because of an excess of neutrality. Nevertheless, it has been accepted as *bhakti* because it is somewhat favorable. Besides this, the other four moods possess an abundance of spontaneous attachment. According to *Bhagavad-gītā* (4.11): "*ye yathā māṁ prapadyante tāṁs tathaiva bhajāmy aham* – I reciprocate with everyone according to their individual degree of surrender to Me." Those who cultivate attachment in the form of anger, fear and delusion attain salvation in the form of *sāyujya-mukti*, the impersonal aspect of liberation in which one imagines that he has merged with Brahman. By *śānta-bhāva* one attains a body suitable for remaining absorbed in Brahman and Paramātmā, like the four Kumāras, headed by Sanaka and Sanātana, or like Śukadeva Gosvāmī. By *dāsya* and *sakhya-bhāva* one attains an appropriate male or female form in accordance with one's eligibility. By *vātsalya-bhāva* one acquires a fatherly or motherly form corresponding to one's mode of service. A pure, transcendental body of a *gopī* is attained by those in *śṛṅgāra-bhāva.*

Verse 56

श्रियः कान्ताः कान्तः परमपुरुषः कल्पतरवो
द्रुमा भूमिश्चिन्तामणिगणमयी तोयममृतम् ।
कथा गानं नाट्यं गमनमपि वंशी प्रियसखी
चिदानन्दं ज्योतिः परमपि तदास्वाद्यमपि च ॥

स यत्र क्षीराब्धिः स्रवति सुरभीभ्यश्च सुमहान्
निमेषार्द्धाख्यो वा व्रजति न हि यत्रापि समयः ।
भजे श्वेतद्वीपं तमहमिह गोलोकमिति यं
विदन्तस्ते सन्तः क्षितिविरलचाराः कतिपये ॥५६॥

śriyaḥ kāntāḥ kāntaḥ parama-puruṣaḥ kalpa-taravo
drumā bhūmiś cintāmaṇi-gaṇa-mayī toyam amṛtam
kathā gānaṁ nāṭyaṁ gamanam api vaṁśī priya-sakhī
cid-ānandaṁ jyotiḥ param api tad āsvādyam api ca

sa yatra kṣīrābdhiḥ sravati surabhībhyaś ca su-mahān
nimeṣārdhākhyo vā vrajati na hi yatrāpi samayaḥ
bhaje śvetadvīpaṁ tam aham iha golokam iti yaṁ
vidantas te santaḥ kṣiti-virala-cārāḥ katipaye

Anvaya

yatra – where; *kāntāḥ* – the beloveds; *śriyaḥ* – (are) Mahā-Lakṣmīs (who are none other than Śrī Kṛṣṇa's dearmost beautiful *vraja-gopīs*); *kāntaḥ* – (where) the sole hero; *parama-puruṣaḥ* – (is) the primeval Supreme Person, Śrī Govinda; *drumā* – (where) the trees; *kalpa-taravaḥ* – fulfill all desires; *bhūmiḥ* – (where) the land; *cintāmaṇi-gaṇa-mayī* – (is) wish-fulfilling stone; *toyam* – (where) water; *amṛtam* – (is) immortal nectar; *kathā* – (where) speech; *gānam* – (is) song; *api* – and; *gamanam* – movement; *nāṭyam* – (is) dance; *vaṁśī* – (where) Śrī Kṛṣṇa's bamboo flute; *priya-sakhī* – acts as a dear friend; *jyotiḥ* –

(where) the *svarūpa* of light; *cid-ānandam* – is a substance of cognizance and bliss; *param api tat* – in that place even ordinary items that are usually illuminated from outside illuminate all other objects like the sun and moon, because their nature is supreme, meaning full of knowledge and bliss; *āsvādyam api ca* – and they are also relishable, i.e. enjoyable; *ca* – and; *saḥ su-mahān* – (where) a very great; *kṣīra-abdhiḥ* – ocean of milk; *surabhībhyaḥ* – from the udders of millions upon millions of Surabhī cows, who are absorbed in the vibration of Kṛṣṇa's flute; *sravati* – incessantly flows; *yatra api* – where also; *samayaḥ* – time; *hi na vrajati* – certainly does not pass away (i.e. eternal spiritual time, which is free from the influence of material time, is an eternal unbroken present without past or future); *vā* – even; *nimeṣa-ardha-ākhyaḥ* – to the extent of half a moment; *aham bhaje* – I render service; *tam* – to that; *śveta-dvīpam* – white island of Śvetadvīpa; *yam* – which; *te* – those; *katipaye* – very few; *santaḥ* – saints whose faith (*niṣṭhā*) for Śrī Bhagavān is firmly established; *kṣiti-virala-cārāḥ* – wandering on the face of the Earth; *iha* – in this world; *vidantaḥ* – know; *iti* – as; *golokam* – Goloka.

Translation

I worship that supreme abode of Śvetadvīpa, where the beloved heroines are a host of transcendental goddesses of fortune, and the Supreme Personality Śrī Kṛṣṇa is the only lover; where all the trees are spiritual desire-trees, and the earth is made of transcendental wish-fulfilling *cintāmaṇi* jewels; where the water is nectar, natural speaking is a melodious song, and walking to and fro is an artful dance; where the flute is the dearmost friend; where light is full of knowledge and bliss, and the supreme spiritual substance that comprises all things is relishable; where a vast transcendental ocean of milk is always flowing from millions upon millions of *surabhī* cows; and where time is not subject to passing away, even for half the blink of an eye, because it is not divided into past and

future, but remains in the undivided eternal present. That divine abode, which is practically unknown in this world, is known by the name of Goloka to only a few, rare *sādhus*.

Ṭīkā translation

Brahmājī has thus described in poetic prayers the glories of his worshipable Lord, and how He alone is the supermost object of loving service. Now, in this pair of verses which comprise verse 56, he eulogizes that realm that is beautified by his worshipable deity (*iṣṭadeva*). One should understand the word *śriyaḥ* to mean the beautiful *gopīs* of Vraja. They are Mahā-Lakṣmīs and they are the beloveds of Golokapati Śrī Kṛṣṇa. They have been described in this way by the *mantras* and meditations employed in their worship. The word *kāntaḥ* is singular in number. This means that Śrī Kṛṣṇa alone is the one exclusive lover of countless beautiful Vraja maidens. Therefore, the glories of Śrī Govinda excel even those of other forms of Bhagavān such as Mahā-Nārāyaṇa, and the glories of Govinda-dhāma excel the glories of Mahā-Vaikuṇṭha.

In Mahā-Vaikuṇṭha, Mahā-Lakṣmī continually renders service to Mahā-Nārāyaṇa in a mood of extreme reverence. Mahā-Nārāyaṇa also accepts Her service and bestows an abundance of mercy upon her. However, in Goloka Vṛndāvana the son of Nanda Mahārāja, Śrī Kṛṣṇa, is the lover of innumerable *gopīs*. He dances with them in *rāsa-līlā* and always remains eager to attain their favor. Thus Goloka-dhāma and Śrī Kṛṣṇa, the supreme connoisseur of transcendental mellows (*rasika-śekhara*), are both possessed of the highest and most astonishing glories because they are adorned with a sweetness that covers their opulences.

The trees there are wish-fulfilling trees (*kalpa-taru*), which fulfill all the hearts' desires of everyone. Out of intense love for

Śrī Kṛṣṇa, they have become like inanimate trees, and they bestow sweet fruits upon all. Feeling the anguish of separation from Śrī Kṛṣṇa when He is away, and becoming immersed in *prema* upon meeting Him, they exhibit the eight types of ecstatic bodily symptoms (*aṣṭa-sāttvika-vikāra*). Even the soil of that place fulfills all desires just like a desire-tree, for its touch alone awakens *kṛṣṇa-prema* in the heart. Furthermore, it is composed of transcendental bliss just like Śrī Kṛṣṇa. If even the soil is of this nature, then what can be said of jewels such as the Kaustubha jewel? If the water there is as delectable as nectar, then what can be said of the nectar?

In Goloka-dhāma, *vaṁśī* is the dearmost friend (*priya-sakhī*), because, by the waves of her sweet voice, she first informs Śrī Kṛṣṇa's beloved *gopīs* about where Śrī Kṛṣṇa is happily engaged in His pastimes and then, exerting a powerful attraction upon them, she brings them to that very place. Furthermore, every substance in that abode is the embodiment of transcendental joy. Every article is self-effulgent like the sun and moon. Thus it is stated in the *Gautamīya-tantra*: "*samānodita candrārkam* – the sun and moon rise at the same time there, and all the substances of that abode possess the power of self-illumination like the sun and moon. The moon displays sixteen phases every night there, and all the objects illuminated by that full moon are themselves self-effulgent. Being composed of *cit-śakti*, they are all highly relishable.

darśayām āsa lokaṁ svam
gopānāṁ tamasaḥ param

Śrīmad-Bhāgavatam (10.28.14)

From this verse it is understood that Śrī Kṛṣṇa granted to Śrī Nanda and the other Vrajavāsīs *darśana* of His own planet, which is situated beyond the material energy. By the expression *surabhībhyaś ca*, it should be understood that when the cows hear the sweet sound of Śrī Kṛṣṇa's flute, they are helplessly overwhelmed with feelings of parental affection, and a stream of milk flows automatically from their udders. They forget to chew and swallow the lush, green grass in their mouths. Instead, they close their eyes and with an insatiable thirst drink the nectar of the sound of Śrī Kṛṣṇa's flute through the vessels of their ears.

The confidential purport of the expression *vrajati na hi* is that because all the Vrajavāsīs are perpetually immersed in the absorption of condensed *prema* for Śrī Kṛṣṇa, they forget everything about their bodies and everything related to the body. They have no time for meditation. There, the great ocean of transcendental blissfulness, which is completely devoid of material afflictions such as birth, death, old age, disease, lamentation and fear, is incessantly moving in endless waves. There is no influence of time in that realm: *na ca kāla-vikramaḥ* (*Śrīmad-Bhāgavatam* 2.9.10).

The word *śveta* means *śuddha*, absolutely pure and untouched by the association of anything else. Therefore Śrī Kṛṣṇa's abode is called Śvetadvīpa or Śuddhadvīpa. It has also been stated in the *Gopāla-tāpanī*: "*yathā sarasi padmaṁ tiṣṭhati tathā bhūmyāṁ hi tiṣṭhati* – just as a lotus flower remains in water and yet is untouched by it, similarly, although Śvetadvīpa-dhāma (Vṛndāvana-Navadvīpa) is apparently located on the surface of the earth, it remains untouched by earthly defects."

The word *kṣitīti* indicates that very few rare persons in this world know about the factual existence of Śrī Goloka. The *ṛṣis* headed by Sanaka Kumāra said: "*yaṁ na vidyo vayaṁ sarve pṛcchanto 'pi pitāmaham* – although we all posed questions before our great father, Brahmājī, we could not understand Goloka Vṛndāvana-dhāma." Therefore, Goloka Vṛndāvana-dhāma is the most inaccessible abode. It can only be understood by those who are the recipients of Śrī Kṛṣṇa's mercy.

Tātparya

The *dhāma* is completely transcendental, full of the most excellent transcendental mellows, and easily attained by those living entities who perform *bhajana*. It cannot be referred to as devoid of attributes (*nirviśeṣa*). The impersonal *brahma-dhāma* is attained through anger, fear and delusion. The devotees attain either Paravyoma Vaikuṇṭha in the spiritual universe or above that, Goloka-dhāma, depending on their *rasa*, or individual devotional inclination. Goloka-dhāma is called Śvetadvīpa (the white isle) because it is absolutely pure. In this world, those who perform worship on the path of *viśuddha-bhakti* attain *viśuddha-prema-bhakti*. Only they have *darśana* of the aforementioned *śvetadvīpa-tattva* in Gokula Vṛndāvana and Navadvīpa situated in this world. Those rare devotees refer to that *śvetadvīpa-tattva* as Goloka.

In that Goloka one will find the everlasting, exquisite beauty of the transcendentally qualified lover and beloved, trees and creepers, land (with mountains, rivers and forests), water, speech, movement, flute-song, moon, sun, the enjoyed and enjoyment (the inconceivable variegated wonders of the sixty-four arts), cows, nectar in the form of a flowing ocean of milk, and spiritual time characterized by the eternal present. This Goloka is described in numerous places in *śāstra* such as the Vedas, Purāṇas and *tantras*.

It is stated in the *Chāndogya Śruti*: *brūyād yāvān vā ayam ākāśas tāvān eṣa antar hṛdaye ākāśaḥ uta asmin dyāv āpṛthivī antar eva samāhite ubhāv agniś ca vāyuś ca sūrya-candra-masāv ubhau vidhun nakṣatrāṇi yac cānyad ihāsti yac ca nāsti sarvaṁ tasmin samāhitam iti.*

The purport is that, just as there are so many attributes and varieties in the world of *māyā*, similarly all those variegated features and even more are present in that transcendental abode.

The harmonious combination of the diverse facets of the spiritual world produces blissfulness, whereas the discord between the diverse features of the material world produces mixed happiness and distress. Through the Vedas and the principles of knowledge contained therein, the Vedas personified and the saintly devotees of Bhagavān adopt the pure and uncontaminated state of consciousness. Thus, they adopt the *yoga* system of the trance of pure devotion, in which they attain the *darśana* of that Goloka-dhāma. By the mercy of Śrī Kṛṣṇa, the faculty of their insignificant consciousness attains an unlimited nature of enjoyment on the same level as Śrī Kṛṣṇa in His abode; that is, they relish the happiness of loving service.

The expression *param api tad āsvādyam api ca* has a hidden meaning. The words *param api* indicate that among all the transcendentally blissful varieties within Goloka, Śrī Kṛṣṇa is the Supreme Absolute Truth (*para-tattva*). The words *tad āsvādyam api* indicate that all the other transcendentally blissful varieties are the objects of Śrī Kṛṣṇa's enjoyment; that is, they are Śrī Kṛṣṇa's *āsvādya-tattva*, meaning they are to be tasted by Him. Śrī Kṛṣṇa attains the condition of possessing a golden complexion when He relishes the following three *bhāvas*: the greatness of Śrīmatī Rādhikā's intimate love (*praṇaya*), the *rasa* of Śrī Kṛṣṇa that is realized by Her, and the happiness She feels upon realizing that *rasa*. In other words, He assumes the form of Śrī Gaurasundara, whose body is adorned with the emotions and luster of Śrī Rādhā, and engages in tasting His own glories. That condition is the happiness of His own *rasa-sevā*, service imbued with transcendental mellows. This happiness of *rasa-sevā* is also eternally present in Śvetadvīpa.

Verse 57

अथोवाच महाविष्णुर्भगवन्तं प्रजापतिम् ।
ब्रह्मन् महत्त्वविज्ञाने प्रजासर्गे च चेन्मतिः ।
पञ्चश्लोकीमिमां विद्यां वत्स दत्तां निबोध मे ॥५७॥

athovāca mahā-viṣṇur
bhagavantaṁ prajāpatim
brahman mahattva-vijñāne
prajā-sarge ca cen matiḥ
pañca-ślokīm imāṁ vidyāṁ
vatsa dattāṁ nibodha me

Anvaya

atha – thereafter, i.e. after hearing the prayers of Brahmā; *mahā-viṣṇuḥ* – Mahā-Viṣṇu, i.e. Śrī Kṛṣṇa, the controller of all controllers; *uvāca* – said; *bhagavantam prajāpatim* – to Bhagavān Brahmā; *brahman* - O Prajāpati (protector of the universal population); *cet* – if; *matiḥ* – your mind desires; *mahattva-vijñāne* – realized knowledge of My glories, i.e. specific knowledge of the transcendental nature; *ca* – and; *prajā-sarge* – the process of generating universal progeny; *vatsa* – (then) dear child; *nibodha* – know; *me* – from Me; *imām* – this; *vidyām* – knowledge; *dattām* – given; *pañca-ślokīm* – in five verses.

Translation

On hearing this prayer, which contains so many essential truths, Bhagavān Śrī Kṛṣṇa said to Brahmā, "O Brahmā, if you desire to create progeny by employing the transcendental realization of My glories, then My dear child, I will bestow upon you this knowledge, contained in five verses. You should take it up in practice."

Ṭīkā translation

Thus, the mercy bestowed on Brahmājī by Śrī Bhagavān upon hearing his prayers is related in this one and a half *ślokas* beginning with *athovāca*. Everything is clear in this verse.

Tātparya

Until this point, Brahmājī has offered with a burning expectation many types of prayers containing names such as Kṛṣṇa and Govinda, which indicate Bhagavān's form, qualities and pastimes, and when Svayam Bhagavān Śrī Kṛṣṇa heard this, He was very pleased. At that time Brahmā also had a desire in his heart to create progeny. Bhagavān Śrī Kṛṣṇa understood his mood, and explained how *jīvas* may perform the *sādhana* of pure, unalloyed *bhakti* while carrying out His orders in the material world. Śrī Bhagavān said, "O Brahmā, knowledge of the transcendental reality is the essential science. If you want to create progeny while remaining situated in this realized knowledge of transcendence, then listen to the instruction on *bhakti-vidyā* that I will impart in the following five *ślokas*."

Bhagavān will explain how one should practice *śuddha-bhakti* while performing one's worldly duties in pursuance of His order.

Verse 58

प्रबुद्धे ज्ञानभक्तिभ्यामात्मन्यानन्दचिन्मयी ।
उदेत्यनुत्तमा भक्तिर्भगवत्प्रेमलक्षणा ॥५८॥

prabuddhe jñāna-bhaktibhyām
ātmany ānanda-cin-mayī
udety anuttamā bhaktir
bhagavat-prema-lakṣaṇā

Anvaya

ātmani prabuddhe – when the soul becomes awakened; *jñāna-bhaktibhyām* – through knowledge of the transcendental *tattvas* of Śrī Bhagavān and devotion for Him; *anuttamā* – (then) the most exalted of all; *bhaktiḥ* – devotion; *ānanda-cin-mayī* – which is the *rasa-svarūpa* of transcendental bliss; *bhagavat-prema-lakṣaṇā* – and is characterized by love for Śrī Kṛṣṇa; *udeti* – arises.

Translation

When one realizes the transcendental subject through knowledge, and through devotion whose goal is affection for Śrī Kṛṣṇa, there is an awakening of *prema* for Bhagavān. That *prema* is characterized by extremely elevated *bhakti* in the form of transcendental *rasa* in relation to the soul's beloved Śrī Kṛṣṇa.

Ṭīkā translation

Now, in these five verses, the mercy of Bhagavān is being described. Bhagavān begins to bestow His mercy with this verse beginning *prabuddhe*. "O Brahmā, being imbued with knowledge and realization by My mercy, you may engage in My service with ecstatic devotional sentiments."

For example, Bhagavān said to Uddhavajī: *jñāna-vijñāna-sampanno bhaja māṁ bhakti-bhāvitaḥ* (*Śrīmad-Bhāgavatam* 11.19.5). The meaning is: "*mām eva bhaja anyat-sarva-tyaja* – abandon everything and engage exclusively in My service." (Śrīdhara Svāmipāda)

"Service is the embodiment of knowledge (*jñāna*), and one who serves is the embodiment of realized knowledge (*vijñāna*). The highest auspiciousness for the *jīvas* lies in rendering service to Bhagavān in knowledge of the constitutional nature of the served and the servant. Therefore the prime duty is to engage in His service with knowledge of relationship (*sambandha-jñāna*). One cannot attain love for Bhagavān by rendering the unsightly service that results from the absence of *sambandha-jñāna*." (Prabhupāda Śrīla Bhaktisiddhānta Sarasvatī Ṭhākura)

Tātparya

The meaning of *jñāna* is *sambandha-jñāna*, or knowledge of the mutual relationship between spiritual substance (in the form of the living entities), dull matter and the supreme transcendental reality who is Śrī Kṛṣṇa. Here *jñāna udeti* does not refer to knowledge of the body and mind, because that knowledge is opposed to *bhakti*. The statements of the Vedas and literature in pursuance of the Vedic conclusion, received through the spiritual hierarchy of *guru-paramparā*, constitute the only immaculate evidence. The seven principles of *Daśa-mūla* that constitute *sambandha-jñāna* are as follows: (1) Śrī Hari is the Supreme Absolute Truth. (2) He is omnipotent. (3) He is the nectarean ocean of all transcendental mellows. (4) The living entities are His separated expansions. (5) Some of those *jīvas* are conditioned. (6) Most of the living entities exist before and beyond this material world and are liberated. (7) The relationship between Bhagavān, the *jīvas* and the creation is one of inconceivable difference and non-difference.

Bhakti is the only process to attain the goal of life, and among the many limbs of *bhakti*, nine are prominent. Activities such as hearing about Śrī Kṛṣṇa, glorifying Him, remembering Him, serving His lotus feet, worshiping Him, offering Him prayers, carrying out His orders, relating to Him as a friend and fully surrendering oneself to His will are called *kṛṣṇānuśīlana*, the cultivation of endeavors directly for Śrī Kṛṣṇa or in connection with Him. One should understand that such *kṛṣṇānuśīlana* is the only process to attain the goal of life. Its limbs and sub-limbs have been described elaborately in *Śrī Bhakti-rasāmṛta-sindhu*. Only by this type of knowledge and devotion can one attain the enlightenment characterized by the awakening of *prema-bhakti* within the heart. Such *prema* is the highest form of *bhakti*, and the ultimate goal for the living entities.

Verse 59

प्रमाणैस्तत्सदाचारैस्तदभ्यासैर्निरन्तरम् ।
बोधयन्नात्मनात्मानं भक्तिमप्युत्तमां लभेत् ॥५९॥

pramāṇais tat-sad-ācārais
tad-abhyāsair nirantaram
bodhayann ātmanātmānaṁ
bhaktim apy uttamāṁ labhet

Anvaya

tad-abhyāsaiḥ – through the *sādhaka's* repeated practice; *tat-sad-ācāraiḥ* – in accordance with the pure standards of *bhakti* that have been previously established by the examples of *sādhu-bhaktas*; *pramāṇaiḥ* – and with the evidence given in all *śāstras* that teach the philosophical conclusions of pure *bhakti*; *nirantaram* – incessantly; *bodhayan* – realizing; *ātmānam* – oneself; *ātmanā api* – through one's own self (in the form of a purified *jīva* who has taken shelter of Śrī Bhagavān); *labhet* – one can attain; *uttamām bhaktim* – pure devotion.

Translation

One may attain incessant realization of one's constitutional identity by continuously observing the codes of appropriate behavior, and by practicing the *sādhana-bhajana* prescribed by the authentic scriptures. Understanding oneself to be under the shelter of Bhagavān, one may offer oneself fully at His lotus feet. A *sādhaka* who does so attains *uttama-bhakti*.

Ṭīkā translation

Sādhana-bhakti is the only method to attain *prema-bhakti*. Therefore the subject of *sādhana-bhakti* is being described in this verse beginning *pramāṇais tat*. The term *sat* or *sādhu* refers to the great transcendentally realized personalities who conduct themselves perfectly in accordance with the precepts of *śuddha-bhakti*, and with the etiquette prescribed by authentic devotional scriptures such as the Vedas, Purāṇas, *Bhagavad-gītā* and *Śrīmad-Bhāgavatam*. When the *sādhaka-bhakta* continuously practices the limbs of *bhakti* – such as *śravaṇa*, *kīrtana* and *smaraṇa* – in accordance with the standards set by such realized personalities, he realizes within his heart that he is a pure spirit soul under the shelter of Bhagavān. *Śuddha-bhakti* is actually *rāgānuga-bhakti*; that is, *bhakti* following the moods of Śrī Kṛṣṇa's eternal associates in Goloka who are by nature deeply attached to Him. One who engages in the uninterrupted cultivation of this *śuddha-bhakti* attains within his pure heart a transcendental manifestation of his eternal spiritual form as a servant of Bhagavān, by the mercy of a pure devotee or by the direct mercy of Bhagavān Himself. Subsequently he achieves the highest stage of *prema-bhakti*.

A lucid analysis of this occurrence can also be found in the prayers by the Vedas personified in *Śrīmad-Bhāgavatam* (10.87.20):

sva-kṛta-pureṣv amīṣv abahir-antara-saṁvaraṇaṁ
tava puruṣaṁ vadanty akhila-śakti-dhṛto 'ṁśa-kṛtam
iti nṛ-gatiṁ vivicya kavayo nigamāvapanaṁ
bhavata upāsate 'ṅghrim abhavam bhuvi viśvasitāḥ

The living entities are internally and externally controllers of their bodies and populate the entire universe. They are not independent, but are fragmentary parts (*vibhinnāṁśa*) of Your energy. Those who attain a true understanding, and who are in knowledge of the desired goal of the greatly realized souls, utterly reject the fruitive activities mentioned in the Vedas. With complete faith they cultivate unalloyed, transcendental *bhakti* in the form of worshiping You without the slightest expectation of material remuneration. In this way, although they remain in the world, they easily cross over the insurmountable ocean of material existence and come to You by engaging in the loving service of Your lotus feet. Your divine lotus feet are the only cure for the fear experienced in the endless chain of birth and death.

Tātparya

The word *pramāṇa* (reliable evidence) refers to the *bhakti-śāstras* such as the Vedas, Upaniṣads, Purāṇas, *Bhagavad-gītā* and *Śrīmad-Bhāgavatam*. The word *sadācāra* should be understood to indicate the behavior of Vaiṣṇavas who are practicing pure *bhakti*, and whose activities are based on deep, spontaneous attachment to Śrī Kṛṣṇa. *Tad-abhyāsa* denotes the process of acquiring a clear understanding of the ten fundamental principles (*daśa-mūla-tattva*) described in *bhakti-śāstra*, and then, as prescribed by the *śāstra*, receiving *harināma*, which is the embodiment of Śrī Kṛṣṇa's names, form, qualities and pastimes. After that one should continuously cultivate the practice of chanting *harināma* throughout the day and night. This is the meaning of *abhyāsa*. Thus, this verse stresses that it is absolutely necessary to adopt the process of spiritual cultivation in accordance with the instructions of *śāstra*, and under the guidance of *sādhus*. Cultivating the practice of chanting *harināma* along with appropriate conduct dispels the ten kinds of offenses against the holy name. *Abhyāsa* means to follow the uninterrupted and offenseless cultivation of *harināma* practiced by *śuddha-bhaktas*. If one practices in this way, the desired result, namely *prema-bhakti*, will manifest in the heart.

Verse 60

यस्याः श्रेयस्करं नास्ति यया निर्वृतिमाप्नुयात् ।
या साधयति मामेव भक्तिं तामेव साधयेत् ॥६०॥

yasyāḥ śreyas-karaṁ nāsti
yayā nirvṛtim āpnuyāt
yā sādhayati mām eva
bhaktiṁ tām eva sādhayet

Anvaya

na asti – there is nothing else; *śreyaḥ-karam* – which is more potent in promoting auspiciousness; *yasyāḥ* – than that (*śuddha-bhakti*); *yayā* – (because) by that; *āpnuyāt* – one can attain; *nirvṛtim* – supreme bliss; *eva* – certainly; *yā sādhayati* – it captivates; *mām* – Me; *eva* – indeed; *sādhayet* – one should practice *sādhana*; *tām bhaktim* – for that *śuddha-bhakti*.

Translation

***Prema-bhakti* is the aim and object of life, and there is nothing more auspicious than this. The platform of supreme bliss is attained only through *prema-bhakti*. This *prema-bhakti*, which leads to Me, is only achieved through *sādhana-bhakti*.**

Ṭīkā translation

Prema-bhakti is the only aim and object of life (*sādhya*), and there is nothing more auspicious than this for the living entities. Bhagavān is attained by *prema-bhakti*, which is the embodiment of the highest transcendental bliss. This has also been stated in *Śrīmad-Bhāgavatam* (4.24.55):

taṁ durārādhyam ārādhya
satām api durāpayā
ekānta-bhaktyā ko vāñchet
pāda-mūlaṁ vinā bahiḥ

O Bhagavān, Your unalloyed devotional service is extremely difficult to attain, even for *sādhus*. After worshiping Your lotus feet, which are rarely attained, what kind of unfortunate person in this world could give up loving service to them and desire anything else born of ignorance, such as the happiness derived from the gross physical body, from elevation to heaven, or from liberation?

Those who wish to know more about this subject can refer to *Bhakti-sandarbha*.

Tātparya

There is nothing more auspicious for the living entities than *prema-bhakti*. This stage of accomplished devotion constitutes the *jīvas'* highest bliss. The lotus feet of Śrī Kṛṣṇa are attained only by *prema-bhakti*. Only those who cultivate *sādhana-bhakti* with a grief-stricken and desperate hankering to attain accomplished devotion can become successful in achieving it. *Prema-bhakti* can never be attained by others.

Verse 61

धर्मानन्यान् परित्यज्य मामेकं भज विश्वसन् ।
यादृशी यादृशी श्रद्धा सिद्धिर्भवति तादृशी ॥

कुर्वन्निरन्तरं कर्म लोकोऽयमनुवर्त्तते ।
तेनैव कर्मणा ध्यायन् मां परां भक्तिमिच्छति ॥६१॥

dharmān anyān parityajya
mām ekaṁ bhaja viśvasan
yādṛśī yādṛśī śraddhā
siddhir bhavati tādṛśī

kurvan nirantaraṁ karma
loko 'yam anuvartate
tenaiva karmaṇā dhyāyan
māṁ parāṁ bhaktim icchati

Anvaya

parityajya – completely renouncing; *anyān* – other; *dharmān* – forms of constitutional activity centered around the principles of religious conduct, economic development, sense gratification and liberation, which are practiced out of ignorance; *bhaja* – render service; *mām* – to Me; *ekam* – exclusively; *viśvasan* – with faith; *yādṛśī yādṛśī* – in accordance with the degree; *śraddhā* – of faith; *bhavati* – there is achieved; *tādṛśī* – a corresponding; *siddhiḥ* – perfection; *ayam lokaḥ* – the people of this material world; *nirantaram* – incessantly; *kurvan* – engaging in action; *karma anuvartate* – follow this process of work; *eva* – certainly; *tena karmaṇā* – through performing such activities; *dhyāyan* – while contemplating; *mām* – Me; *icchati* – one hankers; *parām bhaktim* – for the supreme stage of *bhakti*, i.e. *prema-bhakti*.

Translation

O Brahmā, abandon all varieties of *dharma* and engage exclusively in My *bhajana* with unwavering determination and faith. Perfection is attained according to one's faith. Human beings in this world are continuously engaged in occupational duties. They should desire to attain *prema-bhakti* by being absorbed in thoughts of Me through the performance of their respective duties.

Ṭīkā translation

To further fortify the resolve of Brahmājī in the practice of *śuddha-bhakti*, Śrī Bhagavān said, "O Brahmā, engage in My service with unflinching faith. Others who desire sense gratification or liberation should also think exclusively of Me and nothing else while carrying out their respective duties. In this way everyone may worship Me, the Supreme Personality, through unalloyed *bhakti-yoga*."

This has also been stated in *Śrīmad-Bhāgavatam* (2.3.10):

akāmaḥ sarva-kāmo vā
mokṣa-kāma udāra-dhīḥ
tīvreṇa bhakti-yogena
yajeta puruṣaṁ param

Those who are desireless, those who have all desires, those who desire liberation and those who desire unalloyed devotion should all simply worship Me, the Supreme Enjoyer, Śrī Kṛṣṇa, through the performance of unadulterated *bhakti-yoga*.

Tātparya

Śuddha-bhakti is the only transcendental occupation for the living entities, and is therefore called the eternal constitutional occupation of the living entity (*jaiva-dharma*). All other constitutional activities apart from this are engagements arising from the influence of material designations. There are many types of such materially designated occupations current in the world, such as the *dharma* of knowledge of Brahman aimed at attaining impersonal liberation; *yoga-dharma* such as the eightfold *yoga* process aimed at oneness with Brahman; the *dharma* of mundane piety to acquire bodily sense pleasure; the *dharma* of *jñāna-yoga* as a mixture of fruitive activity with the cultivation of intellectual knowledge; and the *dharma* of dry renunciation. Here Bhagavān is saying, "Reject all these superficial *dharmas* and engage in My service by taking shelter of *bhakti-dharma*, which is based on transcendental faith. Exclusive faith in Me is called *viśvāsa*. When that conviction gradually matures, it assumes the form of steadiness (*niṣṭhā*), taste (*ruci*), attachment (*āsakti*) and ecstatic transcendental emotion (*bhāva*). The degree of one's attainment of spiritual perfection depends on the extent to which faith matures or becomes intensified."

One might raise the question: how will a person protect his body and maintain his life if he always remains absorbed in the constant endeavor for perfection in *bhakti*? Death is inevitable when activities for physical preservation and maintenance are arrested, and how will it be possible to endeavor for perfection in *bhakti* when one has died? To dispel this doubt, Bhagavān is saying, "If human beings maintain their lives and protect their bodies with the sole intention of attaining Me, the reactive quality of the activities they perform is eliminated, and these activities become acts of devotion. The survival and sustenance of the human being is accomplished through three types of activity, namely, bodily, mental and social. Bodily activities include eating, drinking, sitting, walking, reclining, dressing and activities for purifying oneself, such as bathing. Mental activities include thinking, remembering, concentrating, realizing and feeling happiness and distress. There are many types of social activities such as marriage, mutual obligations between the king and his subjects, fraternity, assemblies for performing sacrifice, activities related to one's home and temple, fulfilling desires by constructing hospitals and digging wells for public welfare, maintaining family members, receiving guests, observing customs and honoring others according to their social status. When all these activities are performed for the sake of one's own enjoyment, they can be called *karma-kāṇḍa*. When one attempts to accumulate knowledge through the performance of these activities, they can be called *karma-yoga* or *jñāna-yoga*. But when all such activities are favorable to *sādhana-bhakti*, they are called the indirect application of *bhakti* (*gauṇa-bhakti-yoga*).

"Only activities that are purely based on service to Me may be called the direct application of devotion. According to the circumstances, one may sometimes engage in the activities of direct devotion, and at other times, one may be engaged in indirect *bhakti* while meeting worldly obligations. In either case, every activity is effectively a meditation upon Me. In such a condition, one does not become indifferent to Me, even while being engaged in activities." In this method, although work is performed, one remains internally fixed. *Śrī Īśopaniṣad* (1) states:

īśāvāsyam idaṁ sarvaṁ
yat kiñcij jagatyāṁ jagat
tena tyaktena bhuñjīthā
mā gṛdhaḥ kasya svid dhanam

Our revered commentator has stated, *tena īśa-tyaktena visṛṣtena*. The essential purport is that whatever one receives should be accepted with the understanding, "By good fortune I have attained this mercy personally given by Bhagavān." If one accepts everything in this way, the reactive quality of *karma* is eliminated and the activity takes on the quality of devotion. Therefore, the verse beginning with *īśāvāsya* conveys the following sense:

kurvann eveha karmāṇi
jijīviṣec chataṁ samāḥ
evaṁ tvayi nānyatheto 'sti
na karma lipyate nare

Śrī Īśopaniṣad (2)

By observing this method, a human being may work throughout a life extending over thousands of years, without being tainted by *karma*.

The *jñānīs* interpret both of these *mantras* as advocating the renunciation of the fruits of work. However, the devotees interpret them to mean that one can attain the mercy of Bhagavān by completely offering everything unto Him. Bhagavān is saying, "Perform your worldly duties along with meditating upon Me and worshiping Me on the path of formal deity worship."

Within Brahmā's heart there is a desire to create. If Brahmā considers the task of creation to be Bhagavān's order, and carries it out while meditating upon Him, then, because he is surrendered to Bhagavān, this may be included within *bhakti* as a secondary function favorable to the nourishment of devotion. Thus it was appropriate for Bhagavān to instruct Brahmā in this way, although this type of instruction is not required for a living entity who has attained *bhāva*, because he is naturally detached from any subject other than Śrī Kṛṣṇa.

Verse 62

अहं हि विश्वस्य चराचरस्य
बीजं प्रधानं प्रकृतिः पुमांश्च ।
मयाहितं तेज इदं विभर्षि
विधे विधेहि त्वमथो जगन्ति ॥६२॥

ahaṁ hi viśvasya carācarasya
bījaṁ pradhānaṁ prakṛtiḥ pumāṁś ca
mayāhitaṁ teja idaṁ vibharṣi
vidhe vidhehi tvam atho jaganti

iti śrī brahma-saṁhitāyāṁ bhagavat-siddhānta-saṅgrahe
mūla-sūtrākhyaḥ pañcamo 'dhyāyaḥ

Anvaya

aham – I; *hi* – alone; *bījam* – (am) the seed; *viśvasya* – of this universe; *cara-acarasya* – of moving and non-moving beings; *pradhānam* – the unmanifest aggregate of material elements; *prakṛtiḥ* – the external potency (which is unmanifest to the conditioned souls) consisting of the three binding qualities; *ca* – and; *pumān* – the Supreme Person (overseer of everything); *idam* – this; *tejaḥ* – spiritual power; *vibharṣi* – you hold; *āhitam* – is endowed; *mayā* – by Me; *vidhe* – O Creator (Brahmā); *atho* – now; *vidhehi* – (through that power) furnish all necessities; *jaganti* – for the worlds.

Translation

O Brahmā, listen to Me. I alone am the seed and the root principle of this universe of moving and non-moving entities. Only I am the unmanifest aggregate of the material elements. Only I am the predominated (*prakṛti*)

as well as the predominator (*puruṣa*). The brahminical power that is concealed within you has been given by Me. Therefore, employ this power in creating the universe of animate and inanimate entities.

Ṭīkā translation

In this verse beginning *ahaṁ hi*, Bhagavān tells Śrī Brahmā with sound logic, "Thus your desire to create will also be successful. Only I am the seed of the unmanifest aggregate of material elements, the embodiment of the highest cause of all causes, the full and complete Brahman, and the complete truth, or Svayam Bhagavān. I am the external energy (*prakṛti*), which is composed of three material modes, and which is called unmanifest. I am also the Supreme Male who glances upon that energy. What more can I say? You are also employing the potency that was bestowed by Me. Therefore, O Brahmā, create the whole universe of mobile and stationary beings by that potency."

It is mentioned in *Brahma-saṁhitā* and other scriptures that the text of *Brahma-saṁhitā* comprises one hundred chapters. This fifth chapter is the essential purport of *Brahma-saṁhitā*, also called *Śrī Kṛṣṇopaniṣad*, compiled by Brahmājī, because it is the collected essence of the entire text of one hundred chapters. Although many different interpretations and meanings can be given, we have defined the pure interpretation and significance, along with the philosophical analysis according to the eternally established conclusions received through the genuine succession of realized spiritual preceptors. Intelligent and learned readers will make a meticulous study of this text with implicit faith. Just as the eternal Supreme Personality is the ultimate refuge, similarly that Śrī Rūpa Gosvāmipāda, whose elder brother is Śrī Sanātana Gosvāmipāda and whose younger brother is Śrī Vallabha, is my exclusive shelter.

Thus ends the translation of Śrī Jīva Gosvāmipāda's commentary on *Śrī Brahma-saṁhitā.*

Tātparya

According to some opinions, the superlative principle of truth is the formless, undifferentiated Brahman, which is devoid of qualities. Those who adhere to this conception think as follows: "It is only due to bewilderment that the impersonal substance known as Brahman appears to have attributes. Otherwise, when the illusory nature is divided, it is called material existence (*saṁsāra*), and in the undivided state it is called Brahman. Alternatively, Brahman is the object and the material world is its reflection." Another idea is, "Everything is simply the *jīva's* illusion. It is only in the *jīva's* deluded condition that the mistaken conception of the *jīva* and the material world is present in the impersonal Brahman." Some say, "By nature *īśvara* is one entity, the *jīva* is another and the universe of five gross elements is another *tattva.* They all exist with eternal and separate independence." Others support the following theory: if *īśvara* can be compared to a noun, then the *jīva* and the universe can be compared to its adjectives. Thus the noun of the Absolute Truth, being qualified by the adjectives of *jīva* and *jagat,* is the embodiment of qualified monism (*viśiṣṭādvaita*), and that specifically non-dual Brahman is the Supreme Truth. Some philosophers are of the opinion that the Supreme Truth appears sometimes in oneness and sometimes in duality by the influence of inconceivable potency. Some conclude that the monistic conception of a truth without potency is meaningless and illogical: "Thus, Brahman is the eternally pure, non-dual principle, replete with pure potency."

All such philosophies have come into being on the basis of statements from the Vedas with support from the *Vedānta-sūtra.*

Although they do not represent the genuine all-encompassing conclusion of the Vedas, they certainly contain some contextual aspects of the Vedic truth of qualified monism (*viśiṣṭādvaita*). Philosophies such as *sāṅkhya, pātañjala, nyāya* and *vaiśeṣika* are contrary to the Vedas, and the *pūrva-mīmāṁsa* philosophy conforms to the section of the Vedas that deals with the *dharma* of mundane piety.

Not to mention such philosophies which only externally take Vedānta as their basis, the philosophies of monism (*advaita*), qualified monism (*viśiṣṭādvaita*), dualism-with-non-dualism (*dvaitādvaita*), purified non-dualism (*śuddhādvaita*) and pure dualism (*śuddha-dvaita*) outlined previously have come into being on the basis of Vedānta.

"O Brahmā, leave behind those statements of the Vedas that are relevant to a particular context, or that are not universally applicable. You and your pure *sampradāya* should accept that complete philosophical conclusion that is consistent with the entirety of the Vedas, namely the highest principle of inconceivable difference and non-difference (*acintya-bhedābheda*). By doing so, you will be able to become a *śuddha-bhakta*. The essential significance of this statement is that the animate world is composed of *jīvas*, and the inanimate world is composed of matter. My superior potency has manifested the *jīvas* from the marginal potency, and My inferior potency has manifested the inert material world. I am the seed of everything. In other words, My desire potency, which is part of the predominated potency and which is non-different from Me, regulates everything. The transformations of the predominated potencies have become the unmanifest aggregate of the material energy (*pradhāna*), the predominated potency (*prakṛti*) and *puruṣa*. Although manifest as the potency of *pradhāna, prakṛti* and *puruṣa*, I am also eternally separate from them as the possessor and controller of the potency. In this way, the principle of simultaneous difference and non-difference is manifested in its fullest and most complete sense by the influence of My inconceivable potency. The statements of the Vedas descending in the succession of realized spiritual preceptors are called *āmnāya*. Therefore, may the *āmnāya* teaching of the preceptorial succession in your *sampradāya* be concerned exclusively with the attainment of *kṛṣṇa-prema* through that pure *bhakti-yoga* that is complete with knowledge of the mutual relationship between *jīva*, matter and Kṛṣṇa, on the basis of the philosophy of inconceivable distinction with non-distinction (*acintya-bhedābheda-tattva*). In this way, let the followers of your Śrī Brahma *sampradāya* also adopt this conception of *śuddha-bhakti* and bring auspiciousness to the world."

jīvābhaya-pradā vṛttir
jīvāśaya-prakāśinī
kṛtā bhaktivinodena
surabhī-kuñja-vāsinā

This *Prakāśikā-vṛtti*, which reveals the intention of Śrī Jīva Gosvāmī and bestows fearlessness upon the *jīvas*, has been published by Śrī Saccidānanda Bhaktivinoda Ṭhākura, a resident of Surabhī-kuñja.

Thus ends the Gauḍīya commentary entitled *Prakāśinī* on the original *sūtras* of the fifth chapter of the collected theistic conclusions that comprise *Śrī Brahma-saṁhitā*.

Śrīla Jīva Gosvāmī's Sanskrit Commentary

Verse 1 Ṭīkā

śrī śrī rādhā-kṛṣṇābhyāṁ namaḥ

śrī kṛṣṇa-rūpa-mahimā
mama citte mahīyatām
yasya prasādād vyākartum
icchāmi brahma-saṁhitām

duryojanāpi yuktārthā
suvicārād ṛṣi-smṛtiḥ
vicāre tu mamātra syād
ṛṣiṇāṁ sa ṛṣir gatiḥ

yadyapy adhyāya-śata-yuk
saṁhitā sā tathāpy asau
adhyāyaḥ sūtra-rūpatvāt
tasyāḥ sarvāṅgatāṁ gataḥ

śrīmad-bhāgavatādyeṣu
dṛṣṭaṁ yan mṛṣṭa-buddhibhiḥ
tad evātra parāmṛṣṭaṁ
tato hṛṣṭaṁ mano mama

yad yac chrī-kṛṣṇa-sandarbhe
vistarād vinirūpitam
atra tat punar āmṛśya
vyākhyātuṁ spṛśyate mayā

atha śrī-bhāgavate yad uktam – "ete cāṁśa-kalāḥ puṁsaḥ kṛṣṇas tu bhagavān svayam" iti, tad eva tāvat prathamam āha – īśvara iti. atra 'kṛṣṇa' ity eva viśeṣyaṁ tan nāma eva – 'kṛṣṇāvatārotsava' ity ādau śrī-śukādi-mahājana-prasiddhyā, "kṛṣṇāya vāsudevāya devakī-

nandanāya" ity ādi sāmopaniṣadi ca prathama-pratītatvena, tan nāma varṇāvirbhāva-kṛtā gargeṇa prathamam uddiṣṭatvena, tathā ca mantram adhikṛtya 'payasā kumbhaṁ pūrayati' iti nyāyena tatrāgrataḥ paṭhitatvena, mūla-rūpatvāt. tad uktaṁ prabhāsa-khaṇḍe padma-purāṇe ca śrī nārada-kuśadhvaja-saṁvāde śrī bhagavad uktau – "nāmnāṁ mukhyatamaṁ nāma kṛṣṇākhyaṁ me parantapa" iti. ataeva brahmāṇḍa-purāṇokta-kṛṣṇāṣṭottara-śatanāma-stotre – "sahasra-nāmnāṁ puṇyānāṁ trir āvṛttyā tu yat phalam. ekāvṛttya tu kṛṣṇasya nāmaikaṁ tat prayacchati." ity atra śrī-kṛṣṇasyety evoktam. yat tv agre 'govinda' nāmnā stoṣyate, tat khalu kṛṣṇatve 'pi tasya gavendratva-vaiśiṣṭya-darśanārtham eva. tad evaṁ rūḍhi-balena, prādhānyāt tasyaiva 'īśvaraḥ' ity ādīni viśeṣaṇāni. atha guṇa-dvārāpi tad dṛśyate; yathāha gargaḥ – "āsan varṇās trayo hy asya gṛhṇato 'nuyugaṁ tanuḥ. śuklo raktas tathā pīta idānīṁ kṛṣṇatāṁ gataḥ. bahūni santi nāmāni rūpāṇi ca sutasya te. guṇa-karmānurūpāṇi tāny ahaṁ veda no janāḥ." – 'asya' kṛṣṇatvena dṛśyamānasya 'pratiyugaṁ' nānā 'tanuḥ' avatārān 'gṛhṇataḥ' prakāśayataḥ śuklādayo 'varṇās trayaḥ' 'āsan' prakāśam avāpuḥ; satyādau śuklādir avatāra 'idānīṁ' sakṣād asyāvatāra-samaye 'kṛṣṇatāṁ gataḥ' etasminn evāntarbhūtaḥ. ataeva kṛṣṇe kartṛtvāt sarvotkarṣakatvāt kṛṣṇeti mukhyaṁ nāma; tasmād asyaiva tāni rūpāṇīty āha – bahūnīti. tad evaṁ guṇa-dvārā tan nāmni prādhānya-sūcakasya kṛṣṇasya tan nāmnaḥ prādhanye labdhe "kṛṣir bhū-vācakaḥ śabdo ṇaś ca nirvṛti-vācakaḥ. tayor aikyaṁ paraṁ brahma kṛṣṇa ity abhidhīyate." iti yoga-vṛttitve 'pi tasya tadṛśatvaṁ labhyate. na cedaṁ padyamany aparam. tad upāsanā-tantra-gautamīya-tantre 'ṣṭādaśākṣara-mantra-vyākhyāyāṁ tad etat tulyaṁ padyaṁ dṛśyate – "kṛṣi-śabdaś ca sattārtho ṇaś cānanda-svarūpakaḥ. sukha-rūpo bhaved ātmā bhāvānandamayas tataḥ." iti. tasmād ayam arthaḥ – 'bhavanty asmāt sarve 'rthāḥ' iti bhū-dhātv-artha ucyate bhāva-śabdavat. sa cātra karṣater evārthaḥ; gautamīye bhū-śabdasya sattā-vācakatve 'pi tad dhātv-arthaḥ sattaivocyate. ghaṭa-śabdasya pratipādyamānatvena saha sāmānādhikaraṇyāsambhavād dhetumat tāvad bhedopacāraḥ kāryaḥ. tac cākarṣābhiprāyaḥ. ghaṭatvaṁ sattā-vācakam ity ukter ghaṭa-sattaiva gamyate, na tu paṭa-sattā, na sāmānya-satteti. atha 'nirvṛttiḥ' ānandaḥ; tayor aikyaṁ sāmānādhikaraṇyena vyaktam. yat 'paraṁ brahma' sarvato 'pi sarvasyāpi bṛṁhaṇaṁ vastu tat bṛhattamam. 'kṛṣṇa ity abhidhīyate' īryate iti vā pāṭhaḥ. kintu kṛṣer ākarṣa-mātrārthakena ṇa-śabdasya ca pratipādyenānandena saha sāmānādhikaraṇyāsambhavād dhetu-hetumator abhedopacāraḥ kāryaḥ. tac cākarṣa-prācuryārtham 'āyur ghṛtam' itivat. para-brahma-śabdasya tat tad arthaś ca – "bṛhattvād bṛṁhaṇatvāc ca yad brahma paramaṁ viduḥ" iti viṣṇu-

purāṇāt; "atha kasmād ucyate brahma bṛṁhati bṛṁhayati" iti śruteś ca. evam evoktaṁ bṛhad-gautamīye – "kṛṣi-śabdo hi sattārtho ṇaś cānanda-svarūpakaḥ. sattā-svānandayor yogāt tat paraṁ brahma cocyate." iti. advaya-brahmavādibhir api sattānandayor aikyaṁ tathā mantavyam. śābdikair bhinnābhidheyatvena pratīteḥ sattā-śabdena cātra sarveṣāṁ satāṁ pravṛtti-hetur yat paramaṁ sat tad evocyate – "sad eva saumyedam agra āsīt" iti śruteḥ. abhinnābhidheyatve 'vṛkṣaḥ taruḥ' itivad viśeṣeṇa viśeṣyatvāyogād ekasya vaiyarthyāc ca. gautamīya-padyaṁ caivaṁ vyakhyeyaṁ – pūrvārdhe sarvākarṣaṇa-śakti-viśiṣṭa ānandātmā kṛṣṇa ity arthaḥ; tad uttarārdhe yasmād evaṁ sarvākarṣaka-sukha-rūpo 'sau tasmād ātmā jīvaś ca tatra sukha-rūpo bhavet. tatra hetuḥ – 'bhāvaḥ' premā, tan mayānandatvād iti. tad evaṁ svarūpa-guṇābhyāṁ parama-bṛhattamaḥ sarvākarṣaka ānandaḥ kṛṣṇa-śabda-vācya iti jñeyam. sa ca śabdaḥ śrī-devakī-nandana eva rūḍhaḥ. asyaiva sarvānandakatvaṁ vāsudevopaniṣadi dṛṣṭaṁ – "devakī-nandano nikhilam ānandayet" iti. ānando 'trāvikāro 'nanya-siddhaḥ. tataś cāsau śabdo nānyatra saṅkramaṇīyaḥ; yathāha bhaṭṭaḥ – "labdhātmikā satī ruḍhir bhaved yogāpahariṇī. kalpanīyā tu labhate nātmānaṁ yoga-vādhataḥ." iti. para-brahmatvaṁ ca bhāgavate – "gūḍhaṁ paraṁ brahma manuṣya-liṅgam" iti, "yan mitraṁ paramānandaṁ pūrṇaṁ brahma sanātanam" iti ca; śrī-viṣṇu-purāṇe – "yatrāvatīrṇaṁ kṛṣṇākhyaṁ paraṁ brahma narākṛti"; gītāsu – "brahmaṇo hi pratiṣṭhāham" iti; tāpanīṣu ca – "yo 'sau paraṁ brahma gopālaḥ" iti.

atha mūlam anusarāmaḥ – yasmād etādṛk kṛṣṇa-śabda-vācyas tasmād 'īśvaraḥ' – sarva-vaśayitā. tad idam upalakṣitaṁ bṛhad-gautamīye kṛṣṇa-śabdasyaivārthāntareṇa – "athavā karṣayet sarvaṁ jagat sthāvara-jaṅgamam. kāla-rūpeṇa bhagavāṁs tenāyaṁ kṛṣṇocyate." iti; – kalayati niyamayati sarvam iti hi 'kāla'-śabdārthaḥ; tathā ca tṛtīye tam uddiśyoddhavasya pūrṇa eva nirṇayaḥ – "svayantv asāmyātiśayas tryadhīśaḥ svārājya-lakṣmyāpta-samasta-kāmaḥ. baliṁ haradbhiś cira-loka-pālaiḥ kirīṭa-koṭīḍita-pāda-pīṭhaḥ." iti; gītāsu – "viṣṭabhyāham idaṁ kṛtsnam ekāṁśena sthito jagat" iti; tāpanyāṁ ca – "eko vaśī sarvagaḥ kṛṣṇa īḍyaḥ" iti. yasmād etādṛk īśvaras tasmāt 'paramaḥ' parāḥ sarvotkṛṣṭā mā lakṣmī-rūpāḥ śaktayo yasmin; tad uktaṁ śrī bhāgavate – "reme ramābhir nija-kāma-samplutaḥ" iti; "nāyaṁ śrīyo 'ṅga u nitānta-rateḥ prasādaḥ" ityādi; tatrāti śuśubhe tābhir bhagavān devakī-sutaḥ" iti ca; atraivāgre vakṣyate – "śriyaḥ kāntāḥ kāntaḥ parama-puruṣaḥ" iti; tāpanyāṁ ca – "kṛṣṇo vai paramaṁ daivatam" iti. yasmād etādṛk paramas tasmāt 'ādiḥ' ca; tad uktaṁ śrī-daśame – "śrutvājitaṁ jarāsandhaṁ nṛpater dhyāyato hariḥ. āhopāyaṁ tam evādya uddhavo yam uvāca ha." iti; ṭīkā ca – "ādyo hariḥ śrī-kṛṣṇaḥ" ity eṣā; ekādaśe tu tasya śreṣṭhatvam ādyatvaṁ ca yugapad āha – "puruṣam ṛṣabham ādyaṁ kṛṣṇa-saṁjñaṁ nato 'smi" iti. na caitad āditvaṁ tad avatārāpekṣaṁ, kintu 'anādiḥ' – na vidyate ādir yasya tādṛśam; tāpanyāṁ ca – "eko vaśī sarvagaḥ kṛṣṇa īḍyaḥ" ity uktvāha – "nityo nityānām" iti. yasmād etādṛśatayā ādis tasmāt 'sarva-kāraṇa-kāraṇam' – sarveṣāṁ kāraṇaṁ mahat-sraṣṭā puruṣas tasyāpi kāraṇam; tathā ca daśame taṁ prati devakī-vākyaṁ – "yasyāṁśāṁśa-bhāgena viśvotpatti-layodayā. bhavanti kila viśvātmaṁs taṁ tvādyāhaṁ gatiṁ gatā." iti; ṭīkā ca – "yasyāṁśaḥ puruṣas tasyāṁśo māyā tasyā aṁśā guṇās teṣāṁ bhāgena paramāṇu-mātra-leśena viśvotpatty ādayo bhavanti; taṁ tvā tvāṁ gatiṁ śaraṇaṁ gatāsmi" ity eṣā. tathā ca brahma-stutau – "nārāyaṇo 'ṅgaṁ nara-bhū-jalāyanāt" iti; narāj jātāni tattvāni nārāṇīti vidur budhaḥ. tasya tāny ayanaṁ pūrvaṁ tena nārāyaṇaḥ smṛtaḥ." ity anena lakṣito nārāyaṇas tavāṅgaṁ tvaṁ punaraṅgīty arthaḥ. gītāsu – "viṣṭabhyāham idaṁ kṛtsnam ekāṁśena sthito jagat" iti. tad evaṁ kṛṣṇa-śabdasya yaugikārtho 'pi sādhitaḥ. ye ca tac chabdena kṛṣi-ṇābhyāṁ paramānanda-mātraṁ vācayanti, te 'pi īśvarādi-viśeṣaṇais tatra svābhāvikīṁ śaktiṁ manyeran. tasmin tasmān na dvitīyatvena sarva-kāraṇatvena ca vastv-antara-śaktyāropāyogāt. tathā ca śrutiḥ – "ānandaḥ brahmeti", "ko hy evānyāt kaḥ prāṇyād ya ākāśa ānando na syāt", "ānandād dhīmāni bhūtāni jāyante", "na tasya kāryaṁ karaṇaṁ ca vidyate na tat samaś cābhyadhikaś ca dṛśyate. parāsya śaktir vividhaiva śrūyate svābhāvikī jñāna-bala-kriyā ca." iti. nanu sva-mate yoga-vṛttau ca sarvākarṣakaḥ parama-bṛhattamānandaḥ kṛṣṇa ity abhidhānād avigraha eva sa ity avagamyate, ānandasya vigrahān avagamāt? satyaṁ, kintv ayaṁ paramāpūrvaḥ pūrva-siddhānanda-vigraha iti. 'sac-cid-ānanda-vigrahaḥ' iti – sac-cid-ānanda-lakṣaṇo yo vigrahas tad rūpa evety arthaḥ; tathā ca śrī-daśame brahmaṇa-stave – "tvayy eva nitya-sukha-bodha-tanau" iti; tāpanī-hayaśīrṣayor api – "sac-cid-ānanda-rūpāya kṛṣṇāyākliṣṭa-kāriṇe" iti; brahmāṇḍe cāṣṭottaraśata-nāma-stotre – "nanda-vraja-janānandī sac-cid-ānanda-vigrahaḥ" iti. etad uktaṁ bhavati – 'sattvaṁ' khalv avyabhicāritvam ucyate; tad rūpatvaṁ ca tasya śrī-daśame brahmādi-vākye – "satya-vrataṁ satya-paraṁ tri-satyam" ity atra vyaktam; devakī-vākye ca – "naṣṭe loke dviparārdhāvasāne mahā-bhūteṣv ādi-bhūtaṁ gateṣu. vyakte 'vyaktaṁ kāla-vegena yāte bhavān ekaḥ śiṣyate śeṣa-saṁjñaḥ." iti, martyo mṛtyur vyāla-bhītaḥ palāyan sarvāl̐ lokān nirbhayaṁ nādhyagacchat" ityādi; "eko 'si prathamam" ityādi; brahmaṇo vākye – "tad idaṁ brahmādvayaṁ śiṣyate" iti; śrī-gītāsu – "brahmaṇo hi pratiṣṭhāham" iti, "yasmāt kṣaram atīto 'ham akṣarād api cottamaḥ.

ato 'smi loke vede ca prathitaḥ puruṣottamaḥ." iti; tāpanyām – "janma-jarābhyāṁ bhinnaḥ sthāṇur ayam acchedyo 'yaṁ yo 'sau saurye tiṣṭhati, yo 'sau goṣu tiṣṭhati, yo 'sau gāḥ pālayati, yo 'sau gopeṣu tiṣṭhati" ityādi, "govindān mṛtyur bibheti" ityādi cātra pūrvatra 'saurya' iti – saurī yamunā-tad-adūra-bhava-deśa-vṛndāvana ityarthaḥ. atha 'cid-rūpatvaṁ' – sva-prakāśatvena para-prakāśatvam; tac coktaṁ śrī-daśame brahmaṇā – "ekas tvam ātmā" ityādau "svayaṁ jyotiḥ" iti, tāpanyāṁ – "yo brahmaṇā vidadhāti pūrvaṁ yo brahma-vidyāṁ tasmai gāḥ pālayati sma kṛṣṇaḥ. taṁ hi devam ātma-vṛtti-prakāśaṁ mumukṣur vai śaraṇam amuṁ vrajet." iti, "na cakṣuṣā paśyati rūpam asya" "yam evaiṣa vṛṇute tena labhyas tasyaiṣa ātmā vivṛṇute tanuṁ svām" iti śruty-antaravat. atha 'ānanda-rūpatvaṁ' – sarvāṁśena nirupādhi-parama-premāspadatvam. tac ca śrī-daśame brahma-stavānte – "brahman parodbhave kṛṣṇe" ityādi praśnottarayor vyaktam. tathā cānubhūtam ānakadundubhinā – "vidito 'si bhavān sākṣād īśvaraḥ prakṛteḥ paraḥ. kevalānubhavānanda-svarūpaḥ sarva-buddhi-dṛk." iti; – "ānandaṁ brahmaṇo rūpam" iti śruty-antaravat. tad evaṁ sac-cid-ānanda-vigraha-rūpatve siddhe vigraha evātmā tathātmaiva vigraha iti siddham. tato jīva-vad dehitvaṁ tasya netyapi siddhāntitam; yathoktaṁ śrī-śukena – "kṛṣṇam enam avehi tvam ātmānam akhilātmānām. jagad-dhitāya so 'py atra dehī vābhāti māyayā." iti; tathāpi tasya dehi-val-līlā kṛpā-paravaśatayaivety arthaḥ – "māyā dambhe kṛpāyāṁ ca" iti viśva-prakāśaḥ.

tad evam asya tathā tal-lakṣaṇaṁ, śrī-kṛṣṇa-rūpatve siddhe cobhaya-līlābhiniviṣṭatvena kvacid vṛṣṇīndratvaṁ kvacid govindatvaṁ ca dṛśyate. yathāha dvādaśe sūtaḥ – "śrī-kṛṣṇa kṛṣṇa-sakha vṛṣṇy ṛṣabhāvani-dhrug rājanya-vaṁśa-dahanānapavarga-vīrya. govinda gopavanitā-vraja-bhṛtya-gīta-tīrtha-śravaḥ śravaṇa-maṅgala pāhi bhṛtyān." iti. tad evaṁ svābhīṣṭa-rūpa-līlā-parikara-viśiṣṭatayā govindatvam eva svārādhyatvena yojayati – govinda iti. yathātraivāgre stoṣyate – "cintāmaṇi-prakara-sadmasu-kalpa-vṛkṣa-lakṣāvṛteṣu" ityādi; śrī-daśame śrī-govindābhiṣekārambhe surabhi-vākyaṁ – "tvaṁ na indro jagat pate" iti; abhiṣekānte "govinda iti cābhyadhāt" ity uktvā tat prakaraṇānte śrī-śuka-prārthanā – "prīyān na indro gavām" iti – 'gavāṁ' sarvāśrayatvād gavendratvenaiva sarvendratva siddheḥ. na cedaṁ nyūnaṁ mantavyam. tathā hi gosūktaṁ – "gobhyo yajñāḥ pravartante, gobhyo devāḥ samutthitāḥ. gobhir vedāḥ samudgīrṇāḥ saṣaḍaṅga-pada-kramāḥ." iti. astu tāvat parama-golokād avatīrṇānāṁ tāsāṁ gavām indratvam iti, tāpanīṣu ca brahmaṇā tadīyam eva svenārādhitaṁ prakāśitaṁ – "govindaṁ sac-cid-ānanda-vigrahaṁ sura-bhū-ruha-talāsīnaṁ satataṁ sa-marud-gaṇo 'haṁ toṣayāmi" iti; tathaiva śrī-daśame – "tad bhūri-

bhāgyam iha janma kim apy aṭavyāṁ yad gokule" ityādi. tatra śrī nanda-nandanatvenaiva ca tal labdham. tat prārthanā – "naumīḍya te 'bhra-vapuṣe taḍid-ambarāya" ityādau "paśupāṅgajāya" iti. tad evaṁ govindādi-śabdasya paramaiśvarya-mayasya sārthakatāpi tenābhimatā. tathā coktaṁ īśvaratva-parameśvaratvānuvāda-pūrvaka-tātparyāvasānatayā gautamīya-tantre śrīmad-daśākṣara-mantrārtha-kathane – "gopīti prakṛtiṁ vidyāj janas tattva-samūhakaḥ. anayor āśrayo vyāptyā kāraṇatvena ceśvaraḥ. sāndrānandaṁ paraṁ jyotir vallabhena ca kathyate. athavā gopī prakṛtir janas tad-aṁśa-maṇḍalam. anayor vallabhaḥ proktaḥ svāmī kṛṣṇākhya īśvaraḥ. kārya-kārāṇayor īśaḥ śrutibhis tena gīyate. aneka-janma-siddhānāṁ gopīnāṁ patir eva vā. nanda-nandana ity uktas trailokyānanda-vardhanaḥ. iti. – 'prakṛtim' iti māyākhyāṁ jagat kāraṇa-śaktim ity arthaḥ; 'tattva-samūhakaḥ' mahad-ādi-rūpaḥ; 'anayor āśrayaḥ' 'sāndrānandaṁ paraṁ jyotiḥ' īśvaro 'vallabha'-śabdena kathyate; īśvaratve hetuḥ – 'vyāptyā' 'kāraṇatvena' ceti; 'prakṛtiḥ' iti svarūpa-bhūtā māyātītā vaikuṇṭhādau prakāśamānā mahā-lakṣmyākhyā śaktir ity arthaḥ; 'aṁśa-maṇḍalaṁ' saṅkarṣaṇādi-trayam; 'aneka-janma-siddhānām' ityatra 'bahūni me vyatītāni janmāni tava cārjuna" iti bhagavad-gītā-vacanād anādi-janma-paramparāyām eva tātparyam. tad evam atrāpi nanda-nandanatvenābhimatam; śrī gargeṇa ca tathoktaṁ – "prāg ayaṁ vasudevasya kvacij jātas tavātmajaḥ" iti. yuktaṁ ca tat; – ātmajatvaṁ hi tasya śrī-vasudevasyāpi manasyāvirbhūtatvam eva matam – "āviveśāṁśa-bhāgena mana ānaka-dundubheḥ" iti. vrajeśvarasyāpi tathāsīd eva – śrī-bhagavat-prādurbhāvasya pūrvāvyavahita-kālaṁ vyāpya tathā sarvatra darśanāt. kintv ātmani tasyāvirbhāve saty apy ātmajatvāya pitṛ-bhāvamaya-śuddha-mahā-premaiva prayojakam; yathā brahmaṇaḥ sakāśād varāhadevasyāvirbhave 'pi brahmaṇi varāhadeve loke ca tad-avagamādarśanāt. tādṛśa-śuddha-premā tu śrī-vrajarāja eva; śrī-vasudeve tv aiśvarya-jñāna-pratibandha iti sādhūktaṁ "prāg ayaṁ vasudevasya" iti. ataḥ śrīmad-daśākṣara-viniyoge 'pi tan-maya eva dṛśyate.

Ṭīkā 2

atha tasya tad-rūpatā-sādhakaṁ nityaṁ dhāma pratipādayati – sahasra-patram ityādinā. sahasrāṇi patrāṇi yatra tat kamalam ityādinā "bhūmiś cintāmaṇi-gaṇamayī" iti vakṣyamāṇāc cintāmaṇi-gaṇamayaṁ padmaṁ tad rūpaṁ. tac ca 'mahat' sarvotkṛṣṭaṁ 'padaṁ' sthānam; 'mahataḥ' śrī-kṛṣṇasya mahā-bhāgavato vā 'padaṁ' mahā-vaikuṇṭha-rūpam ity arthaḥ. tat tu nānā-prakāraṁ śrūyate ity āśaṅkya viśeṣaṇatvena niścinoti –

gokulākhyām iti. 'gokulam' ity ākhyā rūḍhir yasya tat gopā-vāsa-rūpam ity arthaḥ – "rūḍhir yogam apaharati" iti nyāyena tasyaiva pratīte. etad abhipretyoktaṁ śrī-daśame – "bhagavān gokuleśvaraḥ" iti. ataeva tad-anukūlatvenottara-granthe 'pi vyākheyam. tasya śrī-kṛṣṇasya śrī-nanda-yaśodādibhiḥ saha vāsa-yogyaṁ mahāntaḥ puram. taiḥ saha vāsitā tv agre samuddekṣyate. tasya svarūpam āha – tad iti. 'anantasya' baladevasya 'aṁśena' jyotir vibhāga-viśeṣeṇa 'sambhavaḥ' sadāvirbhāvo yasya tat; tathā tantreṇaitad api bodhyate; – ananto 'ṁśo yasya tasya śrī-baladevasyāpi sambhavo nivāso yatra tad iti.

Ṭīkā 3–4

sarva-mantra-gaṇa-sevitasya śrīmad-aṣṭādaśākṣarākhya-mahā-mantra-rāja-pīṭhasya mukhya-pīṭham idam ityāha – karṇikāram iti dvayena. 'mahad yantram' iti – yat pratikṛtir eva sarvatra yantratvena pūjārthaṁ likhyata ityarthaḥ. yantratvam eva darśayati – ṣaṭ-koṇāny abhyantare yasya tat; 'vajra-kīlakaṁ' karṇikāre bīja-rūpa-hīraka-kīlaka-śobhitam; mantre ca 'ca'-kāropalakṣitā catur-akṣarī kīlaka-rūpā jñeyā. ṣaṭ-koṇatve prayojanām āha – ṣaṭ aṅgāni yasyāḥ sā ṣaṭ-padī śrīmad-aṣṭādaśākṣarī, tasyāḥ sthānam. 'prakṛtiḥ' mantra-sadma-rūpaṁ svayam eva śrī-kṛṣṇaḥ kāraṇa-rūpatvāt; tac coktaṁ ṛṣy-ādi-smaraṇe – "kṛṣṇaḥ prakṛtiḥ" iti; puruṣaś ca; – sa eva tad adhiṣṭhatṛ-devatā-rūpaḥ; tābhyām 'avasthitam' adhiṣṭhitam. sa hi caturthā pratīyate – mantrasya karaṇatvena, varṇa-samudāya-rūpatvena, adhiṣṭhatṛ-devatā-rūpatvena, ārādhya-rūpatvena prāg uktaḥ – "īśvaraḥ paramaḥ kṛṣṇaḥ" iti. varṇa-rūpatvenāgrata uddhariṣyate – "kāmaḥ kṛṣṇāya" iti. yathoktaṁ hayaśīrṣa-pañcarātre – "vācyatvaṁ vācakatvaṁ ca devatā-mantrayor iha. abhedenocyate brahman tattvavidbhir vicārite." iti; gopāla-tāpanī-śrutiṣu "vāyur yathaiko bhuvanaṁ praviṣṭo rūpaṁ rūpaṁ pratirūpo babhūva. kṛṣṇas tathaiko 'pi jagad-dhitārthaṁ śabdenāsau pañca-pado vibhāti. iti.

kvacid durgāyā adhiṣṭhātṛtvaṁ tu śakti-śaktimator abheda vivakṣayāḥ; ataevoktaṁ gautamīya-kalpe – "nārado 'sya ṛṣiḥ proktaś chando virāḍ iti smṛtam. śrī-kṛṣṇo devatā vāsya durgā 'dhiṣṭhātṛ-devatā. yaḥ kṛṣṇaḥ saiva durgā syād yā durgā kṛṣṇa eva saḥ. anayor antarādarśī saṁsārān no vimucyate." ityādi. ataḥ svayam eva śrī-kṛṣṇas tatra svarūpa-śakti-rūpeṇa durgā-nāma; tasmān neyaṁ māyāṁśa-bhūtā durgeti gamyate. niruktiś cātra – "kṛcchreṇa durārādhanādi-bahu-prayāsena gamyate jñāyate" iti. tathā ca śrī-nārada-pañcarātre śruti-vidyā-saṁvade – "jānāty ekā parā kāntā saiva durgā tadātmikā. yā parā paramā śaktir mahā-

viṣṇu-svarūpiṇī. yasyā vijñāna-mātreṇa parāṇāṁ paramātmanaḥ. muhūrtād eva devasya prāptir bhavati nānyathā. ekeyaṁ prema-sarva-svabhāvā śrī-gokuleśvarī. anayā sulabho jñeya ādi-devo 'khileśvaraḥ. bhaktir bhajana-sampattir bhajate prakṛtiḥ priyam. jñāyate 'tyanta-duḥkhena seyaṁ prakṛtir ātmanaḥ durgeti gīyate sadbhir akhaṇḍa-rasa-vallabhā. asya āvarikā śaktir mahā-māyā 'khileśvarī. yayā mugdhaṁ jagat sarvaṁ sarva-dehābhimāninaḥ." iti. tathā ca sammohana-tantre – "yan nāmnā nāmni durgāhaṁ guṇair guṇavatī hy aham. yad vaibhavān mahā-lakṣmī rādhā nityā parā-dvayā." iti durgā-vākyaṁ kiṁ ca, prema-rūpā ya ānanda-mahānanda-rasās tat paripāka-bhedātmakena. tathā 'jyotī-rūpeṇa' svaprakāśena 'manunā' mantra-rūpeṇa 'kāma-bījena saṅgatam' iti mūla-mantrāntargatatve 'pi kāma-bījasya pṛthag uktiḥ kutra ca na svātantryāpekṣayā.

tad evaṁ tad dhāmoktvā tadāvaraṇāny āha – tad ity arddhena. tasya karṇikā-rūpa-dhāmnaḥ 'kiñjalkaṁ' – 'kiñjalkāḥ śikharāvali-valita-prācīrapaṅktayaḥ' ityarthaḥ; tat tu 'tad aṁśānāṁ' – tasminn aṁśādayo vidyante yeṣāṁ parama-prema-bhājāṁ sajātīyānāṁ dhāmety arthaḥ. 'gokulākhyam' ity ukter eva teṣāṁ tat sajātīyatvaṁ coktaṁ svayaṁ śrī-bādarāyaṇinā – "evaṁ kakudminaṁ hatvā stūyamānaḥ svajātibhiḥ. viveśa goṣṭhaṁ sabalo gopīnāṁ nayanotsavaḥ." iti. ataeva tasya kamalasya 'patrāṇi' 'śriyāṁ' tat-preyasīnāṁ gopī-rūpāṇāṁ śrī-rādhādīnam upavana-rūpāni dhāmānīty arthaḥ. gopī-rūpatvaṁ cāsāṁ – mantrasya tan nāmnā liṅgitatvāt; rādhāditvaṁ ca – "devī kṛṣṇamayī proktā rādhikā para-devatā. sarva-lakṣmī-mayī sarva-kāntiḥ sammohinī parā." iti bṛhad-gautamīyāt, "rādhā vṛndāvane vane" iti matsya-purāṇāt; "rādhayā mādhavo devo mādhavenaiva rādhikā" iti ṛk-pariśiṣṭāc ca. tatra 'patrāṇām' ucchritaprāntānāṁ sandhiṣu vartmāny agrim asandhiṣu goṣṭhāni jñeyāni. akhaṇḍa-kamalasya gokulatvāt tathaiva gokula-samāveśāc ca goṣṭhaṁ tathaiva. yat tu sthānāntare vacanam asti – "sahasrāraṁ padmaṁ dalitatiṣu devībhir abhitaḥ parītaṁ gosaṅghair api nikhila-kiñjalka-militaiḥ. kavāṭe yasyāsti svayam akhila-śakti-prakaṭita-prabhāvaḥ sadyaḥ śrī-parama-puruṣas taṁ kila bhaje." iti – tatra 'go-saṅkhaiḥ' iti tu pāṭhaḥ samañjasaḥ. go-saṅkhyāś ca gopā iti – 'gopā gopāla-go-saṅkhya-godhu-gābhīra-ballavāḥ' ity amaraḥ. kavāṭa iti kavāṭānām abhyantare karṇikā-madhyadeśa ity arthaḥ. akhila-śaktyā prakaṭitaḥ prabhāvo yena sa parama-puruṣaḥ śrī-kṛṣṇa ity arthaḥ.

Ṭīkā 5

atha gokulāvaraṇāny āha – caturasram iti caturbhiḥ. tasya gokulasya bahiḥ sarvataḥ 'catur asraṁ' catuṣ-koṇātmakaṁ sthalam śvetadvīpākhyam. tad etad upalakṣaṇaṁ gokulākhyaṁ cety arthaḥ. yadyapi gokule 'pi śvetadvīpatvam asty eva tad evāntara-bhūmi-mayatvāt, tathāpi viśeṣa-nāmnā svātantryatvāt tenaiva tat pratīyata iti tathoktam. kintu catur asre 'py antar maṇḍalaṁ vṛndāvanākhyaṁ jñeyam. tathā ca svāyambhūvāgame – "dhyāyet tatra viśuddhātmā idaṁ sarvaṁ krameṇaiva" ity ādikam uktvā tan madhye "vṛndāvanaṁ kusumitaṁ nānā-vṛkṣair vihaṅgamaiḥ saṁsmaret" ity uktam. tathā ca bṛhad-vāmana-purāṇe śrī-bhagavati śrutīnāṁ prārthanā-pūrvakāni padyāni – "ānanda-rūpam iti yad vidanti hi purā vidaḥ. tad rūpaṁ darśayāsmākaṁ yadi, deyo varo hi naḥ. śrutvaitad darśayām āsa gokulaṁ prakṛteḥ param. kevalānubhavānanda-mātram akṣara-madhvagam. yatra vṛndāvanaṁ nāma vanaṁ kāma-dughair drumaiḥ." ityādīni. tac ca catur asraṁ 'catur mūrteḥ' catur-vyūhasya śrī-vāsudevādi-catuṣṭayasya 'catuṣ-kṛtaṁ' caturdhā vibhaktaṁ 'caturdhāma'. kintu deva-līlatvāt tad upari vyoma-yāna-sthā eva te jñeyāḥ. 'hetubhiḥ' tat tat puruṣārtha-sādhanaiḥ 'manu-rūpaiḥ' sva-sva-mantrātmakair indrādibhiḥ sāmādayaś catvāro vedās tair ity arthaḥ. 'śaktibhiḥ' vimalādibhir goloka-nāmāyaṁ lokaḥ śrī-bhāgavate sādhitaḥ. tad evaṁ tasya loko varṇitaḥ; tathā ca śrī-bhāgavate – "nandas tv atīndriyaṁ dṛṣṭvā loka-pāla-mahodayam. kṛṣṇe ca sannatiṁ teṣāṁ jñātibhyo vismito 'bravīt. te cautsukya-dhiyo rājanmatvā gopās tam īśvaram. api naḥ svagatiṁ sūkṣmām upādhāsyad adhīśvaraḥ. iti svānāṁ sa bhagavān vijñāyākhiladṛk svayam. saṅkalpa-siddhaye teṣāṁ kṛpayaitad acintayat. jano vai loka etasminn avidyā-kāma-karmabhiḥ. uccāvacāsu gatiṣu na veda svāṁ gatiṁ bhraman. iti sañcintya bhagavān mahā-kāruṇiko vibhuḥ. darśayām āsa lokaṁ svaṁ gopānāṁ tamasaḥ param. satyaṁ jñānam anantaṁ yad brahma jyotiḥ sanātanam. yad dhi paśyanti munayo guṇāpāye samāhitāḥ. te tu brahma-hṛdaṁ nītā magnāḥ kṛṣṇena coddhṛtāḥ. dadṛśur brahmaṇo lokaṁ yatrākrūro 'dhyagāt purā. nandādayas tu taṁ dṛṣṭvā paramānanda-nirvṛtāḥ. kṛṣṇaṁ ca tatra cchando 'bhistūyamānaṁ su-vismitāḥ." iti – 'atīndriyam' adṛṣṭa-pūrva, 'svagatiṁ' svadhāma; 'sūkṣmāṁ' durjñeyāṁ; 'upādhāsyat' upadhāsyati asmān prāpayiṣyatīty arthaḥ saṅkalpitavanta iti śeṣaḥ. 'jano' 'sau vrajavāsī mama svajanaḥ – "sālokya-sārṣṭi" ityādi-pade "janāḥ" itivad ubhayatrāpy anya-janatvam aśrutam iti, vraja-janasya tu tadīya-svajanatamatvaṁ tena svayam eva vibhāvitaṁ – "tasmān mac-charaṇaṁ goṣṭhaṁ man-nāthaṁ mat-parigraham. gopāye svātma-yogena so 'yaṁ me vrata āhitaḥ." ity anena; sa 'etasmin' prāpañcike loke avidyādibhir yā 'uccāvacāḥ' deva-tiryag-ādi-rūpā gatayas tāsu 'svāṁ gatiṁ' 'bhraman' tan-miśratayābhivyaktes tan nirviśeṣatayā jānan tām eva svāṁ gatiṁ na vedety arthaḥ; madīya-laukika-līlā-viśeṣeṇa jñānāṁśa tirodhānād iti bhāvaḥ; – "iti nandādayo gopāḥ kṛṣṇa-rāma-kathāṁ mudā. kurvanto ramamāṇāś ca nāvidan bhava-vedanām." iti daśamokter avidyā-kāma-karmaṇāṁ tatrāsāmarthyāt. gopānāṁ 'svaṁ lokaṁ' golokam arthāt tān pratyekaṁ darśayām āsa 'tamasaḥ' prakṛteḥ 'paraṁ' svarūpa-śakty-abhivyaktatvāt. ṛta eva sac-cid-ānanda-rūpa evāsau loka ityāha – satyam iti. atha śrī-vṛndāvane ca tādṛśa-darśanaṁ katham anya-deśaḥ sthitānāṁ teṣāṁ jātam ity āha – 'brahma-hradam' akrūra-tīrthaṁ kṛṣṇena nītāḥ punaś ca tenaiva 'magnāḥ' majjitāḥ punaś ca tasmāt tenaiva 'uddhṛtāḥ' uddhṛtya punaḥ sva-sthānaṁ prāpitāḥ santo 'brahmaṇaḥ' parama-bṛhattamasya tasyaiva lokaṁ gokulākhyaṁ dadṛśuḥ – "mūrdhabhiḥ satya-lokas tu brahma-lokaḥ sanātanaḥ" iti dvitīye vaikuṇṭhāntarasyāpi tat tathā 'hyāteḥ. ko 'sau brahma-hradas tatrāha – yatreti, tat tīrtha-mahimānaṁ lakṣam eva vidhātuṁ seyaṁ paripāṭīti bhāvaḥ. atra 'svāṁ gatim' iti tadīyatā-nirdeśaḥ, 'gopānāṁ svaṁ lokam' iti ṣaṣṭhī-sva-śabdayor nirdeśaḥ, 'kṛṣṇaṁ' iti sākṣān nirdeśaś ca vaikuṇṭhāntaraṁ vyavacchidya śrī-golokam eva vyavasthāpitavān iti. tathā ca harivaṁśe śakra-vacanaṁ—"svargād ūrdhvaṁ brahma-loko brahmarṣi-gaṇa-sevitaḥ. tatra somagatiś caiva jyotiṣāṁ ca mahātmanām. tasyopari gavāṁ lokaḥ sādhyās taṁ pālayanti hi. sa hi sarva-gataḥ kṛṣṇo mahākāśa-gato mahān. upary upari tatrāpi gatis tatra tapomayī. yāṁ na vidmo vayaṁ sarve pṛcchanto 'pi pitāmaham. gatiḥ śama-damāḍhyānāṁ svargaṁ sukṛta-karmaṇām. brāhme tapasi yuktānāṁ brahma-lokaḥ parā gatiḥ. gavām eva hi yo loko durārohā hi sā gatiḥ. sa tu lokas tvayā kṛṣṇa sīdamānaḥ kṛtātmanā. dhṛto dhṛtimatā vīra nighnato 'padravān gavām. iti. atrāpātapratītārthāntare 'svargād ūrdhvaṁ brahma-lokaḥ' ity uktaṁ syāt 'loka-trayam atikramya' ity ukteḥ 'tatra somagatiś caiva' iti na sambhavati candrasyānyeṣām api 'jyotiṣāṁ' dhruvalokād adhastād eva gates tathā 'sādhyās taṁ pālayanti' ity api nopapadyate; deva-yoni-rūpāṇāṁ teṣāṁ svarga-lokasyāpi pālanam asambhavaṁ, kim uta tad upari lokasya surabhilokasya. tathā tasya lokasya surabhilokatve 'sa hi sarvagataḥ' ity anupapannaṁ syāt, śrī-bhagavad-vigraha-lokayor acintya-śaktitvena vibhutvaṁ ghaṭeta, na punar anyasyeti. ataeva sarvātītatvāt 'tatrāpi tava gatiḥ' iti 'api' – śabdo vismaye prayuktaḥ; 'yaṁ na vidmo vayaṁ sarve' ity ādikaṁ coktam tasmāt prākṛta-golokād anya evāsau goloka iti siddham. tathā ca mokṣa-dharme nārāyaṇīyopākhyāne śrī-bhagavad-vākyam – "evaṁ bahu-vidhai rūpaiś carāmīha vasundharām. brahma-lokaṁ ca kaunteya golokaṁ ca sanātanam." iti tasmād ayam arthaḥ – 'svarga'-śabdena, "bhūr-lokaḥ kalpitaḥ padbhyāṁ bhuvar-loko 'sya nābhitaḥ. svar-lokaḥ kalpito mūrdhnā iti vā loka-kalpanā." iti bhāgavate dvitīyoktānusāreṇa, svar-lokam ārabhya satya-loka-

paryantaṁ loka-pañcakam ucyate. tasmāt 'ūrdhvam' upari 'brahma-lokaḥ' brahmātmako lokaḥ sac-cid-ānanda-rūpatvāt, brahmaṇo bhagavato lokaḥ iti vā – "mūrdhvabhiḥ satyalokas tu brahma-lokaḥ sanātana" iti dvitīyāt; ṭīkā ca – "brahma-loko vaikuṇṭhākhyāḥ sanātano nityaḥ, na tu sṛṣṭi-prapañcāntarvartī" ity eṣā; śrutiś ca – "eṣa brahma-loka eṣa ātma-lokaḥ" iti. sa ca "brahmarṣi-gaṇa-sevitaḥ" – brahmaṇo mūrtimanto vedāḥ, ṛṣayaḥ śrī-nāradādayaḥ, gaṇāś ca śrī-garuḍa-viṣvaksenādayaḥ; taiḥ sevitaḥ. evaṁ nityāśritānuktvā tad-gamanādhikariṇa āha – 'tatra' brahmaloke, umayā saha vartate iti 'somaḥ' śrī-śivas tasya 'gatiḥ' – "svadharma-niṣṭhaḥ śata-janmabhiḥ pumān viriñcatām eti tataḥ paraṁ hi mām. avyākṛtaṁ bhāgavato 'tha vaiṣṇavaṁ padaṁ yathāhaṁ vibudhāḥ kalātyaye." iti caturthe rudra-gītāt. someti supāṁ supalugity-ādinā ṣaṣṭhīluk chāndasaḥ. tad uttaratrāpi gatir ity anvayaḥ. 'jyotiḥ' brahma, tadaikātma-bhāvānāṁ muktānām ity arthaḥ, na tu tādṛśānām api sarveṣāṁ, kintu 'mahātmanāṁ mahāśayānāṁ mokṣānādaratayā bhajatāṁ śrī-sanakādi-tulyānām ity arthaḥ; – "muktānām api siddhānāṁ nārāyaṇa-parāyaṇaḥ. sudurlabhaḥ praśāntātmā koṭiṣv api mahā-mune." iti ṣaṣṭhataḥ, "yoginām api sarveṣāṁ mad-gatenāntarātmanā. śraddhāvān bhajate yo māṁ sa me yuktatamo mataḥ." iti gītābhyaś ca teṣv eva mahattva-paryavasānāt. 'tasya' brahma-lokasya 'upari gavāṁ lokaḥ' śrī-goloka ity arthaḥ. taṁ ca golokaṁ 'sādhyāḥ' prāpañcika-devānāṁ prasādanīyā mūla-rūpā nitya-tadīya-devagaṇāḥ 'pālayanti' dik-pāla-rūpatayā vartante – "te ha nākaṁ mahimānaḥ sacantas tatra pūrve sādhyāḥ santi devāḥ" iti śruteḥ; "tatra pūrve ye ca sādhyā viśve devāḥ sanātanāḥ. te ha nākaṁ mahimānaṁ sacantaḥ śubha-darśanāḥ." – iti mahā-vaikuṇṭha-varṇane pādmottara-khaṇḍāc ca; yad vā; "tad bhūri-bhāgyam iha janma kim apy aṭavyāṁ yad gokule 'pi" iti śrī-brahma-stavānusāreṇa tad-vidha-parama-bhaktānām api sādhyāḥ tādṛśa-siddhi-prāptaye prasādanīyāḥ śrī-gopa-gopī prabhṛtayas taṁ pālayanti. tad evaṁ sarvopari gatatve 'pi 'hi' prasiddhau, 'sa' śrī-golokaḥ 'sarva-gataḥ' śrī-nārāyaṇa iva prāpañcikā prāpañcika-vastu-vyāpakaḥ. kaiścit krama-mukti-vyavasthayā tathā prāpyamāno 'py asau dvitīya-skandha-varṇita-kamalāsana-dṛṣṭa-vaikuṇṭhavat śrī-vrajavāsibhir atrāpi yasmād dṛṣṭa iti bhāvaḥ. ataeva 'mahān' bhagavad-rūpa eva – "mahāntaṁ vibhum ātmānam" iti śruteḥ. atra hetuḥ – 'mahākāśaṁ' parama-vyomākhyaṁ brahma viśeṣaṇa-lābhāt, "ākāśas tal liṅgāt" iti nyāya-siddheś ca; 'tad agataḥ' – brahmākārodayānantaram eva vaikuṇṭha-prāpter yathājāmilasya. tad evam 'upary upari' sarvopary api virājamāne 'tatra' śrī goloke 'pi 'tava gatiḥ' śrī-govinda-rūpeṇa krīḍā vartata ity arthaḥ. ataeva sā gatiḥ sādhāraṇī na bhavati, kintu 'tapomayī' – tapo 'trānavacchinnaiśvaryam; sahasra-nāma-bhāṣye 'pi

– "paraṁ yo mahat-tapaḥ" ity atra tathā vyākhyātam; "sa tapo 'tapyata" iti parameśvara-viṣayaka-śruteḥ – aiśvaryaṁ prakāśayad iti hi tatrārthaḥ. ataeva brahmādibhir durvitarkatvam āha – yām iti. adhunā tasya gokula ity ākhyā bījam abhivyañjayati – gatir iti. 'brāhme' brahma-loka-prāpake 'tapasi' śrī kṛṣṇa-viṣayaka-manaḥ-praṇidhāne 'yuktānāṁ' rata-cittānāṁ tad eka-prema-bhaktānām ity arthaḥ – "yasya jñānamayaṁ tapaḥ" iti śruteḥ. 'brahma-lokaḥ' vaikuṇṭha-lokaḥ, 'parā' prakṛty-atītā. 'gavāṁ' vrajavāsi-mātrāṇāṁ – "mocayan vraja-gavāṁ dina-tāpam" iti śrī-daśamāt – teṣāṁ svatas tad-bhāvitānāṁ ca sādhana-vaśād ity arthaḥ. atas tad-bhāvasyāpy asulabhatvād 'dūrārohā' duṣprāpyānyeṣāṁ tapa ādinā. 'dhṛtaḥ' rakṣitaḥ śrī-govardhanoddharaṇe 'pi tathā sa cakṣuṣām eva lokaḥ pradṛṣṭaḥ. "tā vāṁ vāstūny uśmasi gomadhyai yatra gāvo bhuri-śṛṅgā ayāsaḥ. atrāha tad urugāyasya kṛṣṇaḥ paramaṁ padam avabhāti bhūri." iti; vyākhyātaṁ ca – 'tā' tāni 'vāṁ' yuvayoḥ kṛṣṇa-rāmayoḥ, 'vāstūni' līlā-sthānāni 'gomadhyai' prāptum 'uśmasi' kāmayāmahe. tāni kiṁ viśiṣṭāni? – "yatra yeṣu 'bhuri-śṛṅgāḥ' mahā-śṛṅgāḥ gāvo vasanti; yathopaniṣadi – bhūri-vākye dharma-pareṇa bhūri-śabdena mahiṣṭham evocyate, na tu bahutaram iti bahu-śubha-lakṣaṇa iti vā. 'ayāsaḥ' śubhāḥ – "ayaḥ śubhāvaho vidhiḥ" ity amaraḥ, 'devāsaḥ' itivat yuṣanta-padam idam. vṛkṣaḥ sarva-kāma-dughasyeti. 'atra' bhūmau tal loko vede prasiddhaḥ śrī-golokākhyaḥ. 'urugāyasya' svayaṁ bhagavataḥ 'padaṁ' sthānaṁ 'bhūri' bahudhā avabhāti iti 'āha' veda iti; yathā yajuḥsu mādhyandinīye stūyate – "dhāmāny uśmasīti iti viṣṇoḥ paramaṁ padam avabhāti bhūri" iti cātra prakaraṇāntaraṁ paṭhanti. śeṣaṁ samānam.

Ṭīkā 6

atha mūla-vyākhyām anusarāmaḥ. virāṭ-tad-antaryāminor abheda-vivikṣayā puruṣa-suktādāv eka-puruṣatvaṁ yathā nirūpitaṁ, tathā goloka-tad-adhiṣṭhātror apy āha – evam iti. 'devaḥ' golokas tad-adhiṣṭhātṛ-śrī-govinda-rūpaḥ. 'sadānandam' iti tat-svarūpam ity arthaḥ; napuṁsakatvaṁ – "vijñānam ānandaṁ brahma" iti śruteḥ. 'ātmārāmasya' anya-nirapekṣasya; 'prakṛtyā' māyayā na samāgamaḥ", yathoktaṁ dvitīye – "na yatra māyā kim utāpare" iti.

Ṭīkā 7

atha prapañcātmanas tad-aṁśyasya puruṣasya tu na tādṛśatvam ity āha – māyayeti prākṛta-pralaye 'pi tasmiṁs tasyā layāt – "yasyāṁśāṁśāṁśa-bhāgena" ity ādeḥ. nanu tarhi jīvavat tal-liptatvenānīśvaratvaṁ syāt? tatrāha – ātmaneti. sa tu 'ātmanā' antarvatnyā tu 'ramayā' svarūpa-śaktyaiva 'reme' ratiṁ prāpnoti, bahir eva māyayā sevya ity arthaḥ; – "eṣa prapanna-varado ramayātma-śaktyā yadyat kariṣyati gṛhīta-guṇāvatāraḥ" iti tṛtīye brahma-stavāt; "māyāṁ vyudasya cic-chaktyā kaivalye sthita ātmani" iti prathame śrīmad-arjuna-vākyāc ca. tarhi tat preraṇaṁ vinā kathaṁ sṛṣṭiḥ syāt? tathāha – 'sisṛkṣayā' sraṣṭum icchayā 'tyaktaḥ' sṛṣṭy-arthaṁ prahitaḥ 'kālaḥ' yasmāt tādṛśaṁ yathā syāt tathā reme. prathamānta-pāṭhas tu sugamaḥ. tat-prabhā-rūpeṇa tenaiva sā sidhyatīti bhāvaḥ; – 'prabhāvaṁ pauruṣaṁ prāhuḥ kālam eke yato bhayam" iti, "kāla-vṛttyā tu māyāyāṁ guṇa-mayyām adhokṣajaḥ. puruṣeṇātma-bhūtena vīryam ādhatta vīryavān". iti ca tṛtīyāt.

Ṭīkā 8

nanu ramaiva sā kā? tatrāha – niyatir atyardhena. niyamyate svayaṁ bhagavaty eva niyatā bhavatīti 'niyatiḥ' svarūpabhūtā tac-chaktiḥ; 'devī' dyotamānā svaprakāśa-rūpā ity arthaḥ; tad uktaṁ dvādaśe – "anapāyinī hareḥ śaktiḥ śrīḥ sākṣād ātmano hareḥ" iti; ṭīkā ca – "anapāyinī hareḥ śaktiḥ; tatra hetuḥ – sākṣād ātmana iti; svarūpasya cid-rūpatvāt tasyās tad-abhedād ity arthaḥ" ity eṣā. atra sākṣāc chabdena – "vilajjamānayā yasya sthātum īkṣā-pathe 'muyā" ityādyuktā māyā neti dhvanitam. tatra 'anapāyinītvaṁ' yathā viṣṇu-purāṇe – "nityaiva sā jagan-mātā viṣṇoḥ śrīr anapāyinī. yathā sarvagato viṣṇus tathaiveyaṁ dvijottama." iti, "evaṁ yathā jagat-svāmī deva-devo janārdanaḥ. avatāraṁ karoty eṣā tathā śrīs tat-sahāyinī." iti ca.

nanu kutrāpi śiva-śaktyoḥ kāraṇatā śrūyate? tatra virāḍ-varṇanavat kalpanayā te tad-aṅga-viśeṣaṇatvenāha – tal liṅgam iti. "tasyāyutāyutāṁśāṁśe viśva-śaktir iyaṁ sthitā" iti viṣṇu-purāṇānusāreṇa prapañcātmanas tasya mahā-bhagavad-aṁśasya svāṁśa-jyotir ācchannatvād aprakaṭa-rūpasya puruṣasya 'liṅgaṁ' liṅga-sthānīyo yo 'ṁśaḥ prapañcotpādakāṁśaḥ, sa eva śambhuḥ; anyas tu tad-āvirbhāva-viśeṣatvād eva śambhur ucyata ity arthaḥ. vakṣyati ca – "kṣīraṁ yathā dadhi-vikāra-viśeṣa-yogāt" ity ādi. tathā tasya vīryādhāna-sthānīya-māyāyā apy aprakaṭana-rūpāyā yā 'yoni' sthānīyo 'ṁśaḥ, saiva 'aparā' pradhānākhyā śaktir iti pūrva-vat. tatra ca 'hare' tasya puruṣākhya-haryaṁśasya 'kāmo' bhavati – sṛṣṭy-arthaṁ tad-didṛkṣā jāyata ity arthaḥ. tataś ca 'mahat' iti sajīva mahat-tattva-rūpaṁ sa-prapañca-rūpaṁ bījam āhitaṁ bhavatīty arthaḥ; – "so 'kāmayata" iti śruteḥ, "kālavṛttyā" ityādi tṛtīyāc ca.

Ṭīkā 9

ataḥ śiva-śāstram api tad-viśeṣā-vivekād eva svātantryeṇa pravartate, vastutas tu pūrvābhiprāyatvam evety āha – liṅgety ardhena. 'māheśvarī' māheśvaryaḥ.

Ṭīkā 10

śaktimān ity ardhena tad evānūdya tasmin pūrvoktasyāprakaṭa-rūpasya prakaṭa-rūpatayā punar abhivyaktir ity āha – tasminn ity ardhena. tasmāliṅga-rūpī prapañcotpādakas tad-aṁśo 'pi śaktimān puruṣo maheśvara ucyate. tataś ca 'tasmin' bhūta-sūkṣma-paryantatāṁ prāpte 'liṅge' svayaṁ tad-aṁśī 'mahā-viṣṇur āvirabhūt' prakaṭa-rūpeṇāvirbhavati; yato 'jagat-patiḥ' jagatāṁ sarveṣāṁ parāvareṣāṁ jīvānāṁ sa eva patir iti.

Ṭīkā 11

tad eva rūpaṁ vivṛṇoti – sahasra-śīrṣeti. sahasram aṁśā avatārā yasya sa 'sahasrāṁśaḥ'; sahasraṁ sūte sṛjati yaḥ sa 'sahasrasūḥ', sahasra-śabdaḥ sarvatrāsaṅkhyatāparaḥ. dvitīye ca rūpam idam uktam – "ādyo 'vatāraḥ puruṣaḥ parasya" ity asya ṭīkāyāṁ – "parasya bhūmnaḥ puruṣaḥ prakṛti-pravartakaḥ, 'yasya sahasra-śīrṣa' ity ādy ukto līlā-vigrahaḥ sa ādyo 'vatāraḥ" iti.

Ṭīkā 12

ayam eva kāraṇarṇavaśāyītyāha – nārāyaṇa iti sārdhena. ataḥ āpa eva 'kāraṇārṇo-nidhir āvirāsīt'. sa tu nārāyaṇaḥ 'saṅkarṣaṇātmakaḥ' iti; – pūrvaṁ golokāvaraṇatayā yaś caturvyūha madhye saṅkarṣaṇaḥ sammatas tasyaivāṁśo 'yam ity arthaḥ. atha tasya līlām āha – yoga-nidrām iti; svarūpānanda-samādhiṁ gata ity arthaḥ. tad uktaṁ – "āpo nārā iti proktā āpo vai nara-sūnavaḥ. tasya tā ayanaṁ pūrvaṁ tena nārāyaṇaḥ smṛtaḥ." iti.

Ṭīkā 13

tasmād eva brahmāṇḍānām utpattim āha – tad rometi. 'tat' iti tasyety arthaḥ. tasya saṅkarṣaṇātmakasya yad bījaṁ yoni-śaktāvadhyas taṁ, tad eva bhūta-sūkṣma-paryantatāṁ prāptaṁ sat paścāt tasya 'roma-bila-jāleṣu' vivareṣu antarbhūtaṁ ca sat 'haimāni aṇḍāni jātāni' tāni cāpañcīkṛtāṁśair mahā-bhūtair āvṛtāni jātānīty arthaḥ. tad uktaṁ daśame brahmaṇā – "kvedṛgvidhāvigaṇitāṇḍa-parāṇucaryā vātādhvaroma-vivarasya ca te mahitvam" iti; tṛtīye ca – "vikāraiḥ sahito yuktair viśeṣādibhir āvṛtaḥ. aṇḍa-koṣo bahir ayaṁ pañcāśat-koṭi-vistṛtaḥ. daśottarādhikair yatra praviṣṭaḥ paramāṇuvat. lakṣyante 'ntargatāś cānye koṭiśo hy aṇḍa-rāśayaḥ." iti.

Ṭīkā 14

tataś ca teṣu brahmāṇḍeṣu pṛthak pṛthak svarūpaiḥ rūpāntaraiḥ sa eva praviveśety āha – praty-aṇḍam iti. 'ekāṁśād ekāṁśāt' ekenaikenāṁśenety arthaḥ.

Ṭīkā 15

punaḥ kiṁ cakāra? tatrāha – vāmāṅgād iti. viṣṇvādaya ime sarveṣām eva brahmāṇḍānāṁ pālakādayaḥ prati-brahmāṇḍāntaḥ sthitānāṁ viṣṇvādīnāṁ ceśvarāṇāṁ prayoktāraḥ. yathā prati-brahmāṇḍaṁ tathādhibrahmāṇḍa-maṇḍalam abhyupagantavyam iti bhāvaḥ; yeṣu prajāpatir ayaṁ hiraṇyagarbha-rūpa eva na tu vakṣyamāṇa caturmukha-rūpa eva; so 'yaṁ tat-tad-āvaraṇagata-tat-tad-devānāṁ sraṣṭeti. viṣṇu-śambhū api tat-tat-pālana-saṁhāra-kartārau jñeyau. 'kūrca-deśāt' bhruvor madhyāt. eṣāṁ jalāvaraṇa eva sthānāni jñeyāni.

Ṭīkā 16

tatra śambhoḥ kāryāntaram apy āha – ahaṅkārātmakam ity ardhena. 'etad viśvaṁ' tasmād eva 'ahaṅkārātmakaṁ' 'vyajāyata' babhūva – viśvasyāhaṅkārātmakatā tasmāj jātety arthaḥ; sarvāhaṅkārādhiṣṭhātṛtvāt tasya.

Ṭīkā 17

brahmāṇḍa-praviṣṭasya tu tat-tad-rūpasya līlām āha – atha tair ity ādi. 'taiḥ' tat-sadṛśaiḥ 'trividhaiḥ' prati-brahmāṇḍagata-viṣṇvādibhiḥ 'veśaiḥ' rūpaiḥ 'līlāṁ' brahmāṇḍāntargata-pālanādi-rūpām 'udvahataḥ' brahmāṇḍāntargata-puruṣasyeti tām udvahati tasminn ity arthaḥ. 'yoga-nidrā' pūrvokta-mahā-yoga-nidrāṁśa-bhūtā 'bhagavatī' svarūpānanda-samādhi-mayatvād antarbhūta-sarvaiśvaryaiḥ, 'saṅgatā śrīr iva' iti – tatra yathā śrīr apy aṁśena saṅgatā tathā sāpīty arthaḥ.

Ṭīkā 18

tataś ca sisṛkṣāyām iti. 'nālaṁ' nāla-yuktaṁ tat 'hema-nalinaṁ,' brahmaṇo janma-śayanayoḥ sthānatvāt 'lokaḥ' ity arthaḥ.

Ṭīkā 19

tathāsaṅkhya-jīvātmakasya samaṣṭi-jīvasya prabodhaṁ vaktuṁ punaḥ kāraṇārṇo nidhiśāyinas tṛtīya-skandhoktānusāriṇīṁ sṛṣṭi-prakriyāṁ vivṛty āha – attvānīti trayeṇa. tatra dvayamāha – 'māyayā' sva-śaktyā 'parasparaṁ tattvāni yojayan' iti yojanāntaram eva nirīhatayā 'yoga-nidrām' eva svīkṛtavān ity arthaḥ.

Ṭīkā 20

atha tṛtīyaṁ – yojayitveti. 'yojayitvā' tad-yojana-yoga-nidrayor antarasāv ity arthaḥ. 'guhāṁ' prati; virāḍ-vigraho 'pratibudhyate' pralaya-svāpāj jāgarti.

Ṭīkā 21

tayoḥ svābhāvikīṁ sthitim āha – sa nitya ity ardhena. 'nityaḥ' anādy-ananta-kāla-bhāvī, 'nitya-sambandhaḥ' bhagavatā saha nityaḥ sambandhaḥ samavāyo yasya saḥ, sūryeṇa tad-raśmi-jālasyeveti bhāvaḥ. "yat taṭasthantu cid-rūpaṁ saṁvedāt tu vinirgatam rañjitaṁ guṇa-rāgeṇa sa jīva iti kathyate." – iti śrī-nārada-pañcarātrāt; tathā ca śrī-gītāsu – "mamaivāṁśo jīvaloke jīva-bhūtaḥ sanātanaḥ" iti. ataeva 'prakṛtiḥ' sākṣi-rūpeṇa svarūpa-sthita eva bimba-pratibimba-pramātṛ-rūpeṇa prakṛtim iva prāptaś cety arthaḥ – "prakṛtiṁ viddhi me parāṁ jīva-bhūtām" iti śrī-gītāsv eva ca, "dvā suparṇā sayujā sakhāyā" iti śrutiś ca nitya-sambandhaṁ darśayati.

Ṭīkā 22

atha tasya samaṣṭi-jīvādhiṣṭhānatvaṁ guhā-praviṣṭāt puruṣatvād upapannam ityāha – evam iti. tataḥ samaṣṭi-dehābhimāninas tasya hiraṇya-garbha-brahmaṇas tasmāt bhoga-vigrahādy-utpattim āha – tatreti.

Ṭīkā 23

atha tasya catur-mukhasya ceṣṭām āha – sañjāta iti sārdhena. spaṣṭam.

Ṭīkā 24

atha tasmin pūrvopāsanā-labdhāṁ bhagavat-kṛpām āha – uvāceti sārdhena. spaṣṭam.

Ṭīkā 25

etad eva "sparśeṣu yat ṣoḍaśam eka-viṁśam" iti tṛtīya-skandhānusāreṇa yojayati – tapas tvam ity ardhena. spaṣṭam.

Ṭīkā 26

sa tu tena mantreṇa sva-kāmanā-viśeṣānusārāt sṛṣṭi-kṛc-chhakti-viśeṣa-viśiṣṭatayā vakṣyamāṇa-stavānusārād gokulākhya-pīṭha-gatatayā śrī-govindam upāsitavān ity āha – atha tepa iti caturbhiḥ. 'guṇa rūpiṇyā' sattva-rajas-tamo-guṇamayyā; 'rūpiṇyā' mūrtimatyā 'paryupāsitaṁ' paritas tal-lokād bahiḥ sthitayopāsitaḥ dhyānādinārcitam – "māyā parety abhimukhe ca vilajjamānā" iti, "balim udvahanty samadanty ajayānimiṣā" iti ca śrī-bhāgavatāt. 'aṁśaiḥ' tad-āvaraṇasthaiḥ parikaraiḥ.

Ṭīkā 27

tad evaṁ dikṣātaḥ parastād eva tasya dhruvasyeva dvijatva-saṁskāras tadābādhitatvāt tat-tan-mantrādhidevāj jāta ity āha – atha veṇv iti dvayena. 'trayī murtiḥ' gāyatrī vedamātṛtvāt, dvitīya-padye tasyā eva vyaktibhāvitvāc ca, tan-mayī; 'gatiḥ' paripāṭī. mukhābjāni praviveśa ity aṣṭabhiḥ karṇaiḥ praviveśety arthaḥ. ādi-guruṇā śrī-kṛṣṇena sa brahmā saṁskṛta iti karma-sthāne prathamā.

Ṭīkā 28

tataś ca trayīm api tasmāt prāpya tam eva tuṣṭāvety āha – trayyeti spaṣṭam.

Ṭīkā 29

stutim āha – cintāmaṇīty ādi. tatra goloke 'smin mantra-bhedena tad-ekadeśeṣu bṛhad-dhyāna-mayādiṣv ekasya mantrasya vā samayādiṣu ca pīṭheṣu satsv api madhya-sthatvena mukhyatayā prathama gokulākhya-pīṭha-nivāsa-yogya-līlayā stauti – cintāmaṇīty ekena. 'abhi' sarvatobhāvena vana-nayana-cāraṇa-gosthānānayana-prakāreṇa 'pālayantaṁ' sa-snehaṁ rakṣantam. kadācid rahasi tu vailakṣaṇyam ity āha – lakṣmīti. lakṣmyo 'tra gopa-sundarya eveti vyākhyātam eva.

Ṭīkā 30

tad eva cintāmaṇi-prakara-sadma-mayaṁ 'kathā gānaṁ nāṭyaṁ gamanam api' iti vakṣyamāṇānusāreṇa gokulākhya-vilakṣaṇa-

pīṭhagatāṁ līlām uktvā. eka-sthāna-sthitikāṁ kathāṁ gamanādi-rahitāṁ bṛhad-dhyānādi-dṛṣṭāṁ dvitīya-pīṭhagatāṁ līlām āha – veṇum iti dvayena. tatra veṇum iti sarvaṁ spaṣṭam.

Ṭīkā 31

āloletyādi. praṇayapurvako yaḥ keliḥ parihāsas tatra yā kalā vaidagdhī, saiva vilāso yasya taṁ – "drava-keli-parihāsāḥ" ity amaraḥ.

Ṭīkā 32

tad eva līlā-dvayam uktvā paramācintya-śaktyā vaibhava-viśeṣeṇāha – aṅgānīti caturbhiḥ. tatra tatra vigrahasyāha – aṅgānīti. hasto 'pi draṣṭuṁ śaknoti, cakṣur api pālayituṁ pārayati, tathānyad-anyad apy aṅgam anyat kalayituṁ prabhavatīti; evam evoktaṁ – "sarvataḥ pāṇi-pādaṁ tat sarvato 'kṣi-śiro-mukham" ity ādi. 'jaganti' iti līlā-parikareṣu tat tad aṅgaṁ yathā svayam eva vyavaharatīti bhāvaḥ. tatra ca tasya vigrahasya vailakṣaṇyam eva hetur ity āha – ānandeti.

Ṭīkā 33

vailakṣaṇyam eva puṣyati – advaitam iti tribhiḥ. 'advaitaṁ' pṛthivyām ayam advaito rājetivad atulyam ity arthaḥ – "vismāpanaṁ svasya ca" iti tṛtīya-sthoddhava-vākyāt. 'acyutaṁ' – "kaṁso vatādyākṛta me 'tyanugrahaṁ drakṣye 'ṅghri-padmaṁ prahito 'munā hareḥ. kṛtāvatārasya duratyayaṁ tamo purve 'taran yan nakha-maṇḍala-tviṣā. yad arcitaṁ brahma-bhavādibhiḥ suraiḥ śriyā ca devyā" ity ādi daśama-sthākrūra-vākyāt, "yā vai śriyārcitam ajādibhir āpta-kāmair yogeśvarair api yadātmani rāsa-goṣṭhyām. kṛṣṇasya tad bhagavataś caraṇāravindaṁ nyastaṁ staneṣu vijahuḥ parirabhya tāpam" iti śrīmad-uddhava-vākyāt – "darśayām āsa lokaṁ svaṁ gopānāṁ tamasaḥ param" ity uktvā "nandādayas tu taṁ dṛṣṭvā paramānanda-nirvṛtāḥ. kṛṣṇaṁ ca tatra chandobhiḥ stūyamānaṁ suvismitāḥ". iti śuka-vākyāc ca. 'anādim' āditrayaṁ; yathaikādaśe sāṅkhya-kathane – "kālo māyā-maye jīve" ity ādau mahā-pralaye sarvāvaśiṣṭatvena brahmopadiśya tad api tasya draṣṭā tvaṁ svayaṁ bhagavān asminn āha – "eṣa sāṅkhya-vidhiḥ proktaḥ saṁśaya-granthi-bhedanaḥ. pratilomānulomābhyāṁ parāvara-dṛśā mayā." iti. 'purāṇa puruṣaṁ' – "ekas tvam ātmā puruṣaḥ purāṇaḥ" iti brahma-vākyāt, "gūḍhaḥ purāṇa-puruṣo vana-citra-mālyaḥ" iti māthura-vākyāc ca. tathāpi 'nava-yauvanaṁ' – purāpi navaḥ puraṇa iti nirukteḥ, "gopyas tapaḥ kim acaran yad amuṣya rūpam" ity ādau "anusavābhinavam" iti śrī-daśamāt, "yasyānanaṁ makara-

kuṇḍalam" ity ādi navamāt "satyaṁ śaucam" ityādau "kauśalaṁ kāntir dhairyam" ādīni paṭhitvā "ete cānye ca bhagavan nityā yatra mahā-guṇāḥ. prārthyā mahattvam icchadbhir na viyanti sma karhicit" iti prathamāt; bṛhad-dhyānādau tathā śravaṇāt, "gopa-veśam abbhrābhaṁ taruṇaṁ kalpa-drumāśritam" iti tāpanī-śrutau tad dhyāne 'taruṇa'-śabdasya 'nava yauvana' eva śobhā-nidhānatvena tātparyāt. 'vedeṣu durlabhaṁ' – "bhejur mukunda-padavīṁ śrutibhir vimṛgyām" iti "adyāpi yat pada-rajaḥ śruti-mṛgyam" iti ca śrī-daśamāt. 'adurlabham ātma-bhaktau' "bhaktyāham ekayā grāhyaḥ" ity ekādaśāt, "pureha bhūman" ity ādi śrī-daśamāc ca.

Ṭīkā 34

panthās tv iti. 'prapada-sīmni' caraṇāravindayor agre – "citram bataitad ekena vapuṣā yugapat pṛthak. gṛheṣu dvy-aṣṭa-sāhasraṁ striya eka udāvahat" iti śrī-nāradokteḥ. "eko vaśī sarvagaḥ kṛṣṇa īḍya eko 'pi san bahudhā yo vibhāti" iti gopāla-tāpanyām. tatra siddhāntam āha – avicintya-tattva iti; "ātmeśvaro 'tarkya-sahasra-śaktiḥ" iti tṛtīyāt, "acintyāḥ khalu ye bhāvā na tāṁs tarkeṇa yojayet. prakṛtibhyaḥ paraṁ yac ca tad acintasya lakṣaṇam." iti skāndād bhāratāc ca, "śrutes tu śabda-mūlatvāt" iti brahma-sūtrāt, "acintyo hi maṇi-mantra-mahauṣadhīnāṁ prabhāvaḥ" iti bhāṣya-yukteś ceti bhāvaḥ.

Ṭīkā 35

eko 'py asau iti – "tāvat sarve vatsa-pālāḥ paśyato 'jasya tat kṣaṇāt vyadṛśyanta ghanaśyāmāḥ" ity ārabhya tair vatsapālādibhir evānanta-brahmāṇḍa-sāmagrī-yuta-tat-tad-adhipuruṣāṇāṁ tenāntarbhāvāt; 'jagadaṇḍa-cayāḥ' iti – "na cāntar na bahir yasya" ity ādeḥ, "aṇor aṇīyān mahato mahīyān" ityādi-śruteḥ, "yo 'sau sarveṣu bhūteṣv āviśya bhūtāni vidadhāti sa vo hi svāmī bhavati. yo 'sau sarva-bhūtātmā gopāla eko devaḥ sarva-bhūteṣu gūḍhaḥ" ity ādi tāpanībhyaḥ.

Ṭīkā 36

atha tasya sādhaka-cayeṣv api bhakteṣu vadānyatvaṁ vadan nityeṣu kaimutyam āha – yad bhāveti. yathā gopaiḥ samāna-guṇaśīla-vayo-vilāsa-veśaiś cety āgama-vidhinetyādi-nitya-tat-saṅgināṁ tat sāmyaṁ śrūyate, tathaiva sambhāvyety arthaḥ; "vaireṇa yaṁ nṛpatayaḥ śiśupāla-śālva-pauṇḍrādayo gati-vilāsa-viloka-nādyaiḥ. dhyāyanta ākṛti-dhiyaḥ śayanāsanādau tad bhāvam āpur anurakta-dhiyāṁ punaḥ kim." ity ekādaśāt.

Ṭīkā 37

tat preyasīnāṁ tu kiṁ vaktavyam? yataḥ parama-śrīṇāṁ tāsāṁ sāhityenaiva tasya tal-lokavāsa ityāha – ānandeti. 'ānanda-cinmayo rasaḥ' parama-premamaya ujjvala-nāmā, tena 'pratibhāvitābhiḥ'; yadvā, pūrvaṁ tāvad yo rasas tan nāmnā rasena so 'yaṁ bhāvita upāsito jatas tataś ca tasya tena rasena yāḥ pratibhāvitās tābhiḥ sahety arthaḥ pratiśabdāl labhyate; yathā akhilānāṁ goloka-vāsinām anyeṣām api priya-vargāṇām ātmataḥ parama-śreṣṭhatayātmavad avyabhicāry api tābhir eva saha nivasatīti tāsām atiśāyitvaṁ darśitam. tatra hetuḥ – 'kalābhiḥ' hlādinī-śakti-vṛtti-rūpābhiḥ. tatrāpi vaiśiṣṭyam āha – praty-upakṛtaḥ sa ity uktes tasya prāg upakāritvam āyāti, tadvat. tatrāpi 'nija-rūpatayā' svadāratvenaiva, na tu prakaṭa-līlāvat paradāratva-vyahāreṇety arthaḥ. parama-lakṣmīṇāṁ tāsāṁ tat-para-dāratvāsambhāvad asya svadāratvamaya-rasasya kautukāvaguṇṭhitatayā samutkaṇṭhayā pauruṣārthaṁ prakaṭa-līlāyāṁ māyayaiva tādṛśatvaṁ vyañjitam iti bhāvaḥ. 'ya eva' ity evakāreṇa yat prāpañcika-prakaṭa-līlāyāṁ tāsu paradāratāvyavahāreṇa nivasati so 'yaṁ ya eva tad aprakaṭa-līlāspade goloke nijarūpatāvyavahāreṇa nivasatīti vyajyate. tathā ca vyākhyātaṁ gautamīya-tantre pada-prakaṭa-nitya-līlāśīlamaya-daśārṇa-vyākhyāne – "aneka-janma-siddhānāṁ gopīnāṁ patir eva vā" iti. "goloka eva" ity eva-kāreṇa seyaṁ līlā tu kvāpi nānyatra vidyata iti prakāśyate.

Ṭīkā 38

yadyapi goloka eva nivasati, tathāpi premāñjaneti. "acintya-guṇa-svarūpam" api premākhyaṁ yad-añjanaṁ yena churitavad uccaiḥ prakāśamānaṁ bhakti-rūpaṁ vilocanaṁ tenety arthaḥ.

Ṭīkā 39

sa eva kadācit prapañce nijāṁśena svayam avataratīty āha – rāmādīti. yaḥ kṛṣṇākhyaḥ 'paramaḥ pumān kalā niyamena' tatra niyatānām eva śaktīnāṁ prakāśena 'rāmādi-mūrtiṣu tiṣṭhan' tat-tan-mūrtīḥ 'prakāśayan nānāvatāram akarot' ya eva 'svayaṁ samabhavat' avatatāra. taṁ līlā-viśeṣeṇa govindam ahaṁ bhajāmīty arthaḥ. tad uktaṁ śrī-daśame devaiḥ – "matsyāśva-kacchapa-varāha-nṛsiṁha-haṁsa-rājanya-vipra-vibudheṣu kṛtāvatāraḥ. tvaṁ pāsi nas tribhuvanaṁ ca yathādhuneśa bhāraṁ bhuvo hara yadūttama vandanaṁ te." iti.

Ṭīkā 40

tad evaṁ tasya sarvāvatāritvena pūrṇatvam uktvā svarūpeṇāpyāha – yasyeti. dvayor eka-rūpatve 'pi viśiṣṭatayāvirbhāvāt śrī-govindasya dharmi-rūpatvam aviśiṣṭatayāvirbhāvād brahmaṇo dharma-rūpatvaṁ tataḥ pūrvasya maṇḍala-sthānīyatvam iti bhāvaḥ. ataeva gītāsu – "brahmaṇo hi pratiṣṭhāham" iti; ataevaikādaśe sva-vibhūti-gaṇanāyāṁ tad api svayaṁ gaṇitaṁ – "pṛthivī vāyur ākāśa āpo jyotir ahaṁ mahān. vikāraḥ puruṣo vyaktaṁ rajaḥ sattvaṁ tamaḥ param". iti. ṭīkā cātra – "paraṁ brahma ca" ity eṣā. śrī-matsya-devenāpy aṣṭame tathoktaṁ – "madīyaṁ mahimānaṁ ca paraṁ brahmeti śabditam. vetsyasy anugṛhītaṁ me saṁpraśnair viditaṁ hṛdi". iti. ataevāha dhruvaś caturthe – "yā nirvṛtis tanu-bhṛtāṁ tava pāda-padma-dhyānād bhavaj-jana-kathā śravaṇena vā syāt. sā brahmaṇi sva-mahimany api nātha mā bhūt kiṁ tv antakāsi lulitāt patatāṁ vimānāt." ataevātmārāmāṇām api tad guṇenākarṣaḥ śrūyate –"ātmārāmāś ca munayo nirgranthā apy urukrame. kurvanty ahaitukīṁ bhaktim ittham-bhūta-guṇo hariḥ." iti. atra viśeṣa-jijñāsā cet śrī-bhāgavata-sandarbho dṛśyatām ity alam-ativistareṇa.

Ṭīkā 41

tad evaṁ tasya svarūpa-gataṁ māhātmyaṁ darśayitvā tad-gata-māhātmyaṁ darśayati dvābhyāṁ. tatra bahiraṅga-śakti-māyācintya-kārya-gatam āha – māyā hīti. māyayā hi tasya sparśo nāstīty āha – sattveti. sattvasya rajas-tamo-miśritasyāśrayi yat paraṁ tad amiśraṁ śuddhaṁ sattvaṁ cic-chakti-vṛtti-rūpaṁ yasya tam; tathoktaṁ śrī-viṣṇu-purāṇe – "sattvādayo na santīśe yatra ca prākṛtā guṇāḥ. sa śuddhaḥ sarva-śuddhebhyaḥ pumān ādyaḥ prasīdatu. iti. viśeṣataḥ śrī-bhāgavata-sandarbhe tad idam api vivṛtam asti.

Ṭīkā 42

atha tan-maya-mohanatvam āha – ānandeti. 'ānanda-cinmaya-rasa' ujjvalākhyaḥ prema-rasas tad-ātmatayā tad-āliṅgitatayā prānindruṁ manaḥsu prati-phalan sarva-mohana-svāṁśa-cchurita-paramāṇu-pratibimbatayā kiñcid udayann api smaratām upety ādi yojyam yad uktaṁ rāsa-pañcādhyāyāṁ – "sākṣān manmatha-manmatha" iti. "cakṣuṣaś cakṣuḥ" itivat. tad evaṁ tat kāraṇatve 'pi smarāveśasya dṛṣṭatvaṁ jagad-āveśavat.

Ṭīkā 43

tad idaṁ prapañcagataṁ māhātmyam uktvā nija-dhāma-gata-māhātmyam āha – goloketi. devī-maheśetyādi-gaṇanaṁ vyutkrameṇa jñeyam. devy-ādīnāṁ yathottaram ūrdhvordhva-prabhavavatvāt tal-lokānām urdhvordhva-bhāvitvam iti. golokasya sarvordhvagāmitvaṁ sarvebhyo vyāpakatvaṁ ca vyavasthāpi tam asti; bhuvi prakāśamānasya vṛndāvanasya tu tenābhedaḥ pūrvatra darśitaḥ. "sa tu lokas tvayā kṛṣṇaḥ sīdamānaḥ kṛtātmanā. dhṛto dhṛtimatā vīra nighnato 'padravaṁ gavām" ity anenābhedenaiva hi. goloka eva nivasatīty eva kāraḥ saṅghaṭate, yato bhuvi prakāśamāne 'smin vṛndāvane tasya nitya-vihāritvaṁ śrūyate; yathādi-vārāhe – "vṛndāvanaṁ dvādaśakaṁ vṛndayā parirakṣitam. hariṇādhiṣṭhitaṁ tac ca brahma-rudrādi-sevitam." tatra ca viśeṣaḥ – "kṛṣṇa krīḍā-setu-bandhaṁ mahā-pātaka-nāśanam. ballavībhiḥ krīḍanārthaṁ kṛtvā devo gadādharaḥ. gopakaiḥ sahitas tatra kṣaṇam ekaṁ dine dine. tatraiva ramaṇārthaṁ hi nitya-kālaṁ sa gacchati." iti. ataeva gautamīye, śrī-nārada uvāca – "kim idaṁ dvātriṁśad-vanaṁ vṛndāraṇyaṁ viśāmpate. śrotum icchāmi bhagavan yadi yogyo 'smi me vada." śrī-kṛṣṇa uvāca – "idaṁ vṛndāvanaṁ nāma mama dhāmaiva kevalam. atra ye paśavaḥ pakṣi-mṛgāḥ kīṭā narādhamāḥ. nivasanti mayāviṣṭe mṛtā yānti mamālayam. atra yā gopa-kanyāś ca nivasanti mamālaye. gopinyastā mayā nityaṁ mama sevā-parāyaṇāḥ. pañca-yojanam evāsti vanaṁ me deha-rūpakaṁ. kālindīyaṁ suṣumnākhyā paramāmṛta-vāhinī. atra devāś ca bhūtāni vartante sūkṣma-rūpataḥ. sarva-deva-mayaś cāhaṁ na tyajāmi vanaṁ kvacit. āvirbhāvas tirobhāvo bhaven me 'tra yuge yuge. tejo-mayam idaṁ ramyam adṛśyaṁ carma-cakṣuṣā." iti. etad rūpam evāśritya vārāhādau te nitya-kadambādayo darśitā varṇitāś ca. tasmād asmad-dṛśyamānasya eva vṛndāvanasya asmad-dṛśyatādṛśa-prakāśa-viśeṣa eva goloka iti labdham. yadā cāsmad-dṛśyamāne prakāśe sa-parikaraḥ śrī-kṛṣṇa āvirbhavati tadaiva tasyāvatāra ucyate, tad eva ca rasa-viśeṣa-poṣāya saṁyoga-virahaḥ punaḥ saṁyogādi-maya-vicitra-līlayā tayā pāra-dāryādi-vyavahāraś ca gamyate. yadā tu yathātra yathā vānyatra kalpa-tantra-yāmala-saṁhitā-pañcarātrādiṣu tathā dig-darśanena viśeṣā jñeyāḥ. tathā ca śrī-daśame – "jayati jana-nivāso devakī-janma-vādo yaduvara-pariṣat svair dorbhir asyann adharmam. sthira-cara-vṛjina-ghnaḥ su-smita-śrī-mukhena vraja-pura-vanitānāṁ vardhayan kāmadevam." ityādi. tathā ca pādme nirvāṇa-khaṇḍe śrī-bhagavad-vyāsa-vākye – "paśya tvaṁ darśayiṣyāmi svarūpaṁ veda-gopitam. tato paśyāmy ahaṁ bhūpa bālaṁ kālāmbuda-prabham. gopa-kanyāvṛtaṁ gopaṁ hasantaṁ gopa-bālakaiḥ." iti; anenālabdha-strī-dharma-vayaskatādi-bodhakena kanyāpadena tāsām anyādṛśatvaṁ nirākriyate. tathā ca gautamīya-tantre caturthādhyāye – "atha vṛndāvanaṁ dhyāyet" ity ārabhya, tad dhyānaṁ – "svargād iva paribhraṣṭa-kanyakā-śata-maṇḍitam. gopa-vatsa-gaṇākīrṇaṁ vṛkṣa-ṣaṇḍaiś ca maṇḍitam. gopa-kanyā-sahasrais tu padma-patrāyatekṣaṇaiḥ. arcitam bhāva-kusumais trailokyaika-guruṁ param." ity ādi. tad darśana-kārī ca darśitas tatraiva sadācāra-prasaṅge – "ahar niśaṁ japen mantraṁ mantrī niyata-mānasaḥ sa paśyati na sandeho gopa-rūpa-dharaṁ harim." iti; tatraivānyatra "vṛndāvane vased dhīmān yāvat kṛṣṇasya darśanam" iti; trailokya-san-mohana-tantre cāṣṭādaśākṣara-prasaṅge – "japed yas tu mantrī niyata-mānasaḥ. sa paśyati na sandeho gopa-veśa-dharaṁ harim." iti. ataeva tāpanyāṁ brahma-vākyaṁ – "tad u hovāca brahma-savanaṁ carato me dhyātaḥ stutaḥ parārdhānte so 'budhyate gopa-veśo me puruṣaḥ parastād āvirbabhūva." iti. tasmāt kṣīrodaśāyyādy-avatāratayā tasya yat kathanaṁ tat tu tad-aṁśānāṁ tatra praveśopekṣayā. tad alam ati-vistareṇa śrī-kṛṣṇa-sandarbhe darśita-caraṇe prastutam anusarāmaḥ.

Ṭīkā 44

pūrvaṁ devī-maheśa-hari-dhāmnām uparicaradhāmatvaṁ tasya darśitam; samprati tu tat-tad-āśrayatvāt tad eva yogyam iti darśayati – sṛṣṭīti pañcabhiḥ. yathoktaṁ śrutibhiḥ – "tvam akaraṇaḥ svarāḍ akhila-kāraka-śakti-dharas tava balim udvahanti samadantyajayānimiṣā" iti.

Ṭīkā 45

atha krama-prāptaṁ maheśaṁ nirūpayati – kṣīram iti. kārya-kāraṇa-bhāva-mātrāṁśe dṛṣṭānto 'yaṁ dārṣṭāntikasya kāraṇa-nirvikāratvāt cintāmaṇy-ādivat acintya-śaktyaivā tad-ādi-kāryatayāpi sthitatvāt. śrutiś ca – "eko ha vai puruṣo nārāyaṇa āsīn na brahmā na ca śaṅkaraḥ sa munir bhūtvā samacintayat. tata ete vyajāyanta viśvo hiraṇyagarbho 'gni-varuṇa-rudrendra" iti, tathā – "sa brahmaṇā sṛjati rudreṇa nāśayati. so 'nutpattilaya eva hariḥ kāraṇa-rūpaḥ paraḥ paramānandaḥ" iti. śambhor api kāryatvaṁ guṇa-sambalanāt; yathoktaṁ śrī-daśame – "harir hi nirguṇaḥ sākṣāt puruṣaḥ prakṛteḥ paraḥ. śivaḥ śakti-yutaḥ śaśvat-triliṅgo guṇa-saṁvṛtaḥ." iti; etad evoktaṁ – 'vikāra-viśeṣa-yogāt' iti. kutracid bhedoktir yā dṛśyate tām api samādadhāti; tato hetoḥ pṛthaktvaṁ nāstīti. yathoktam ṛg-veda-śirasi – "atha nityo nārāyaṇaḥ, brahmā ca nārāyaṇaḥ, śivaś ca nārāyaṇaḥ, śakraś ca nārāyaṇaḥ, kālaś ca nārāyaṇaḥ, diśaś ca nārāyaṇaḥ, adhaś ca nārāyaṇaḥ, urdhvaṁ ca nārāyaṇaḥ, antar-bahiś ca nārāyaṇaḥ. nārāyaṇa, evedaṁ sarvaṁ jātaṁ jagatyāṁ jagat." ityādi. brahmaṇā tv evam uktaṁ – "sṛjāmi tan niyukto 'haṁ haro harati tad vaśaḥ. viśvaṁ puruṣa-rūpeṇa paripāti triśakti-dhṛk" iti.

Ṭīkā 46

atha krama-prāptaṁ hari-svarūpam ekaṁ nirūpayan guṇāvatāra-maheśa-prasaṅgād-guṇāvatāraṁ viṣṇuṁ nirūpayati – dīpārcir iti. tadṛktve hetuḥ – "vivṛta-hetu-samāna-dharmā." iti. yadyapi govindāṁśāṁśaḥ kāraṇārṇavaśāyī tasya garbhodakaśāyī tasya cāvatāro 'yaṁ viṣṇur iti labhyate, tathāpi mahā-dīpāt krama-paramparayā sūkṣma-nirmala-dīpasyoditasya jyotī-rūpāṁśo yathā tena saha sāmyaṁ tathā govindena rūpāntaraṁ viṣṇur gamyate. śambhos tu tamo 'dhiṣṭhanāt kajjalamaya-sūkṣma-dīpa-śikhā-sthānīyasya na tathā sāmyam iti; tirodhānāt tad ittham ucyate agre tu mahā-viṣṇor api kalā-viśeṣatvena darśayiṣyamāṇatvāt.

Ṭīkā 47

atha kāraṇārṇava-śāyinaṁ nirūpayati – ananta-jagad-aṇḍaiḥ saha roma-kūpāḥ yasya saḥ saha-śabdasya pūrva-nipātābhāva ārṣaḥ. 'ādhāra-śaktimayīṁ' parāṁ sva-mūrtiṁ śeṣākhyām.

Ṭīkā 48

tatra sarva-brahmāṇḍa-pālako yas tavāvatāratayā mahā-brahmādi-sahacaratvena tad abhinnatvena ca mahā-viṣṇur darśitaḥ; tatra ca tam apy evaṁ tal-lakṣaṇatayā varṇayati – 'tat-taj-jagad-aṇḍa-nāthāḥ' viṣṇv-ādayaḥ 'jīvanti' tat-tad-adhikāratayā jagati prakaṭaṁ tiṣṭhanti.

Ṭīkā 49

tad evaṁ devy-ādīnāṁ tad-āśrayakatvaṁ darśayitvā prasaṅga-saṅgatyā brahmaṇaś ca darśayann atīva bhinnatayā jīvatvam eva spaṣṭayati – bhāsvān iti. 'bhāsvān' sūryo yathā 'nijeṣu' nitya-svīyatvena vikhyāteṣu 'aśma-sakaleṣu' sūrya-kāntākhyeṣu svīyaṁ kiñcit tejaḥ prakaṭayati; 'api' – śabdāt tena tad upādhikāṁśena dāhādikāryaṁ svayam eva karoti, tathā ya eva jīva-viśeṣe kiñcit tejaḥ prakaṭayati, tena tad upādhikāṁśena svayam eva brahmā san jagad-aṇḍe brahmāṇḍe vidhāna-kartā vyaṣṭi-srṣṭi-kartā bhavatīty arthaḥ; yad vā, mahā-brahmaivāyaṁ varṇyate, tad-upalakṣito mahā-śivaś ca jñeyaḥ; tataś ca jagad-aṇḍānāṁ vidhāna-kartṛtvaṁ ca yuktam eva. yadyapi durgākhyā māyā kāraṇārṇavaśāyina eva karma-karī, yadyapi ca brahma-viṣṇv-ādyā garbhodakaśāyina evāvatārās tathāpi tasya sarvāśrayatayā te 'pi tad-āśrayitayā gaṇitāḥ. evam uttaratrāpi.

Ṭīkā 50

atha sarve sarva-vighna-nivāraṇārthaṁ prathamaṁ gaṇapatiṁ stuvantīti tasyaiva stutiyogyatety āśaṅkya pratyācaṣṭe – yat pādeti. kaimyutena tad eva dṛḍhīkṛtaṁ śrī-kapiladevena – "yat pāda-niḥsṛta-sarit-pravarodakena tīrthena mūrdhany adhikṛtena śivaḥ śivo 'bhūt."

Ṭīkā 51

tac ca yuktam ity āha – agnir mahīti – sarvaṁ spaṣṭam.

Ṭīkā 52

nanu kecit savitāraṁ sarveśvaraṁ vadanti? tatrāha – yac cakṣur iti. ya eva 'cakṣuḥ' prakāśako yasya saḥ – "yad āditya-gataṁ tejo jagad bhāsayate 'khilam. yac candramasi yac cāgnau tat tejo viddhi māmakam" iti śrī-gītābhyaḥ, "bhīṣāsmād vātaḥ pavate bhīṣodeti sūryaḥ" ity ādi śruteḥ, virāḍ-rūpasyaiva savitṛ-cakṣuṣṭvāc ca."

Ṭīkā 53

kiṁ bahunā? dharma iti. – "ahaṁ sarvasya prabhavo mattaḥ sarvaṁ pravartate." iti śrī-gītābhyaḥ.

Ṭīkā 54

tatra tatra sarveśvaras tu 'parjanyavad draṣṭavyaḥ' iti nyāyena karmānurūpa-phala-dātṛtvena sāmye 'pi bhakte tu pakṣa-pāta-viśeṣaṁ karotīty āha – yas tv indreti. "samo 'haṁ sarva-bhūteṣu na me dveṣyo 'sti na priyaḥ. ye bhajanti tu māṁ bhaktyā mayi te teṣu cāpy aham. iti, "ananyāś cintayanto māṁ ye janāḥ paryupāsate. teṣāṁ nityābhiyuktānāṁ yoga-kṣemaṁ vahāmy aham" iti ca śrī-gītābhyaḥ.

Ṭīkā 55

sa eva ca svayantu vairibhyo 'pyanya-durlabha-phalaṁ dadāti, kim uta sva-viṣayaka-kāmādinā niṣkāma-śreṣthebyaḥ. tataḥ ko vānyo bhajanīya iti? bhajāmīty anta-prakaraṇam upasaṁharati – yaṁ krodheti. 'sahaja-praṇayaḥ' sakhyam; 'vātsalyaṁ' pitry-ādy-ucita-bhāvaḥ; 'mohaḥ' sarva-vismaraṇa-mayo bhāvaḥ, para-brahmatayā sphūrtiḥ; 'guru-gauravaṁ' svasmin pitṛtvādi-bhāvanāmayam; sevya-

bhāvaḥ "sevyo 'yaṁ mameti" bhāvanā – dāsyam ity arthaḥ. 'tasya sadṛśīṁ' krodhāveśino prākṛtatva-mātrāṁśair nānyeṣu tu tat-tad-bhāvanā-yogya-rūpa-guṇāṁśa-lābha-tāratamyena tulyam ity arthaḥ. "adṛṣṭvānyatamaṁ loke śīlaudārya-guṇaiḥ samam" iti śrī-vasudeva-vākyasya, "jagad-vyāpāra-varjam" iti brahma-sūtrasya, "prayojyamāne mayi tāṁ śuddhāṁ bhāgavatīṁ tanum" iti nārada-vākyasya ca dṛṣṭyā sarvathā tat-sadṛśatvāvirodhāt, "vaireṇa yaṁ nṛpatayaḥ" ity ādau "anurakta-dhiyāṁ punaḥ kim" ity anurakta-dhīṣu stutvā tena viśiṣṭaṁ svatas tv iti prāpte teṣv api tat-tad-anurāga-tāratamyenāpi tat tāratamyaṁ labhyata iti. anena golokastha-prapañcāvatīrṇayor ekatvam eva darśitam; tad uktaṁ – "nandādayas tu taṁ dṛṣṭvā" ity ādi.

Ṭīkā 56

tad evaṁ nijeṣṭadevaṁ bhajanīyatvena stutvā tena viśiṣṭaṁ tal lokaṁ tathā stauti – śriyaḥ kāntā iti yugmakena. 'śriyaḥ' śrī-vraja-sundarī-rūpās tāsām eva mantre dhyāne ca sarvatra prasiddheḥ. tāsām anantānām apy eka eva 'kāntaḥ' iti parama-nārāyaṇādibhyo 'pi tasya, tat-tal-lokebhyo 'pi tadīya-lokasya cāsya, māhātmyaṁ darśitam. 'kalpa-taravo drumāḥ' iti – teṣāṁ sarveṣām eva sarva-pradatvāt tathaiva prathitam tadvat 'bhūmiḥ' ity ādikaṁ ca bhūmir api sarva-spṛhāṁ dadāti, kim uta kaustubhādi. 'toyam' apy amṛtam iva svādu, kim utāmṛtam ity ādi. 'vaṁśī' priya-sakhīti sarvataḥ śrī-kṛṣṇasya sukha-sthiti-śrāvakatvena jñeyam. kiṁ bahunā? 'cid-ānanda' lakṣaṇam vastv eva 'jyotiś' candra-sūryādi-rūpam; 'samānodita-candrārkam' iti vṛndāvana-viśeṣaṇaṁ gautamīya-tantra-dvaye; tac ca nitya-pūrṇacandratvāt tathā tad eva param api tat tat prakāśayam apīty arthaḥ. tathā tad eva teṣām 'āsvādyaṁ' bhogyam api ca cic-chakti-mayatvād iti bhāvaḥ – "darśayām āsa lokaṁ svaṁ gopānāṁ tamasaḥ param" iti śrī-daśamāt. 'surabhībhyaś ca sravatīti tadīya-vaṁśī-dhvanyādyāveśād iti bhāvaḥ. 'vrajati na hi' iti tad-āveśena te tad vāsinaḥ' kālam api na jānantīti bhāvaḥ; kāla-doṣās tatra na santīti vā – "na ca kāla-vikramaḥ" iti dvitīyāt. ataeva 'śvetaṁ' śuddhaṁ 'dvīpam' anya-saṅga-rahitaṁ, "yathā sarasi padmaṁ tiṣṭhati tathā bhūmyāṁ hi tiṣṭhati" iti tāpanībhyaḥ. kṣitīti – tad uktaṁ – "yaṁ na vidmo vayaṁ sarve pṛcchanto 'pi pitāmaham" iti.

Ṭīkā 57

tad evaṁ tasya stutim uktvā śrī-bhagavat-prasāda-lābham āha – atheti sārdhena. sarvaṁ spaṣṭam.

Ṭīkā 58

tatra prasāda-rūpāṁ pañca-ślokīm āha – prabuddha iti. "jñāna-vijñāna-sampanno bhaja māṁ bhakti-bhāvitaḥ" ity ekādaśāt.

Ṭīkā 59

prema-lakṣaṇa-bhakteḥ sādhana-jñāna-rūpayor bhaktyoḥ prāpty upāyam āha – pramāṇair iti. 'pramāṇaiḥ' bhagavac-chāstraiḥ 'tat-sadācāraiḥ' tadīyā ye santas teṣām ācārair anuṣṭhānaiḥ 'tad abhyāsaiḥ' teṣām eva paunaḥ-puṇya-bāhulyena, 'ātmanātmānaṁ bodhayati' svayam eva svaṁ bhagavad-āśritaḥ śuddha-jīva-rūpam anubhavati; tato 'py uttamāṁ śuddhāṁ bhaktiṁ labhata iti. tathā ca śruti-stave – "sva-kṛta-pureṣv amīṣv abahirantara-saṁvaraṇaṁ tava puruṣaṁ vadanty akhila-śakti-dhṛto 'ṁśa-kṛtam." iti nṛgatiṁ vivicya kavayo nigamāvapanam bhavata upāsate 'ṅghrim abhavaṁ bhuvi viśvasitāḥ." iti.

Ṭīkā 60

tathā ca prema-bhaktir eva sādhyā, nānyety āha – yasya iti. tad uktam caturthe – "ato māṁ sudurārādhyaṁ satām api durāpayā. ekānta-bhaktyā ko vāñchet pāda-mūlaṁ vinā bahiḥ." iti.

Ṭīkā 61

punaḥ śuddhām eva sādhana-bhaktiṁ draḍhayann anye kāmair api tām eva kuryād ity āha – dharmān anyān iti. tad uktam – "akāmaḥ sarva-kāmo vā mokṣa-kāma udāra-dhīḥ. tīvrena bhakti-yogena yajeta puruṣaṁ param." iti.

Ṭīkā 62

tasmāt tava sisṛkṣāpi phaliṣyatīti sayuktikam āha – ahaṁ hīti. 'pradhānaṁ' śreṣṭhaṁ, 'bījaṁ' pūrṇa-bhagavad-rūpaṁ, 'prakṛtiḥ' avyaktaṁ, 'pumān' draṣṭā; kiṁ bahunā? tvam api mayā 'āhitam' arpitaṁ tejo vibharṣi, tasmāt tena mat-tejasā 'jaganti' sarvāṇi sthāvara-jaṅgamāni, he vidhe, 'vidhehi' kurv iti.

Sanskrit Glossary

A

abhidheya-tattva – process
abhimāna – self-conception
acara-jagat – inanimate world
acintya – inconceivable
acintya-bhedābheda-tattva – inconceivable distinction with non-distinction
acintya-śakti – inconceivable potency
acintya-tattva – inconceivable Absolute Truth
ādhāra-śakti – all-accommodating potency
adhikāra – qualification
ādhikārika-devatā – delegated authority
adhiṣṭhātṛ-deva, adhiṣṭhātṛ-devatā, adhiṣṭhātṛ-devī – presiding deity
ādhyātmika-jñāna – knowledge of the nature of the self
ādi-puruṣa – primeval personality
advaya-jñāna akhaṇḍa-tattva – non-dual undivided principle
ahaṅkāra – false ego
aiśvarya – sense of awe and reverence
akhaṇḍa-pūrṇa-cinmaya-tattva – indivisible, complete and perfect transcendental principle
aṁśa – part and parcel
aṁśāvatāras – partial incarnations
anādi – beginningless
ānanda – bliss
ānanda-cinmaya-rasa – blissful transcendental mellows
ananta-dharma – unlimited in nature
ananya-bhakti – exclusive devotion
apara-śakti – inferior potency
aprakaṭa – unmanifest
aprakaṭa-līlā – unmanifest pastimes
aprakaṭa-nitya-līlā – eternal unmanifest pastimes
aprākṛta – supramundane

aprākṛta-anaṅga – transcendental Cupid
aprākṛta-jagat – transcendental world
ārādhana – worship
ārādhyadeva – personality who is to be worshiped by a *mantra*
arcana – formal worship with auspicious articles
arcana-mārga – path of reverent worship of the deity
ārṣa-prayoga – use by authoritative *ṛṣis*
artha – economic development
āsakti – attachment
asamordhva-tattva – incomparable and unsurpassed reality
āśrama – spiritual order
āśrita-tattva – beings under His shelter
aśuddha-sattva – impure goodness
aṣṭāṅga-yoga – eightfold yoga process
aṣṭa-sāttvika-bhāvas – eight symptoms of transcendental ecstasy
ātmārāmatā – self-satisfaction
ātma-tattva – essential reality of the self
āveśa-avatāras – empowered incarnations
avidyā – ignorance
avyakta – unmanifest

B

bahiraṅgā – external
bahiraṅga-śakti – external potency
bahirmukha-jīva – living entities who have turned away from Kṛṣṇa
bhagavad-rasa – mellows of transcendental service to Bhagavān
bhagavat-tattva-jñāna – knowledge of the essential reality of the Supreme Personality
bhagavat-tattva – supreme personal Absolute Truth
bhakta-vatsala – caring and affectionate to His devotees
bhakti-mārga – path of *bhakti*
bhakti-tattva-jñāna – knowledge of the essential reality of *bhakti*
bhāṣya – commentary
bhauma-gokula – earthly Gokula, which is the manifestation of Śrī Kṛṣṇa's eternal abode, Goloka Vṛndāvana, on the surface of this Earth.

bhauma-navadvīpa – earthly Navadvīpa, which is the manifestation of Śrī Śacīnandana Gaurahari's eternal abode, Śvetadvīpa, on the surface of this Earth.

bhāva – transcendental sentiment

bhaya – fear

bheda – differentiation

brahma-dhāma – abode of the impersonal Brahman. This is the region which has no feature other than the infinite light of the *brahmajyoti.*

brahmāṇḍa – egg-shaped material universe

brahma-jñāna – impersonal knowledge

brahmajyoti – the effulgence of the bodily form of Śrī Kṛṣṇa. It is one aspect of the Supreme Absolute Truth, and is considered by monists to be the ultimate goal of self-realization.

brahmajyoti – transcendental effulgence

brahmalaya – dissolving the self in Brahman

brahma-teja – brahminical power

bṛhad-dhyānamayī – subject of expanded meditation

buddhi – intelligence

C

caṇḍāla – dog-eater, outcaste

cara-jagat – animate world

catuḥ-ślokī – four original verses

cid-ābhāsa – semblance of transcendence

cid-aiśvarya – transcendental opulence

cid-vilāsa – transcendental pleasure-pastimes

cinmaya – transcendental

cinmaya-dhāma – transcendental abode

cinmaya-prakṛti – spiritual dominated potency

cinmaya-tattva – Absolute Transcendence

cintāmaṇi – desire-fulfilling gem

cit – knowledge

cit-śakti – transcendental potency; knowledge potency

cit-jagat – transcendental realm

citta – consciousness

cit-tattva – transcendental reality

D

daiva-vāṇī – transcendental Sarasvatī. Sarasvatī is manifest within this world as the goddess of learning, but is also present in an eternal spiritual form in the spiritual world. That transcendental Sarasvatī spoke the eighteen-syllable *gopāla-mantra* to Brahmājī.

daśa-mūla-tattva – ten fundamental principles

dāsya-bhāva – mood of servitorship

deva – demigod

devatā – demigod

devī-dhāma – the mundane world, the abode of Durgā-devī

dhāma – transcendental abode

dharma – constitutional nature; principles of religious conduct; religiosity; righteous prescription

Divya-Sarasvatī – transcendental Sarasvatī. See *daiva-vāṇī.*

dravya – aggregate of material elements

dṛśyamāna bhauma – visible earthly

E

ekādaśa-indriya – eleven senses

ekapāda-vibhūti – one-fourth of Bhagavān's opulence

G

gauṇa-dharma – secondary function

Gadādhara – (1) A name of Kṛṣṇa which means "wielder of the club" or "one who plays sweetly upon His flute." (2) Gadādhara Paṇḍita, one of the principle associates of Śrī Caitanya Mahāprabhu.

gandharva – a class of demigods who are celestial musicians

goloka-tattva – essential Reality of Goloka

gopa-kanyā – cowherd damsel

gopa-ramaṇī – charming cowherd girl beloveds

goṣṭha – residence and pasture of the cows

grantha – book

guṇa – modes of material nature

guṇa-avatāras – presiding deities of the material modes

guru-gaurava – reverence

H

Hiraṇyagarbha – the Viṣṇu expansion called Hiraṇyagarbha or Mahā-Brahmā from whom Brahmā is manifest. When there is no *jīva* qualified for the post of Brahmā, sometimes Viṣṇu Himself becomes Brahmā, and sometimes Hiraṇyagarbha performs the functions of Brahmā.

hlādinī-śakti – transcendental pleasure potency

hlādinī-svarūpa – internal pleasure potency

hlādinī-vṛtti – bliss function

I

icchā-śakti – desire potency

indragopa – the name of a species of minute insect

iṣṭadeva – worshipable deity

īśvara – Supreme Lord

J

jaiva-dharma – eternal constitutional occupation of the living entity

Janas – one of the higher planetary systems situated above Maharloka. Also called Janoloka.

jīva-śakti – potency comprised of the living entities

jñāna – knowledge

jñāna-mudrā – a finger position indicating wisdom, formed by joining the thumb and middle finger and exhibited with the first and third fingers pointing upright with the palm of the hand facing outward

jñāna-vṛtti – faculty of knowledge

jñāna-yoga – the process for spiritual elevation based on philosophical introspection and cultivation of knowledge. See also *neti neti.*

K

kaivalya – impersonal liberation; merging into the Absolute; oneness with Brahman

kājala – black eye-cosmetic

kalā – phase
kāla – time
kalā-viśeṣa – specific expansion of an expansion
kalpa-vṛkṣa – desire-tree
kāma – lust; transcendental desire; sense gratification
kāma-bīja – desire seed
kāmadhenu – wish-fulfilling cow
kāraṇa – cause
Kāraṇodakaśāyī – Mahā-Viṣṇu, who lies down on the waters of the Causal Ocean. See also Mahā-Viṣṇu.
kārya-nimitta – instrumental cause
kṛṣṇa-tattva – fundamental Reality of Kṛṣṇa
karma – activity; fruitive activities
karma-cakra – wheel of fruitive activities
karma-kāṇḍa – *dharma* of mundane piety
karma-phala – the fruit of action
kartā – performer of activities
kārya-kāriṇī-śakti – potency of cause and effect
kāya-vyūha – direct expansions of the personal form
kinnara – a race whose individual members possess the figure of a human and the head of a horse
krodha – anger
kuñja – bower

L

līlā-kathā – narrations of pastimes
līlā-pīṭha – arena of pastimes
līlā-śakti – pastime potency
līlā-vigraha – pastime expansion
loka – planet

M

madhura-bhāva – amorous love
mādhurya-maṇḍala – sweet realm of Vraja
mahābhāva – highest spontaneous love

Mahā-Brahmā – another name for Hiraṇyagarbha, the Viṣṇu expansion from whom Brahmā is manifest. See also Hiraṇyagarbha.

mahākāśa – the spiritual sky within which the Vaikuṇṭha planets are situated

mahā-mādhurya – immense sweetness

mahānanda-rasa – supremely blissful transcendental mellows

mahāpuruṣa – great personality

Mahar – one of the higher planetary systems, the residence of great sages. Also called Maharloka.

mahā-śakti – great potency

mahat-tattva – aggregate material energy

Mahā-Viṣṇu – the immense Viṣṇu form who lies down on the waters of the Causal Ocean, and in the duration of whose breathing all the universes are created and annihilated

maheśa-dhāma – the abode of Maheśa, Lord Śiva

maheśvara-tattva – Supreme Controller

manas – mind

Manmatha-manmatha – a name of Kṛṣṇa, meaning that He churns the heart of Cupid, who churns the hearts of all living beings

mantra – a verse possessing extraordinary power

mantra-japa – recitation of a *mantra*

mantra-rāja – king of transcendental invocations

māyā – illusory energy

māyā-śakti – illusory potency

māyika – illusory

māyika-jagat – material worlds

moha – delusion

mūla-prakṛti – original potency

mūla-puruṣa – original enjoyer

N

nāga – a race of serpent-beings who inhabit planetary systems below the earthly plane. Vāsuki is chief of the *nāgas*.

nāgara – hero

nāgarī – heroine

naimittika-avatāra – occasional incarnation
navayauvana-svarūpa – ever-fresh adolescent form
nāyaka – hero
neti neti – literally, "not this, not this." This phrase refers to the process in *jñāna-yoga* of eliminating the mundane through philosophical analysis. After eliminating all mundane, temporary objects, only the eternal spiritual principle should remain.
nimitta – instrument or immediate cause
nimitta-kāraṇa – instrumental cause. Creation involves an instrumental cause and an ingredient cause (*upādāna*). The instrumental cause activates the ingredient cause.
niṣkāma – freedom from desire
niṣṭhā – steadiness
nirguṇa – free from material qualities; transcendental to the material modes
nirvāṇa – impersonal liberation. See also *kaivalya*.
nirviśeṣa – devoid of specific attributes
nirviśeṣa-jñāna – impersonal knowledge. See also *brahma-jñāna*.
nirviśeṣa-vāda – philosophy that the Absolute Truth is formless and impersonal
nitya-parikaras – eternal associates
nitya-kiśorī – eternal adolescents
nitya-sevā – eternal service

P

pañca-mahā-bhūta – five gross elements
pañcama-puruṣārtha – fifth goal of human existence
pañca-tan-mātra – five sense-objects
parā prakṛti – superior potency
parabrahma – Supreme Brahman
para-dāra – wife of another
parakīya-bhāva – paramour mood
parakīyā-ramaṇī – another's wife
paramānanda-svarūpa – intrinsic form of supreme, transcendental bliss
parama-puruṣa – Supreme Personality

parama-puruṣottama – Supreme Personality and Enjoyer
parama-tattva – Supreme Absolute Truth
parameśvara – Supreme Controller
para-tattva – supreme, transcendental Reality
pariṇāma – transformation
parikara – associate
pārṣada – see *parikara*
pati-bhāva – mood of being married
pīṭha – place of pastimes; seat
phala-śruti – benediction for readers
prabhāva – influence
pradhāna – unmanifest aggregate of the material elements
praṇaya – intimate love. Śrīla Rūpa Gosvāmī defines *praṇaya* in *Ujjvala-nīlamaṇi* as that state where the lover and beloved become one due to the intensity of their affection.
prāṇāyāma – controlling the breathing process
prakāśa – manifestation; illumination
prakaṭa – manifest
prakaṭa-līlā – manifest pastimes
prakṛti – predominated potencies; predominated principle; external energy; material nature
prakṛti-śakti – predominated potency
prasāda – mercy
prema – transcendental love
premānanda – bliss of pure, spiritual love
priya-sakhī – intimate female companion
pūjā – formal worship
pūrṇa-brahma – complete Brahman
puruṣa – male; the enjoyer; the predominator
puruṣa-avatāra – one of the three Viṣṇu expansions involved in the creation, maintenance and annihilation of this world: Kāraṇodakaśāyī Mahā-Viṣṇu, Garbhodakaśāyi Viṣṇu and Kṣīrodakaśāyi Viṣṇu.

R

rāga – spontaneous attachment; intense passion

rāgānuga-bhakti – *bhakti* that follows Kṛṣṇa's eternal associates in Goloka
rajas – material mode of passion
rākṣasa – a type of man-eating demon
rākṣasī – man-eating demoness
ramaṇa – lover
rasa – transcendental mellows
rasa-pīṭha – abode of divine rapture
rasika – connoisseur of ecstatic transcendental mellows
rasika-śekhara – crown jewel of connoisseurs of ecstatic transcendental mellows
ruci – taste

S

sac-cid-ānanda – eternity, knowledge and bliss
sadācāra – appropriate conduct
sādhaka-jīva – living entity engaged in spiritual practice
sādhana-bhakti – devotional service in practice
sādhya – aim and object of life
sādhya-bhakti – accomplished devotion
sahaja-praṇaya – natural intimacy
sakāma – with desire
sakhā – cowherd friend
sakhya-bhāva – the mood of friendship
śakti – potency
śaktimān – possessor of potency
śānta-bhāva – passive or neutral adoration
samadarśī – equally disposed to all
samādhi – trance
samavāya-sambandha – a relationship of aggregation, where a group of things are meaningful when taken as a whole, more so than individually.
samaṣṭi-dehābhimānī – possessor of the collective bodily identification
sambandha-jñāna – knowledge of relationship

saṁhitā – a compilation of *mantras*. *Mantra* refers specifically to a verse that possesses extraordinary power. Not all verses are *mantras*, and therefore not all compilations of verses can be called *saṁhitā*.

saṁsāra – material existence

saṁskāra – impressions; reformatory process

sāṅkhya – the process of enumeration. *Śrīmad-Bhāgavatam* provides an elaborate description of *sāṅkhya* philosophy in the teachings of Śrī Kapiladeva in the Third Canto.

sannyāsa – renounced order

sannyāsa-dharma – duties of the renounced order

Sarasvatī – the goddess of speech and learning. She exists in a form in this mundane world, and is worshiped for success in learning and education. She also exists in a transcendental form in the spiritual world.

sarva-kāraṇa-kāraṇa – cause of all causes

sarvāvatārī – source of all incarnations

sarveśvara – controller of all

sattva – existence; material mode of goodness

Satya – the topmost planetary system within the material world, and the residence of Brahmājī. Also called Satyaloka and Brahmaloka.

satya-kāma – whose every desire comes to fruition

sa-viśeṣa – endowed with specific attributes

sāyujya-mukti – liberation of merging into Bhagavān's existence

sevā-pīṭha – service location

sevya-bhāva – servitude

siṁhāsana – throne

siddhānta – philosophical conclusion

siddhi – perfection; spiritual perfection

smaraṇa – meditative remembrance

smṛti – Vedic scriptures such as the Purāṇas and histories such as the *Rāmāyaṇa* and the *Mahābhārata*. The word *smṛti* means "that which is remembered." Also see *śruti*.

sphūrti – manifestation; realization

śraddhā – transcendental faith

śruti – Vedic scriptures such as the four Vedas and the Upaniṣads. The word *śruti* means "that which is heard." Also see *smṛti.*
stava-stuti – prayers and verses
strī-śakti – the passive feminine potency
śuddha-bhakti – pure, unalloyed devotional service
śuddha-bhakti-samādhi – trance of pure devotion
śuddha-bhakti-rasa – transcendental mellows of pure *bhakti*
śuddha-parakīyā-rasa – pure paramour mellow
śuddha-sattva – pure existence
śuddha-svarūpa – pure, intrinsic form and nature
śuddha-tattva – pure absolute reality
śuṣka-vairāgya – dry renunciation
svāṁśa – personal expansion
svāṁśa-ābhāsa – semblance of a plenary portion
svāṁśa-bhāvābhāsa – semblance of an expansion of the Supreme Godhead
svabhāva – acquired nature
sva-dāra – own wife
svajātīya – intimate, having the same mood
svakīya-bhāva – wedded conjugal love
svarūpa – intrinsic form and nature
svarūpa-bhūta-śakti – intrinsic, personal potency
svarūpa-śakti – personal intrinsic potency
svarūpa-tattva – intrinsic fundamental reality
svayaṁ-rūpa – original personal form

T

Tapas – the planetary system of great sages such as the four Kumāras, situated just below Satyaloka. Also called Tapoloka.
tapasya – austerities
tamas – material mode of ignorance
tāmasa-ahaṅkāra – tamasic phase of false ego
taṭastha – marginal. When there is a point on the bank of a river which is exactly on the boundary between air and water, it is called the marginal position. It may sometimes be submerged beneath the water and may sometimes be exposed to the air.

This same adjective is applied to the living entity, who is the marginal potency of Śrī Kṛṣṇa, and who may be submerged in the darkness of the material energy, or may remain forever under the shelter of Kṛṣṇa's personal energy. The living entity can never remain in the marginal position, but must take shelter of the spiritual energy or be subjected to the material energy.

taṭastha-prakṛti – marginal potency

taṭastha-śakti – marginal potency

taṭastha-vikrama – marginal prowess

tattva – essential realities; philosophical principles; truth

tattva-siddhānta – philosophical conclusions of the Absolute Truth

ṭīkā – commentary

tribhaṅga-lalita – enchanting threefold-bending

tripāda-vibhūti – three-fourths of Bhagavān's opulence

U

ujjvala-rasa – resplendent mellow of amorous love

upādāna – ingredient cause. The ingredient cause of creation is the material nature (*prakṛti*), which furnishes the raw ingredients which are activated by the reflected effulgence of Mahā-Viṣṇu in the form of Śambhu. See also *nimitta-kāraṇa*.

upavana – sub-forests

V

vaiśiṣṭhya – unique qualities

vanitā – young woman

vātsalya-bhāva – parental affection

veda-mārga – Vedic path

vibhinnāṁśa – separated expansion. This refers to the living entities, who are minute expansions. Although the separated expansions in the form of living entities are eternal, full of knowledge and blissful by nature, due to their minuteness they are prone to be overwhelmed by the illusory energy. Thus they are also called *taṭastha*, or marginal. See also *taṭastha*.

vibhrama-vilāsa – deceptive pastimes; divine delusion

vibhu – Supreme Master

vibhūti – opulence
vidyā-vṛtti – knowledge function
vikāra – transformation
vilāsa – pleasure-pastimes
vilāsa-mūrti – pastime form
vilāsa-vigraha – pastime expansion
virajā – literally, "free from the influence of *rajo-guṇa*, the material mode of passion." The Virajā, sometimes referred to as the River Virajā, is the boundary between the material and spiritual worlds.
virāṭ-puruṣa – universal form
viśeṣaṭā – unique qualities. See *vaiśiṣṭhya*.
viśuddha – absolutely and perfectly pure; transcendentally pure
viśuddha-sattva – perfectly pure existence; unalloyed pure goodness; the mixture of the knowledge potency (*saṁvit-śakti*) and pleasure potency (*hlādinī-śakti*) which enters into the heart of the *sādhaka* when one enters the stage called *rati*.
viśvedevas – a class of demigods. The names of the ten Viśvedevas are given in the *Vācaspati-abhidhāna* as follows: Ṛtu, Dakṣa, Vasu, Satya, Kāma, Kāla, Dhuri, Rocana, Umādravā and Purūravā.
vyaṣṭi-antaryāmī – indwelling witness

Y

Yogamāyā – pastime potency
yoga-pīṭha – place of pastimes

English Glossary

The following terms have been adopted as rough translations of important Sanskrit words and phrases.

abode of divine rapture (*rasa-pīṭha*)
abode of the impersonal Brahman (*brahma-dhāma*)
absolute transcendence (*cinmaya-tattva*)
absolutely and perfectly pure (*viśuddha*)
accomplished devotion (*sādhya-bhakti*)
acquired nature (*svabhāva*)
activity (*karma*)
aggregate material energy (*mahat-tattva*)
aggregate of material elements (*dravya*)
aim and object of life (*sādhya*)
all-accommodating potency (*ādhāra-śakti*)
amorous love (*madhura-bhāva*)
anger (*krodha*)
animate world (*cara-jagat*)
another's wife (*parakīyā ramaṇī*)
appropriate conduct (*sadācāra*)
arena of pastimes (*līlā-pīṭha*)
associate (*parikara* or *pārṣada*)
associates (*parikara-jana*)
attachment (*āsakti*)
austerities (*tapasya*)
beginningless (*anādi*)
being satisfied in the self (*ātmārāmatā*)
beings under His shelter (*āśrita-tattva*)
benediction for readers (*phala-śruti*)
bhakti that follows Kṛṣṇa's eternal associates in Goloka (*rāgānuga-bhakti*)
black eye-cosmetic (*kājala*)
bliss (*ānanda*)

bliss function (*hlādinī-vṛtti*)
bliss of pure, spiritual love (*premānanda*)
blissful transcendental mellows (*ānanda-cinmaya-rasa*)
bower (*kuñja*)
brahminical power (*brahma-teja*) – this refers to the mystical power attained by a *brāhmaṇa* through penance, austerity and knowledge of the Vedas
caring and affectionate to His devotees (*bhakta-vatsala*)
cause of all causes (*sarva-kāraṇa-kāraṇa*)
charming cowherd girl beloveds (*gopa-ramaṇī*)
commentary (*bhāṣya, ṭīkā*)
complete Brahman (*pūrṇa-brahma*)
connoisseur of ecstatic transcendental mellows (*rasika*)
consciousness (*citta*)
conscious realm (*cit-jagat*)
constitutional nature (*dharma*)
controller of all (*sarveśvara*)
controlling the breathing process (*prāṇāyāma*)
cowherd damsels (*gopa-kanyā*)
cowherd friends (*sakhās*)
crown jewel of connoisseurs of ecstatic transcendental mellows (*rasika-śekhara*)
dearly beloved intimate companion (*priya sakhī*)
deceptive pastimes (*vibhrama-vilāsa*)
delegated authority (*ādhikārika-devatā*)
deluding material potency (*māyā-śakti*)
delusion (*moha*)
demigods (*devas, devatās*)
desire potency (*icchā-śakti*)
desire seed (*kāma-bīja*)
desire-fulfilling gem (*cintāmaṇi*)
desires (*kāma*)
desire-tree (*kalpa-vṛkṣa*)
devoid of attributes (*nirviśeṣa*)
devoid of specific attributes (*nirviśeṣa*)
devotional scripture (*grantha*)

devotional service in practice (*sādhana-bhakti*)
dharma of mundane piety (*karma-kāṇḍa*)
differentiation (*bheda*)
direct expansions of the personal form (*kāya-vyūha*)
dissolving the self in Brahman (*brahmalaya*)
divine delusion (*vibhrama-vilāsa*)
dog-eater (*caṇḍāla*)
dry renunciation (*śuṣka-vairāgya*)
duties of the renounced order (*sannyāsa-dharma*)
earthly Gokula (*bhauma-gokula*)
earthly Navadvīpa (*bhauma-navadvīpa*)
economic development (*artha*)
egg-shaped universe (*brahmāṇḍa*)
eight symptoms of transcendental ecstasy (*aṣṭa-sāttvika-bhāvas*)
eightfold yoga process (*aṣṭānga-yoga*)
eleven senses (*ekādaśa-indriya*)
emperor of transcendental invocations (*mantra-rāja*)
empowered incarnations (*āveśa-avatāras*)
enchanting threefold-bending (*tribhaṅga-lalita*)
endowed with attributes (*saviśeṣa*)
equally disposed to all (*samadarśī*)
essential realities (*tattvas*)
essential reality of Bhagavān (*bhagavat-tattva*)
essential reality of Goloka (*goloka-tattva*)
essential reality of the self (*ātma-tattva*)
eternal adolescent (*nitya-kiśorī*)
eternal associates (*nitya-parikaras*)
eternal constitutional occupation of the living entity (*jaiva-dharma*)
eternal reality of spiritual existence (*cit-tattva*)
eternal service (*nitya-sevā*)
eternal unmanifest pastimes (*aprakaṭa-nitya-līlā*)
eternity, knowledge and bliss (*sac-cid-ānanda*)
ever-fresh adolescent form (*nava-yauvana-svarūpa*)
exclusive devotion (*ananya-bhakti*)
existence (*sattva*)
external (*bahiraṅgā*)

external potency (*bahiraṅga-śakti*)
faculty of knowledge (*jñāna-vṛtti*)
false ego (*ahaṅkāra*)
fear (*bhaya*)
fifth goal of human existence (*pañcama-puruṣārtha*)
five gross elements (*pañca-mahā-bhūta*)
five sense-objects (*pañca-tan-mātra*)
formal worship (*pūjā*)
formal worship with auspicious articles (*arcana*)
four original verses (*catuḥ-ślokī*)
free from material qualities (*nirguṇa*)
freedom from desire (*niṣkāma*)
fruit of action (*karma-phala*)
fruitive activities (*karma*)
fundamental reality of Kṛṣṇa (*kṛṣṇa-tattva*)
great personality (*mahāpuruṣa*)
great potency (*mahā-śakti*)
hero (*nāyaka*)
heroine (*nāyikā*)
highest spontaneous love (*mahābhāva*)
ignorance (*avidyā*)
illusory (*māyika*)
illusory energy (*māyā*)
illusory nature (*māyā*)
illusory potency (*māyā, māyā-śakti*)
immense sweetness (*mahā-mādhurya*)
impersonal knowledge (*brahma-jñāna, nirviśeṣa-jñāna*)
impersonal liberation (*kaivalya, nirvāṇa*)
impressions (*saṁskāra*)
impure goodness (*aśuddha-sattva*)
inanimate world (*acara-jagat*)
incomparable and unsurpassed reality (*asamordhva-tattva*)
inconceivable (*acintya*)
inconceivable Absolute Truth (*acintya-tattva*)
inconceivable distinction with non-distinction (*acintya-bhedābheda-tattva*)

inconceivable potency (*acintya-śakti*)
indivisible, complete and perfect transcendental principle (*akhaṇḍa-pūrṇa-cinmaya-tattva*)
indwelling witness (*vyaṣṭi-antaryāmī*)
inferior potency (*apara-śakti*)
influence (*prabhāva*)
ingredient cause (*upādāna*)
instrumental cause (*nimitta, nimitta-kāraṇa, kārya-nimitta*)
intelligence (*buddhi*)
intense passion (*rāga*)
internal pleasure potency (*hlādinī-svarūpa*)
intimate female companion (*priya-sakhī*)
intimate love (*praṇaya*)
intimate, having the same mood (*sva-jātīya*)
intrinsic form and nature (*svarūpa*)
intrinsic form of supreme bliss (*paramānanda-svarūpa*)
intrinsic fundamental reality (*svarūpa-tattva*)
intrinsic nature (*svarūpa*)
intrinsic nature of eternity, knowledge and bliss (*sac-cid-ānanda-tattva*)
intrinsic, personal potency (*svarūpa-śakti, svarūpa-bhūta-śakti*)
jīva engaged in spiritual practice (*sādhaka-jīva*)
jīvas who have turned away from Kṛṣṇa (*bahirmukha-jīvas*)
king of transcendental invocations (*mantra-rāja*)
knowledge (*cit, jñāna, vidyā*)
knowledge function (*vidyā-vṛtti*)
knowledge of relationship (*sambandha-jñāna*)
knowledge of the essential reality of *bhakti* (*bhakti-tattva-jñāna*)
knowledge of the essential reality of the Supreme Personality (*bhagavat-tattva-jñāna*)
knowledge of the nature of the self (*ādhyātmika-jñāna*)
liberation of merging into Bhagavān's existence (*sāyujya-mukti*)
lover (*ramaṇa*)
male (*puruṣa*)
man-eating demoness (*rākṣasī*)
manifest (*prakaṭa*)

manifest pastimes (*prakaṭa-līlā*)
manifestations (*prakāśa*)
marginal potency (*taṭastha-prakṛti, taṭastha-śakti*)
marginal prowess (*taṭastha-vikrama*)
material existence (*saṁsāra*)
material mode of goodness (*sattva*)
material mode of ignorance (*tamas*)
material mode of passion (*rajas*)
material universe (*brahmāṇḍa*)
material world (*māyika-jagat*)
meditative remembrance (*smaraṇa*)
mellows of transcendental service to Bhagavān (*bhagavad-rasa*)
mercy (*prasāda*)
merging into the Absolute (*kaivalya*)
mind (*mana*)
modes of material nature (*guṇa*)
monarch of transcendental invocations (*mantra-rāja*)
mood of being married (*pati-bhāva*)
mood of friendship (*sakhya-bhāva*)
mood of servitorship (*dāsya-bhāva*)
narrations of pastimes (*līlā-kathā*)
natural intimacy (*sahaja-praṇaya*)
non-dual undivided principle (*advaya-jñāna-akhaṇḍa-tattva*)
occasional incarnations (*naimittika-avatāras*)
one without a second (*advitīya*)
one-fourth of Bhagavān's opulence (*ekapāda-vibhūti*)
oneness with Brahman (*kaivalya*)
opulence (*vibhūti*)
original enjoyer (*mūla-puruṣa*)
original form (*svayaṁ-rūpa*)
original personal form (*svayaṁ-rūpa*)
original potency (*mūla-prakṛti*)
own wife (*sva-dāra*)
paramour mood (*parakīya-bhāva*)
parental affection (*vātsalya-bhāva*)
part and parcel (*aṁśa*)

partial incarnations (*aṁśa-avatāras*)
passive or neutral adoration (*śānta-bhāva*)
pastime expansion (*vilāsa-vigraha, līlā-vigraha*)
pastime form (*vilāsa-mūrti*)
pastime potency (*līlā-śakti, yoga-māyā*)
path of *bhakti* (*bhakti-mārga*)
path of reverent worship of the deity (*arcana-mārga*)
perfection (*siddhi*)
perfectly pure existence (*viśuddha-sattva*)
performer of activities (*kartā*)
pericarp (*karṇikāra*) – this is the central seed-pod of a lotus flower, which is in the shape of an inverted cone
personal expansion (*svāṁśa*)
personal intrinsic potency (*svarūpa-śakti*)
personality who is to be worshiped by the *mantra* (*ārādhyadeva*)
phases (*kalās*)
philosophical conclusions (*siddhāntas*)
philosophical conclusions about essential reality (*tattva-siddhānta*)
philosophical conclusions regarding the Absolute Truth (*tattva-siddhānta*)
philosophical principles (*tattva*)
philosophy that the Absolute Truth is formless and impersonal (*nirviśeṣa-vāda*)
place of pastimes (*līlā-pīṭha, pīṭha, yoga-pīṭha*)
planet (*loka*)
pleasure potency (*hlādinī-śakti*)
pleasure-pastimes (*vilāsa*)
plenary portion (*aṁśa*)
possessor of all potencies (*śaktimān*)
possessor of potency (*śaktimān*)
possessor of the collective bodily identification (*samaṣṭi-dehābhimānī*)
potency (*śakti*)
potency of cause and effect (*kārya-kāriṇī śakti*)
potency that produces the *jīvas* (*jīva-śakti*)
prayers and verses (*stava-stuti*)

predominated potency (*prakṛti, prakṛti-śakti*)
predominated principle (*prakṛti*)
presiding deities (*adhiṣṭhātṛ-devas* and *devīs*)
presiding deities of the material modes (*guṇa-avatāras*)
primeval personality (*ādi-puruṣa*)
principles of religious conduct (*dharma*)
process (*abhidheya-tattva*)
pure absolute reality (*śuddha-tattva*)
pure devotion (*śuddha-bhakti*)
pure devotional service (*śuddha-bhakti*)
pure existence (*śuddha-sattva*)
pure, intrinsic form and nature (*śuddha-svarūpa*)
pure paramour mellow (*śuddha-parakīya-rasa*)
pure, unalloyed devotional service (*śuddha-bhakti*)
purely transcendental *svarūpa* (*śuddha-svarūpa*)
qualification (*adhikāra*)
reformatory process (*saṁskāra*)
religiosity (*dharma*)
renounced order (*sannyāsa*)
residence and pasture of the cows (*goṣṭha*)
resplendent mellow of amorous love (*ujjvala-rasa*)
reverence (*guru-gaurava*)
righteous prescription (*dharma*)
sacred literatures (*granthas*)
seat (*pīṭha*)
secondary function (*gauṇa-dharma*)
sees with equal vision (*samadarśī*)
self-conception (*abhimāna*)
self-satisfaction (*ātmarāmatā*)
semblance of a plenary portion (*svāṁśa-abhasa*)
semblance of an expansion of the Supreme Godhead (*svāṁśa-bhāvābhāsa*)
semblance of transcendence (*cid-ābhāsa*)
sense gratification (*kāma*)
sense of awe and reverence (*aiśvarya*)
separated expansion (*vibhinnāṁśa*)

servitude (*sevya-bhāva*)
source of all incarnations (*sarvāvatārī*)
special manifestation (*prakāśa*)
special transforming agent (*vikāra-viśeṣa*)
specific expansion of an expansion (*kalā-viśeṣa*)
spiritual dominated potency (*cinmaya–prakṛti*)
spiritual order (*āśrama*)
spiritual perfection (*siddhi*)
spontaneous attachment (*rāga*)
steadiness (*niṣṭhā*)
sub-forests (*upavana*)
subject of expanded meditation (*bṛhad-dhyānamayī*)
superior potency (*para-prakṛti*)
supramundane (*aprākṛta*)
Supreme Absolute Truth (*parama-tattva*)
Supreme Brahman (*parabrahma*)
supreme controller (*maheśvara-tattva, parameśvara*)
Supreme Lord (*īśvara*)
Supreme Master (*vibhu*)
supreme personal Absolute Truth (*bhagavat-tattva*)
Supreme Personality (*parama-puruṣa*)
Supreme Personality and Absolute Truth (*bhagavat-tattva*)
Supreme Personality and enjoyer (*parama-puruṣottama*)
supreme reality (*para-tattva*)
supreme, transcendental reality (*para-tattva*)
supremely blissful transcendental mellows (*mahānanda-rasa*)
sweet realm of Vraja (*mādhurya-maṇḍala*)
tamasic phase of false ego (*tāmasa-ahaṅkāra*)
taste (*ruci*)
ten fundamental principles (*daśa-mūla-tattva*)
three-fourths of Bhagavān's opulence (*tripāda-vibhuti*)
throne (*siṁhāsana*)
time (*kāla*)
trance (*samādhi*)
trance of pure devotion (*śuddha-bhakti-samādhi*)
transcendental (*cinmaya*)

transcendental abode (*cinmaya-dhāma, dhāma*)
transcendental Cupid (*aprākṛta-anaṅga*)
transcendental desire (*kāma*)
transcendental effulgence (*brahmajyoti*)
transcendental faith (*śraddhā*)
transcendental knowledge potency (*cit-śakti*)
transcendental love (*prema*)
transcendental manifestation (*sphūrti*)
transcendental mellows (*rasa*)
transcendental mellows of pure *bhakti* (*śuddha-bhakti-rasa*)
transcendental mood (*bhāva*)
transcendental opulence (*cid-aiśvarya*)
transcendental pastimes (*cid-vilāsa*)
transcendental pleasure potency (*hlādinī-śakti*)
transcendental pleasure-pastimes (*cid-vilāsa*)
transcendental potency (*cit-śakti*)
transcendental reality (*cit-tattva*)
transcendental realm (*cit-jagat*)
transcendental sentiment (*bhāva*)
transcendental to the material modes (*nirguṇa*)
transcendental world (*aprākṛta-jagat, cij-jagat*)
transcendental, spiritual abode (*cinmaya-dhāma*)
transcendentally pure (*viśuddha*)
transformation (*pariṇāma, vikāra*)
unalloyed pure goodness (*viśuddha-sattva*)
unconscious realm (*māyika-jagat*)
unique qualities (*vaiśiṣṭhya, viśeṣaṭā*)
universal form (*virāṭ-puruṣa*)
universe (*brahmāṇḍa*)
unlimited in nature (*ananta-dharma*)
unmanifest (*aprakaṭa, avyakta*)
unmanifest aggregate of the material elements (*pradhāna*)
unmanifest pastimes (*aprakaṭa-līlā*)
unmanifested external energy (*prakṛti*)
use by authoritative *ṛṣis* (*ārṣa-prayoga*)
Vedic path (*veda-mārga*)

visible earthly (*dṛśyamāna bhauma*)
wedded conjugal love (*svakīya-bhāva*)
wheel of fruitive activities (*karma-cakra*)
whose every desire comes to fruition (*satya-kāma*)
wife of another (*para-dāra*)
wish-fulfilling cow (*kāmadhenu*)
with desire (*sakāma*)
worship (*ārādhana*)
worshipable deity (*iṣṭadeva*)
young woman (*vanitā*)

Verse Index

Index

C

D

H

I

J

K

L

M

O

P

R

S

T

W

BOOK CATALOG 2003

Gauḍīya Vedānta Publications

Śrī Śrīmad Bhaktivedānta Nārāyaṇa Mahārāja

— and —

Śrī Śrīmad A.C. Bhaktivedānta Swami Prabhupāda

Books by Śrī Śrīmad Bhaktivedānta Nārāyaṇa Mahārāja

Jaiva-Dharma

The groundbreaking spiritual novel
by Śrīla Bhaktivinoda Ṭhākura

Jaiva-dharma reveals the ultimate development of the path of pure devotion to the English-speaking world.

Hardbound, 5 x 7.5", 1077 pages, Bible paper, 8 color plates, glossaries of terms, indexes of quoted verses and general index. Code JDC $15.00

Śrīmad Bhagavad-Gītā

With extensive commentaries

This edition of *Bhagavad-gītā* contains two commentaries: the *Sārārtha-varṣiṇī Ṭīkā* by Śrīla Viśvanātha Cakravartī Ṭhākura and the *Sārārtha-varṣiṇī Prakāśikā-vṛtti* by Śrīla Bhaktivedānta Nārāyaṇa Mahārāja.

Hardbound, 5.5 x 8.5", 1120 pages, 12 color plates. Code SBG $15.00

Śrī Śrīmad Bhakti Prajñāna Keśava Gosvāmī

His Life and Teachings

A unique biography of a contemporary saint, the spiritual master of Śrīla Bhaktivedānta Nārāyaṇa Mahārāja and the *sannyāsa-guru* of Śrīla A.C. Bhaktivedānta Swami Prabhupāda.

Softbound, 5.5 x 8.5", 580 pages, 22 color illustrations. Code PKGB $15.00

Pinnacle of Devotion

An introduction to the most powerful yoga system

We all have a tendency to love, and no one can live without loving someone. The problem is, however, where to place our love.

Hardbound, 5.5 x 8.5", 200 pages.
Code POD $10.00

Veṇu-Gīta

Tenth Canto, Chapter 21 of Śrīmad-Bhāgavatam

"By just hearing that flute-song that attracts the hearts of the whole universe, Sanaka and Sanandana and other *ātmārāma munis* became overwhelmed with joy and lost consciousness."

Softbound, 5.5 x 8.5", 188 pages, 8 color illustrations. Code VG $10.00

Bhakti-rasāmṛta-sindhu-bindu

A drop of the nectarean ocean of bhakti-rasa

This book is Viśvanātha Cakravartī Ṭhākura's summary of Śrīla Rūpa Gosvāmī's classic *Bhakti-rasāmṛta-sindhu* (*Nectar of Devotion*).

Softbound, 6 x 9", 305 pages, numerous diagrams. Code BRSB $8.00

Śrī Bhajana-rahasya

Deep analysis of the Hare Kṛṣṇa mahā-mantra

This revolutionary work by Śrīla Bhaktivinoda Ṭhākura presents an astounding analysis of the Hare Kṛṣṇa *mantra*, based on the eight verses of *Śrī Śikṣāṣṭakam*, covering all stages of *bhakti*.

Softbound, 5.5 x 8.5", 497 pages, 4 color plates. Code SBR $10.00

The Origin of Ratha-yātrā

The world's most ancient religious festival

Lectures by Śrīla Bhaktivedānta Nārāyaṇa Mahārāja on the Ratha-yātrā, or the Cart Festival of Lord Jagannātha.

Softbound, 5.5 x 8.5", 372 pages, 8 color plates. Code ORY $10.00

Śrī Brahma-saṁhitā

Lord Brahmā's prayers of devotion to Kṛṣṇa

These prayers offered at the dawn of creation by Brahmā, the secondary creator of the universe, contain all the essential truths of Vaiṣṇava philosophy.

Softbound, 5.5 x 8.5", 452 pages. Code SBS $10.00

Śrī Gauḍīya Gīti-guccha

An unprecedented collection of devotional songs

Sanskrit, Bengali and Hindi devotional poems, prayers, songs and *bhajanas* written by the Gauḍīya Vaiṣṇava *ācāryas* and compiled for the practicing devotee.

Spiral bound, 6 x 9", 224 pages.
Code GGG $10.00

Śrī Manaḥ-śikṣā

Instructions to the mind by
Śrīla Raghunātha dāsa Gosvāmī

Śrī Manaḥ-śikṣā consists of twelve verses composed by Raghunātha dāsa Gosvāmī that instruct the mind on how to make progress on the path of *bhajana*.

Softbound, 5.5 x 8.5", 153 pages. Code SMS $5.00

Jaiva-dharma, Part One

Part one of a spiritual novel by
Śrīla Bhaktivinoda Ṭhākura

"Out of all the books of Śrīla Ṭhākura Bhaktivinoda, *Jaiva-dharma* is considered to be the quintessence by religious thinkers of different countries."
– Śrīla Nārāyaṇa Mahārāja

Softbound, 5.5 x 8.5", 288 pages, 10 color illustrations.
Code JD1 $5.00

Secret Truths of the Bhāgavatam

Discourses on Śrīmad-Bhāgavatam

A series of lectures by Śrīla Nārāyaṇa Mahārāja at the New Vraja community in Badger, California, in June 1999.

Softbound, 5.5 x 8.5", 192 pages, 16 color illustrations. Code STB $5.00

Bhakti-tattva-viveka

The true nature of devotion

Śrīla Bhaktivinoda Ṭhākura has presented the grave and deep conclusions of devotional service, pure *bhakti*, in simple language that is accessible to any sincere reader.

Softbound, 5.5 x 8.5", 112 pages. Code BTV $4.00

Rays of Hope

A compilation of divine discourses, 1996–99

"The real connection with *guru* is through *bhāgavata-paramparā*. Even if one is not initiated by him in *guru-paramparā*, such a qualified disciple has understood his *guru's* mood."
– Śrīla Nārāyaṇa Mahārāja

Softbound, 5.5 x 8.5", 192 pages, 18 color photos and numerous illustrations. Code ROH $5.00

My Śikṣā-guru & Priya-bandhu

Remembrances by Śrīla Bhaktivedānta Nārāyaṇa Mahārāja

A deep and revealing account of the intimate relationship between Śrīla Bhaktivedānta Nārāyaṇa Mahārāja and his instructing spiritual master and dear friend, Śrīla A.C. Bhaktivedānta Swami Prabhupāda, from 1947 up until final instructions given in 1977.

Softbound, 5.5 x 8.5", 49 pages. Code SGPB $2.00

Their Lasting Relation

An Historical Account

A detailed and nectarean account of Śrīla A.C. Bhaktivedānta Swami Prabhupāda's long-standing relationship with both his *sannyāsa-guru*, Śrīla Bhakti Prajñāna Keśava Gosvāmī, and Śrīla Bhaktivedānta Nārāyaṇa Mahārāja.

Softbound, 5.5 x 8.5", 49 pages. Code TLR $2.00

Guru-Devatātmā

Accepting Śrī Guru as One's Life and Soul

Śrīla Bhaktivedānta Nārāyaṇa Mahārāja speaks on the importance of accepting a bona fide *guru*, who is more dear than life itself, the absolute necessity of second initiation, and other topics of *guru-tattva*.

Softbound, 5.5 x 8.5", 52 pages. Code GD $2.00

Our Gurus: One in Siddhānta, One in Heart

Clearing up the confusion

Nowadays some persons claim there are differences in the conclusions taught by Śrīla Bhaktivedānta Nārāyaṇa Mahārāja and Śrīla A.C. Bhaktivedānta Swami Prabhupāda. These authoritative responses to many of the objections will help the reader understand things as they are, without any politically motivated interpretation.

Softbound, 5.5 x 8.5", 61 pages. Code OIS $2.00

Śrī Hari-Nāma Mahā-Mantra

The transcendental holy name of the Lord

"When a qualified person chants *harināma*, this light diffuses, thus keeping the darkness of illusion away from the soul."

Softbound, 5.5 x 8.5", 64 pages. Code SHN $2.00

Happiness in a Fool's Paradise

The futility of material enjoyment

"Everyone wants to be happy, but generally we can find only a little happiness and affection in this world."

Softbound, 5.5 x 8.5", 32 pages, 6 color illustrations.
Code HFP $2.00

To Be Controlled By Love

The guru–disciple relationship

"Even Kṛṣṇa, the Supreme Personality of Godhead, wants to be controlled by love and affection."
– Śrīla Nārāyaṇa Mahārāja

Softbound, 5.5 x 8.5", 32 pages. Code CBL $2.00

The Butter Thief

The true nature of devotion

This book describes Kṛṣṇa's sweet childhood pastimes, in which He plays with Mother Yaśodā as an ordinary child.

Softbound, 5.5 x 8.5", 64 pages, 8 color illustrations.
Code TBT $2.00

The Essence of Bhagavad-gītā

Absorbing the mind in Śrī Kṛṣṇa

"Absorb your mind and heart in Me, become My devotee, worship Me, offer your obeisances to Me, and certainly you will come to Me."

Softbound, 5.5 x 8.5", 32 pages, 4 color illustrations.
Code EBG $2.00

Books by Śrīla A.C. Bhaktivedānta Swami Prabhupāda

These special editions are the authorized and approved versions, with the artwork and format specially designed by Śrīla Prabhupāda for introducing the Western world to Kṛṣṇa consciousness. Not one word or picture has been changed from Śrīla Prabhupāda's original version.

Kṛṣṇa: The Supreme Personality of Godhead

Who is Kṛṣṇa?

Śrīla Prabhupāda's summary of the entire Tenth Canto of *Śrīmad-Bhāgavatam*

Volume 1: hardbound, 7.5 x 10.5", 425 pages, 84 plates. Code KB1 $15.00
Volume 2: hardbound, 7.5 x 10.5", 400 pages, 24 plates. Code KB2 $15.00

Bhagavad-gītā As It Is

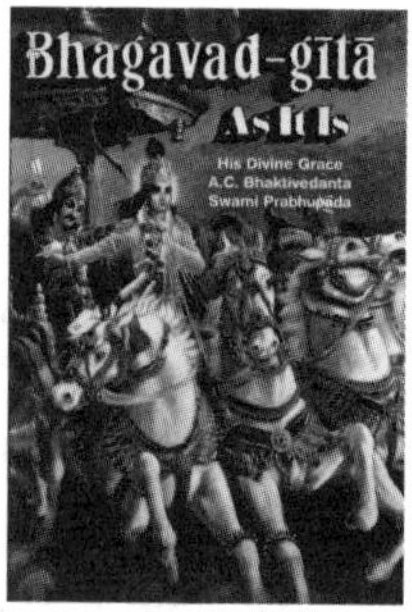

The most beloved of all Vedic literatures

Reprint of the historic original, authorized and approved 1972 Macmillan Complete Edition, with the original Sanskrit text, Roman transliteration, English synonyms, translation and elaborate purports.

Hardbound, 6.25 x 9.25", 1000 pages, 40 color illustrations. Code BG $15.00

Teachings of Lord Caitanya

The Golden Avatar

Lord Caitanya Mahāprabhu appeared in Bengal, India, in 1486, and began a revolution in spiritual consciousness that has profoundly affected the lives of millions.

Hardbound, 440 pages, many original color illustrations. Code TLC $15.00

Kṛṣṇa, the Reservoir of Pleasure

Eternal enjoyment through transcendental sound

"Kṛṣṇa – this sound is transcendental. Kṛṣṇa means the highest pleasure. All of us, every living being, seeks pleasure. But we do not know how to seek pleasure perfectly." – Śrīla Prabhupāda

Softbound, 5.5 x 8.5", 32 pages. Code ROP $1.00

The Perfection of Yoga

"There have been many *yoga* systems popularized in the Western world, especially in this century, but none of them have actually taught the perfection of *yoga*." The original, authorized and approved version.

Softbound, 4 x 7", 56 pages, 8 color plates. Code POY $2.00

U.S. Regional Book Distributors

Northwest (Seattle)

Mark Haines
11321 74th Ave. E
Puyallup, WA 98373
Attn: Maitreya Muni Prabhu
Phone: (866) HARIBOL (427-4265)
Email: maitreyamuni@yahoo.com

California Northern (Berkeley)

Westside & Company
5659 Telegraph Ave. #D
Berkeley, CA 94609
Attn: Kavidatta & Kṛtakarma Prabhus
Phone: (510) 655-5018, 883-0736
Email: kavidatta2000@yahoo.com

California Central (Badger)

Mt. Kailāsa Foundation
PO Box 99
Badger, CA 93603
Attn: Nanda-gopāla Prabhu
Phone: (559) 337-2448
Email: nandagopal@gaudiya.net

California Southern (Los Angeles)

IGVS
111 Dudley Ave
Venice, CA 90291
Attn: Jaga-mohana Prabhu
Phone: (310) 450-5371
Email: purebhakti@hotmail.com

California Southern (San Diego)

Padayatra America
PO Box 2179
La Jolla, CA 92038
Attn: Jayanta Prabhu
Phone: (858) 518-5209
Email: jayantadasa@yahoo.com

South (Houston)

IGVS - Houston
16119 Abergreen Trail
Houston, TX 77095
Attn: Kṛṣṇa dāsa Prabhu
Phone: (281) 550-2940
Email: kris4basics@hotmail.com

Eastern (Washington DC)

Rupa Raghunath Gaudiya Math
6925 Willow St. NW
Washington, DC 20012
Attn: Vamsivadana & Mukunda
Phone: (301) 864-3354
Email: ruparaghunatha@hotmail.com

Southeast (North Carolina)

Maria Christopher
4619 Timberwood Terr.
Efland, NC 27243
Attn: Rāma dāsa Prabhu
Phone: (919) 563-9464
Email: ramdas@mebtel.net

South (Florida)

Acolapissa Foundation
PO Box 1689
Alachua, FL 32616-1689
Attn: Bhāgavata Prabhu
(386) 418-2046 (800) 814-7316 Ext. 00
Email: Bhagavatdasa@msn.com

International Book Distributors

Canada - Western (Vancouver)

Stanley A. Gill
#25 - 15030 58th Ave.
Surrey, B.C. CANADA V3S 9G3
Attn: Prasasya Prabhu
Phone: (866) 575-9438
Email: stannshel@shaw.ca

Europe - UK (England)

Gour Govinda Gaudiya Math
32 Handsworth Wood Rd.
Birmingham B20 2DS, UK
Attn: Jīva-pāvana Prabhu
Phone: (44) 121 682 9159
Email: gourgovinda@hotmail.com

International Spanish Distributors

Vedic Cultural Association
1002 S. Austin St.
Santa Ana, CA 92704 USA
Attn: Haridāsa Prabhu
Phone: (714) 775-8760
Email: hsalas1@prodigy.net

For information on becoming a distributor in your area: e-mail vd@regalgift.com or isani@mail.com, or call Niścintya at 310-837-3518

Book Order Form

Book Code	Price each	Copies	Subtotal
	$		$
	$		$
	$		$
	$		$
	$		$
	$		$
	$		$
	$		$
	$		$
	$		$

Books Total $ ____________

Add 10% Shipping + $3 Handling $ ____________

Grand Total: $ ____________

hip to:

ame ______________________________

ddress ______________________________

____

elephone______________________________

mail ______________________________

nstructions: Fill in the book codes of the books you want to order, the price ach, and the total number of copies you want. **Calculate the Grand Total and ail this form and a check or money order to the Regional Distributor near- t to you (listed on the previous page). Make your check or money order ayable to the name listed in bold type.** Please allow two weeks for delivery— ore for international orders.

CENTERS AROUND THE WORLD

AUSTRALIA • **Murwillumbah** • Sri Giriraja Govardhan Gaudiya Matha • 56 Brisbane Street • Murwillumbah N.S.W 2482 ☎ +61 66-728499 ✉ lilasuka@bigpond.com • **GERMANY** • **Berlin** • Gaudiya Vedanta Samiti Berlin • Emserstrasse 70 • 12051 Berlin ☎ +49 30 62 00 87 47 ✉ gvsberlin@yahoo.com • **INDIA** • **Mathura** • Sri Keshavaji Gaudiya Matha • Opp. Dist. Hospital • Jawahar Hata • Mathura (U.P.) 281001 ☎ +91 565 250-2334 ✉ mathuramath@gaudiya.net ♦ **Navadwipa** • Sri Devananda Gaudiya Matha • Tegharipada, PO Navadwipa, D/O Nadiya, West Bengal ☎ +91 343 240-068 ♦ **New Delhi** • Sri Ramanvihari Gaudiya Math • OCF pocket, Block B-3, near musical fountain park • Janakpuri, New Delhi ☎ +91 11 2553-3568 ☎ +91 11 3230-2159 ♦ **Vrindavan** • Sri Rupa-Sanatana Gaudiya Matha • Danagali, Vrindavana U.P. ☎ +91 565 244-3270 • **INDONESIA** • **Bali** • Ananta Gaudiya Math • Br. Juntal, Desa Kaba-Kaba • Kediri, Tabanan • Bali, Indonesia ☎ +62 361 830986 ☎ +62 361 830987 • **NETHERLANDS** • **Rotterdam** • Preaching Center Rotterdam • 1e Pijnackerstraat 98 • 3035GV Rotterdam ☎ +31 010-2650405 ✉ sanga@worldmail.nl • **NEW ZEALAND** • **Auckland** • Hare Krishna Vegetarian Restaurant • 214 Karangahape Road • Auckland ☎ +64 9 303-1560 ♦ **Wellington** • IGVS Wellington • 22 Wrights Hill Road • Karori, Wellington ☎ +64 4 476-6784 ✉ benhc@hotmail.com ♦ **Kati Kati & Whangamata** • IGVS Bay of Plenty • Kati Kati & Whangamata ☎ +64 7 552-0073 ✉ bhadradasi@hotmail.com • **PHILIPPINES** • **Manila** • International Gaudiya Vedanta Society of the Philippines • Radha Krsna Gopala Mandir • 96 ROTC Hunters Clusters 23 Tatalon • Quezon City, Metro Manila 1113 ☎ +63 2783 0267 ☎ +63 91873-32659 ✉ jaipur_art@mailcity.com • **UNITED KINGDOM** • **Birmingham** • Sri Gour Govinda Gaudiya Matha • 32 Handsworth Wood Road • Birmingham, B20 2DS ☎ +44 121 682 9159 ✉ gourgovinda@hotmail.com • **USA** • **Los Angeles** • Sri Sri Radha-Govinda Gaudiya Math • 111 Dudley Ave. • Venice, CA 90291 ☎ +1 310-450-5371 ✉ purebhakti@hotmail.com ♦ **Miami** • Institute for Gaudiya Vaishnavism • 934 N. University Drive, #102 • Coral Springs, FL 33071 ☎ +1 754-245-2345 ✉ Mbuddhi@cs.com ♦ Sri Gaudiya Vedanta Samiti of South Florida • 701 N.W. 16th Ave. • Pompano Beach, FL 33069 ☎ +1 954-344-5404 ✉ alankar@adelphia.net ♦ **New York** • The Bhaktivedanta Gaudiya Matha • 134-06 95th Ave. • South Richmond Hill, NY 11419 ☎ +1 718-526-9835 ✉ unclepuru108@yahoo.com ♦ **Washington, DC** • Rupa Raghunath Gaudiya Math • 6925 Willow Ave. NW • Washington, DC 20012 ☎ +1 301-864-3354 ✉ ruparaghunatha@hotmail.com • **VENEZUELA** • Sri Venezuela Kesavaji Gaudiya Math and Gaudiya Vedanta Publications (spanish) • Carrera 17, entre calles 50-51 • #50-47, Barquisimeto • Edo. Lara ☎ +58 51-452574 ✉ janardana@postmark.net

For more information please visit the following web sites: **www.gaudiya.net** and **www.purebhakti.com**